Securing Borders

Law and Society Series
W. Wesley Pue, General Editor

The Law and Society Series explores law as a socially embedded phenomenon. It is premised on the understanding that the conventional division
of law from society creates false dichotomies in thinking, scholarship,
educational practice, and social life. Books in the series treat law and
society as mutually constitutive and seek to bridge scholarship emerging
from interdisciplinary engagement of law with disciplines such as politics,
social theory, history, political economy, and gender studies.

A list of the books in this series appears at the end of this book.

Anna Pratt

Securing Borders
Detention and Deportation in Canada

UBCPress · Vancouver · Toronto

15 14 13 12 11 10 09 08 07 06 05   5 4 3 2 1

Printed in Canada on acid-free paper

Library and Archives Canada Cataloguing in Publication

Pratt, Anna, 1964-
  Securing borders : detention and deportation in Canada / Anna Pratt.

(Law and society ISSN 1496-4953)
Includes bibliographical references and index.
ISBN 0-7748-1154-4 (bound); ISBN 0-7748-1155-2 (pbk.)

  1. Deportation – Canada – History – 20th century. 2. Detention of persons –
Canada – History – 20th century. 3. National security – Canada. I. Title. II. Series:
Law and society series (Vancouver, B.C.)

KE4454.P73 2005   342.7108'2   C2005-901497-0
KF4483.I5P73 2005

Canadä

UBC Press gratefully acknowledges the financial support for our publishing program
of the Government of Canada through the Book Publishing Industry Development
Program (BPIDP), and of the Canada Council for the Arts, and the British Columbia
Arts Council.

This book has been published with the help of a grant from the Canadian Federation
for the Humanities and Social Sciences, through the Aid to Scholarly Publications
Programme, using funds provided by the Social Sciences and Humanities Research
Council of Canada.

Printed and bound in Canada by Friesens
Set in Stone by Artegraphica Design Co. Ltd.
Copy editor: Dallas Harrison
Proofreader: Gail Copeland
Indexer: Christine Jacobs

UBC Press
The University of British Columbia
2029 West Mall
Vancouver, BC V6T 1Z2
604-822-5959 / Fax: 604-822-6083
www.ubcpress.ca

For Lucas

Contents

Acknowledgments

I am deeply grateful to the many people who facilitated and contributed to this book. I am especially appreciative of those individuals from non-governmental refugee support and legal advocacy groups, ethnocultural community organizations, the CIC, the IRB, the RCMP, and municipal law enforcement agencies who gave generously of their time and who supported and participated in this project in a variety of invaluable ways. In particular, I would like to thank Fred Franklin of the detention committee of the Toronto Refugee Affairs Council, who facilitated and supported my research and whose tireless work on behalf of those in detention and whose commitment to working for social justice and human rights have been both effective and inspiring. I would also like to thank Ali Mohamud, Kelly Grover, Maggie Smith, Peter Crosbie, Joan Simalchik, and Ursula Franklin for sharing their expertise and for their varied and important contributions to this project over the years.

Many people have made this book possible by reading chapters, making suggestions, pointing out errors and weaknesses, and engaging in helpful conversations. I am particularly grateful to Tony Doob, Peter Fitzpatrick, Nicola Lacey, Dan O'Connor, Wes Pue, Jonathan Simon, Peter Solomon, Carolyn Strange, and the anonymous readers for their generous input into my work as it took shape. I am especially grateful to Mariana Valverde, whose work and thought have been inspirational and who has so generously offered her guidance and support in this and many other of my endeavours. Her sharp insights and willingness to read my work have helped build my confidence and improve my scholarship over the years. Special thanks are also owed to Randy Lippert for the many coffees and conversations that we have shared and for his ever thoughtful and sage advice. I have so enjoyed the energetic participation of graduate students Sara Thompson and Dale Ballucci, who have not only been a terrific help but also injected my work with a healthy and motivating measure of enthusiasm, companionship, and goodwill.

I am also grateful for the encouragement and guidance extended to me by Wes Pue and Randy Schmidt of the Law and Society Book Series at UBC Press. I am very thankful to the York University Faculty of Arts Research Grant program for its contribution to the production of this book. Portions of this book have been published elsewhere. My thanks go to Sage Publications for granting permission to reprint a revised version of "Dunking the Doughnut: Discretionary Power, Law, and the Administration of the Canadian Immigration Act," which originally appeared in *Social and Legal Studies* 8, 2 (1999): 199-226, © Sage Publications. Thanks also to Elsevier Publications for granting permission to reprint a revised version of "Sovereign Power, Carceral Conditions, and Penal Practices: Detention and Deportation in Canada," which originally appeared in *Studies in Law, Politics, and Society* 23 (2001): 45-78, ISBN 0-7623-0792-7/1059-4337 (Series), © Elsevier Publications. And thanks to the *Canadian Journal of Sociology* for granting permission to reprint "'From Deserving Victims to Masters of Confusion': Redefining Refugees in the 1990s," coauthored with Mariana Valverde, which originally appeared in the *Canadian Journal of Sociology* 27, 2 (2002): 135-61. The CIC detention and removal tables have been reproduced with permission from Crown Copyright and Licensing, Public Works and Government Services Canada.

Thanks to my very smart friends, Kirsten Kramar, Kim Varma, and Kimberley White, whose friendships have nourished me over the years, through so many changes, in so many ways. Thanks also to my dear friend Meg for sticking close despite the distance. I am deeply grateful to have shared in the flash and sparkle of Guy Lahaie, with whom I shared a dear friendship that lasted from the day we met in 1989 until the day he died 22 February 2004.

I am indebted to my family. My brothers, Gerhard and Marcus, have each in their own way helped me achieve more than I thought I could. My parents, Cranford and Renate, have been my biggest fans. They have always been keen, careful, and sympathetic readers of my work. I have benefited greatly from my father's kind and generous support and extensive editorial skills. My mother, Renate, lives her life with a guiding and deep-felt concern for the wellbeing of others. Her compassion underlies not only her many great accomplishments but also each and all of her everyday interactions and engagements. It is what has made her a powerful activist, a dear friend to so many, and such a wonderful, devoted mother. She has infused my world with her endless love, her sense of justice, beauty, and humour.

My partner Brian brings me more joy than I ever imagined possible. Words cannot thank him enough for his unfailing patience, tireless support, and willingness to help as I worked on this book. But more important still are his generous spirit, easy smile, deep wisdom, and sense of adventure, which forever sustain and energize me. Finally, I dedicate this book to our wee son Lucas Alexander, whose gummy smile lights up my world.

Acronyms

AFIS	Automated Fingerprint Identification System
API/PNR	Advanced Passenger Information and Passenger Name Recognition Systems
CAVEAT	Canadians against Violence Everywhere Advocating Its Termination
CBA	Canadian Bar Association
CBSA	Canada Border Services Agency
CCC	*Criminal Code of Canada*
CCRA	Canada Customs and Revenue Agency
CDSA	*Controlled Drug and Substances Act*
CEIU	Canada Employment and Immigration Union
CEUDA	Customs Excise Union Douanes Accise
CFIA	Canadian Food Inspection Agency
CFSEU	Combined Forces Special Enforcement Unit
CIC	Citizenship and Immigration Canada
CMB	Case Management Branch (CIC)
CPIC	Canadian Police Information Centre
CPO	Case Presenting Officer
CSIS	Canadian Security Intelligence Service
CUSP	Canada-United States Partnership
EDO	Enforcement Detention Officer
EIC	Employment and Immigration Commission
EU	European Union
FAST	Fast and Secure Trade program
FCC	Federal Court of Canada
FCTD	Federal Court Trial Division
FOSS	Field Operational Support System
IAB	Immigration Appeal Board
IBETs	Integrated Border Enforcement Teams
IPC	Immigration, Passport and Citizenship Program (RCMP)

IRB	Immigration and Refugee Board (of Canada)
IRPA	*Immigration and Refugee Protection Act* (2002)
ITF	Immigration Task Force (RCMP)
IWRC	Immigration Warrant Response Centre
JPAUs	Joint Passenger Analysis Units
LRAG	Legislative Review Advisory Group (Immigration)
LTTE	Liberation Tigers of Tamil Eelam
MADD	Mothers against Drunk Driving
MOU	Memorandum of Understanding
NAFTA	North American Free Trade Agreement
NCMS	National Case Management System
NDP	New Democratic Party
OCU	Organized Crime Unit
PASS	Passenger Accelerated Service Systems
PIP	Partners in Protection
PRRA	Pre-Removal Risk Assessment
RCMP	Royal Canadian Mounted Police
SCC	Supreme Court of Canada
SIO	Senior immigration officer
SIRC	Security Intelligence Review Committee
TRAC	Toronto Refugee Affairs Council
UCRCC	Undocumented Convention Refugees in Canada Class
UN	United Nations
UNHCR	United Nations High Commissioner for Refugees
UNHRC	United Nations Human Rights Committee
USA PATRIOT	*Uniting and Strengthening America by Providing Appropriate Tools Required to Intercept and Obstruct Terrorism Act* (2001)
USINS	United States Immigration and Naturalization Service
WTM	World Tamil Movement

Securing Borders

1
Overview and Orientations

It is not a brand-new world. The denigration and distrust of refugee claimants, heightened anxieties about crime, security, and fraud, and efforts to fortify the border and deflect risky outsiders have been prominent features of Canadian border control, refugee policy, and immigration enforcement for decades.

These preoccupations fuel and are fuelled by the endless quest for security – of borders, of the nation, and of the public. The multiple and intersecting authorities, technologies, forms of knowledge, and modes of rule engaged in and defined by this quest constitute an "immigration penality." Immigration penality is heterogeneous and diverse; it includes but is not limited to legal regimes or formal institutions of government. Detention and deportation are the two most extreme and bodily sanctions of this immigration penality, which constitutes and enforces borders, polices noncitizens, identifies those deemed dangerous, diseased, deceitful, or destitute, and refuses them entry or casts them out. As such, detention and deportation and the borders that they sustain are also key technologies in the continuous processes that "make up" citizens and govern populations.

This book maps the transitions in the governance of immigration penality over the past fifty years and explores the relationships between Canadian policies and practices of detention and deportation and the transitions from welfare liberal to neoliberal regimes of government. I do not provide a general or total history of this field or a detailed institutional analysis of the development of Canadian immigration and refugee law and policy. Neither do I engage in a comprehensive critical analysis of Canadian detention and deportation law, policy, and practice. Rather, I engage in a close study of the shifting and historically specific discursive formations, transformations, and technologies of power that have surrounded the development and promotion of detention and deportation in Canada. While not explicitly prescriptive, this study is not merely descriptive. Although I do not provide a specific set of policy recommendations, by making visible the less visible dimensions of immigration penalty and border control this study demonstrates the need to unsettle and accept less readily the taken-for-granted myths and truths that shape policies and practices in this domain.

Over the past fifty years, as human rights doctrine became more consequential and legal "rights talk" more established, explicitly racist, moralistic, and ideological grounds for exclusion were delegitimized. Instead, the categories of crime and criminality proliferated and merged with a reconfigured and expanded understanding of national security. Over the past three decades in particular, the very category of security has come to include an increasing number of criminal threats to the population that are judged to have a significant international dimension. This expansion contrasts sharply with the formerly dominant conception of security, primarily concerned with threats posed by a variety of subversives to the "political state." This crime-security nexus coupled with distinctly neoliberal preoccupations with certain kinds of fraud and system abuse has produced a powerful hybrid rationale for the policies and practices of border control and immigration penalty. By the twenty-first century, immigration penalty in general and the practices of detention and deportation in particular had come to be governed through crime-security. What followed 11 September 2001 was a major refocusing on international terrorism in the context of a trend toward governing through crime that was already well entrenched.[1]

The crime-security nexus and linked preoccupations with risk and fraud have converged upon refugees in particular and troubling ways. A process has taken place in which the primary importance of identifying and protecting the refugee, the deserving victim "at risk," has been deemphasized and made contingent in the first instance on identifying and excluding the undeserving, possibly deceitful, and likely criminal "risky" refugee claimant.

Technologies of border control and immigration penalty, including both "hard technologies" and "innovations in social practices,"[2] manifest the effort to tame uncertainty and to know the unknowable. The intense preoccupation with certain kinds of fraud – welfare claims, refugee claims, documentation, identity – has become intertwined with guiding concerns about crime-security. The spectre of fraud and related concerns about identity are also consistent with a construction of dangerousness that is constituted by criminality and the unpredictable and therefore unmanageable risks linked with "unknowability." As observed by John Pratt in relation to the dangerous classes of the 1800s, "the shifting identities of these criminals also made the risks they posed all the more incalculable. Their very rootlessness, their ability to shrug off one identity as it suited them and then assume another rendering them, as it were, 'unknowable,' confirmed their status as dangerous."[3] Just as dangerous offenders in the 1800s were dangerous and ungovernable because of their criminality, unknowability, and unpredictability, so too are refugees: their "real" identities presumed unknown, their credibility always suspect, and their links with criminality, security, and fraud continually reconstituted. Refugees have become the "folk devils" of the twenty-first century.[4] In the EU as in North America, the mobilization of these folk devils provides the occasion and the justification for stricter border controls and the intensification of immigration enforcement.

The Canadian Context: "Closing the Back Door"

On 6 April 2000, when the twin towers of New York City's World Trade Center were still standing, then Minister of Citizenship and Immigration Elinor Caplan tabled new legislation (Bill C-31) to replace the 1976 *Immigration Act*.[5] In February 2001, a slightly revised version of this bill was reintroduced (Bill C-11), it received royal assent in November 2001, and in June 2002 the new *Immigration and Refugee Protection Act (IRPA)* came into effect.[6] When this legislation was first contemplated, its exclusionary concerns were animated by the linked threats posed to national security by crime and fraud ("criminal abuse") in the shape of organized crime. After the tragic events of 11 September 2001, this focus on organized crime was supplemented by the reinvigorated threat of terrorism.

The preoccupation with criminality, security, and fraud and the heavy emphasis on enforcement measures that pervade *IRPA* evidence the degree to which crime-security and fraud had already become the dominant justifications for the policies and practices of national exclusions prior to September 11th. That Bill C-11, prepared well before September 11th, was already embedded in these discourses enabled its representation after that date as an almost clairvoyant, cutting-edge response to the new terrorist threat. The proposed reforms were quickly promoted as an important part of Canada's much-needed antiterrorist, national security arsenal. The government, far from countering the fear-laced expressions of anti-immigrant, anti-refugee sentiments that followed the attacks, thus mobilized and affirmed this fear, further entrenching the associations between crime-security and fraud and new immigrants and refugees.

September 11th gave new life to long-standing domestic and American concerns about Canada's immigration and refugee determination systems. Facing hyperbolic criticisms that Canada is a "haven for terrorists" because of its allegedly porous borders and its lax immigration and refugee determination systems, the Canadian government responded in December 2001 with sweeping new legislation targeting the terrorist threat within. Bill C-36, the *Anti-Terrorism Act*, dramatically expanded the powers of law enforcement and national security agents to target, monitor, arrest, and detain without warrant Canadian citizens on the basis of suspicions relating to terrorist activity.[7] As promoted by the Canadian Department of Justice, this act "creates measures to *deter, disable, identify, prosecute, convict and punish* terrorist groups ... [and] provides *new investigative tools* to law enforcement and national security agencies."[8] The *IRPA* and the *Anti-Terrorism Act* were promoted as Canada's hard-hitting, two-pronged contribution to the post-September 11th "War against Terrorism."

Canada has long been involved in a host of national and transnational border security, interdiction, and prevention initiatives. While many of these originated prior to 11 September 2001, a number were formalized and widely publicized after September 11th, including the widely proclaimed thirty-point "Canada-US Smart Border Accord" and the "Joint Statement on Co-operation and Regional Migration Issues" signed with much fanfare on 3 December 2001 by the Canadian solicitor general and minister of citizenship and immigration and the attorney general of the United States.[9] These measures have received unprecedented support and have been pursued by the governments of Canada and the United States with vigour. This support has been framed and fuelled by the interaction of two quite different justifications: the protection of national security and public safety and the economic necessity of ensuring that the free flow of goods and services across the border is not significantly impaired. These political and economic imperatives, operating in the shadow of the crime-security nexus, the spectre of fraud, and a pervasive culture of fear, effectively overpowered the cautionary voices of civil libertarians, legal critics, nongovernmental advocates for new immigrants and refugees, and those anxious to preserve independent Canadian immigration and refugee policies and Canadian sovereignty more generally.

Nevertheless, *IRPA* was by no means universally welcomed. Not only was it criticized by those who thought that it did not go far enough in the enforcement direction, but it was also roundly criticized by those who objected to its negative stereotyping of new immigrants and refugees and its heavy enforcement emphasis, which, for example, expanded inadmissibility and exclusion provisions as well as powers of detention. The framework approach of the legislation leaves most of the details to extensive regulations that can be changed without the involvement of Parliament. Concerns were raised that *IRPA* has the effect of placing limits on the discretion of frontline officers while significantly expanding the discretion of bureaucrats. This concern is of interest in that the former legislation had been criticized for delegating *too much* discretion to frontline officers.[10] While the legislation does include more prominent references to Canada's human rights obligations than the former legislation, it also expands the categories of people who are to be denied these protections. By excluding those deemed to be "serious criminals, terrorists, traffickers and security risks," there is, as cautioned by Amnesty International, "a real danger of sending some of them back to face serious human rights violations such as torture."[11] The bill had originally provided for a new independent appeal for denied refugee claims, a provision that had to a certain degree assuaged some of the concerns of its critics. However, as of March 2005, this appeal had yet to be implemented.

Despite its title, *IRPA* is not primarily about protecting refugees. What guides this legislation is the protection of the Canadian public, nation, borders, and integrity of Canada's administrative systems. It is Canadians who need to be protected from the threats posed by "foreign nationals" – the manifestly alienating term used in the legislation to refer to prospective immigrants and refugees who are noncitizens of Canada. The needs of refugees for protection and for a place to live are very much in second place.

To the extent that this legislation affords protection to refugees, it is simply assumed that this inclusionary humanitarian aim will be addressed more or less automatically by more extensive enforcement-oriented provisions to detect, detain, and deport "criminal abusers" that will free up the system to deal with those who are truly in need of protection. This effect is captured by the analogy of closing and opening doors, as offered by the minister of citizenship and immigration: "Closing the back door to those who would abuse the system allows us to ensure that the front door will remain open both to genuine refugees and to the immigrants our country will need to grow and prosper in the years ahead."[12] The closure of the back door, and the removal of "undesirables" who have managed to sneak through it, are to be achieved through tough proactive measures included in the legislation. However, other than closing the back door, relatively few measures are offered in the legislation that would enable refugees to reach, let alone enter through, the front door. Instead, the Canadian government, along with the rest of the Western world, has simultaneously bolstered prevention and interdiction policies that have precisely the opposite effect.

Europe, Australia, and the United States: Building Fortresses
Canada is not alone in these preoccupations. Over the past decade, Australia, the United States, and many countries in Western Europe have been engaged in sustained efforts to deflect refugees and undesirable migrants from their borders.

On 18 June 1990, the *Schengen Convention* was signed in the European Union (EU).[13] It commits its members to the elimination of internal border checks, permitting free movement between participating countries, to the harmonization of visa policies, and to the strengthening and standardization of external border controls. Schengen countries have access to an integrated security information system (the Schengen Information System), and there are close links and networks between different law enforcement and judicial authorities. Member states have also committed to joint efforts to combat drug and other threats. The 1990 *Dublin Convention* created standardized criteria for determining in which country refugees had to make their claims. These criteria are based largely on assigning cases to the country of first arrival.[14] This convention entered into force for all fifteen EU member states in 1995.[15]

European countries had already been strengthening border enforcement and implementing stricter immigration and refugee controls for some time. A few examples. In 1993, Germany amended its *Asylum Law,* making access to German asylum procedures much more difficult and facilitating the removal of, as put by the German Embassy, "bogus refugees." It instituted "safe third country" and "safe country of origin" amendments and enhanced border checks and patrols. The law designated all of the countries that border Germany as safe third countries, with the result that all asylum seekers who travel overland to Germany are denied the right to apply for asylum and may be turned back by border guards. The effects of these changes were immediate. In 2001, there were 88,000 asylum applications, down from 104,353 the year before.[16]

In response to September 11th, Germany quickly passed antiterrorist legislation. It extends substantially the powers of state authorities to carry out security checks on noncitizens and to monitor them while they are in the country. In addition, the new legislation excludes more varieties of criminals and security threats from asylum procedures and facilitates detention and deportation procedures.[17]

In France, under the 1992 and 1994 "Waiting Zone" legislation, noncitizens who have been refused admission and asylum seekers may be held (or, if refugee claimants in transit from a safe third country, will be held) in waiting zones (*zones d'attentes*) for up to twenty days, provided judicial permission is obtained after four days. Asylum seekers have no access to their files, and access to interpreters is reportedly poor. They also have no legal status and do not receive any financial or other assistance while their claims are pending.[18] France has been particularly concerned to prevent undocumented asylum seekers from entering France via the Eurotunnel from England, just as England has been concerned to prevent undocumented asylum seekers from entering England through the same route. The 2001 Anglo-French Agreement posted French police officers at the British point of departure to remove undocumented people from trains destined for France, and later the same year the two countries agreed again to toughen up enforcement practices at the tunnel.[19]

A series of enforcement-oriented and increasingly restrictive reforms to British immigration legislation was introduced over the 1990s. The *Asylum and Immigration Appeals Act* of 1993, the 1996 *Asylum and Immigration Act,* and the 1999 *Immigration and Asylum Act* all introduced increasingly tough and restrictive measures to crack down on system abuse and false refugee claims and, more generally, to "stem the flow" of migrants and asylum seekers to the United Kingdom.[20] In 2002, the government passed yet another tough piece of legislation, the *Nationality, Immigration, and Asylum Act,* which restricted the right to deportation appeals, introduced new border control measures and technologies to identify those using false identities, introduced new criminal offences for assisting illegal immigration and harbouring unlawful immigrants, and enhanced powers of detention.[21] Barely a year later, the government introduced the *Asylum and Immigration Bill 2003,* which further removes legal safeguards for refugee claimants, restricts access to appeals, facilitates removals based on safe third country provisions, and removes support for unsuccessful asylum seekers.[22]

In the same year, the UK government made plans to relocate refugee claimants to "Asylum Transit Camps" to be located outside the EU. It also proposed the establishment of "Regional Protection Centres" or "Zones of Protection" in regions close to the world's "trouble spots" for those seeking refuge, arguing that this way the refugees would be much closer to their countries of origin, making their return that much easier and more convenient. Both proposals were greeted with strong opposition from human rights and advocacy groups as efforts to put refugees "out of sight, out of mind,"[23] and to shift "responsibility for asylum seekers and refugees to some of the poorest countries in the world."[24] While this effort to deflect refugees from Europe received support from Denmark, Austria, and the Netherlands, in the face of opposition and the lack of support from other European countries, the government subsequently announced that it was no longer considering establishing the transit camps.[25]

Australia has an exceptionally punitive approach to immigration, refugee, and border-related issues. Its "Pacific Solution" intercepts ships carrying undocumented migrants and asylum seekers and sends them to Australian-funded detention facilities located in Nauru, Papua New Guinea, and Australia's Christmas Island.[26] Australia's navy and coast guard monitor surrounding waters to prevent vessels carrying asylum seekers from landing.[27]

Australia's inland detention facilities are bulging as a result of its long-standing policy of automatic detention of all asylum seekers. Under the 1958 *Migration Act* and the 1994 *Migration Regulations,* all noncitizens who "unlawfully" enter Australia are detained. Those who claim asylum are usually detained for the duration of the adjudication process, which can take months or even years.[28] Many of the detention facilities are located in isolated and remote areas, including the now-closed notorious camp at Woomera.[29]

In 1996, the United States passed the *Illegal Immigration Reform and Immigrant Responsibility Act.* It introduced tough new criminal sanctions for immigration offences, increasing the number of enforcement personnel and posting more Immigration and Naturalization Service (INS) enforcement officers at the border. Like British reforms, the act also restricted eligibility for benefits and imposed tougher requirements relating to sponsorship.[30] INS officers are required to detain virtually all noncitizens who are the subjects of removal proceedings as well as "all asylum seekers in the expedited removal process until the claimants have established a credible fear of persecution; all arriving aliens who appear inadmissible; and all persons who have been ordered removed for at least 90 days following the order."[31] According to the US Committee for Refugees in 2001, an average of 20,000 individuals were in immigration detention each day, including 3,000 asylum seekers.[32]

The 1996 legislation introduced the expedited removal process for "inadmissible aliens" seeking entry to the United States. Under this process, an INS officer may summarily order the immediate removal of a noncitizen ("alien") if the officer concludes that the person in question is undocumented or improperly documented, unless that person makes a refugee claim. If a claim is made, the case is referred to an asylum officer, who determines if the claim has a "credible basis." If no such basis is found, the officer may order the immediate removal of that individual "without further hearing or review." There are no appeals of expedited removal decisions.[33]

Since September 11th, the US has introduced additional and extreme enforcement measures. The *Uniting and Strengthening America by Providing Appropriate Tools Required to Intercept and Obstruct Terrorism Act (USA PATRIOT)* of 2001 expands the definitions of terrorist-related threats and creates new measures to facilitate the detention and deportation of those identified as terrorists. New rules were also introduced that provide for the indefinite detention of noncitizens for reasons of national security.[34] In perhaps the most extreme move, President George Bush issued an order that allows military tribunals to try noncitizens charged with terrorism. This order gives the tribunals the authority to develop their own trial procedures, the trials may be held anywhere in the world, and the proceedings are secret. The tribunals require only a two-thirds majority to convict and impose sentence, and they are empowered to impose the death penalty. Under the order, there is no right to appeal a decision to any other court.[35]

The developments sketched here rest upon and reproduce the discursive associations between security, criminality, and fraud that have converged upon "foreigners" in general and refugee claimants in particular. These efforts do not provide protection or find safe and enduring solutions for refugees; rather, they have the effect of deflecting people in need, people attempting to escape poverty or famine or drought or war, people fleeing persecution, people looking for a safe place to live.[36]

While not a novel observation, it is nonetheless remarkable that, at the same time as Western, industrialized countries have been pursuing interdiction with such vigour, the same states have urged the breaking down of national economic borders to facilitate the free flow of capital. Just as transnational efforts to achieve a borderless global economy have taken place, so too have national efforts to fortify and secure territorial borders against "undesirable" outsiders through the intensification and proliferation of technologies of control and enforcement. These developments and their associated emphases on rooting out fraud and identifying who is and who is not a citizen may also be indicative of what John Torpey has termed the state monopolization of the legitimate means of movement, a historically contingent process that contributes to the continual constitution of nation-states and "their" citizens.[37] William Walters has identified these and related developments as part of the international police of population. From this perspective, the "allocation of subjects to their proper sovereigns ... serves to sustain the image of a world divided into 'national' populations and territories, domiciled in terms of state membership."[38] Understood in this broader context, Canadian efforts to crack down on "criminals and others who would abuse Canada's openness and generosity"[39] are thus neither new nor exceptional.

A Few Conceptual Notes

While this study is not in any strict sense a "governmentality study," I am nonetheless guided in this work by a number of insights that derive from the work of Michel Foucault and from the analytics of government that his work has inspired.

Penality, Power, and the State

Foucault urged that systems of punishment, penality, be analyzed as social phenomena with a variety of effects rather than as merely the consequence of legal theory.[40] The material and political dimensions of the subjugation of human bodies should be attended to, as should the discourses, the ways of thinking and acting upon social relations, which turn these bodies into objects of knowledge. Discourses neither reflect nor disguise "true" social realities. As explained by Alan Hunt and Gary Wickham, discourse "constitutes social subjects, the subjectivities and identities of persons, their relations and the field in which they exist, but only within a context of institutional practices."[41]

Immigration penality and the borders that it sustains may be understood as an assemblage, as a historically constituted regime of practices "composed of heterogeneous elements having diverse historical trajectories, as polymorphous in their internal and external relations, and as bearing upon a multiple and a wide range of problems and issues."[42] Formal institutions of government and the law play but a part in their operations; neither immigration penality nor the border is reducible to "the state" or law. Foucault was expressly concerned to decentre the state as the locus of power and of law as its instrument: "I don't want to say that the state isn't important;

what I want to say is that relations of power, and hence the analysis that must be made of them, necessarily extend beyond the limits of the state."[43]

Following Foucault, the focus shifts from the state to a conception of government that is not limited to formal institutions but understood more broadly as "all endeavours to shape, guide, direct the conduct of others."[44] Government also includes how we are urged, incited, educated to govern ourselves. It thus involves a plurality of aims and means that are not reducible to the unified state, to the sovereign, or to juridical law. It is, as explained by Nikolas Rose and Peter Miller, "the historically constituted matrix within which are articulated all those dreams, schemes, strategies and manoeuvres of authorities that seek to shape the beliefs and conduct of others in desired directions by acting upon their will, their circumstances or their environment."[45] Often the more general term "governance" is used to connote this decentred understanding of government as the conduct of conduct.

The force of Foucault's critique of conventional state-centred analyses of power does not, however, preclude the application of Foucauldian tools to a domain that does coincide with the formal institutions of government, that is governed by law, and that clearly does display negative and interdictory qualities. Such analyses, however, must be particularly sensitive to the heterogeneity and complexity of governing programs, discourses, forms of knowledge, authorities, and technologies that are at play.[46]

Power is not something that is owned or wielded by the powerful against the powerless. It is ubiquitous and dispersed. Foucault directs attention not to the source of power but to its techniques, strategies, and effects. His rejection of state-centred analyses is supplemented by his rejection of the view that power is exclusively negative, interdictory, and repressive. Relations of power are also and directly productive: "We must cease once and for all to describe the effects of power in negative terms: it 'excludes,' it 'represses,' it 'censors,' it 'abstracts,' it 'masks,' it 'conceals.' In fact power produces; it produces reality; it produces domains of objects and rituals of truth. The individual and the knowledge that may be gained of him belong to this production."[47] Thus, attention to the negative and coercive effects of border practices and immigration penalty should not obscure their productive and positive effects. Indeed, immigration penalty actively produces historically specific conceptions of "the border," national identity, citizenship, and the desirable/undesirable citizen.

Contemporary developments in the domain of border control and security, including "deterritorialization," "securitization," the proliferation of hard and soft border control technologies, the expansion of networks and alliances between national and international agencies, and the expansion of the very category of "security," have been addressed in a variety of ways.[48]

In this study, the border is regarded as at once, but not simply, a physical, built environment, a line on a map, a sociolegal construct, a political invention, and a mechanism of inclusion/exclusion. The border is a contingent and artful accomplishment. It is continuously constituted and reconstituted at a variety of sites through an assemblage of intersecting authorities, technologies, forms of knowledge, and regimes of rule. Furthermore, the border is a flexible and elastic sociolegal construct that plays a central part in the ongoing constitution and regulation of identities (refugees, citizens, criminals, victims, deportees, etc.) and the welfare of the population. The Canadian "border" is constituted by diverse practices that effectively decide who and who may not enter the country. It defines both insiders and outsiders. It is a historically specific creation erected through shifting state and extra-state rationales and practices of governance. Yet this sociotechnological complexity of the border has been obscured by its self-evidence. It has been, to borrow from Bruno Latour, "black boxed."[49] This study begins in a preliminary way to pry open the black box of the border and unsettle its self-evidence.

Sovereignty, Discipline, and Governmentality

> The traveller glanced casually at the man, who, when pointed at by the officer, had kept his head lowered and now seemed to be all ears, trying to catch something. But the movements of his pressed, pouting lips made it obvious that he could understand nothing. The traveller had wanted to put various questions to the officer, but at the sight of the condemned man, asked only: "Does he know his judgement?"
>
> "No," said the officer, about to continue his explanations; but the traveller broke in: "He doesn't know his own judgement?"
>
> "No," the officer repeated, pausing for an instant as if demanding a more detailed explanation of the question. The officer then said: "It would be no use informing him. He's going to experience it on his body anyway."[50]

As Foucault famously demonstrated, sovereign punishments were bodily, bloody, and spectacular. They literally and painfully inscribed the "judgement," the power of the king, on the bodies of the condemned. Sovereign punishments were occasioned by transgressions of sovereign authority and sought "spectacularly, spasmodically and violently"[51] to reestablish the authority of the sovereign over his territory and subjects in the face of such transgressions. The sovereign mode of punishment, characteristic of premodern and early modern times, aimed to reaffirm "the dissymmetry between the subject who has dared to violate the law and the all powerful sovereign who displays his strength."[52]

The sovereign could also withhold punishment, "suspend law and vengeance,"[53] "decide on the exception."[54] Giorgio Agamben explores the power to rule on the exception as a key feature of sovereign power. He explores "the camp" as a liminal zone of "bare life," neither outside nor inside the polity. It is at this "threshold of indistinction" that exceptional measures become the norm,[55] where "violence passes over into law and law passes over into violence."[56] The detention centre, like the camp, is a zone of exclusion that manifests this sovereign power to decide on the exception.[57] It is a liminal and exceptional space governed by exceptional measures operating outside the usual parameters of juridical rule. The constituent features of sovereign power thus include negative and bodily punishments, the capacity to decide the exception, the defence or control of territory, and an affinity for spectacle.[58]

Foucault proposed that the sovereign mode of power characteristic of premodern and early modern feudal societies had been reconfigured by the emergence of disciplinary and governmental regimes.[59] Whereas sovereignty is characterized by the discontinuous exercise of power through spectacle, by law as command, and by sanctions as negative, bodily, and deductive, disciplinary regimes feature "the continuous exercise of power through surveillance, individualization and normalization."[60] Disciplinary regimes in modern prisons, as in factories, schools, and asylums, "worked to instil obedience and social utility in their inmates by encouraging them to internalize methods of self-scrutiny and control. No longer merely an enemy of the king's peace, the criminal in this historical period came to represent a deviation from a social norm to be corrected and restored."[61] Thus, in the modern period, there emerged a "higher aim" of punishment: to transform or "normalize" offenders through the gentler techniques of discipline and surveillance. This aim was linked with the development of new knowledges in the emergent human sciences and with the rise of a new conception of political rule as distinct from sovereign rule.[62] Discipline is a distinct form of power that entails a range of governing techniques that do not rest upon force or coercion and that thus contrast sharply with the "majestic rituals of sovereignty."[63]

Foucault draws attention to new forms of governmentalities (governing mentalities) that became more important than sovereignty in the eighteenth and nineteenth centuries. Unlike the negative and deductive power of sovereignty, which from the Middle Ages is characterized by the "transcendent singularity"[64] of the authority of the sovereign over his territory and subjects with the law as its "singular instrument,"[65] the art of government, also referred to as governmentality, that flourished in the eighteenth century follows a "productive logic."[66] Governmental rule seeks to shape and guide the conduct of citizens in the name of the health, wealth, happiness, and welfare of the population.[67] The economy, formerly conceived as "the correct manner of managing individuals, goods and wealth within the family," is introduced "into the management of the state."[68]

Governmental rule is linked to the emergence of "apparatuses of security," which include "the use of standing armies, police forces, diplomatic corps, intelligence services and spies" but also "health, education and social welfare systems and the mechanisms of the management of the national economy."[69] Governmental rule is also linked to the development of statistics as a science of government and to the new science of political economy. It entails the development of complex and vast administrative state apparatuses to achieve these diverse aims.

Foucault cautions against understanding the growth of the administrative state in terms of ever-expanding state domination of society; rather, he characterizes the process as the "governmentalization of the state."[70] More specifically, this refers to the rise of the administrative state, the process through which "the discursive, legislative, fiscal, organizational and other resources of the public powers have come to be linked in varying ways into networks of rule. Mobile divisions and relations have been established between political rule and other projects and techniques for the calculated administration of life."[71] Governmentality has not replaced sovereignty or discipline; rather, it has rearticulated them "within this concern for the population and its optimization."[72]

The domain of immigration is multidimensional and expansive, coercive and enabling, harsh and humanitarian. While inclusionary and enabling governmental technologies certainly act upon those deemed worthy of citizenship who are ushered into "zones of inclusion," coercive and despotic practices persist in relation to those deemed unworthy and who are confined within "zones of exclusion" and ultimately expelled from the nation. Sovereign power is thus not merely a "fiction" or an "archaic residue of the past." Indeed, it is a distinctly sovereign regime that is paramount in the governance of the particular sites and practices of immigration detention and deportation. No efforts are needed to transform "deficient" outsiders into desirable, governable citizen-subjects.[73] Those deemed unwanted are physically confined and forcefully expelled. In this zone of exclusion, rules, not norms, are the central feature of the regimes that govern this site, and it is the bodies, not the souls, habits, or risks, of noncitizens that are directly targeted.

Still, contemporary regimes of sovereign power are more complicated than the mode that Foucault described. The spectacle of punishment has been reconfigured. Detention in an airport motel is a far cry from the scaffold in the town square. While detention at the Celebrity Inn immigration detention centre in Mississauga, Ontario, is rather low-profile and out of sight, there are occasional broadcasts of widely publicized, high-profile detentions and deportations that have become more frequent as deterrence and prevention objectives have become more entrenched. One such spectacle surrounded the high-profile interception, detention, and subsequent deportation of 599 Chinese nationals from Fujian, China, who arrived on the West Coast of Canada in four boats in the summer of 1999. After those who arrived on the first boat disappeared after being released once bond was posted, immigration officials detained the remainder of the arrivals as flight risks, most in correctional facilities.[74] The massive media coverage of this event provided frequent images of the migrants being subjected to various criminal justice technologies: barbed wire, shackles, guard dogs, prison uniforms, and guards. Despite being identified as victims of people smugglers, they were simultaneously represented in popular and political discourse as system abusers, queue jumpers, bogus refugees, and even criminals. Most of the migrants were eventually deported with similar fanfare and sensationalized media coverage. While the numbers of those targeted were more concentrated than usual, they were not exceptionally large. This event demonstrates not only the easy slippage between the categories of refugees, frauds and criminals, victims and offenders, but also speaks to the continued, albeit modified, operations of spectacle in the application of sovereign power in this field.

It is nonetheless the case that detention and deportation cannot be understood exclusively in terms of sovereignty; they lie at the intersection of sovereignty and governmentality.[75] Indeed, even in the context of these seemingly straightforward sites of negative, coercive, and interdictory sovereign practices, there is still the coexistence and commingling of different authorities, regimes, and technologies. For example, while not new, the role of third parties, "partners," and community members in the governance of immigration penality has become more prominent.[76] Indeed, when one considers the domain of immigration penality and border control more broadly, the interpenetration of sovereign and governmental technologies is much in evidence. This multiplicity and intersectionality of state, quasi-state, and "community" players and the diversity of practices and technologies at work display one way in which detention and deportation have become "governmentalized."

Furthermore, if one examines the changes over time in the grounds for and justifications surrounding detention and deportation, another dimension of the governmentalization of detention and deportation becomes apparent. Certainly, while political enemies of the state have long been and continue to be the targets of detention and deportation, the categories of those to be excluded or expelled have expanded dramatically over the past century to encompass a variety of potential threats to the economy and the welfare of the population.[77] As documented in the chapters that follow, even as racist, moralistic, and otherwise discriminatory grounds for exclusion were delegitimized, the grounds for exclusion based on criminal threats posed to the population proliferated in Canada. Moreover, the very category of security, once associated in virtually singular relation with the protection of the political state from the threats posed by subversion, treason, and espionage, has been reconfigured to include an expanding roster of criminal threats to the public. Public safety, economic security, and system integrity are key constituents of contemporary concerns for the safety and welfare of the population that surround the programs and practices of immigration penalty and border control.

Liberalism, Law, and Discretion

Liberalism takes on a slightly different meaning within the perspective of governmentality. Rather than being understood as a theory, a juridical or political philosophy, an ideology or a set of policies, liberalism is understood as a political rationality: "the changing discursive field within which the exercise of power is conceptualized, the moral justifications for particular ways of exercising power by diverse authorities, notions of the appropriate forms, objects and limits of politics, and conceptions of the proper distribution of such tasks among secular, spiritual, military and familial sectors."[78] Put differently, liberalism is a broad historical discourse that rationalizes and systematizes specific governmental programs and policies for the ordering of social life in particular, historically specific ways. Rationalities and programs depend upon the existence of governmental technologies (strategies, techniques, devices, and procedures) that give them practical effect. As explained by Rose, "a technology of government, then, is an assemblage of forms of practical knowledge, with modes of perception, practices of calculation, vocabularies, types of authority, forms of judgement, architectural forms, human capacities, non-human objects and devices, inscription techniques and so forth, traversed and transected by aspirations to achieve certain outcomes in terms of the conduct of the governed."[79]

Liberal rationality sets out the limits of state powers, the freedom of rights-bearing subjects under the law, and carves out private domains of social life that lie outside the appropriate reach of direct political interference and control. Liberalism is thus characterized by indirect rule – "governing at a distance." As explained by Rose and Miller, it "identifies a domain outside of politics and seeks to manage it without destroying its existence and autonomy" through independent agents and alliances.[80] Liberalism is also characterized by the foundational problematic of security and liberty linked to the exercise of rights. As emphasized by Kevin Stenson, "liberalism has involved a difficult balance between a recognition of the need to promote freedom and diversity, yet impose a secure, unified field of state and juridical authority."[81]

While the specific practices of border control and immigration penality are perhaps less creatures of liberalism than they are of sovereignty,[82] they have nonetheless had to accommodate liberal political discourses relating to autonomy, accountability, the social contract, and the limits of state rule as well as related liberal legal doctrines of rights, the rule of law, and due process. These discourses have served to democratize sovereignty, to legitimize coercive practices, and have themselves played a central part in facilitating the emergence of new forms of disciplinary power.[83] Even noncitizens are rights-bearing subjects, in Canada at any rate, and their treatment must, to a certain degree, negotiate the political and legal dictates of liberal government.

Under liberalism, law is no longer the singular instrument of the sovereign; the elected parliament assumes the "mantle of sovereignty."[84] Liberal forms of legality (liberal legality) are constituted by the ideals of the rule of law, the separation of powers, and related conceptions of individual autonomy and free will. As put by George Pavlich, "liberal legality presumes the primordial existence of free, rational individuals – the bearers of its rights, duties and freedoms. This implies that such individuals exist naturally and merely require political structures to vindicate their natural form."[85]

Furthermore, rather than seeing law as an autonomous system of orders backed up by coercive sanctions that operates as an instrument of negative and oppressive power, scholars such as Alan Hunt have encouraged the view of law as one of many intersecting modes of regulation. In this view, law and social relations are mutually constitutive. The regulation approach encourages attention to both the positive and the negative dimensions of power – regulation makes possible and facilitates certain forms of social relations while discouraging and disadvantaging others.[86]

These observations about "law" should not be read to imply that there is a single, monolithic, and homogeneous body of law. Indeed, pluralistic analyses of law have effectively unsettled such a view, urging recognition that there is no totalizing unity to the "complex of written codes, judgements, institutions and agents and techniques of judgement that make up 'the law.'"[87] The diversity and historically specific context of law must be taken seriously.

Liberal legality may be understood as a metanarrative that construes law in terms of "universal principles grounded in the dictates of reason deemed intrinsic to all human subjects."[88] Under the conditions of liberal legality, administrative discretion becomes a key governmental technology that carves out a domain of freedom that negotiates or "accommodates" the apparent contradiction between the universality and particularity of liberal law and that reconciles the gap between law and equity.[89]

In the context of immigration penalty and border control, the practices of classifying and filtering the high from the low risk, the undeserving and undesirable from the deserving and desirable, produce borders and "make up" citizens. Just as the moralizing categorization of the deserving and undeserving poor legitimizes differential treatment on the basis of these categories, so too do the distinctions between the deserving and undeserving refugee and the desirable and undesirable immigrant. As explained by Hunt, the moral element of these categories "involves any normative judgment that some conduct is intrinsically bad, wrong or immoral. It is an important supplement that moralising discourses frequently invoke some utilitarian consideration linking the immoral practice to some form of harm."[90] These "dividing practices" are given practical effect through the operations of discretion under liberal legal regimes of government.[91]

Welfare Liberalism, Neoliberalism, and Technologies of Risk

Government is a problematizing activity that "poses the obligations of rulers in terms of the problems they seek to address."[92] Welfare liberalism as a political rationality conceptualizes and acts upon social problems that are understood in terms of the population and the economy – the declining birthrate, delinquency, the dysfunctional family, ill health, and so on. It is centrally linked to "the social" as a basis for thinking about and acting upon the population. The form of social government dominant from the late nineteenth century to the mid-twentieth century seeks to foster and enhance social solidarity through a variety of programs and objectives: social order, social welfare, social insurance, social security, social justice, social citizenship. Welfare liberalism emphasizes the collective rights and duties of citizenship and privileges social notions of risk management and risk sharing.[93] As put by Rose, it "seeks to encourage national growth and wellbeing through the promotion of social responsibility and the mutuality of social risk."[94] The mutuality of social risk refers to practices of nation-wide risk pooling that provide all individuals with some measure of security in the event of loss or interruption of income so long as the misfortune that occasions this need, whether it be sickness, unemployment, injury, or disability, is experienced "through no fault of their own." At the same time, individuals are stitched into a relation of mutual obligation and social responsibility; "individuals are constituted as citizens bound into a system of social solidarity and mutual interdependency."[95] Welfare liberalism entrenches moralistic distinctions between earned and unearned benefits, between the deserving and the undeserving poor. It teaches citizens moral lessons about thrift, hard work, responsibility, and obligation.

In contrast, neoliberal forms of government recast social responsibility and mutual obligation as dependency and passive citizenship.[96] The primacy accorded to social solidarity and the social citizen is displaced by the constitution of the independent, active, and entrepreneurial citizen. The state is judged to be too large, too intrusive, and too costly. Its role should be limited to maintaining law and order and to empowering "entrepreneurial subjects of choice in their quest for self-realization."[97] The role of individual citizens, on the other hand, is to actively promote their own well-being through ceaseless enterprise, responsible choices, and individual risk management techniques. Under neoliberal forms of rule, the "social state" gives way to the "enabling state." Individuals, families, organizations, schools, et cetera become "partners" who take on responsibility for their own well-being.[98] As defined by Rose, risk management involves "the identification, assessment, elimination or reduction of the possibility of incurring misfortunes or loss."[99] Neoliberal risk management technologies are individualized rather than social. In place of nation-wide risk pools, much smaller, differentiated risk pools have emerged. As observed by Jacques Donzelot, this modified conception of risk "shifts the emphasis from the principle of collective indemnification of ills and injuries attendant on life in society, towards a greater stress on the individual's civic obligation to moderate the burden of risk which he or she imposes on society."[100]

The "decline of the social" and the rise of neoliberalism have inflected the development and promotion of the laws, policies, and practices of immigration penality and border control in a variety of ways. For example, the rights-bearing claimant of social benefits, in the context of refugee claims, just as in the context of welfare claims, has been unsettled and rendered always and already suspect. Rather than being received as an entrepreneurial, self-governing, risk-taking potential citizen, the deserving figure of the refugee "at risk" has been widely recast as the "risky" refugee. As pointed out by Rose, "while social notions of risk were universalizing, these risk agencies focus upon 'the usual suspects' – the poor, the welfare recipients, the petty criminals" – who, along with refugees, are now constituted as actually or potentially "risky" individuals.[101] And the manifestly neoliberal spectre of fraud has come to occupy a central place in the exercise of government in the domains of welfare, refugee determination, and border control. In the same domains, as in that of criminal justice, increasingly punitive laws and policies are promoted according to the neoclassical logics of deterrence and dessert.

The "risk society" thesis[102] has generated considerable scholarly interest in risk "as a way of thinking about and trying to order our world."[103] Risk technologies are forward looking; "the centre of risk consciousness lies not in the present but *in the future* ... In risk society, the past loses the power to determine the present. Its place is taken by the future ... We become active today in order to prevent, alleviate or take precautions against the crises and problems of tomorrow and the day after tomorrow."[104] Scholars working in a variety of disciplines have investigated the content and practical uses of risk knowledges and risk management strategies in various settings.[105] Some, for example, have suggested the contemporary emergence of a "new penology" in which actuarial regimes of risk management have become more prominent than disciplinary regimes of "correction."[106] Robert Castel explains that "a risk does not arise from the presence of particular precise danger embodied in a concrete individual or group. It is the effect of a combination of abstract factors which render more or less probable the occurrence of undesirable modes of behaviour."[107] It is revealing to note that in the mid-1960s national exclusions that were formerly based on the dangers thought to inhere in certain subjects (prostitutes, homosexuals, criminals, beggars, chronic alcoholics) came to be justified instead on the basis of their "associated risks." While meaningful conclusions about the variety of uses and forms of risk knowledges and practices in the domain of border control and immigration penality remain a question for empirical investigation,[108] this study certainly points to the prominence of risk management technologies in the development and justification of contemporary practices of border control and immigration penality.

Governing *through* Crime

As observed by Jonathan Simon, "we govern through crime to the extent to which crime and punishment become the occasions and the institutional contexts in which we undertake to guide the conduct of others (or even of ourselves)."[109] Crime and punishment have become increasingly prominent themes in the promotion and justification of a broad range of law and social policy. Immigration penality has not been immune to this. The threats constituted by the crime-security nexus, blended with concerns about fraud and "system abuse" ("criminal abuse"), have become the primary occasion and justification for the development and application of increasingly enforcement-oriented immigration law and policy reforms and practices. Immigration penality and border control have been reconstituted under the banner of crime.

Governing through crime is linked to the decline of the social and the rise of neoliberal regimes of rule. On a broad level, it can be read as reflecting the emergent neoliberal view of law and order as the last remaining legitimate domain of interventionist state authority. It may also be read as a technique for the exclusion of those who are regarded as ungovernable, as unable or unwilling to "enterprise their lives or manage their own risk, incapable of exercising responsible self government, attached to no moral community or to a community of anti-morality."[110] Governing through crime is part of the construction and exclusion of a criminal population consisting of the poor, the dispossessed, the unemployed, and welfare recipients.[111] With the governance of immigration penality through crime, marginalized migrants and refugees are similarly targeted.

Chapter Outline

So easily accepted is the official rhetoric that the detention and deportation of noncitizens is not punishment that the first task of this book is to make visible the material conditions, concrete practices, and punitive dimensions of the detention and expulsion of undesirable, undeserving noncitizens. Chapter 2 provides a detailed examination of the carceral conditions and penal practices of immigration detention in the "Celebrity Budget Inn" in Mississauga, Ontario, near Pearson International Airport. This microstudy reveals that, while a sovereign regime of coercive, negative, and bodily power predominates at this liminal zone, there is nonetheless a multiplicity of authorities and technologies involved in its day-to-day administration.

Discretion has always been central to the operation of immigration penalty in Canada. A guiding concern of this work is the shifting roles of law and discretion in national exclusions. The conventional legal view of law/ discretion as a zero-sum game is an inadequate frame for thinking about the operations of power in this field. I therefore consider in some detail in Chapter 3 the limits imposed by this conventional view of law versus discretion and seek to avoid these limits by considering discretion as an *active* form of governmental power rather than a residual space created by law.

In Chapter 4, I document the way that, as previously legitimate grounds for exclusion – race, morality, political ideology – were socially, politically, and legally delegitimized over the postwar period, the crime-security nexus articulated through the language of risk emerged as the guiding logic of border control and immigration penalty. While the waning of the Cold War undermined the legitimacy of exclusions justified by a strictly political conception of "the state," the logic of national security expanded to include an ever-widening roster of criminal threats to the population. This reconfiguration of national security, along with broad tracts of discretionary power dedicated to its protection, reveal the transition from a sovereign construction of the state to one that is more strongly associated with governmental concerns for public safety and the economic welfare and protection of the population.

The production and inclusion of the desirable immigrant (the independent, talented, entrepreneurial, and skilled newcomer with high economic "establishment potential") and the deserving refugee (the credible and genuine victim of persecution "through no fault of their own") only become possible through the criminalization, repression, and exclusion of undesirable, undeserving new immigrants and refugees. Alongside the figure of the genuinely deserving refugee emerged that of the unscrupulous, fraudulent, risky, and even downright criminal refugee claimant – each produced and maintained in contradistinction to the other, the latter excluded in the name of the former. Chapter 5 details this emergence of the "bogus refugee" over the 1980s and the forging of its association with that of the "criminal foreigner."

The protection of rights-bearing and deserving (genuine) refugees has become contingent upon the identification and exclusion of dangerous criminals, security threats, and opportunistic system abusers. Neoliberal preoccupations with fraud, also evident in the domain of social services, are seen to converge with crime-security to produce a powerful new threat, "the fraudulent criminal refugee." The corollary concern for victims and victim rights that has become more and more prominent in most areas of public policy has had no echo in relation to refugees and migrants. Instead, it has been the state, state systems, and the public that have been constructed as the victims of unscrupulous, criminal, and otherwise risky refugees. In Chapter 6, I examine this redefinition of refugees from being "at risk" to being "risky" through a mini case study of the Somali community in Toronto, Ontario.

In Chapter 7, I return to the specific question of discretion and examine the legal construction of dangers to the public and threats to national security. In 1995, those deemed a danger to the public joined those deemed threats to national security as the only two categories of people denied access to the usual processes of deportation appeal. The implications of these crime-security-based national exclusions are examined through analysis of the 2002 Supreme Court of Canada (SCC) *Suresh* decision. The articulation and resolution of issues relating to serious criminality/national security, international human rights, and national sovereignty in the Canadian courts are found to be thoroughly embedded in and shaped by the powerful binaries of law versus discretion, liberty versus security, and freedom versus authority.

Immigration enforcement, border control, and the policies and practices of detention and deportation have been reshaped under the banner of crime. In Chapter 8, I review the prominent national and transnational crime-security threats that have animated immigration penalty over the past decade and the proliferation of national and international initiatives to counter these threats.

In Chapter 9, I begin to pry open the "black box" of the border. I explore the range of intersecting and diverse authorities, networks, and technologies that are engaged in immigration penalty and that both control the border and continually constitute it. Border control and immigration penalty more generally are situated in relation to the endless quest for security, and I pay particular attention to the prominence of risk management strategies in this quest.

Finally, I conclude the book with reflections on a number of conceptual and empirical issues that emerge from this study: the centrality of discretion and dividing practices in systems of liberal rule and in the operations of immigration penality; the relationship of immigration penality with transitions from welfare liberal to neoliberal forms of governance; the continuing importance of sovereign power and its intersections with governmental, risk-based strategies of rule in the domain of immigration penality and the regulation of borders; and the emergence of criminality and punishment (detention and deportation) as central to the promotion and development of border control and immigration penality.

2

Detention at the Celebrity Inn

The Celebrity Inn, part hotel and part immigration detention centre, is a Kafkaesque "centre of confinement."[1] The "prisoners of passage" confined within Celebrity are quasi-criminal transgressors of quasi-judicial law or quasi-rights-bearing noncitizen subjects who are subjected to quasi-legal, quasi-administrative, quasi-criminal rituals of exclusion. The boundaries here are blurred; one finds public servants, private security, private health care, government authorities, nongovernmental volunteers, community representatives, public legal aid, private counsel, law enforcement, administrative policy, protection, punishment, paternalism, hospitality, and incarceration. This zone of exclusion exhibits a strange blend of governing rationales, technologies, and authorities, from shackles to child care. Despite this multiplicity, this is nonetheless sovereign power in action. The forcible confinement of these individuals does not aim to "correct," "reform," or "transform" souls, habits, or risks. It has no official purpose other than to confine and ultimately expel the actual bodies of undesired noncitizens.

Confinement at Celebrity is not technically carceral criminal punishment: it is administrative detention. Notwithstanding the historical legal distinction between administrative detention and criminal justice punishment, those who are suspected of violating immigration law for whatever reason, criminal or otherwise, are acted upon as criminals – a trend that, as detailed in the chapters to follow, has intensified since the early 1990s. That Celebrity is a "holding" as opposed to a "detention" centre, that the detainees are "administratively" rather than "punitively" confined, and that they are specifically classified as "noncriminals" are largely irrelevant to those who are held there.

The Death of Michael Akhimien

On 17 December 1995, in the Celebrity Inn Immigration Holding Centre, thirty-nine-year-old Michael Akhimien's naked body was found in a bathtub overflowing with water. He had slipped into a coma from which he would not awake.[2] After claiming refugee status on 28 October, Akhimien, a Nigerian, was detained by Citizenship and Immigration Canada (CIC).[3] He was held for two days at the CIC holding centre in Niagara Falls and then transferred to Celebrity on 30 October. He never left. Shortly before his death, Akhimien had written the following words to immigration officials: "[I would rather] die in Nigeria for a reason than waste away in [detention in Canada] when I had done nothing wrong."[4]

Akhimien had become increasingly unwell while in immigration detention. His pleas for medical attention were either ignored or disbelieved by the facility's security guards. On several occasions, he had been placed in solitary confinement after verbal confrontations with the guards. Twice before his death, Akhimien had been found unconscious by security guards in this segregated room.[5] He suffered from nausea, dizziness, fuzzy vision, and fatigue. He lost weight and was having difficulty eating solid foods. Akhimien made twelve written requests for medical treatment and many verbal ones. He even offered to pay for a checkup with his own money. On the one occasion that he was seen by the private doctor contracted by Celebrity, the doctor found nothing seriously wrong with him, although no tests were carried out to confirm this conclusion.[6] After his death, it was determined that Akhimien had been suffering from a diabetic disease (diabetic ketoacidosis) that, according to the coroner's jury that heard the inquest, had caused his death.[7] In desperation, Akhimien indicated that he would rather return to Nigeria than remain in detention in Canada, and he made two applications to withdraw his refugee application. This request was finally granted on 15 December.

On 17 December, Akhimien asked the security guards for some water. When they did not bring him any, he went without security escort to the kitchen to get it himself. A symptom of the diabetes that he was suffering from is extreme thirst. Upon finding him outside his room without security escort, guards forcibly returned him to solitary confinement and left him there. The coroner's synopsis of the case indicates that Akhimien was found lying on the floor and was "reported not to be eating or drinking." One hour later he was found unconscious lying in an overflowing bathtub. Akhimien never regained consciousness. Hours later, alone and still in solitary confinement, he slipped into a coma and died. Finding him at 11:35 p.m. without any vital signs, security officers attempted CPR and called 911. Akhimien was finally transferred to hospital, where he was pronounced dead at 12:15 a.m., 18 December 1995.

Michael Akhimien had sought protection in Canada in accordance with national and international human rights law. Concerns about his identity cast official doubt on his claim to be a credible and genuinely deserving victim and led to the decision to detain him. From first contact, Akhimien was surrounded by and subjected to a pervasive culture of disbelief. This profound distrust extended even to his claims of intense physical suffering while in detention. The coroner's inquest ruled that Akhimien died of "natural causes" and did not address the harm of solitary confinement, thereby ignoring the punitive and coercive circumstances and practices that had at the least exacerbated his suffering before he died and at the worst actually contributed to his death. In accordance with the limitations set out in the *Coroners Act,*[8] the coroner's court jury made no findings relating to legal responsibility, nor did it express any "conclusion of law."[9] The jury did, however, make twenty-nine recommendations. Most of these were directed toward the need to improve health care at the facility and to improve communication between medical staff, security staff, and immigration officers at the centre. From these recommendations, it is clear, for example, that there was confusion whether Akhimien was in solitary confinement for punitive or medical reasons and whether he was being disciplined or treated. There was no doubt, at least, that the multiplicity and often oppositional nature of authorities, rationales, and technologies at play and the fragmentation and miscommunication that this multiplicity entailed were "problems" requiring attention.

The Nigerian Canadian Association immediately applied for judicial review of the inquest on the ground that it had been conducted in a biased and discriminatory manner. However, Akhimien's family lacked the resources required to complete this legal process. In December 1996, the surviving relatives of Michael Akhimien submitted a communication to the United Nations Committee against Torture alleging that Akhimien had been subjected to "cruel, inhuman or degrading treatment" while in detention; that his death was preventable; that the acts or omissions of the employees of the immigration detention centre were the cause of his death; and that the government of Canada therefore bore responsibility for his death. The committee decided that the communication was inadmissible at that time as all domestic remedies had not been exhausted.[10]

Zones of Exclusion

Michael Akhimien died in the zone of exclusion that is immigration detention. Immigration detention facilities that confine undesirable non-citizens are very exceptional sites of government. They exist at the edges, the boundaries, on the very borders that demarcate territory, "topographizing it, investing it with powers, bounding it by exclusions, defining who or what can rightfully enter."[11] As Nikolas Rose notes, perhaps fancifully but certainly intriguingly, the term "territory" derives from *terre* but also perhaps from *"terrere,"* meaning "to frighten, terrorize, exclude, warn off."[12]

Those confined within these facilities are literally and metaphorically "prisoners of passage" confined at a distinctly liminal site evocative of Michel

Foucault's work on madness and asylums.[13] Speaking of the space within which the madman was confined, Foucault notes that "it simply develops, across a half-real, half-imaginary geography, the madman's *liminal* position on the horizon of medieval concern – a position symbolized and made real by the madman's privilege of being *confined* within the city *gates:* his exclusion must enclose him; if he cannot and must not have another *prison* than the *threshold* itself, he is kept at the point of passage. He is put in the interior of the exterior, and inversely."[14] Like the asylums that Foucault describes, and the camps that are the concern of Giorgio Agamben, the detention centre represents a "third order of repression," a peculiar sovereign power that is established "between the police and the court, at the limits of the law."[15] It is a quasi-judicial, administrative entity, a "centre of confinement" that "decides, judges and executes" and that exercises "quasi-absolute sovereignty."[16] Those who occupy this in-between space are the "naked lives" of Agamben's camp – without political voice, status, or protection, they are bare life, barely alive.[17]

Detention facilities are a liminal space, a "zone of exclusion," the boundaries of which separate those destined for inclusion and those for whom exclusion is "inexorable." Those who do not qualify for inclusionary governmental interventions (including, for example, citizenship tests and rituals, settlement programs, public services, and job training), those who "exist outside of this nexus of activity," are the "underclass, the marginalized, the truly disadvantaged."[18]

A number of characteristics make immigration detention a distinct field of study: those in detention are noncitizens; they occupy the liminal space of the border; and, while the mode of power predominant at these centres of confinement is sovereign, the authorities, techniques, and processes that are entailed in the administration and operation of this mode of power are multiple and diverse, and its effects are similarly varied. While immigration detention is situated metaphorically and symbolically in the liminal space of the border, the Celebrity Inn is not physically located at, or even very near, the Canadian border. The practices of detention and deportation are distinctly negative and coercive, but they are also productive. Detention and deportation continuously constitute and reconstitute the sovereignty of the expelling nation, the sovereignties of receiving nations, the "proper" national citizenship of subjects, the identities of citizens, noncitizens, and nations, and the conceptions of borders.

In what follows, I pay careful attention to the specific, technical, and material conditions and practices of immigration detention at Celebrity. Even at this apparently uncomplicated and obvious site of "state" authority, conventional boundaries are blurred, and a multiplicity of authorities and technologies coexist and intersect.[19]

The Celebrity Inn Immigration Holding Centre

"Travellers under Cloud Stay at the Inn of Unhappiness"
Welcome to the Celebrity Inn – an Immigration Holding Centre, in bureaucratic parlance. In reality it is an immigration jail for the unlucky, the fraudulent and the suspect.[20]

In the United States, hotels that double as immigration holding centres have been referred to as "Kafka hotels,"[21] no doubt because of Franz Kafka's powerful depiction of the absurd, seemingly senseless, though ultimately punitive qualities of modern bureaucracy.

The Celebrity Inn in Mississauga is Canada's own Kafka hotel, complete with Kafkaesque name. It is located in one wing of the fully functioning and busy airport hotel, the Celebrity Budget Inn. Conveniently located less than a kilometre from Toronto's Pearson International Airport, Celebrity promises to "treat all guests as celebrities."[22]

There are two entrances for those who stay at Celebrity, one for those who can leave freely and one for those who cannot. The included and the excluded bunk in different wings of the same hotel, illustrating dramatically the contrasting destinies of those deemed to be deserving and/or desirable and those deemed otherwise who are ushered into this distinct zone of exclusion.

The Celebrity Inn is one of the three principal immigration holding centres in Canada. The other two are located in Vancouver, British Columbia, and Laval, Quebec. In 2004, Vancouver operated a centre for short-term detentions (under seventy-two hours). Laval's facility, officially designated the "Immigration Prevention Centre," is located in a refurbished former prison. Generally speaking, there are between 75 and 100 people detained at Celebrity, which has the capacity to detain 100 people "comfortably."[23] In contrast, Vancouver and Montreal Laval each hold approximately twenty to forty people.[24]

These immigration "holding centres" are for the detention of noncriminal noncitizens, people who have come to the attention of the authorities, who have violated or are suspected of having violated Canadian immigration law, and who are judged, initially by immigration officers and subsequently by adjudicators, to represent a "flight risk." Individuals whose cases involve criminality and who are deemed to be a "danger to the public" are not sent by Immigration to the Celebrity Inn but to provincial jails. Detention is *for* deportation: "The intention with the non-criminal is that detention be as short as possible. In most cases it really is to facilitate removal, so there is not a justification for a long detention."[25]

While one might expect that those confined in more secure correctional institutions for reasons of criminality would likely be subjected to the coercive and punitive dimensions of criminal justice incarceration, "temporary hold-ing centres" for the administrative detention of *noncriminal* immigration cases might reasonably be expected to operate under a different, noncarceral regime. However, notwithstanding the absence of "criminals," and notwith-standing official declarations to the contrary, immigration detention – even in a holding centre for noncriminals located in a busy hotel – is a distinctly carceral experience.

The presence of a secure detention facility in the isolated rear wing of the Celebrity Budget Inn would likely come as a surprise to most of the hotel's paying customers. From the main entrance to the inn, there are few visual clues that it doubles as a medium-security detention centre. Around the side of the building, a keen observer might notice a surveillance camera mounted on the outside wall, just above a steel door entrance with a coded locking mechanism just beside it. This is the visitor's entrance to the deten-tion facility. It is permanently locked. To enter, visitors ring a buzzer, and their images are recorded and transmitted to a security officer within who may then deactivate the lock and allow entry.

The door opens into a large, dingy, yellowish room empty of furniture except for the chairs that line the walls. There is another surveillance cam-era and a pay phone in this room. One corner of the room has been sec-tioned off, and a security guard permanently posted behind fortified Plexiglas acts as the facility's "visits officer." Just behind this security post is the "de-tainee visiting area" in which detainees sit at cubicles and meet their visi-tors through Plexiglas barriers and communicate through a telephone. There are twelve visiting "stations."

To enter the inner regions of the centre, the locks on two more steel doors need to be deactivated by security. A metal detector lines the frame of one of these doors. Immediately on the other side are blue tiled stairs that lead up to the second floor of the detention wing. It is a gloomy place indeed: dim lighting, nondescript beige/brown walls, long empty corridors. It is exceptionally clean – not new, not necessarily in good repair, but clean. The detention centre is serviced by the cleaning staff of the Celebrity Inn. The detainees' rooms and every floor of every room are cleaned daily, in the win-ters sometimes twice or three times a day because of the snow and salt tracked in from outside. The disinfectant smell of ammonia and cleaning fluids hovers throughout. The walls, inside and out, are frequently painted. The air quality within the facility can only be described as terrible due to the per-manently sealed windows and lack of ventilation and fresh-air circulation.

Located at the top of the immaculate but gloomy stairway are the sepa-rate entrances to the male and female dining and smoking rooms and the cafeteria-style kitchen. A long, dimly lit hotel hallway leads away from the dining rooms to the detainees' rooms. There are security posts at each end

of the hallway and at each entrance to the dining areas. There are surveillance cameras in the hallway and in each of the common areas. Escape, not
violence, is the primary security concern. Each room has an outside window,
which is sealed with reinforced Plexiglas. Beds have also been modified so
that the iron frames cannot be removed and used as pry bars or weapons.

The enforcement detention officers (EDOs) who run the facility, and their
support staff, work primarily out of three rooms across from the dining
areas. In addition to admission and release powers, the EDOs at the Celebrity Inn are responsible for every aspect of the daily management and administration of the facility, including hearing and investigating complaints;
taking disciplinary action against unruly detainees; making visitation decisions; managing transportation to and from detention reviews and refugee
hearings; managing contracts with private suppliers; and communicating
with a range of other agencies, including government departments, law
enforcement, airport authorities, the Immigration and Refugee Board (IRB),
foreign embassies, legal counsel, community advocates, media, and the
public.

Across from the immigration office is a rather sparsely equipped "children's
playroom." It was created in response to pressure from members of the
Toronto Refugee Affairs Council (TRAC). The detention of minors is a matter of considerable concern and has long been the subject of sustained criticism by nongovernmental advocates. The official response is that it is not
the practice to *detain* young children; they are there with their detained
parent(s) as *guests* of Immigration.[26]

On the first floor of the detention wing, the rooms that line the hallway
are used for a variety of purposes. Several are designated as "meeting rooms"
for detainees and their lawyers or other "professional" contacts. In 1999, a
few were adapted to function as "video-conferencing" detention review
rooms. Before then, all detainees had to be transported off site to attend
these reviews. They may now be done at Celebrity with the technology of
video-conferencing. This manner of conducting the reviews further undermines a detainee's ability to make a case persuasively. As observed by one of
TRAC's case workers, because so much of each detention release decision
depends on the perceived credibility of the detainee, the disconnected and
impersonal medium of video-conferencing presents a further obstacle to
detainees.[27]

In addition to the video-conferencing rooms, the contract community
doctor and duty nurses work out of two rooms. There is also a detainee
baggage room, a room for the TRAC case worker, and finally several rooms
used for segregation and solitary confinement for either health or security/
disciplinary purposes. It was in one of these rooms that Michael Akhimien
died. The beige and brown hallway on the first floor of the detention wing

leads to the main security (or supervisor's) office, the admissions and discharge office, and the holding room, which form a triangle at the end of the hall. The supervisor of security and the head guard are more or less permanently posted at the main security desk. The supervisor's desk faces a wall of monitors that continuously transmit the images generated by the facility's five internal and seven external surveillance cameras. Here the gaze of surveillance is not coupled with discipline or the collection and classification of information about the detainees.

Across the hall from the security office is the detainee holding room. Of all the rooms at Celebrity, this one most closely resembles and evokes the popular image of a police cell. It is small, no more than eight to ten feet square. It is a dirty shade of pale, institutional yellow and has fluorescent lights, no windows. Wooden benches are bolted to the walls. There is a large Plexiglas window in the door to permit viewing of the room from the outside when the door is closed. Once closed, the door cannot be opened from the inside. The third room in the security triangle is the admissions and discharge office.

Just beyond these rooms is the third entrance to the inn, the detainees' entrance. It opens into the "loading and unloading" area of the compound that forms a corner of the detainees' "exercise yard," which used to be the parking lot for the hotel rooms in this wing. It measures about 25 feet wide by 100 feet long. It is empty save for two picnic benches bolted to the pavement and a poorly situated basketball hoop. The yard is monitored by several cameras mounted to the outside walls of Celebrity. Other than the basketball hoop and the occasional soccer ball, the only exercise equipment provided for those detained are a StairMaster and a fitness bike located in the children's playroom and in dubious states of repair.

The exercise yard and the loading and unloading area are encircled by two wire fences. The outside fence is twelve feet high and is capped with "ordinary" barbed wire as opposed to the "razor" variety. The inside fence is eight feet high and fitted with an inward-leaning overhang covered with mesh to prevent detainees from climbing up and over.

Detention and Release Decision Making

Immigration officers, who are civil servants employed by Citizenship and Immigration Canada, and adjudicators, who are order-in-council appointees to the IRB, an independent adjudicative tribunal, have broad statutory powers to detain noncitizens (under *IRPA*, adjudicators are now members of the new "Immigration Division" of the IRB). Parliament has established two main grounds that justify detention: a likelihood that the person poses a danger to the public or, if not detained, is likely not to appear for examination, inquiry, or removal.[28] Prior to *IRPA*, other grounds did exist, although, according to the 1998 IRB *Guidelines on Detention*,[29] they were rarely applied.

They relate to port of entry cases in which a person is unable to satisfy an immigration officer with respect to that person's identity or when, in the opinion of the deputy minister or a person designated by the deputy minister, there is reason to suspect that the person may be a member of an inadmissible class.[30]

The *IRPA* and regulations have substantially expanded the detention powers of immigration officers and made identity-based detentions much more prominent.[31] The regulations further expand the powers of immigration officers to arrest without warrant, even when removal is not imminent. In addition to flight risk and danger to the public, under the new regulations "foreign nationals" may be detained *at any point* in the process if an Immigration officer is not satisfied in terms of identity. The new regulations also allow for the continued detention of individuals if they are deemed to be "uncooperative" in efforts to establish their identities. Also new is the power to detain if it is deemed necessary to complete an examination, what some have called "detention based on convenience."[32]

The Federal Court ruled in *Sahin* (1995)[33] that, in addition to making a determination as to whether one or both of the acceptable grounds for detention exist, the decision maker must also consider whether the length of detention is likely to be reasonable and therefore in accordance with section 7 of the *Canadian Charter of Rights and Freedoms*.[34] This means that, while the legislation itself does not limit the total length of detention, there is the implicit restriction that the length of detention must be "reasonable." As stated in the 1998 IRB guidelines, "if a detention appears unduly lengthy, *the reasonableness of the delay* should be considered in order to ensure that the detention is not in fact an 'indefinite detention.' Such detentions constitute deprivations of liberty that come into conflict with the principles of fundamental justice."[35] However, in the CIC *Detention Policy* issued in October 1998,[36] as well as the October 2002 guidelines on detention under *IRPA*, much more prominence is given to the Federal Court ruling in *Kidane* (1996). This ruling held that prolonged and effectively "indefinite" detention *is* justified under the *Charter* in cases involving people who have been found to be a danger to the public by an adjudicator in a detention review, who have "hampered" efforts to remove them, and where there are no real alternatives to detention.[37]

International legal instruments are also relevant to the governance of immigration detention. CIC acknowledged and incorporated them in the development of its national detention standards.[38] These standards include relevant provisions of the *United Nations High Commissioner for Refugees (UNHCR) Guidelines on Detention of Asylum Seekers*,[39] the *United Nations (UN) Body of Principles for the Protection of All People under Any Form of Detention or Imprisonment*,[40] and the *UN Standard Minimum Rules for the Treatment of Prisoners*.[41]

CIC carried out a national review of its detention practices in 2000. A key recommendation of this review called for the strengthening of the management of the detention program. Subsequently, CIC created the Detentions Directorate and the National Detention Management Committee. The objectives of this initiative were to "promote consistency; provide strategic direction; develop and maintain national standards and principles for the treatment of detained people; and support regional operations." However, according to CIC, these initiatives were subsequently "overtaken by the events of September 11."[42]

While government agents are centrally involved in immigration enforcement and the administration of immigration detention, and while detention and release are carried out under the authority of immigration legislation and policy, national and international human rights instruments, in actuality a variety of authorities, technologies, and discretionary powers are involved. The discretionary powers exercised in the detention of noncitizens are multiple, diverse, and dispersed, both within and outside the "formal institutions of the state."[43] While it is true that those authorities and discretionary powers associated most closely with the formal institutions of government are likely to be particularly influential, others are also noteworthy. The ultimate decision to detain – or to release – is not a singular event. The "case" is constructed over time and is contributed to by a myriad of practices and decisions carried out by different agents at different points in the process. These discretionary decisions are not in any simple way merely top-down decisions; rather, they are multiple, cumulative, and issue from diverse locations.

Canada Customs and Revenue Agency (CCRA) officers who carry out primary inspections on behalf of CIC make the first referral to Immigration for more in-depth examination.[44] At the secondary inspection, immigration officers make the initial recommendation to arrest and/or detain. All detention cases must then be reviewed by a senior immigration officer (SIO) within forty-eight hours of the initial detention. The SIO reviews the case to determine whether release is appropriate. In exercising their power, SIOs have considerable discretion to impose terms or conditions of release. If a person is not released within forty-eight hours of the initial detention, the decision to detain is reviewed again seven days later. If the detention is continued, subsequent reviews take place at thirty-day intervals until the case is resolved.[45]

This review and each subsequent review are carried out by a member of the Immigration Division of the IRB who hears submissions from a case presenting officer (CPO), the person seeking release from detention, the person's representative if he or she has one (legal or not), and/or other interested parties. It is this member who decides whether to continue detention or order release subject to any terms and conditions that the member deems appropriate.

Because of the high costs of detention, CIC has increasingly emphasized the need to consider alternatives to detention in cases where safety and security are not a concern. Such alternatives include the issuance of terms and conditions, cash or performance bonds, or third-party risk programs. These programs entail a third person or a group of persons (who must be Canadian citizens or permanent residents) who sign a deposit or a "guarantee for compliance." They are held responsible for ensuring that the person released from detention obeys the conditions of release. If any terms are broken, the third party loses its deposit or, in the case of a guarantee, is required to pay the specified amount.[46] Release from Celebrity may also be facilitated by the Immigration Bail Program, also an example of a third-party release program that provides surveillance and imposes and enforces conditions on selected "low-risk" detainees released into the community. The use of electronic bracelets to monitor people released from detention has also been explored.

It is not only the authority of the adjudicator that is important in the resolution of detention cases. Also important are whether or not the detainee is represented in the detention review and, if so, the quality of the representation – whether by a lawyer, paralegal, or immigration consultant. The authority of legal aid to grant or deny funding for legal counsel for a detention review is critical. The assessment made of a particular case by legal or nongovernmental advocates and agencies in order to decide whether, in the context of limited resources, they should take it on is also central to the release decision, as is whether or not the EDO decides to make some phone calls and pull some strings on behalf of the detainee. Access to support and resources in the building of a case is critical to its outcome – this may be as seemingly simple as access to a telephone or contacts in the community and a place to stay, or it may involve media coverage and political mobilization. The risk assessment and decision making carried out by the Immigration Bail Program are significant as well. The individual's past dealings with the police are important considerations in a decision to release. In addition, legal, ethnocultural, religious, and other community organizations are important since they are increasingly called upon to offer third-party assistance (bonds, sureties, a place to stay) as part of the release process and to participate in the postrelease control and "risk management" of the person in question.

In addition to this involvement of community groups and individual citizens in release decision making and in the governance of those released from detention, immigration officials have allowed TRAC to maintain a presence at Celebrity since 1985. CIC provides TRAC with office space within

Celebrity and facilitates detainees' access to TRAC for assistance. While TRAC volunteers are not allowed to do advocacy work on behalf of individual detainees, volunteer TRAC case workers posted at the detention centre interview people in detention, assess their needs, provide information, help fill out forms, liaise with immigration officials, and make appropriate referrals to a wide range of community and legal contacts. TRAC also holds "detention review seminars" to provide information and guidance to detainees relating to the detention review process. CIC leaves all programming and special service delivery to TRAC's volunteers. Depending on the availability of volunteers, these services have included, for example, English as a second language, spiritual counselling, art therapy, post-traumatic stress counselling, and assistance in filling out official forms. As put by an EDO, "If TRAC doesn't do it, then it isn't done."[47]

Private Security

In light of the proliferation of privatization projects in many fields of public policy, including correctional services, the blurring of the boundaries between immigration enforcement and criminal law enforcement as well as the increasing prominence of law and order programs in most areas of public policy, it should not come as much of a surprise that CIC contracts Wackenhut Corrections Corporation, an American private security corporation that specializes in prison security, to police Celebrity.

Wackenhut Corporation was first founded in 1954 by a former FBI agent, George Wackenhut, and was quickly supported by FBI Director J. Edgar Hoover. Wackenhut Corrections is a subsidiary company created in 1984 that specializes in prisons, immigration detention centres (including the notorious centre in Woomera, Australia), and more recently the business of running psychiatric hospitals. It operates prisons for profit internationally, including the United States, Australia, the United Kingdom, South Africa, Canada, and Puerto Rico.[48] Speaking of its operations in Australia, former Chairman and CEO George Wackenhut is quoted as stating, "Australian operations are very important to us. They're really starting to punish people the way they should have done all along. The do-gooders say no, punishment is not the answer, but I can't think of a better one."[49]

Wackenhut, which changed its name in November 2003 to the Global Expertise in Outsourcing (GEO) Group, boasts that it is not only "a world leader in privatized correctional and detention management"; as Chair and CEO George Foley asks visitors to the website, "did you also know that we offer a wide range of other diversified services – from home detention and electronic monitoring to the development of medical and mental health facilities?"[50]

In 2004, the GEO Group reported that it had forty-three contracts representing forty-one facilities in the United States, Australia, South Africa, and

New Zealand. It administered approximately 36,000 beds around the world as well as provided a range of other related services.[51] Business for the GEO Group is good – very good – in these days of law and order and post-September 11th crackdowns. In 2003, it grossed $617.5 million, with a net income of $45.3 million.[52] As Foley explained in 2002, "the North American market is growing rapidly, and we are focused on expanding Federal procurement opportunities. The Federal Bureau of Prisons is operating at 131 percent capacity, and a recently enacted Federal law authorizes longer term contracts than ever before, resulting in more favorable financing alternatives for new privatized development. Pending new Homeland Security and anti-terrorism legislation may help drive business growth as well. We expect to have the opportunity to bid on more than 18,000 new beds in North America over the next 12-18 months."[53]

Widespread concerns have been raised in the context of criminal justice about the impacts of privatization on the conditions of imprisonment, the quality of care (including nutritional concerns), the humane treatment of prisoners, and the attention given to rehabilitative programming.[54] Private security's primary concern with the bottom line has been found to detract from these objectives, substituting instead those relating to efficient and economical risk management. Wackenhut promises 20-30 percent savings in facility development and 10-20 percent savings in facility management.[55] While the privatization of security in the area of immigration detention does not raise parallel concerns about the quality and quantity of rehabilitative programs because, in short, such enabling, reform projects have no meaningful place in the context of immigration detention, the use of private contracts in the areas of security, food, and health unavoidably raises concerns about the sacrifice of humane treatment, quality, care, and conditions of labour in the name of cost cutting and profit maximization.

Private companies are also involved in deportations. In 1999, five "manacled and shackled" Nigerians were deported from Canada aboard a US federal service flight nicknamed "Con Air." CIC paid $4,800 US for each one-way ticket, reportedly only a third of the cost of using commercial airlines.[56] The US leases planes that are used in a fleet officially known as the Justice Prisoner and Alien Transportation System. The flights carrying "aliens and criminals" are heavily guarded by armed US marshals. "Con Air is an Airline with a Difference. The standard operating procedure by the flight attendants – armed US Marshals clad in bullet proof vests – is to handcuff obstreperous passengers to their seats. Really disruptive ones have their handcuffed hands taped around tennis balls."[57]

In 2001, it was reported that CIC had hired Protecting and Indemnity Associates International (Pty) to assist in three "extremely difficult" removals of individuals to Africa.[58] While the government announced at the time that it had stopped the practice in the face of criticisms, in 2003 CIC reported that it had removed 130 "high risk or uncooperative individuals" on fifteen charter flights. Seven of these were joint charters with the US. Rather than conceding to any concerns, CIC defends this privatization move as evidence of successful efforts to "share best practices and coordinate efforts to expedite removals."[59] As put by a government spokesperson, "It's a very good initiative for us to collaborate with [the US] ... and put our individuals on the same plane ... It's a cost effective means of removing these people."[60]

The contracting of private companies to carry out removals and the role of private agents in the forcible detention and confinement of people being deported are concerns for the variety of reasons that I have touched on here. They also raise the more general question of the legitimacy of contracting out the coercive powers of government to private industry: punishing for profit. From a governmental perspective, it points to the theme of "governing at a distance"; the hiring of private companies indicates again the ways in which government is not in any simple way reducible to its formal institutions. It involves a multiplicity of alliances, networks, and technologies. These developments also speak to the rise of neoliberal rationalities that justify such practices in terms of cost cutting, efficiency, and building partnerships.

In 2000, fourteen Wackenhut guards were on site at Celebrity during the day, including three drivers, the security supervisor, the head guard, the visits guard, and the admissions and discharge guard. During the evening and midnight shifts, the number of guards on site is reduced to nine or ten.[61] Wackenhut has its own training regimens that CIC supplements with a five-day specialized training session. The guards, who in 2000 were paid about $9.50 an hour, must also pass a minimally demanding physical fitness test. They receive training in basic defence, proper use of body restraints, and security "post orders." While guards are instructed to respect the principle of nondiscrimination, in 2000 they were not receiving any form of cultural sensitivity training from CIC.[62]

The CIC *Post Orders* detail the operational procedures relating to the security aspects of immigration detention. In true Kafkaesque fashion, the *Post Orders* are not publicly posted and accessible to all but chained to the security posts in the facility and accessible only to security and CIC staff. The elusive and mysterious nature of the *Post Orders* was even noted in the verdict of the coroner's inquest into Michael Akhimien's death: "It has been said over and over by witnesses that while they are aware of a manual entitled 'Post Orders' they have never read it."[63]

The 1996 CIC *Post Orders* summarized the responsibilities of the Wackenhut security contractor:

- Supervise persons being detained.
- Admit/release detainees from the Holding Centre.
- Provide information to new detainees concerning rules of the Centre.
- Take control and be responsible for the personal effects of detainees.
- Order meals and verify delivery.
- Conduct frequent and unscheduled room checks.
- Admit visitors and ensure that visitors are not in possession of weapons, alcohol, etc.
- Obtain medical treatment for detainees as required.
- Evacuate the Centre in the event of an emergency.
- Operate metal detecting devices.
- Complete reports.
- Transport all persons under order of detention as requested by Citizenship and Immigration.
- Prevent escapes.
- Apply restraints.[64]

Carceral Practices

The technologies used by private security guards in the policing of immigration detention resemble those conventionally associated with criminal justice punishment. While the degree to which nineteenth-century reforms to the criminal justice system actually "humanized" prison practices should not be overstated, the emergence of new modes of power that aimed to transform rather than merely control and punish prisoners had no echo in the context of immigration penality. The only objectives of the penal practices used in immigration detention are bodily subjection, control, and ultimately expulsion. Of course, there are clear and compelling arguments to be made that point to the continuing primacy of bodily and coercive technologies of control and subjection in prisons. The argument can certainly also be made that criminal justice technologies have come to resemble immigration technologies – that they are less transformative than exclusionary, less oriented toward integration and rehabilitation than toward segregation and management, less about discipline than about risk. These important questions notwithstanding, there is an unmistakable commingling and sharing of exclusionary and coercive technologies of control between criminal justice and immigration enforcement authorities.

Of particular importance is the use of body restraints. Their use is standard policy and practice during transport to and from the Celebrity detention facility. In particular, handcuffs and leg irons or shackles constitute the "standard" from which deviations may arise.[65] Exceptions may be made with the preauthorization of the EDO or the security supervisor. In general, reduction of the standard uses of body restraints may be made in the case of "children, old people, very pregnant women, disabled persons or persons who should not be handcuffed for a specific reason."[66]

The standard must be applied in full in the case of male detainees being transferred to or from a more secure correctional facility (jail). In such cases, handcuffs and leg irons may be supplemented with a "transportation belt" if the guards judge that there is a risk of violence. A transportation belt works to secure handcuffed wrists at the waist level, thereby eliminating the danger of the person using cuffed wrists as weapons. Exceptions to this standard must be approved by an EDO. Female detainees being transported from a correctional facility are also always cuffed but are spared the leg irons unless specifically directed by the EDO or the security supervisor.[67] Handcuffs and shackles are also standard fare for deportees. The use of these restraints is guided by the principle of "safe restraint" and is justified by reference to the need to protect safety and prevent escape.[68]

Handcuffs, leg irons, and transportation belts cannot help but evoke images of criminal justice penality and forcible subjection, confinement, and punishment. The corporeality and brute forcefulness of these instruments of restraint are also powerfully reminiscent of medieval penality, particularly when linked with expulsion. Yet these technologies are not merely negative and repressive but also productive; as put by Alison Young, the use of body restraints on detainees and deportees is part of a program out "to produce 'docile subjects'" and "to train the individual body, the social body and the nation."[69]

This association of forced bodily restraint and expulsion with premodern and early modern sovereign modes of penality (stocks, exile, and banishment) is heightened by tales of abuses and extreme bodily interventions that occasionally come to light – tales that also and further highlight the diversity of technologies and authorities at work. In 1990, there were reports of "uncooperative" deportees who were forcibly drugged and sedated during their removal. Enforcement officers have also reportedly sealed the mouths of particularly unruly and vociferous deportees with duct tape.[70]

The symbolic importance of the use of restraints on deportees is powerfully depicted in the following description of a deportation incident: "The newspapers have reported actual cases where persons were drugged before being sent back without any medical supervision, or handcuffed for their return flight, or even put in leg irons ... It is hard to forget the case of a young Dominican who was deported a short while ago from Canada. Despite the fact that both of his feet had been amputated, he was nevertheless handcuffed."[71]

The use of body restraints in the direct and physical subjection and control of bodies by force is commonly associated with criminal justice enforcement. Their use in the noncriminal, administrative context of immigration enforcement both evidences and reproduces the association between immigration and crime and the coercive edge of traditionally sovereign power that permeates immigration penality. For those physically subjected, the use of body restraints is experienced as a distinctly penal practice: coercive, punitive, humiliating, and undeserved.[72] The use of private agents in this subjection and control once again complicates the conventional view of power and state authority and indicates, again, the multiplicity of authorities at play. The delegation of coercive powers and technologies of control to private authorities is indeed remarkable. Moreover, the fact that private security guards, private airlines, public police, clinic doctors, prison nurses, hotel staff, civil servants, and nongovernmental activists and advocates are all involved in the administration of immigration detention and deportation indicates a blurring and meshing of conventional boundaries in this domain.

Penal Regimes

The penal character of the regimes at Celebrity Inn is established from the moment the detainees are transported by an immigration enforcement van through the gate in the doubled, twelve-foot-high, barbed-wire fence into the "loading and unloading" area of the compound. The new detainees are "unloaded" and escorted by the private security guards into the facility.[73] Body restraints are removed, and detainees are placed in the holding room, where their shoes are removed and checked, they are frisked ("pat-searched"), and a handheld metal detector is passed over their bodies by a guard of the same sex. Any luggage is seized, searched (in the presence of the owner), tagged, and stored in the permanently locked baggage room. All valuables and any money are recorded and locked in safety deposit boxes. If any identification documents are found in the possession of detainees, regulations detail which are to be seized and to whom they are to be forwarded. Detainees may take clothes and other "nonthreatening" items to their rooms. They may keep up to thirty dollars on hand for personal use. Detainees have access to their seized luggage and valuables between 1800 and 1900 hours or by special authorization. New detainees are assigned a log number and a room number, and the time of their admission is recorded.[74]

Detainees are provided with two information handouts: "Rules for Detainees" and "Information for Persons Detained." They do not contain the same information as, nor are they summaries of, the *Post Orders*. The "Rules for Detainees" is largely prohibitive and governs their behaviour while in detention. It includes, for example, rules concerning the seizure of certain belongings, restrictions on mobility, visiting hours, doctor's hours, television volume controls, the expectation that detainees keep their rooms "neat and clean," and lights out at 11:30 p.m. Mention is also made of the presence of TRAC and the complaints process.

Before being escorted to their rooms, new detainees must be frisk-searched one more time. From this point on, detainees may not leave their rooms except under security escort and only for certain regularly scheduled and carefully coordinated and controlled movements and activities (meals, "fresh air," "telephone time," visitor's hours) or with permission for special requests such as a visit with the doctor or a lawyer. Visits with other detainees in their rooms are prohibited.[75]

The movement of detainees within the facility is carefully coordinated and controlled by security.[76] Detainees must have a security officer escort when being moved from one location of the facility to another. They must have special permission to leave their rooms at unscheduled times, and if permission is granted they must be escorted by a guard at all times. Private security officers also carry out frequent, unscheduled floor patrols and regular outside patrols, room checks, and room searches.[77]

The use of force by CIC staff and private security personnel at Celebrity is governed by the relevant provisions of the *Criminal Code of Canada*. They are empowered to use "necessary force" to prevent an escape and/or to protect themselves against an assault. They are prohibited from using "excessive force": that is, force intended to or likely to cause "death or grievous bodily harm."[78]

The policing and control of detainees is also effected through punitive measures taken against disruptive or otherwise unruly detainees. When presented with a relatively minor disciplinary problem, the preferred initial action by the EDO is "talking to the guy and finding out what happened, what the problem is and trying to resolve it."[79] If that doesn't work, the EDO may order confinement in one of the "isolation/overflow" rooms. The ultimate, and arguably the most powerful, sanction available to an EDO at Celebrity is the threat of transfer to jail. Indeed, the spectre of jail is a key and powerful technology at Celebrity, so powerful that it is explicitly detailed in the final rule in the "Rules for Detainees": "These rules are designed for the safety, security and comfort of all persons in the Centre. You are expected to respect them. Disruptive behaviour, including damage of property, will not be tolerated. Such behaviour may lead to your transfer to a more secure detention facility."[80]

The threat of isolation or transfer to jail is frequently employed to govern unruly detainees. Actual transfer to a prison is generally assured in the case of a more serious "disciplinary problem" such as that posed by a violent or abusive detainee or someone who has attempted escape. However, in 1999 and again in 2000, several people detained at Celebrity went on a hunger strike. They, too, were transferred to prison.[81]

In a symbolically evocative arrangement, the isolation/overflow rooms on the main floor are used for both punitive/disciplinary reasons (solitary confinement) and reasons relating to the health of detainees (quarantine).

This ominous duality was implicated during the coroner's inquest into the death of Michael Akhimien when it was noted that there was some confusion whether his confinement in one of these rooms was for punitive or health care reasons. It is equally grim that the sanction of transfer to prison may also be imposed for either punitive/disciplinary reasons or "health and safety" reasons. Detainees thought to pose a "suicide risk" are transferred to prison. It is not uncommon to have the threat of transfer to jail used in the context of the provision of medical care.[82] For example, a sick Chinese man was told by one immigration officer that if he refused to take his medication he would be transferred to jail.[83]

Increased attention was paid to the health care conditions of detention at Celebrity after the death of Akhimien. The coroner made several recommendations that CIC subsequently implemented, including first-aid training for the security guards and routine examinations of detainees being held longer than a week. Still, concerns about the quality of care persist.

As a matter of policy, ill or injured detainees, except for minor cases, are transferred to a medical facility.[84] However, many of those in detention exhibit serious depressive symptoms, and suicide is an ever-present concern. The preferred way of dealing with those feared to be suicidal is to transfer them to jail. If a detainee is deemed to be a "low-risk suicide threat case," he or she may be confined to one of the isolation rooms under special watch; "the person's status ... will be checked every 10 minutes on all shifts."[85]

The justification for the transfer of suicidal detainees to jail is that unlike Celebrity jails have special "suicide watch rooms." However, there is some doubt that jail is the best place for a seriously depressed or suicidal person. This is particularly true for refugee claimants who may have experienced torture and other human rights violations while being detained by authorities in their countries of origin.

There are no on-site provisions for assisting detainees with psychological problems. While the medical staff may refer those with psychological problems to an outside clinic or counsellor, the practice is rare. It is more common to transfer such cases to jail. A case recounted in a report on detention at Celebrity sheds some light on the attitudes that inflect the provision of health care there. In 1997, a young female refugee claimant, one of Celebrity's many "long-term" detainees (over thirty days), was increasingly depressed and suffered from serious physical symptoms. In response to queries made by the on-site TRAC representative regarding her health, medication, and possible need for psychiatric referral, the on-site nurse argued, "Why should we pay for a psychiatrist when she should be deported anyways?"[86]

The daily lives of detainees at Celebrity are organized by and revolve around various "schedules":[87] the daily time schedule, the visiting schedule, the baggage access schedule, the telephone time schedule, the medical services schedule. The daily time schedule sets out meal times, telephone times, fresh-air time, and bedtime (televisions off).

Visitation is strictly regulated.[88] Different visiting conditions apply to two different categories of visitors, those classified by CIC as "professional" visitors and those classified as "unprofessional" visitors. No direct, physical contact is allowed between detainees and unprofessional visitors. They must meet in the designated visiting area of Celebrity. They are separated by Plexiglas and communicate through telephones. The CIC *Post Orders* stipulate that in addition to family and friends "immigration consultants, church groups, doctors, Amnesty International personnel and other similar groups are not to be treated as Professional Visitors without prior approval from the EDO. They are not to be allowed access into the Centre unless previous authorization has been obtained. These groups will use the detainee visiting area to conduct their business."[89]

In contrast, "professional" visitors may enter the inner regions of the facility. They include lawyers, embassy and consulate officials, police, interpreters, representatives of the UN Commission for Refugees, and approved nongovernmental organizations such as TRAC. Unlike "unprofessional" visitors, professional visitors are allowed into the centre anytime to meet with detainees in the "boardrooms" on the first floor.

The 2000 draft of Celebrity's new *Post Orders* amended the professional and unprofessional visitor categories. The restrictions on access to the facility by Amnesty International "and other similar groups" as well as by physicians were particularly contentious.[90] In the new *Post Orders*, Amnesty International representatives and clergy were upgraded to the category of professional visitors. Doctors, psychiatrists, and other medical specialists deemed unprofessional visitors in the 1996 *Post Orders* now comprise a hybrid category. They will be allowed into the facility but only with a referral or recommendation from the facility's on-site doctor.[91] The restrictions on the access afforded to consultants and paralegals, however, remained in force. As with most of the rules and regulations of Celebrity, the EDO has the discretion to make exceptions to the restrictions on visitation. For example, for humanitarian reasons, an EDO might allow a detainee scheduled for imminent removal to meet directly with loved ones to say good-bye more intimately. This is done "from time to time."[92]

Regulations limit access to telephones.[93] Telephones are a vital part of the detainees' existence. Contact with and access to friends and family members, lawyers and advocates, ethnic and religious community groups, embassies and shelters are critical for detainees seeking release. Incoming telephone calls are received by security guards, who are to pass messages to detainees "as soon as practical."[94]

The Scope of Detention in Canada

In 1994, CIC detained just over 9,000 people (including "criminals" and "noncriminals").[95] This figure reflects the heightened preoccupation with enforcement triggered by the 1994 shootings of Georgina Leimonis and Constable Todd Baylis by black men in Toronto, Ontario.[96] Significantly, the enforcement response that ensued (including the "Criminals First" detention and deportation policy) resulted in longer lengths of detention in both criminal and noncriminal cases in both correctional institutions and holding centres. In the crackdown that followed the 1994 killings, the total number of immigration "jail days" in Ontario correctional institutions rose from just under 35,000 in 1992-93 to approximately 82,000 in 1995-96.[97] Over the same period, the total number of "holding centre days" in Ontario also rose dramatically, from 37,000 in 1992-93 to 48,000 in 1995-96.[98]

In 1996-97, CIC detained a total of 6,400 people, and in 1997-98, detentions rose again to 7,080.[99] The majority of immigration detention cases in Ontario involve criminality issues. For example, between 1994 and 1997, for every one person in detention at Celebrity, three were being held in correctional institutions.[100] By 2000-1, CIC reported that the number of people detained had reached 8,786.[101] Of these, 5,755 people were unsuccessful refugee claimants, and 1,701 people (20 percent) were detained for reasons of criminality.[102] In 2001-2, the year of the suicide air attacks in the United States, CIC reported that it had detained 9,542 people and that the "total detention days" had increased by 3.6 percent from the previous year to 141,307. This increase, it claimed, highlights "the positive role of judiciously applied detention practices in the Government of Canada's security agenda and response to terrorism."[103] In 2002-3, the numbers rose again. CIC detained 11,503 people for a total of 165,070 detention days, an increase of about 20 percent in the number of those detained and an increase of 17 percent in the number of detention days over the previous year.[104]

A review of CIC's "Weekly Detention Snapshots" provides a little more detail regarding the use of detention after September 11th. In 2002, on any one day, an average of 440 people were in immigration detention across Canada. On average, approximately 284 were being held in provincial jails, and 156 were in Immigration holding centres. Seventy-two percent of detainees were in Ontario, 20 percent in Quebec, 3 percent in the Prairies and Territories, 5 percent in British Columbia and the Yukon, and less than 1 percent in the Atlantic provinces. Most (232) of those in detention in Ontario were held in correctional facilities as compared with an average of 84 held in the Celebrity Inn holding centre. In Quebec, the relationship was reversed; most (sixty-nine) were held in the immigration centre as compared with eighteen held in jails. On average, there were eleven minors in detention across Canada, two of whom, on average, were unaccompanied.

Figure 2.1

National detention days

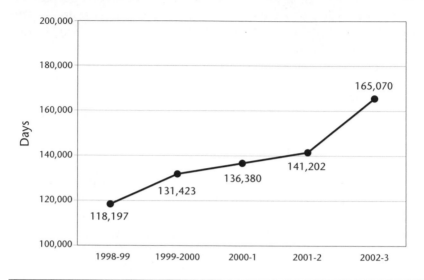

Source: CIC, *Department Performance Report for the Period Ending March 31st, 2003* (Ottawa: Minister of Public Works and Government Services, 2003).

Figure 2.2

Persons detained: National totals

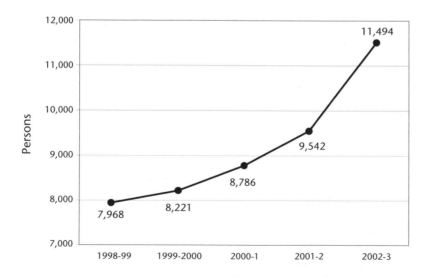

Source: CIC, *Department Performance Report for the Period Ending March 31st, 2003* (Ottawa: Minister of Public Works and Government Services, 2003).

During the same period, on any one day, an average of five people were being held in detention under a security certificate issued by the attorney general and the minister of citizenship and immigration.[105] Three of these people had been detained in Ontario prior to September 11th, and one had been detained in Quebec after September 11th. After September 11th, there were also "a handful" of security-related short detentions in which no security certificate was issued.[106]

During 2003, the numbers and distributions remained fairly steady. Between 9 January 2003 and 27 March 2003, CIC reported that the average number of detainees across Canada rose slightly to 521. Of these, an average of 323 people were in provincial jails, and 198 were in immigration holding centres. Sixty-seven percent of detainees were in Ontario, 21 percent in Quebec, 3 percent in the Prairies and Territories, 9 percent in British Columbia and the Yukon, and less than 1 percent in the Atlantic provinces. In Ontario, an average of 241 people were held in jail, compared with 107 in the Celebrity Inn detention centre. During this period, the average number of minors in detention dropped from eleven to seven. Five people were in detention under a security certificate during this period, two of whom had been detained prior to September 11th and three of whom had been detained after September 11th.[107]

Who Is in Detention at Celebrity?

People detained in each of the three national holding centres include those who have been refused entry for a variety of noncriminal reasons, including, for example, those suspected of not being "genuine visitors," those who have been found working in Canada without authorization, those who have overstayed temporary visas, and those whose refugee claims have been rejected. Approximately half of those detained at Celebrity have been detained at the "front end" of the immigration process at an airport or port of entry. The other half have been detained at the "back end" within Canada, usually after a routine encounter with the police or some other local authority.[108]

The vast majority of those detained at Celebrity are nonwhite, male, and between the ages of twenty and forty. In early 2000, it was reported that China, Somalia, Iran, India, and "the Caribbean" were the countries most commonly represented among the detainees.[109] While statistics on the composition of the detainee population at Celebrity over time are not available, the following numbers provide a snapshot of the composition of the detainee population at Celebrity on one day, 3 February 2000. On this day, there were a total of eighty-five people in detention. Thirty-two (37 percent) were from Asia (China [14], India [7], Korea [4], Philippines [2], Vietnam [1], Malaysia [1], Sri Lanka [2], Pakistan [1]). Nineteen (22 percent) were from Central and South America (Suriname [1], Guyana [4], Costa Rica

[2], Venezuela [2], Mexico [4], Honduras [2], Argentina [1], El Salvador [2], Brazil [1]). Fourteen (16 percent) were from Africa (Nigeria [5], Zimbabwe [3], Ivory Coast [1], Senegal [1], Somalia [1], Uganda [2], Namibia [1]). Nine (11 percent) were from the West Indies (Dominican [2], St. Lucia [2], Jamaica [4], Grenada [1]). Eight (9 percent) were from Eastern Europe (Ukraine [1], Russia [2], Poland [1], Albania [1], Hungary [2], Uzbekistan [1]). One was from the Middle East (Iraq), one came from Western Europe (Netherlands), and the national origin of one was unavailable.[110] There were at least five preschool-age children in the detention centre as "guests" of CIC and at least one unaccompanied minor.

While these numbers reflect the specific composition of the detainee population at Celebrity on one particular day, the general characteristics remain relatively stable over time: the vast majority are always nonwhite, generally poor, mostly male. Most are without resources, financial or otherwise.[111] The specific countries represented at any one time reflect a combination of factors, including changing migration patterns, the shifting focus of CIC enforcement practices, interdiction initiatives, the targeting of certain airlines, and selective policing practices. There is some consistency over time with respect to the backgrounds of those detained. For example, there are frequently Eastern European sex trade workers at Celebrity,[112] while many of the young women from the West Indies bear the scars of domestic violence.

Detention of Refugee Claimants
Canada does detain people with active refugee claims who have no criminal history. They are never many, but they are a persistent component of those detained. On 3 February 2000, for example, ten of the eighty-four detainees at Celebrity (12 percent) had active refugee claims.[113] The detention of asylum seekers is a matter of considerable concern. CIC officials are quick to emphasize the distinction between the (genuine and deserving) refugee and the (always and already suspect) refugee claimant. CIC, they stress, "does not detain refugees, only refugee *claimants* and of them, only very few."[114] As put by then Minister of Immigration Lucienne Robillard, "We put them in detention only if we have a serious reason to do so, and once there, their conditions – again these are not prisons – are quite acceptable."[115] While in Canada, detention for those with active refugee claims is relatively rare, the majority of the detained Chinese migrants who arrived in 1999 on the West Coast of Canada had refugee claims.

The number of refugee claimants in detention at Celebrity at any one time is usually between ten and fifteen people. TRAC case files indicate that, during the seven-month period between September 1996 and March 1997, of those who sought the assistance of TRAC at Celebrity, thirty-one were front-end refugee claimants, and twenty-six were rejected refugee claimants.[116] The fact that their numbers are relatively small does not diminish the particularly debilitating effects of detention on refugees. Their efforts to find, retain, and communicate with legal counsel for their refugee claims and their ability to prepare their cases are severely restricted by their confinement. Moreover, the impact of detention on their mental health and well-being can be profound: "The detention of refugees who have experienced violent persecution, often including imprisonment and torture, creates a set of circumstances which pose great risk to the well-being of the detained individual. The consequences of being detained again can cause traumatic affectations generally described as post-traumatic stress syndrome ... A vulnerability to retraumatization exists ... These psychological stresses severely limit the efforts of a person to establish a refugee claim. There is no recognition of their special circumstances and no medical treatment to meet their special needs."[117]

Length of Detention

CIC defines a "long-term" detention as one that exceeds thirty days.[118] The majority of long-term immigration detentions are cases in which the adjudicator judges that the release of the individual from detention would pose a danger to the public.[119] As explained by CIC, "the dilemma the department is placed in is that if we release someone who is considered a high risk individual and they go out into public and kill a police officer or a citizen, we're accountable for that."[120]

CIC reported in June 1997 that there were a total of 184 long-term detentions in Ontario. Thirty-five (20 percent) of these were noncriminal "flight risks" being held at Celebrity. The remaining 149 (80 percent) involved criminality and danger issues and were being held in correctional institutions across the province. Of these 184 long-term detentions, 83 (45 percent) had been detained for at least six months, 36 (20 percent) had been detained for at least a year, and 9 (5 percent) had been detained for more than two years.[121] The average length of detention for individual detainees before they were released or deported was eight months (239.9 days). Of these 184 people held in long-term detention, 158 were nonwhite, 90 were of African descent, 50 were Jamaican, and 32 were Vietnamese.[122]

The situation facing long-term immigration detainees was and continues to be of particular concern. Typically, about 60 percent of the long-term detainees have been permanent residents who have been declared by the minister to be a danger to the public under section 70(5) of the former 1976 *Immigration Act*, and about 40 percent are failed refugee claimants who have been detained for reasons of criminality and judged by adjudicators to pose a danger to the public.[123] They have already served their criminal sentences, yet they remain in prison under "immigration hold" while CIC attempts to effect their removal. Sometimes the time spent in prison in immigration hold exceeds the length of the criminal sentence served, a situation referred to as "double punishment." For example, a refugee from Suriname who was granted refugee status in Canada in 1985 was convicted of several narcotics offences that netted him four months in jail. In July 1997, he had been on immigration hold for over two years.[124]

While most of the critical attention paid to long-term detentions focuses on those being held in correctional institutions for reasons of criminality, the concern is also present at Celebrity. While the Celebrity detention centre is designated for the short-term, temporary detention of noncriminal noncitizens, many are confined for periods far exceeding thirty days.[125] On 3 February 2000, for example, 40 percent (thirty-four) of the current detainees were, by CIC's definition, long-term detention cases. Of those, eleven had been detained for a period of one to two months; six had been detained for two to three months; nine had been detained for three to five months; seven had been detained for five to seven months; and one had been in detention for nine months. Of the six held in detention for more than six months, three were from China and three from India.[126]

Long-term detentions at Celebrity are often related to difficulties in obtaining identity and/or travel documents. People are held in detention while their national governments process their applications. Certain countries, for example India, are known for taking a long time to produce the necessary documents. A long-term detention at Celebrity may also be related to an active refugee claim in those circumstances where a claimant is detained for the entire period during which the claim is processed and heard. While the IRB gives priority to detention cases, the wait can still be several months. Like Michael Akhimien, many refugee claimants are driven to withdraw their refugee claim even in the face of danger and loss of protection.[127]

The rationale for the continued detention of refugee claimants resembles a catch-22. TRAC has found that, the more obvious it is to CIC officials and to adjudicators that persons seeking release from detention desperately want to stay in Canada, the more likely it is that they will not be released because they are considered flight risks. Refugees who honestly express fear of returning home in their detention reviews are thus unwittingly strengthening the case for their continued detention. For this reason, TRAC routinely counsels detainees about the difference between the detention review and the refugee hearing and emphasizes the importance of downplaying their fears of persecution were they to be returned home for their refugee hearings. Long-term detentions may also result when individuals refuse to sign the papers needed to apply for the travel document. Indeed, CIC cites the "lack of detainee cooperation" in securing travel documents, alongside the noncooperation of the country of origin, as being the primary reasons for long-term detentions, although noncooperation of detainees is a significantly smaller problem than that of foreign governments.[128] Nonetheless, one of CIC's primary preoccupations is to gain the cooperation of detainees in the effort to apply for the necessary documents. Celebrity officials frequently use the promise of release from detention as an incentive to get detainees to "sign."[129] CIC has also begun to attempt to win this cooperation during the course of detention reviews. In 1997, CIC made every effort to make this cooperation a condition of release.[130]

Moreover, the threat of transfer to jail is sometimes employed to coerce a detainee to sign. In such cases, the refusal of a detainee to sign the application for a travel document is construed as evidence of noncooperation with CIC officials, and this "unruliness" garners a punitive response. As mentioned earlier, under *IRPA* persons may also have detention continued if it is determined that they have not "reasonably cooperated" with the authorities in efforts to establish their identities.[131]

Many refugee claimants do not have the necessary identity/travel documents. For them, the consequences of "signing" have an additional edge. While the lack of requisite documents is commonly interpreted as an indication of potential flight risk or possible danger and therefore justifies continued detention, the credibility of refugee claimants who agree to sign is immediately cast in doubt: "They say, you help us get a passport for you or we will keep you in detention. Then they help get a passport, and then the department turns around and says, you're not a refugee, because you applied for a passport."[132]

The central importance of signing the travel document to immigration penalty bears a strong resemblance to the importance of a confession to sovereign punishments as described by Foucault.[133] Both legitimize and expedite the sanction. Both render the subject of the sanction complicit in their own subjectification. And the withholding of both results in a more onerous challenge for the authorities, who must work harder to achieve their desired objective. Moreover, the refusal to sign is often the only bit of leverage left to some detainees in their efforts to avoid deportation. For all of these reasons, the signing, like the confession, is a key regulatory technique and guiding preoccupation of authorities.

Fiscal Imperatives

The cost of detention is an extremely significant factor in the development of policy and practice. While increasingly intensive enforcement practices imply more detentions, fiscal imperatives increasingly dictate restraint and alternative measures. In 1994-95, the Canadian government spent $21.1 million on immigration detention. In 1995-96, this amount rose to $23.4 million, and in 1997-98, the national budget for detention was capped at $19.8 million. Of this, approximately $13 million was budgeted for immigration detention in Ontario. Of that figure, $4 million was designated for the Celebrity detention centre, leaving $9 million for criminality-based detentions in Ontario. According to CIC, "the cost to detain a person for a full year at the Celebrity Inn is $33,000.00. This is equal to $90.41 per day per person ... Not included in this figure are the medical bills that range from 150,000 to 200,000 at the Celebrity Inn, or transportation costs (to immigration proceedings etc.)."[134] CIC observes that "detention costs a lot of money ... [and] is used quite sparingly and with restraint ... by the domestic regions across the country."[135] The numbers of immigration detainees in Canada are indeed relatively small and those of noncriminal detentions even smaller. In the end, it emerges that fiscal imperatives have governed detention and release decisions at Celebrity. "It is completely resource-driven. If there are no more beds, we pick up the phone and say don't arrest any more people, don't bring any more people here."[136] In February 2000, there was no more room at the inn. Celebrity was over capacity with 119 detainees. Arresting officers were told to "stop arresting people we can't remove; we can't keep them here."[137] The resource-driven nature of detention decisions at Celebrity led one EDO to conclude that detention at Celebrity serves no official policy purpose or objective other than public relations – "so Immigration can say we're doing something."[138]

Current Trends and Policy Initiatives Relating to Detention

The United States has been busy building and opening new detention facilities. There immigration detention is big business. In 1986, the United States passed the *Immigration Reform and Control Act*. One of the consequences of this restrictive piece of legislation was the expanded use of detention for immigration violations. This trend was intensified with the passing of the 1996 *Illegal Immigration Reform and Immigrant Responsibility Act*. It provided that virtually anyone who is to be deported for reasons of criminality be detained without bond, "without regard to age or circumstances." There is no possibility of release even if detainees are likely to appear for proceedings and pose no danger to the public.[139]

US government funding of detention and removal efforts increased from $239 million in 1994 to $733 million in 1998. During the same period, the number of people employed in the work of detention and removals increased from 1,900 to 3,400. In 1995, there were approximately 8,600 beds in INS detention facilities. In 1998, this number increased to 16,000,[140] and by 2002 it reached 21,000.[141] Since the 1980s, the INS has opened more than twenty-six detention centres, some of which have been described as large, "state-of-the-art" facilities.[142] As the increase in detention capacity suggests, the number of those admitted to detention has also risen dramatically. In 1995, there were 86,000 admissions, and in 1998, the number was more than 150,000. The average stay is thirty-four days, although Mexican nationals on average are detained for much shorter periods.[143] As put by Doris Meissner, commissioner of the Immigration and Naturalization Service, in

September 1998, the INS program "is the fastest growing detention operation within the Department of Justice."[144]

As discussed in Chapter 1, immigration detention grew exponentially in the United States after September 11th. For example, the US implemented "Operation Liberty Shield," which mandates the detention of asylum seekers from Iraq and at least thirty-three other countries. The US also widened detention rules to allow FBI agents and US marshals to detain foreign nationals for alleged immigration violations when there is not enough evidence to hold them on criminal charges.

In contrast, Canada has resisted blanket detentions and continues to detain far fewer people than the United States. Nevertheless, a number of legislative reforms and policy initiatives since September 11th directly expand the potential for the use of detention in Canada. For example, as noted, under the provisions of *IRPA*, the use of detention for reasons relating to identity are much more prominent. The powers of immigration officers to arrest without warrant are expanded, and officers are allowed to detain if they believe it necessary to complete the examination.[145] The 2001 "security" budget earmarked $210 million toward detention, removal, and refugee determination over the following five years.[146] And "Project Identity" is a CIC pilot project that aims to detain people whose credibility is doubted, who are "evasive or uncooperative" with immigration officers, or who have no identity documents. The most likely people to be detained under this project are refugee claimants, many of whom lack the requisite documents due to the circumstances of departure from their countries of origin. Critics believe that this initiative, like many other enforcement-oriented developments in this field since September 11th, are less about national security and public safety and more about reassuring the United States that Canada is taking a tough stance in the wake of September 11th.[147]

In January 2003, it was reported that CIC was close to finalizing a deal with the Ontario Ministry of Public Safety and Security to lease a section of the recently opened, 1,200-bed "super jail" in Kawartha Lakes. If this deal goes through, people currently detained in Ontario correctional institutions will be housed in the one location.[148] While government bureaucrats had been persistently exploring the possibility of building, buying, or sharing a facility that would more closely resemble a US-style super detention centre,[149] in December 2003 it was reported that the federal government had awarded a five-year, $20 million contract to a private security company to transform another larger airport hotel, the Heritage Inn, into a detention facility to replace the Celebrity Inn.[150]

Despite the small numbers, immigration detention at Celebrity and elsewhere is a critical instrument for drawing and maintaining "zones of exclusion." Detention at Celebrity is part of the assemblage that produces and reproduces borders, identities, national sovereignties, and citizens. The practices of confinement that have been described here are "social phenomena" that "cannot be accounted for by the juridical structure of society alone."[151] Quasi-judicial, quasi-administrative, and quasi-criminal procedures act upon quasi-criminal detainees in partly punitive, partly paternal ways. Conventional boundaries are blurred, categories are meshed, and technologies are diversified. Always carceral and sometimes compassionate. Public policy and private enterprise. Public enforcement officers and private security personnel. Law and administration. Immigration and criminal justice. Rules and discretion. Hospitality and incarceration. Punitive and paternal. Health care and punishment. Enforcement officers and community members. State and civil society. Risk and refugees. Shackles and mercy. Barbed wire and children.

Yet, despite this diversity and multiplicity, detention and deportation are the most extreme, coercive, and bodily sanctions of immigration penality and do manifest the contemporary persistence of sovereign power. A key feature of the operations of sovereign power in relation to the policies and practices of Canadian detention and deportation is discretion, to which this discussion now turns.

3
Reframing Discretion

"Discretion, like the hole in a doughnut, does not exist except as an area left open by a surrounding belt of restriction."[1] Ronald Dworkin's often-cited "doughnut analogy" sums up the conventional legal view of discretion. This view assumes that law is the primary instrument of regulation, that discretion is a residual category of law,[2] and that this discretion is exercised by essentially free and autonomous rational decision makers. These core assumptions continue to underpin political discussions and policy debates to such an extent that they shape and limit imagined policy and legislative reforms from all sides of the political spectrum.

While the discretionary powers of criminal justice officials have been widely studied, not so the discretionary powers of immigration officials. To a certain extent, this is explained by the analytical preoccupation with judicial settings that issues out of the dominant liberal legal paradigm and by the assumption that the rights normally central to that paradigm are not really applicable to noncitizens. Moreover, despite the proliferation of historical and contemporary works from a variety of disciplinary perspectives on the subject of Canadian immigration policy and practice, few engage in any analysis of discretion and detention as objects of study from other than a strictly legal and/or human rights perspective.[3]

This chapter interrogates the dominant view of law/discretion as a zero-sum game and demonstrates the value of shedding this binary in favour of an alternative approach. Rather than considering discretion as the *absence* of governance, it is considered here as a powerful form *of* governance, one that facilitates the translation of certain social concerns and priorities into immigration law, policy, and practice.[4]

Discretionary power is inflected by shifting, historically specific discourses. As this book demonstrates, at the beginning of the twenty-first century, the crime-security nexus inflected by the spectre of fraud provides the basis and justification for exclusionary immigration law and policy to a degree unprecedented in Canadian history. Exclusionary immigration law and policy refer specifically to those provisions in Canadian immigration legislation and policy that prohibit the entry of certain categories of people into Canada, that sanction the detention and deportation of noncitizens, and that deem certain people ineligible for refugee status in Canada. The preceding discussion of immigration detention at the Celebrity Inn indicates the pervasiveness of discretionary power in this domain. This chapter interrogates this discretion more fully and continues the discussion, which is central to all that follows, of the importance of discretionary power in the processes and practices of national exclusions under a liberal regime of governance.

Law versus Discretion

> When law ends, discretion begins, and the exercise of discretion may mean either beneficence or tyranny, either justice or injustice, either reasonableness or unreasonableness.[5]

For the most part, contemporary legal theorizing on discretion continues to be framed by the liberal preoccupation with the rule of law. This view expresses the legal conceit that discretion is the unruly shadow of law, a space unconstrained to varying degrees by legal or legalistic rules. Ideally, in this space, essentially autonomous individuals make decisions that reflect rational, reasonable, and objective calculations and that apply general legal rules to individual cases. A standard dictionary defines discretion as "the power or right to decide or act, according to one's own judgement or choice."[6] The "freedom to choose" of autonomous decision makers is defined in natural opposition to the constraints imposed by legal rules. The taken-for-grantedness of this relation is expressed in the same dictionary's definition of "arbitrariness," the most prevalent concern associated with discretionary decision making: "subject only to individual will or judgement, without restriction; contingent only on one's discretion: an arbitrary decision ... having unlimited power; uncontrolled or unrestricted by law; despotic; tyrannical."[7] The idea of discretion is thus intertwined with assumptions and ideals relating to the power of law, autonomy, and freedom of choice. Whether discretion is regarded benevolently or critically, its essential and inextricable binary relationship to law is largely taken for granted.

It's a zero-sum game. Discretion and law are constituted as discrete and distinct entities that are negatively correlated in much the same way as liberty/authority and freedom/security: more of one means less of the other. The view that the only meaningful constraint on discretion is law leads to a primary focus on the "surrounding belt of restrictions" rather than on the "hole" of discretion. Where discretion is constructed as a problem (often expressed in terms of "arbitrariness" or "disparity"), solutions are most frequently sought through the development and application of even more legal rules to constrain, shape, and guide the uses of discretion.

In 1915, the dominant view of the relation between law and discretion received its classic articulation by A.V. Dicey, who argued that discretionary decision making by public servants was the antithesis of law and associated with arbitrary might and coercion.[8] With the emergence of the welfare era, many students of jurisprudence came to a more benevolent view of discretionary decision making as a "humanizing" device to permit the general rules of law to be adapted to the circumstances of individual cases. Beginning in the 1960s, many scholars, including most notably Kenneth Culp Davis, returned to earlier preoccupations, again seeing the widening use of administrative discretionary powers as a serious threat, both real and potential, to individual justice.[9]

Despite these shifts – discretion as tyranny, discretion as benevolence, and again discretion as tyranny – the essential binary relationship of law and discretion has rarely been questioned. Consequently, as discretion became increasingly regarded as a "problem," the taken-for-granted solution was to implement more legal or legalistic rules to confine discretion, thereby, as put by Davis, "eliminating and limiting discretionary power ... fixing the boundaries and keeping discretion within them."[10] In contrast to the "arbitrariness" of discretion, the rule of law is seen to promise certainty, objectivity, and fairness. From this perspective, discretion poses particular problems when it threatens individual rights and individual justice. Accordingly, as put by Nicola Lacey, "the issue of control is often represented in terms of the protection of the individual from state or bureaucratic abuse."[11] While most acknowledge that its presence is necessary, indeed inevitable, given the complexity and diversity of the administration of the modern liberal state, the use (and abuse) of discretion has been a matter of growing concern since the 1960s.[12]

Also deeply imbedded in the conventional view of discretion is the liberal conception of individual autonomy and free choice. Where there is a "gap" in the legal rules, it is assumed that individual decision makers are afforded the opportunity to flex their innate autonomy and are, to varying degrees, "free to choose" between possible alternative courses of action.[13] Davis's definition of discretion is still widely cited: "A public official has discretion whenever the effective limits on his power leave him free to make a choice among possible courses of action or inaction."[14]

Legal scholars have increasingly acknowledged that there is in fact no clear distinction between discretion and law. It is today more commonly conceded that laws and their application are suffused with discretion and that administrative discretion is in fact extensively curbed by rules. As stated by Madame Justice Beverly McLachlin of the Supreme Court of Canada, "things are not as simple as Dicey perceived them. The law is not as certain as he would have it, nor are administrators as arbitrary."[15]

This recognition that law and discretion are not related in a zero sum dichotomy is an important development. However, while this acknowledgment modifies and blurs the distinction, conceives of it as overlapping, even porous and shifting, it does not unsettle the basic assumption that discretion is something essentially *outside* law, always and already defined by its conceptual binary opposite, law. While recent legal scholarship on discretion provides a more nuanced version of the relationship between law and discretion, the essential law/discretion binary remains largely undisturbed.

The tendency of traditional legal approaches to treat discretion as a residual category of law has distracted attention from how decisions are actually made and focused it on judicial discretion and review. Whereas legal scholarship has tended to privilege the law side of the dichotomy, social scientists have tended to focus on the discretion side, privileging social forces. The interest in "discretion-centred" studies (as opposed to "law- or rule-centred") has contributed to the gradual "decentring" of law by denying its essential primacy and by focusing analytical attention on "extra-legal" or "nonlegal" influences on discretionary decision making.[16] However, again, while the dividing line between law and discretion has been rendered less definite and the primacy of law less certain, the fundamental binary remains intact.

The limitations of the discussions and debates around discretion, administration, and law suggest the need for the development of new ways of thinking about discretion. The rule-based view of discretion and the automatic recourse to law that the law/discretion dichotomy implies need to be unsettled. The historically specific context of the operations of discretion and the particular objectives that guide its operations must be taken seriously. Robert Goodin draws important attention to the link between discretion and context in his study of discretion and provision of welfare assistance. He argues that problems arise not because of discretion but because of the underlying purpose of welfare decision making: to distinguish between the deserving and the undeserving poor. He concludes provocatively: "Imagine, in contrast, a world in which officials were guided only by the first half of that twin obsession: suppose officials are anxious to ensure that everyone who needs/deserves benefits gets them, but that they are utterly unconcerned to ensure that only they receive them."[17] The uses of discretionary power in the context of immigration exclusions and refugee determinations clearly share much in common with its uses in the context of welfare administration. In each sphere of decision making, discretionary power is deployed in selective distribution of administrative state benefits (welfare payments, citizenship, refugee status). Differential treatment is justified by reference to the oppositional and moralized categories of deserving and undeserving claimants.

As discussed in Chapter 1, in keeping with an understanding of liberalism as a way of governing, rather than a political theory or "ideology,"[18] discretion is here understood as a practical technology in the "dividing practices" of liberalism.[19] Discretion actively and continuously carves out a domain of freedom that negotiates law and equity and that mitigates the apparent gap between the universality and particularity of liberal legality.[20] Thus, while discretion tends to be constructed as "law's rival," it works to reconcile the universality of liberal legal principles and the particularity of specific legal cases and contexts. In the sense developed by Peter Fitzpatrick in relation to law and administration and law and informalism, discretion and law are mutually constitutive and mythical. As he surmises, "it is because of the particularist and pervasive powers of administration that the rule of law can be maintained in all its aspects of universality and equality and seen as marking out fields for free action ... Administration is the necessary 'dark side' of law."[21]

This study of immigration penalty seeks to avoid the problems that issue from the core assumptions that underlie the contemporary debates, namely the primacy of law, the law/discretion dichotomy, and the notion of autonomy and "free choice." It takes seriously the specific context of discretionary decision making. It accepts that the nature and effects of discretionary power must be considered in relation to the historically specific discursive formations that surround and inflect it, the specific institutional and practical dimensions of its existence, the local and dispersed nature of its operations, and the complex, overlapping, and dynamic processes that it traverses.

While the primacy of law has been increasingly questioned, the law/discretion binary is not easily shed. It is a constituent and largely taken-for-granted feature of the dominant legal paradigm in Western liberal regimes. The legal paradigm reinterprets social relations and perceived problems in terms of "legal or quasi-legal categories of thought";[22] problems are thus understood as issuing from inadequate regulation by law or lawlike rules, and therefore solutions are understood to lie in more law or lawlike rules. Moreover, due to its constituent conception of the rule of law and related conceptions of individual autonomy and free will, the legal paradigm is closely associated "with liberalism as a doctrine of political morality."[23] The conventional view that the solution to the "problem" is to make administrative decision making more rule bound and legalistic not only detracts attention from material conditions and the struggle for concrete changes in these conditions but also sustains the primacy of the liberal legal paradigm and the assumption that the imposition of rules will bring increased individual justice. This again reveals the close association of liberalism and the dominant legal paradigm, which together privilege individual justice and regard the rule of law as essential to its attainment. In light of these observations, the phrase "liberal legality" is used to capture and convey, or at least to flag and unsettle, these constitutive features of the still dominant legal paradigm so that they might be a little less taken for granted.

The following discussion demonstrates the centrality of discretion in the domain of immigration detention and deportation. It also aims to make visible the law/discretion binary and the degree to which issues and problems associated with immigration detention and removal are "reinterpreted" as arising from gaps or ambiguities in the law or from inadequate rule-based regulation.

Discretion and Immigration Detention

Administrative law has long been characterized by the breadth of discretion afforded to its administrators. This discretion has been justified primarily on two grounds: (1) discretion allows for the tailored application of general laws to individual cases, facilitating the attainment of individualized justice, and (2) discretionary powers of decision making are essential to the efficient and effective administration of legislation that affects huge numbers of people in complex and varying ways. Discretionary decision making, political and bureaucratic, is today and has always been a central feature of the administration of Canadian immigration and refugee policies.[24]

As outlined in the previous chapter, Canadian immigration legislation sanctions the use of coercive powers against noncitizens who, as a result of a series of broadly discretionary decisions and a complex web of interactions between a variety of authorities, have been targeted for detention and/or deportation. The debates around the uses of discretionary power in the administration of law and policy have been particularly pointed whenever the decisions taken entail serious consequences for the life and liberty of citizens. The administration of immigration legislation, in particular of provisions that deal with the detention and removal of noncitizens, has tended to attract less attention even though it entails the very consequences that have generated so much concern in the administration of criminal law.

In certain respects, the enforcement powers of immigration officers exceed those of police officers. For example, immigration officers may detain a prospective immigrant or refugee if they are of the opinion that the person in question is not likely to appear for future immigration-related proceedings. While those charged with criminal offences may, after a hearing is held, be detained before trial because they are deemed to represent a flight risk or a danger to the public, the detention powers of immigration officers nonetheless exceed those of police officers: "Immigration Officers have powers beyond the range of any policeman or soldier in this country. There is no policeman who can arrest somebody because he thinks the guy won't show up for a hearing next week. If the person doesn't show up, you issue an arrest warrant, but you can't decide Joe Blow isn't going to come next week, then go to his or her house, arrest them in their pyjamas and take them to detention."[25]

The legal distinction between punitive and preventative detention moves immigration detention from the ambit of criminal law into that of civil law. As such, the merely "quasi-judicial" nature of immigration detention decision making does not carry with it the same obligation to provide all the same legal protections required under criminal law. While those who are detained may experience their detention as punishment, they are not accorded the degree of rights and protections that would be theirs if they were actually being punished. For example, in detention review hearings, legal rules of evidence do not apply, access to legal counsel is limited, and the onus of proof is reversed so that the person in detention has to prove that he or she should be released.

The distinction between administrative immigration detention and deportation and criminal punishment as well as the long-standing tradition of judicial restraint in this area of public law and policy hinge in large part on the notion of state sovereignty. The legacy of the ideological national conception of sovereignty and the political conception of the sovereign rights and duties that derive from this legacy are remarkably resilient. As expressed in *Canada v. Chiarelli*, "the most fundamental principle of immigration law is that non-citizens do not have an unqualified right to enter or remain in the country. At common law an alien has no right to enter or remain in the country."[26] This construction of state sovereignty continues to justify even the most coercive of immigration enforcement activities, arrest, detention, and deportation, and works to protect these activities from thorough judicial oversight.[27] This is so despite overwhelming evidence that – from Chinese labourers to Japanese enemy aliens, from communist subversives to the destitute and unemployed, from immoral British nannies to homosexuals – immigration exclusions have more to do with making up citizens, with regulating populations, with enhancing the economy, and therefore with intersecting and historically specific economic conditions, political factors, racism, morality, and international conditions than with political and juridical notions of sovereignty. As explored in the first chapter, immigration penality is a creature of both sovereign and governmental modes of power.

Discourses of national sovereignty continue to be dominant despite (or indeed fuelled by) the growing recognition that global and transnational developments have increasingly unsettled the sovereignty of nation-states and the territorial borders that both constitute and are constituted by them. A global "intensification of interconnectedness"[28] has unsettled conventional constructions of the nation-state "as common territory and time"[29] and as the primary locus of citizenship.[30] Detention and deportation operate to redistribute citizens to their "proper" nations (or substitutions thereof), thereby reconstituting citizenship and reconfiguring sovereignties in a global context, what William Walters refers to as the "international police" of population. From a more state-centred perspective, others regard the increasingly enforcement-oriented policies and practices of immigration penality and border control that remain deeply and defiantly embedded in the principles that affirm the nation's sovereign right to control who gets in as defensive reactions of increasingly insecure nation-states to the changing political geography of the world.[31]

The *IRPA* is even more entrenched in the crime-security nexus than its predecessor. The former 1976 *Immigration Act* included the objective of the promotion of "international justice by denying the use of Canadian territory to persons who are likely to engage in criminal activity."[32] The *IRPA* goes several steps further by explicitly sanctioning the exclusion of refugee claimants in the name of both criminality and security: "to promote international justice and security by denying access to Canadian territory to persons, including refugee claimants, who are security risks or serious criminals."[33] The objectives of both the 1976 *Immigration Act* and the *IRPA* also specify the need to ensure that decision making under the legislation is consistent with the *Charter*, fulfills Canada's international legal obligations with respect to refugees, and upholds Canada's "humanitarian tradition with respect to the displaced and the persecuted." A tension thus pervades the objectives of Canadian immigration legislation between national and international human rights obligations and considerations of safety and security. Those responsible for immigration enforcement tend to regard the obligations relating to the legal and human rights of noncitizens as a constant frustration in their ability to do their job. This is reflected in the official designation of these legal rights as "impediments to removal."[34]

Judicial Review

While it tends to be assumed that judicial review provides an important top-down check on the potential for injustices in administrative decision making, administrative law and policy have always enjoyed a significant degree of protection from judicial oversight. Judicial noninterference is particularly pronounced in the area of immigration decision making: "Immigration law, like the law surrounding parole and prison discipline, has had a reputation among people interested in administrative law as a sort of wasteland in which judges have been loathe to apply the legal principles we normally associate with a sense of justice in Canadian public administration."[35] This is largely attributed to the legally entrenched understanding of the unassailability of the discretion that distinguishes administration and that deflects the intrusion of generally recognized legal principles. As noted by

J.G. Cowan, "cases involving immigrants, prisoners, and parolees are examples of other areas of discretionary power in which the courts are reluctant to interfere. Statutory powers exercised by immigration and prison officials are quite wide, and considerable scope has been given to the purposes for which they may be exercised and the factors that may be considered in reaching a decision, all of which are reflected in decisions in which the principles of natural justice have been modified significantly or ignored."[36]

While the judiciary maintains a residual jurisdiction to review procedural fairness and propriety to ensure that administrative decision making respects a radically trimmed-down version of the principles of fundamental justice and that it operates within the general parameters of due process – that it is not arbitrary or capricious – the substance of administrative immigration decisions is rarely reviewed by the courts. In practice, the courts have long been loathe to interfere with administrative decision making in all issues respecting immigration, national security, public order, and defence.[37] As pointed out by the Canadian Bar Association (CBA), "the vast majority of leave applications are denied, with no judicial review or further appeal being allowed."[38]

The logic of crime-security justifies the further limits imposed on access to judicial review under *IRPA*. For example, permanent residents and "foreign nationals" have no right to appeal a deportation order if they have been found inadmissible on the broadly defined grounds of security, violating human or international rights, serious criminality, or organized criminality.[39] "Serious criminality" that results in the denial of appeal is determined if a person is convicted of an offence punished by at least two years in prison.[40] As noted by the CBA, "The denial of a right to appeal based on an arbitrary rule that does not distinguish between permanent residents who arrived six months ago, and those who arrived 20 years ago, or as children, is fundamentally flawed and unfair."[41] In addition, under the 1976 *Immigration Act*, overseas decisions made by visa officers could be appealed "by right" (without seeking leave) to the Federal Court. Under *IRPA*, the leave requirement is extended to apply to any immigration decision whether arising in Canada or overseas.[42]

The effectiveness of law, in this case in the form of judicial review, as a practical and meaningful "check" on administrative discretion has thus been sorely limited. In the view of the CBA, *IRPA* limits even further the "essential procedural safeguards [that] ... ensure that these critical decisions are made fairly and appropriately."[43] Nonetheless, the relationship of law and the discretionary decision making of administration can be seen as both powerful and productive. The apparent limits of legal oversight in this domain work to sustain the continuing need for judicial review; as observed by Fitzpatrick, discretion is the necessary "dark side" of law. As noted, discretion is a key component in the reconciliation of the universality and

particularity of liberal law. In this view, discretion is erected as an oppositional barrier to fixity; if fixity doesn't exist, then neither does discretion.

Departmental Policy

The ever-present threats of arbitrariness, disparity, and capriciousness posed
by discretionary decision making are also understood to be mitigated by
nonbinding departmental policies and guidelines, including those that govern detention decision making. These do not intend to "fetter" discretion;
rather, they articulate a "recommended" approach in the name of consistency, coherence, and fairness in the making of decisions. Still, even carefully worded, suggestive, and nonbinding guidelines provoke divisive and
defensive opposition.

In the fall of 1996, the CIC issued a new policy on the detention of noncitizens. Due in large part to growing concerns regarding the costs associated with detention, the new policy sought to limit the number of people
in detention by focusing the attention of immigration officials on criminality as the primary public policy reason for detention. Detention, the guidelines sought to instruct, was to be regarded as a last resort, justified only
when there was a real possibility that release would endanger the Canadian
public. The policy also sought to facilitate the release of people already in
detention by setting comparatively low amounts on the sureties/bonds
needed to obtain a release.

The strongest opposition to this policy initiative emanated from those
immigration officers who make detention decisions. They argued that the
policy fettered the discretion that is essential for them to carry out their
duties effectively and efficiently. As a result of their strong opposition, the
CIC drafted another detention policy. This was a particularly challenging
task due in large part to the sensitivity of immigration officers on the question of discretion. For example, the department had wanted to include a
section entitled "Expected Results" but had opted to remove it due to concerns that it represented an unjustified constraint on officers' discretion.[44]
New CIC detention guidelines were eventually released in 1998.[45]

The primary justification for the issuing of departmental guidelines regarding discretionary decision making is the need for greater "consistency"
of decisions in accordance with liberal notions of due process and the principles of fundamental justice. In the view of critics, this lack of consistency
amounts at best to "arbitrariness" and at worst to racism and other forms of
discrimination.

Discretion constitutes an integral part of both the professional identities
and the practices of immigration officers (just as it does for police officers).
In the 1996 policy, discretion is represented as making "good" or "professional" judgments based on the "objective" evaluation of complex issues of
law, fact, and relevant jurisprudence.[46] Interestingly, the 1998 detention

policy adds the requirement that officers exercise "sensible risk management practices" in addition to "good judgement." The section on detention in the CIC immigration manual also includes new mention of risk management: "Sound judgement not only requires individual assessment of the case, but also an assessment of the impact of release on the safety of Canadian society. Additionally, it requires a risk management approach to take decisions within the context of [four] ... priorities." These priorities are listed as safety or security concerns (terrorism, criminality, violent behaviour at the time of examination); identity issues that must be resolved in order to determine whether there are safety and security concerns; flight risks; and the establishment of identity where no reliable documents are available or where the person is "noncooperative."[47]

Different agents involved in detention and removal decision making understand discretion in various ways. Policy officials tend to adhere to the strictly legal view that discretion does not exist unless there are options laid out in the relevant legislation, with the officer having a legislated choice whether or not to exercise authority. In this legalistic view, neither the officers of the Canada Customs and Revenue Agency (CCRA), who carry out the primary inspections on behalf of Immigration (who, as of 2003, are officers of the Canada Border Services Agency [CBSA]), nor immigration officers carrying out the secondary inspection, who may recommend detention, have *any* discretion; if certain "facts" exist, they "must exercise their legislated authority."[48] An alternative view is expressed in the detention policy as set out in the 2001 immigration manual, which states that the decision to detain requires a "sensitive and balanced" approach and that, "*in exercising their discretionary authority to detain,* officers need to consider all reasonable alternatives before ordering the detention of an individual."[49]

In the legal view, it is only the senior immigration officer (SIO) who reviews the initial decision to detain within the first forty-eight hours who has any discretion. This is because the decision of the SIO is not legally tied to the two legislated grounds for detention. Moreover, several options are built into the legislation: the SIO may detain or release and may impose whatever terms and/or conditions on release that he or she deems warranted. Curiously, from this perspective, adjudicators who review the detention decision after seven days, and every thirty days after that, are not regarded as having much discretion. As put by one senior immigration official, "at a detention review there really isn't discretion ... The adjudicator can only release when they are satisfied the grounds [for detention] don't exist. Or, there really is a third element, they [the grounds for detention] can be superseded by the legality of jurisprudence."[50]

This official legalistic view of discretion as created and bound by law differs from a more interpretive understanding held by advocates and even some decision makers. This interpretive view regards discretion, rather than the law, expansively. Discretion here is regarded in relation to the interpretive dimensions of applying general legal rules to individual cases. For example, a former adjudicator with the CIC explained that at detention reviews adjudicators in fact have broad discretionary powers; they interpret both law and policy as well as the "facts," situations, circumstances, characters, et cetera in order to assess the risk (of danger or flight), which ultimately grounds their decision in law.[51] Advocates and nongovernmental commentators tend to share this more expansive, interpretive view of discretion.

Moreover, it would seem that immigration officers themselves disagree with the view that they do not have any discretion in making their initial detention recommendations. Their opposition to the proposed 1996 CIC guidelines on detention rested on their view that the guidelines were a "blatant attempt by management to fetter the actions of Immigration officers."[52] The Canada Employment and Immigration Union (CEIU) takes serious issue with the "fettering" of the discretion of immigration officers by management. As put by the CEIU, "officers' decisions are fettered by management whose decision to over-rule and release detainees is based on cost factors rather than health, safety and security of the Canadian public. There are periodic blitzes of releasing people from ... the Immigration Holding Centre (the Celebrity Inn near Pearson Airport) because the Inn has too many people there."[53]

Thus, there is a stark contrast between the view that discretion is clearly demarcated and defined by law and the differing and often conflicting meanings and perceptions of discretion that vary depending, in this case, on one's professional identity, location, and preoccupations.

Policy Discussions and Debates on Detention

In their 1997 report *Not Just Numbers: A Canadian Framework for Future Immigration,* the government-appointed Immigration Legislative Review Advisory Group (LRAG) recommended that the issues of detention and removal be the subject of CIC Parliamentary Standing Committee hearings.[54] Accordingly, in 1997-98, the CIC Standing Committee received submissions on Canadian detention and removal policy and practice from a wide range of governmental and nongovernmental representatives. LRAG was another step in the ongoing immigration legislation reform efforts of the Liberal Party that had been launched in 1993 with cross-country consultations on immigration by then Minister of Immigration Sergio Marchi. In 1998, Minister of Immigration Lucienne Robillard held consultations on LRAG's report and announced her intention to table new immigration legislation. In the same year, the Liberal government published a white paper entitled "Building on a Strong Foundation for the 21st Century: New Directions for Immigration and Refugee Policy and Legislation."[55] As previously noted, on 6 April 2000, the government introduced Bill C-31, the first *Immigration and*

Refugee Protection Act, but this bill died when the November 2000 election was called. In February 2001, the government introduced Bill C-11, a revised version of Bill C-31. This new *Immigration and Refugee Protection Act* received royal assent on 1 November 2001. The new immigration regulations were prepublished on 15 December 2001 and 9 March 2002. The *IRPA,* together with the regulations, came into force on 28 June 2002.

LRAG's 1997 report, together with the representations and submissions to the 1997-98 Standing Committee, attests to the degree to which discretion is a critical and politically contentious feature of the administration of the detention and removal provisions of Canadian immigration legislation. Also evidenced is the embeddedness of the liberal legal paradigm and the limits that issue from the law/discretion dichotomy.

The rule of law and all that it promises guide LRAG's position that greater consistency and accountability of immigration decision making are necessary to ensure fairness and restore public confidence in the legitimacy of the system. Procedural justice, a key element of the rule of law, requires that laws be announced and that they are transparently and consistently applied. As expressed by LRAG, "immigration and protection laws [should] be implemented in such a way that the criteria used to make decisions are derived directly from the Acts and Regulations, and are readily available to the public in a language they can understand. Transparency is a necessary condition for the effectiveness and efficiency of the immigration and protection programs and the maintenance of public confidence in their administration."[56]

LRAG was particularly concerned with the potential for arbitrariness, disparity, and the obstruction of transparency of discretionary detention decision making under the 1976 *Immigration Act:* "With such broad powers given to officers to deprive persons of their liberty, concern has been expressed by many that in the absence of specificity in the Act, and with virtually no policy guidelines issued by the department, the standards for detention are not transparent and vary greatly from office to office and officer to officer."[57]

Accordingly, LRAG's recommendations are designed in large part to limit and constrain the discretion of decision makers through the development of specific, clear, and coherent law and policy: more law equals less discretion. Decisions must not be, or appear to be, "arbitrary" lest public confidence in the system and hence its legitimacy is diminished. The solution is to fix the boundaries: more law, more rules, more policies, more guidelines.

However, notwithstanding the expressed commitment to the ideals of the rule of law and procedural fairness, LRAG proposed that the IRB, a quasi-judicial, arm's-length tribunal, be dismantled and replaced by a "Protection Agency" staffed by civil servants. This idea resurfaced in 2003 when Minister of Citizenship and Immigration Denis Coderre also proposed that refugee claimants should present their cases in interviews carried out by civil servants in the Immigration department ("refugee protection officers") rather than by IRB board members.[58]

This contentious proposal (in 2003 just as in 1997) articulates a very different mentality from that which had underpinned the 1987 introduction of the *Refugee Reform Bill* (Bill C-55).[59] Bill C-55 had been the government's response to the major, precedent-setting *Singh* decision by the Supreme Court in 1985.[60] *Singh* asserted that fundamental justice requires that determinations of the credibility of refugee claims be made on the basis of an oral hearing. Until that decision, the determination of refugee claims was, for the most part, a paper one. There had been provisions for hearings, but they were neither mandatory nor common. The Supreme Court found that, for citizens and noncitizens alike, an absence of oral hearings was contrary to the *Charter*.

Essentially, *Singh* sought to curb "arbitrary" administrative discretion through the expansion of due process in the determination of refugee cases. Bill C-55 created a refugee determination process with mandatory hearings carried out by an independent adjudicative tribunal, the Immigration and Refugee Board (IRB). It also extended the due process and procedural rights afforded to claimants. A further important dimension of the *Singh* decision was the care taken by the Supreme Court to ensure that the human rights entrenched in the 1982 Canadian *Charter* applied to refugee claimants. It ruled that the "everyone" in section 7 of the *Charter* included not only everyone "physically present in Canada" but also anyone "seeking admission at a port of entry."[61] In effect, this decision extended *Charter* rights to noncitizens on Canadian soil.

Detractors of the current refugee determination system are quick to point out that the *Singh* decision did not actually mandate the creation of the IRB and the current determination process; rather, it mandated the more narrow right of people to state their cases and know the cases against them. As explained by LRAG, "the concern with any procedural scheme was not over the absence of a hearing in and of itself, but over the adequacy of the opportunity the scheme provided for persons to state their case and know the case they had to meet."[62]

LRAG proposed the creation of a *protection* agency. Coderre proposed that refugee *protection* officers should replace IRB board members. Canadian immigration legislation bears the name: *Immigration and Refugee Protection Act*. Still, for all the talk of protection, one can't help but wonder just whose "protection" is being sought. Such proposals focus less on the objective of providing protection to those at risk of persecution and more on the need to protect Canadians, Canadian systems, and Canadian borders from unwarranted or "fraudulent" claims and criminal threats.

While the events of 11 September 2001 undoubtedly had an impact on public attitudes, studies report a general hardening of public attitudes toward new immigrants and refugees over the past few decades. Often cited is the 1991 Angus Reid Poll that found, among other things, that almost half of Canadians believed the country is letting in too many immigrants and that about a third believed immigrants take away jobs, drain health care, and increase crime.[63] A 1994 review of public opinion studies on immigrants and refugees in Canada and Australia confirmed that attitudes toward immigrants and refugees had deteriorated.[64] In November 1999, Ipsos-Reid reported that 60 percent of Canadians believed that Canada's immigration policy priority should be to "stop illegal immigrants, rather than encourage qualified immigrants to come to Canada."[65] In the year prior to the attacks, Ipsos-Reid reported that 45 percent of Canadians thought that the number of immigrants coming to Canada is "too high"; 35 percent believed that immigrants are a drain on the economy; and 50 percent believed that it should be a higher priority to "encourage minority groups to try to change to be more like most Canadians."[66]

After September 11th, there was at least a short-term toughening of attitudes. For example, a 2002 poll showed strong support among Canadians for keeping Muslim immigrants out of the country, detaining all refugee claimants, and automatically deporting people travelling without proper identification.[67] However, this effect did subside, and by September 2002 Canadian views were reportedly consistent with those in the early 1990s.[68] A poll conducted in May 2004 indicated that the attitudes of Canadians toward immigrants had become quite positive, particularly when compared with Japan, the United States, Mexico, and some countries in Europe.[69]

While the government justified the creation of the IRB and the refugee determination process by reference to a commitment to ensuring due process for refugee claimants on Canadian soil, this was accompanied by the introduction of a range of administrative measures (e.g., visa requirements and fresh obligations on airlines) that restricted the numbers of noncitizens who could reach Canadian soil.[70] Moreover, in the years that followed the *Singh* decision, the Supreme Court of Canada effectively undermined its guiding principles, leading some legal critics to charge that, before that decision, "the alien's rights at common law were better than they are now under the Charter."[71] For example, in the 1993 case of *Dehghani v. Canada (Minister of Employment and Immigration)*,[72] the Supreme Court ruled that "a person 'held' at a port of entry and forced to answer questions under the threat of criminal charge if he refused, was not 'detained' for the purposes of right to counsel under s. 10(b) of the Charter."[73]

Not surprisingly, the debates surrounding the discretionary powers of Immigration and refugee officials are reminiscent of those heard in the context of any criminal justice initiatives that have sought to limit the discretion of officials. Immigration officers are vigorously protective of their discretionary powers, while nongovernmental representatives and advocates argue for the need to limit, regulate, and monitor discretion relying largely on recourse to law and legal rules. In this contemporary debate, the obligation of "the state" to abide by international human rights law and to respect the *Charter* rights of all people on Canadian soil, citizens and noncitizens alike, is discursively pitted against its obligation to protect its citizens from danger and its systems from abuse. The coercive powers of detention accorded to immigration officers and adjudicators are largely justified on these latter grounds. As put rather explicitly in 1998 by Lucienne Robillard, minister of immigration at the time, "I have spoken about finding ways to facilitate the movement and the integration of people. That is an important part of what we do, but ... it is only part of what we do, and at CIC we also have a clear responsibility to protect the safety, security and well-being of Canadians. There are criminals and other undesirables who would like to come to a prosperous country like Canada."[74] Two key discursive developments have inflected the operations of discretionary power in the context of exclusionary immigration law and policy. The first of these is the expansion of the category of criminality and its association with a reconfigured construction of national security, and the second is the contemporary and distinctly neoliberal preoccupation with fraud that, together with the crime-security nexus, has entailed a heightened preoccupation with identifying and excluding the fraudulent, criminal, or otherwise "risky" refugee claimant rather than identifying the genuine and therefore deserving refugee "at risk."

The prominence of the law/discretion dichotomy and the related liberal legal concerns that characterized the 1997-98 hearings were given expression in the subsequent Standing Committee on Citizenship and Immigration report entitled *Immigration Detention and Removals*.[75] The report emphasized the need to enhance the consistency of detention decision making (e.g., through new guidelines on detention to counter arbitrariness); assure the independence of decision makers; respect international human rights obligations; and reaffirm the importance of liberty as a foundational principle. It also urged that the use of detention be reduced and that its conditions be improved. At the same time, the report emphasized the problem of identification and recommended that detention be used upon arrival in order to establish identity. It also supported increased overseas interdiction measures in order to block undocumented migrants from getting to Canada. Two years later, the Standing Committee produced another report, entitled *Refugee Protection and Border Security: Striking a Balance*.[76] It is much more organized around the dichotomies of freedom/security and risks/rights. Its recommendations focus first on "strengthening, streamlining and expediting refugee determination processes" and then on "how we may make our borders more secure so those that we wish to keep from coming here will be deterred and those we welcome will be facilitated."[77] This report places a high priority on the need to detain people whose identities are suspect and who refuse to cooperate in establishing their identities, a priority eventually entrenched in *IRPA*.

After September 11th, the Standing Committee produced yet another report, this one entitled *Working Together at Our Shared Border and Abroad to Ensure Safety, Security, and Efficiency.*[78] Not surprisingly, this report and its recommendations were organized much more fully around the quest for security through enforcement, with a focus on the need to protect Canada's immigration and refugee programs from abuses. Detention was now represented as a key technology in this effort, "an enforcement tool to ensure the safety, security and integrity of Canada's immigration and refugee protection programs."[79]

Discretion as Arbitrary and Discriminatory

The dominant discourses accept without question the binary that pits "arbitrary" decision making against liberal ideals of the rule of law. Arbitrary decisions are, by definition, not based on law; rather, they are "subject to individual will or judgement without restriction; contingent solely upon one's discretion"; "unrestricted by law," "despotic," "capricious," "unreasonable."[80] And law, by definition, is not arbitrary. Arbitrary decision making is contrary to the liberal ideal of the rule of law; it undermines the premise that different judges hearing the same case would arrive at the same decision. Most of the critics of discretionary immigration decision making focus on this "problem" of arbitrariness. Whether issuing from a general concern with civil rights and liberties or from a particular concern with discrimination, this focus leads almost inevitably to a legalistic solution achieved through the adoption and application of clear rules and an enforced commitment to the rule of law and due process.

Many critics of detention decision making favour an external review mechanism in addition to adequate avenues of appeal, provisions for judicial review, and more extensive training of decision makers. They stress that some measure of external accountability is required to ensure that rules are followed. As put by TRAC, "because of the high level of discernment and decision-making required in this very difficult area of immigration work, transparency and accountability to an outside body is essential."[81] David Matas, a prominent Canadian immigration lawyer and advocate, made the same point in the following terms: "generally, in Canada, police enforcement systems have some form of civilian oversight and civilian run complaints redress or ombudsman. Immigration enforcement is unique amongst enforcement systems in Canada as a system without any civilian supervision of the policing authorities. The courts with jurisdiction over Immigration enforcement officials can correct errors of law, but they can do nothing about bad policies or inappropriate exercise of discretion."[82]

In the view of many who work on behalf of new immigrants and refugees, arbitrariness not only leads to inconsistent decision making but also
allows for the continuing influence of racist or other discriminatory views.
It is not insignificant, in the judgment of many critics, that the vast majority of people being detained by Immigration are nonwhite. The extensive
discretion of Immigration administrators has often been used in racist and
moralistic ways to exclude "offensive" and "undesirable" groups of people,
including, for example, American and Caribbean blacks, Chinese, communists, anarchists, homosexuals, the unemployed, and "immoral" women.
The refusal of the Canadian government to admit Jewish refugees fleeing
the Holocaust is a particularly harrowing example.[83] This historical legacy,
it is argued, continues to inflect refugee and immigration policy and decision making despite official declarations to the contrary, the removal from
immigration legislation of explicitly discriminatory provisions, and the inclusion in both the legislation and the *Charter* of legal requirements of equality and nondiscrimination.[84] Sensitivity to the possibility that individual
and systemic racism influence the use made by immigration and refugee
officers of their wide discretionary powers adds further urgency to the call
for transparency and independent oversight of the policies and practices of
immigration penality.

Despite considerable changes to the law and policy governing Canadian
immigration penality since the early 1900s, the concerns and criticisms regarding discretion do not appear to have changed much. In her study of
deportation from Canada between 1900 and 1935, Barbara Roberts observes
that in the early part of that century the administration of immigration law
and policy was characterized by arbitrariness, by wide and unchecked discretionary powers, by the relative absence of judicial review, and by a star-
tling degree of public and political ignorance about the system.[85] And, as
today, decision making relating to detention and deportation were then
considered "purely administrative proceedings" that had nothing to do with
punishment.

The persistence of the "problem" of discretion, despite the proliferation
of laws and lawlike rules designed to curtail, shape, and contain discretion
and its associated uses and abuses, suggests that legalistic solutions do not
actually present a meaningful remedy and indeed that discretion may not
be the problem. Nevertheless, concerns about arbitrary decision making
and calls for legal solutions come from across the political spectrum. On
the one side, arbitrary decision making (seen as an expression of misplaced
humanitarian compassion) is faulted for undermining the necessary "tough-
ness" of the system that must protect the Canadian public from dangerous
criminals and system abusers. On the other side, arbitrary decision making
(often seen as an expression of racism and other forms of discrimination) is
regarded as unjust, inconsistent, and capricious, penalizing one of the most

vulnerable and powerless groups within our borders, noncitizens. The solution to the "problem" of discretion advocated by each competing perspective is the same: the application of further rigid, specific, and clear legal rules to guide and constrain its operation.

This is the case despite historical and contemporary experiences that suggest the need for alternative remedies or perhaps a more substantial reframing of the problem. A persuasive contemporary example of the limitations associated with the liberal legal presumption of the effectiveness of "more rules" to regulate the uses of discretion is provided by the adoption of pro-charge and pro-prosecution policies in cases of wife assault. Police discretion was regarded as a vehicle for racist, sexist, and outdated views about gender roles, victims, and violence. The solution, it was argued, was to curtail police discretion through the adoption of more rules. Unfortunately, efforts to do this have had many negative "unintended consequences," not the least of which is that pro-arrest policies may actually deter certain marginalized groups of women from calling the police rather than deter abusers from abusing.[86]

Recent developments further attest to the limitations and circularity that the zero-sum game of law/discretion brings in tow. The call for more law and lawlike rules to deal with the problem of discretion has been incorporated in *IRPA*. Unlike its predecessor, *IRPA* is "framework" legislation. It sets out core principles and concepts, and it delegates the legislative authority to develop detailed regulations that cover administrative and procedural details. The *IRPA* and regulations have attracted the criticism that they seriously limit the discretionary capacity of immigration officers that is needed to ensure that decision making can be tailored to individual circumstances. For example, the CBA has argued that *IRPA* regulations reduce the space for more sensitive, individualized decision making while increasing the likelihood of standardized enforcement responses. Discretion is once again a benevolent, humanitarian quality that bridges the gap between law and equity: "Discretion gives decision makers options, to prevent unintended results that might occur if the law were applied strictly. Discretion exists because no complex set of laws, no matter how well thought out, can possibly take into account the myriad circumstances that may exist in individual cases."[87]

Whereas too much discretion has long been criticized for leading to arbitrariness, disparity, and discrimination, too little is seen to restrict the capacity to humanize and individualize decisions. While the critique has swung to the other end of the pendulum, the discretion/law binary continues to limit both the conversations and the imagined solutions.

The degree of discretionary power that characterizes administrative regulatory frameworks is generally set against the application of and commitment to the rule of law under liberalism. From a conventional perspective, discretion in administrative decision making has been defended as a crucial feature of individualized justice since it allows for the tailored and humane application of general rules and laws to individual cases. The critical but still conventional view regards discretion as a vehicle for arbitrariness, tyranny, caprice, and discrimination and argues that law and lawlike rules are needed to constrain and monitor the exercise of discretion.

To view discretion as a form of power promises to provide a way out of the dichotomous impasse imposed by the law/discretion binary. This view encourages different questions about discretion. Rather than asking why it is used, how it can be eliminated, curtailed or expanded, made more fair or just, the guiding question becomes how does this power *work* in specific empirical contexts? What are its practical purposes and effects? What are the historically specific discourses that inflect and justify its use? What social, political, legal, and economic preoccupations and processes influence its operations? What organizational and institutional networks, channels, and techniques are at play? It is these questions that guide this study of detention and deportation in Canada.

4

From Purity to Security

Different eras in Canada have been dominated by different perceptions of what have constituted the greatest threats posed to the nation and its citizens. Historically specific discursive logics that express dominant national insecurities vis-à-vis perceived external threats have justified exclusionary immigration laws, policies, and practices. While there is much overlap and intermingling of these governing logics, and notwithstanding the limitations associated with historical periodization, a general transition can be discerned over the past fifty years from a primary preoccupation with perceived threats to national racial and moral purity to a guiding preoccupation with putative threats to national security. While national security, understood in terms of political ideology and threats to the political state, had long been a guiding concern, it came to encompass criminality and threats to public safety. As will be further demonstrated in this chapter, discretionary power is, and has always been, a central mechanism giving practical effect to these governing logics.

In this chapter, I map out the transitions in the governance of immigration penality from 1945 to the adoption of the 1976 *Immigration Act*.[1] A process began in the mid-1950s and took hold through the 1960s that elevated human rights discourses and delegitimized the explicitly racist and moralistic immigration categories that had been promoted and rationalized by national purity discourses. The broadly discretionary, moralized, and explicitly racist provisions of the 1952 *Immigration Act* offended increasingly influential legal "rights-based" sensibilities and were contrary to the collectively and socially oriented tangents of welfare liberalism.[2] The influence of these discourses can be seen to peak in the 1970s with the passage of the 1976 *Immigration Act* and the creation of an independent administrative and legalized system of onshore refugee determination. These developments have been conventionally represented as the triumph of liberal, democratic, and progressive values and interests.

Concomitantly, after 1945, the ebb and flow of the Cold War heightened national insecurities and helped to fortify the logic of security and the Canadian security apparatus. At the same time that humanitarian and legal challenges both to the racism of immigration policies and to the scope and uses of discretion gained momentum, the logic of security, supplemented by criminality discourses, emerged as the guiding rationale for immigration enforcement and exclusion. Concerns about national security in the Cold War period revolved around threats to the political state by communist revolution. As the Cold War waned, the logic of security transformed to encompass the threats posed to public safety by international terrorism, organized crime, and less exotic true crimes.

There was then during this period a shift away from explicit, racially based exclusions justified by national purity discourses toward exclusions based increasingly on the risks posed to a reconfigured conception of national security. But these logics and transitions were not clear-cut. The logic of (racial and moral) national purity had long interacted with criminality concerns in the governance of exclusionary immigration law and policy. And, indeed, the influence of the logic of security had been dominant for some time, with wartime insecurities leading to the frequent use of discretionary powers to exclude against "subversives," "enemy aliens," communists, anarchists, and the like. Moreover, ethnic origin and imputed ideological threat were intensely intertwined. And, in the absence of an official exclusionary category of "political subversive" or "ideological enemy," criminality provisions were frequently used to effect the detention and deportation of such "threats."[3] However, the point made here, and substantiated in the following chapters, is that broad transitions have taken place in the dominant logics that govern exclusionary immigration law and policy – from national purity to national security – and that, while criminality has always been to varying degrees a key ground for the exclusion of "undesirables," through the forging of the crime-security nexus it has come to enjoy unprecedented dominance in the governance of immigration penality.

During this period, another dynamic also emerged. Increasingly influential neoliberal preoccupations related to fraud and individualized risk management concerns intersected with these growing concerns about crime-security and the proliferation of law and order programs. As will be demonstrated in later chapters, these associations have become prominent in the development and promotion of contemporary regimes of immigration penality and border control.

As discussed in Chapter 2, discretionary power is not exclusively owned or wielded by the formal institutions of "the state." It is not necessarily created by law, nor does it exist only in relation to law. Nevertheless, the examination of the development and application of the enforcement-related provisions of Canadian immigration law and policy does provide a window through which historically specific dynamics may be examined. What follows in this chapter is a selective review of these developments, beginning with Canadian prime minister Mackenzie King's famous 1947 "Statement on Immigration" and ending with the 1976 *Immigration Act*.

Protecting the "Character of Our Population"

The assertion of Canada's sovereign right to be selective with respect to whom it allows to enter and remain in Canada has always represented the bottom line in the justification of Canadian immigration law, policy, and practice and of the broad tracts of ministerial discretion in this field. In a major speech in 1947, Prime Minister Mackenzie King gave expression to this underlying principle and indicated what were then the government's central concerns. He observed that admission to Canada was a privilege and not a right, that immigration law and policy should not exceed the nation's economic "absorptive capacity," and that immigration law and policy should not interfere with the "character" of the nation:

> The policy of the Government is to foster the growth of the population of Canada by the encouragement of immigration. The Government will seek ... to ensure the careful selection and permanent settlement of such numbers of immigrants as can advantageously be absorbed in our national economy ... I wish to make it quite clear that Canada is perfectly within her rights in selecting persons whom we regard as desirable future citizens. It is not a "fundamental human right" of any alien to enter Canada. It is a privilege. It is a matter of domestic policy ... The people of Canada do not wish, as a result of mass immigration, to make any fundamental alteration in the character of our population ... Any considerable Oriental immigration would ... be certain to give rise to social and economic problems.[4]

While explicit expressions of racism have been removed, concerns about the prevalence of less visible and systemic forms of racism persist, concerns about Canada's economic "absorptive capacity"[5] continue, and the sovereign principle that "entering Canada is a privilege and not a right" remains influential. The fact that King's 1947 statement made explicit and racist reference to the potential threat to the "character of our population" posed by "mass" immigration in general and by "Oriental" immigration in particular speaks to the degree to which racist beliefs, articulated and applied in part through the deployment of national "purity" discourses, had been socially, legally, and politically dominant at that time and earlier. Until the 1960s, racism had intermingled with morality, gender, and class in the constitution of the (un)desirable citizen, and (un)desirability was linked discursively with the need to protect national purity.[6] More generally, the promotion of immigration exclusions as a mechanism for the pursuit of the economic and social welfare of the population, rather than as merely a means to protect the political state, indicates the way in which immigration exclusions were not merely manifestations of sovereign power but also governmentalized.

The 1952 *Immigration Act*

The 1952 act was the first *Immigration Act* since 1910.[7] It codified existing racial and moral bases for exclusion and sanctioned sweeping ministerial discretionary powers to exclude, either through inadmissibility or through deportation. The act gave Cabinet the power to exclude people from Canada on the following grounds:

(i) nationality, citizenship, ethnic group, occupation, class or geographical area of origin
(ii) peculiar customs, habits, modes of life or methods of holding property
(iii) unsuitability having regard to the climatic, economic, social, industrial, educational, labour, health, or other conditions or requirements existing temporarily or otherwise, in Canada or in the area or country from or through which such persons come to Canada, or
(iv) probable inability to become readily assimilated or to assume the duties and responsibilities of Canadian citizenship within a reasonable time after admission.[8]

This section remained virtually unchanged from section 38 (c) of the 1910 act.[9] There is little doubt that these provisions were designed in particular to exclude nonwhites, though other groups were also targeted. Doukhobors, Mennonites, and Hutterites were also prohibited under this section due to "their peculiar customs, habits, modes of living and methods of holding property" and their assumed inability to assimilate. Of note is the inclusion of "unsuitability" in regard to "climatic" conditions. A 1952 letter from Minister of Citizenship and Immigration Walter Harris made the following telling claims:

> It would be unrealistic to say that immigrants who have spent the greater part of their life in tropical or sub-tropical countries become readily adapted to the Canadian mode of life which, to no small extent, is determined by climatic conditions. It is a matter of record ... that natives of such countries are more apt to break down in health than immigrants from countries where the climate is more akin to that of Canada. It is equally true that, generally speaking, persons from tropical or sub-tropical countries find it more difficult to succeed in the highly competitive Canadian economy.[10]

The list of "Prohibited Classes" in the 1952 act was also virtually unchanged from the 1910 act. It included

a) persons who:
   i) are idiots, imbeciles or morons
   ii) are insane or, if immigrants, have been insane at any time
   iii) have constitutional psychopathic personalities, or
   iv) if immigrants, are afflicted with epilepsy;
b) persons afflicted with ... any contagious or infectious disease or with any disease that may become dangerous to the public health ...
c) immigrants who are dumb, blind, or otherwise physically defective ...
d) persons who have been convicted of or admit having committed any crime involving moral turpitude ...
e) prostitutes, homosexuals or persons living on the avails of prostitution or homosexualism, pimps, or persons coming to Canada for these or any other immoral purposes
f) persons who attempt to bring into Canada or procure prostitutes or other persons for the purpose of prostitution, homosexual or other immoral purposes
g) professional beggars or vagrants
h) persons who are public charges or who ... are likely to become public charges
i) persons who are chronic alcoholics
j) persons who are addicted to the use of any substance that is a drug within the meaning of the *Opium and Narcotic Drug Act.*[11]

In addition to the above, the 1952 act excluded people who were members of subversive organizations or who were or were likely to become drug "peddlers," traffickers, spies, saboteurs, and conspirators.

The prohibition against admitting homosexuals was officially justified by Cold War "national security" concerns: "sexual deviants" were not merely morally undesirable but also (re)constructed as national security risks.[12] As argued by Philip Girard, this discursive linkage was largely the result of pressure from the RCMP and the American security establishment that had linked communism and homosexuality as part of Cold War subversions.[13] The exclusion of homosexuals under the 1952 act, and the ease with which this exclusion was accepted,[14] speak not only to the extent of discrimination against gay men and lesbians at the time but also to the growing primacy of the logic of security. Although the exclusion of homosexuals under the logic of security may appear as a new, disguised version of moral exclusions, it indicates the intermingling or "hybridity" of logics of governance in this field. The addition of the exclusionary grounds of "drug addiction" and "drug trafficking" signals the expansion of risky categories as defined by a blend of morality, racism, and criminality.

The 1952 act preserved the wide scope of discretionary power that had characterized the 1910 legislation. Section 39 ensured that the government, acting through the minister and officials, continued to have the ultimate authority over exclusionary decisions. It decreed that there was to be no recourse in law for those deemed undesirable and excludable: "No court and no judge or officer thereof has the jurisdiction to review, quash, reverse, restrain or otherwise interfere with any proceeding, decision or order of the Minister, Deputy Minister, Director, Immigration Appeal Board, Special Inquiry Officer or Immigration officer had, made or given under the authority and in accordance with the provisions of this Act relating to the detention, deportation of any person, upon any ground whatsoever, unless such person is a Canadian citizen or has Canadian domicile."[15]

While the 1952 act provided for Immigration Appeal Boards, they could only decide on a limited category of deportation decisions and then only on matters of law. Given the wide degree of discretion accorded to immigration officials, errors of law were quite rare. Moreover, any decision of an Appeal Board could be overturned by the minister.[16]

During the late 1950s and throughout the 1960s, the 1952 act was increasingly criticized for authorizing exceedingly wide discretionary powers to exclude and for its explicit racism. Indeed, the conventional view of this period stresses liberalization, legalization, and humanitarian progress in the field of immigration. However, the extension and entrenchment of similarly broad tracts of discretionary power to exclude in the name of security did not elicit parallel concerns.[17] There was no sense of contradiction between the legal and humanitarian challenges to discriminatory uses of discretion and the concomitant extension of discretionary exclusions in the name of national security. The extension and enforcement of security-related discretion went largely unchallenged.[18]

The logic of security, already well entrenched during wartime and the postwar period, expanded and intensified, free from scrutiny, at the same time as the logic of (racial) purity was increasingly contested. The 1952 act radically extended the security-related exclusionary provisions: "Broader legislative authority was given to prevent the entry into Canada of persons associated 'at any time' with any group about which there were 'reasonable grounds for believing' that they advocated or promoted 'subversion by force or other means of democratic government, institutions or processes, as they are understood in Canada,' or were 'likely to engage in or advocate' subversion. Moreover, persons 'likely to engage in espionage, sabotage or any other subversive activity' were also to be barred."[19]

The 1952 security provisions not only entrenched wide tracts of discretionary power but also limited access to judicial review for those deemed to represent a threat to national security. Under these provisions, permanent residents had no right to appeal. Written reasons for decisions made under the security provisions did not have to be provided to the individual in question. Moreover, the definitions of the security provisions were vague. "Subversion" and "likelihood to engage in subversion" were as difficult to define then as "terrorism" or "danger to the public" are today.[20] As with the slippage between race, morality, and class in the context of "purity" discourses, "security" discourses were liable to be the channel for the exercise of other prejudices.

Whether governed by the logics of purity, security, and/or criminality, discretionary power is a key technology for the construction, reproduction, and enforcement of dominant conceptions of the desirable citizen under a liberal regime of rule. These "dividing practices" entail a variety of effects. The debates around discretion and the coercive practices of immigration penality as well as efforts to impose legal limits on its exercise are thus also consistent with a liberal regime of governance that is constantly preoccupied with defining its limits vis-à-vis the autonomy, freedom, and equality of individuals. Liberal government cannot legitimately make arbitrary, capricious, or discriminatory decisions, particularly when those decisions result in the coercive and violent infringement of individual liberty, in this case through the bodily detention and deportation of undesirable noncitizens. Liberalism, as a mode of governing, imposes restrictions on the state's power to govern individuals through coercion and force. It governs *through*, not against, the freedom and autonomy of individuals.[21]

Rising Opposition to the 1952 Act

The two problems of racial discrimination and unfettered discretionary power (except when linked with security issues) were the focus of widespread legal, social, and political opposition throughout the 1960s. Most prominent among the critics of the 1952 act were lawyers and Members of Parliament. The former were predominantly concerned with the absence of legal protections afforded to noncitizens in the context of (nonsecurity-related) discretionary exclusions and the "arbitrariness" that this absence produced. The latter were particularly troubled by the discriminatory nature of the existing legislation, a concern in part explained by pressure from increasingly ethnically diverse constituencies.

During this period, legal discourses relating to notions of due process, individual rights, and equality gained currency and converged with humanitarian welfarist discourses relating social responsibility, social citizenship, and international human rights that had emerged and gained social, political, and legal influence after the Second World War. This rise of welfarist and rights discourses has led some to the rather rosy conclusion that, "even if admission to Canada was still considered a privilege and not a right, basic due process protections were coming to be seen as properly extended to aliens ... The values and the interests that were driving immigration policy had taken on ... a much more liberal complexion."[22]

Opposition to the 1952 act also emanated from economic sectors but for quite different reasons. The Economic Council of Canada, sensitive to rising unemployment and recession in the late 1950s, was particularly concerned with the immigration sponsorship program, which in its judgment was issuing in a veritable "flood" of unskilled, dependent immigrants. This concern was fuelled by "the increasing need for skilled manpower in Canada and the very real difficulties experienced by the unskilled in the Canadian labour market."[23] In 1964, the council asserted that "the future prosperity of a nation will depend upon an adequate supply of professional, technical, managerial and other highly skilled manpower."[24] It was these two related issues, the impact of the sponsorship program and the argued need for more highly skilled workers, that underpinned the government's 1966 white paper, discussed in more detail below. Finally, the wide scope for ministerial discretion under the existing legislation was criticized for having created an unmanageable workload for the minister.[25]

As with the widely discretionary "danger to the public" provisions introduced by Bill C-44 in 1995, it was the legal paradigm (individual rights, due process, procedural justice, equality), coupled with emergent national and international humanitarian discourses, that set the parameters of the sustained critique of exclusionary discretionary powers in the 1960s. There were also serious discussions of other contentious questions, such as the need for skilled over unskilled labour, the nature and impact of the sponsorship program, and the need for long-term immigration planning rather than the "tap-on, tap-off," approach. However, the most severe criticisms, which began in the mid-1950s and gained momentum through the 1960s, emanated from lawyers and MPs and focused on individual rights and non-discrimination in the context of exclusions.[26]

Two of the earliest and most effective critics of the 1952 legislation were Conservative MP E. Davie Fulton and John Diefenbaker, leader of the Conservative Party, both lawyers. In 1955, Fulton initiated a debate in the House of Commons on immigration law and policy that in many ways summarized the developing criticisms. His submissions centred primarily on the issue of discretion and the protection of individual legal and human rights. He charged the government with "administrative lawlessness" that denied "simple justice to Canadians and non-Canadians alike."[27] Echoing the contemporary political and legal defence of broad ministerial discretionary powers, the government of the day responded repeatedly that "there were no rights attached to immigration. It was a matter of discretion only and could not be made a matter of law."[28] And again echoing contemporary concerns, Fulton responded, "when reasons for decisions do not have to be given, ... as the government maintains that they do not, and when ministerial discretion, which means in the nature of things, departmental discretion, is the sole arbiter, then error, corruption, favouritism, and injustice are invited and rights and liberties are denied in principle as well as in fact."[29]

The 1962 Immigration Regulations
The 1962 regulations responded to the challenges raised by the legal and humanitarian discourses. They removed the "preferred classes" provision (P.C. 1956-785) that had set out a hierarchy of desirability based on country of nationality.[30] As well, section 31(a) of the regulations removed almost all explicit traces of racial discrimination, relying instead on the principle of "skill over ethnicity." The notable exception was the preservation of a preference for Europeans in sponsorship provisions. While all immigrants could sponsor close relatives, only immigrants from a specified list of countries could sponsor more distant relatives. The relevant clause, section 31(d), "ruled out Asia and all of Africa except Egypt."[31]

The regulations also responded to the insistent concern that the individual legal rights of noncitizens facing deportation should be better protected. They enlarged the jurisdiction of the Immigration Appeal Board (IAB) to allow all people facing deportation the right to appeal, rather than just selected categories, as had been the case. However, the minister could still reverse any decision rendered by the board.[32] In addition, the IAB still could not hear sponsorship appeals, and the minister continued to be "swamped" with individual cases.[33] It was not until the *Immigration Appeal Board Act* was passed in 1967 that a more independent and effective board was created.[34] Nevertheless, the 1962 regulations did contribute to the construction of the noncitizen as a "rights-bearing" subject by responding to the legal concern that noncitizens be accorded due process and that those whom the IAB had ordered deported should be granted a right of appeal.

The Sedgwick Report
In 1964, lawyer Joseph Sedgwick was asked by the minister of justice to investigate twenty-three allegations of unlawful detention (twenty of which were made by Greek sailors who had jumped ship in Canada). Sedgwick was also asked to report more generally on Canadian arrest, deportation, and prosecution procedures and to consider the issue of ministerial discretion. He concluded that the criticisms had been ill-founded and that there had been no unlawful detention or unlawful denial of rights in the detention

cases at hand. He added that the problem of deserting seamen "has developed into a wholesale ... and deliberately planned method of circumventing Canada's immigration laws."[35]

The Sedgwick Report is most commonly regarded as a prescription for the curtailment and "checking" of ministerial discretion and ultimately as a prescription for the revision of the 1952 *Immigration Act.* Sedgwick recommended that the IAB be completely independent and authoritative, subject to a right to appeal to the courts. He also recommended that section 39 of the act, that which preserved the final discretionary authority of the minister, should be eliminated and that "express provision should be made from the IAB to the Exchequer Court of Canada on questions of law with a further appeal to the SCC, with leave of that Court."[36]

Sedgwick's unwavering support for the "state's right to exclude" and his heightened concern for national security are of even greater interest here. Sedgwick firmly believed that due process provisions and respect for the individual legal rights of noncitizens should not unsettle the state's sovereign and absolute right to select desirable citizens and exclude others. The preservation of this sovereign right and the coercive state practices that it entails are justified by the logic of security. He argued that it was "both necessary and proper that every effort be made to exclude aliens who are undesirable for security reasons."[37]

The inherently imprecise meaning of "security reasons" is highlighted by Sedgwick himself. He acknowledged that the concept of security is most easily associated with the communist threat, that it also related to other "totalitarian causes," but that it also encompassed criminals. This provides an early signal of the conflation of the categories of security and criminality. Sedgwick also included several enforcement recommendations, including a system of "alien" registration and fingerprinting – both of which are now part of the contemporary immigration regime. While most commentators have focused on Sedgwick's recommendations regarding the legalization of ministerial discretion, his report can also be read as indicating the forging of the crime-security nexus. Arguably, the lack of attention to this aspect of the report speaks at least in part to the "taken for grantedness" of the guiding logic of security that increasingly stood alone as the logic of racial and moral purity was contested and dismantled.[38]

The White Paper

At the same time that Sedgwick was carrying out his inquiry, the Department of Citizenship and Immigration was preparing its own policy paper on immigration, which appeared in 1966.[39] Most commentators regard this document as a fairly straightforward policy paper centred on the need to better manage and control the sponsorship program, on the need of the

Canadian economy for skilled labour (as argued by the Economic Council[40]), on the need to substitute "skill" for "ethnicity" in immigration selection procedures, and on the need to create a more independent Immigration Appeal Board. It proposed a new board to take over the minister's discretionary power to exclude, which would be limited in its jurisdiction only "by the right to appeal its decisions on questions of law to the SCC with leave of that court."[41] It also recommended that the government accede finally to the 1951 *Convention Relating to the Status of Refugees*[42] and create a domestic system to determine whether individual refugee claimants had a well-founded basis for (were "deserving" of) Canadian protection in the form of refugee status. Although Canada had lobbied hard for its promulgation, the country did not sign the refugee convention until 1969, a full seventeen years after it was drawn up and long after the vast majority of countries had become signatories. Canada's delay in signing the refugee convention is explained by its fear that so doing would undermine its ability to deport refugees for reasons of national security.[43]

The white paper can be read as a contribution to the reconstruction of the dominant conception of undesirability in accordance with new discursive conditions and parameters. The exclusion of "undesirables" could no longer be legitimated through the mobilization of moral and racial national purity discourses; the logic of security articulated through the language of risk and rationalized by reference to the welfare of the population set the new parameters for exclusion. Furthermore, the requisites of liberal legality relating to individual rights, due process, and the need to "check" discretionary power had become too compelling to be ignored.

The white paper addressed the exclusionary preoccupations of the day. It considered in turn the "vexed" question of security;[44] the elimination of moralistic grounds for exclusion; the need to penalize transportation companies that brought "undesirables" to Canadian shores; and finally the need to develop new measures to deal with certain prohibited classes, most notably "organized" criminals and subversives. The white paper in no way suggested any diminution of the government's desire to identify and exclude "undesirables" from Canada. However, like the Sedgwick Report, the white paper does provide an early expression of the important transition occurring in the prevailing governing logics of immigration penalty, a shift away from promoting and justifying immigration exclusions on the basis of race and moral status toward exclusions justified by reference to risk-based considerations of security and criminality.

The reason offered in the white paper for the elimination of certain moralistic, status-based grounds for exclusion is revealing. The white paper did not object to these grounds for reasons of fairness, equality, due process, or humanity. To the contrary, it agreed that the exclusion of immigrant applicants on moral grounds was entirely understandable and appropriate, given Canada's legitimate desire to keep out "misfits," but it believed that it was simply unnecessary to exclude them for explicitly moral and otherwise discriminatory reasons. *The same people could be excluded for the same underlying reasons but on other risk-based grounds:*

> Persons who are undesirable on moral or social grounds ought to be excluded as immigrants but not necessarily as non-immigrants, although any such flexibility must be balanced by a compensating provision for their prompt removal should they attempt to remain permanently or give other cause. The homosexual, the beggar or vagrant and the chronic alcoholic are at present specifically prohibited. Though not particularly desirable as immigrants or non-immigrants, such people are not true dangers to the national interest by virtue simply of their personal failings. *To the extent that they represent an unacceptable risk because of factors associated with their weakness, they will be excludable on health, criminal or subversive grounds, or, as public charges. They therefore could safely be deleted from the specific list of prohibited classes.*[45]

This is indeed a telling justification. There is no effort to disguise support for the continued exclusion of these "misfits" and "undesirables." Even more importantly, this excerpt clearly articulates the transition "from dangerousness to risk," a move away from excluding people on the basis of the dangerousness thought to reside in them toward governing individuals and groups through their "associated risks." As put by Robert Castel, "new strategies dissolve the notion of a *subject* or a concrete individual, and put in its place a combinatory of *factors*, the factors of risk."[46]

While ministerial discretion to exclude on "security grounds" was largely immune from sustained substantive criticism, legal discourses had begun to draw at least some critical attention to the procedural secrecy of these exclusions, in particular to the powers of the RCMP with respect to security screening. Security screening was and continues to be "a vexed problem" and was not easily amenable to the challenges raised by legal discourses. In the zero sum contest between liberal rights and freedoms and "security" concerns, national security tends to triumph. Thus, while there was an internal departmental review in the late 1950s and a Royal Commission on Security in 1969 (the Mackenzie Commission), which coincided generally with a "thawing" of the Cold War, in Reg Whitaker's judgment "neither of these did more than scratch the surface of the immigration security process ... despite the growing disillusionment of Canadians with the old Cold War mould and despite some severe external shocks to the old thinking."[47] These "external shocks" included the waning of the war on communism, the Sino-Soviet split and its consequences, and the arrival in Canada of American draft dodgers during the Vietnam War and of left-wing refugees from right-wing totalitarian violence.[48]

Nonetheless, evidence of the mounting challenge posed by legal discourses is found in the white paper in its important concession that the contemporary legal definition of subversion was unlawfully broad: "It is important that recognition be given to the fact that the holding or expression of unpopular opinions, or sympathy with such opinion, is not in itself indicative of subversive activity."[49] However, beyond this, the question of the processes and practices relating to national security was hardly discussed in the white paper.[50]

Following the appearance of the Sedgwick Report and the white paper, a Special Joint Committee of the Senate and the House of Commons on Immigration was appointed in 1966 to conduct hearings and report on both documents. Following the government's release of the *Green Paper on Immigration and Population* in 1975, there were even more extensive hearings as preparation for the long-awaited 1976 *Immigration Act.* In the 1960s and the first half of the 1970s, Canadian immigration law and policy thus received historically unprecedented critical public and political attention and debate, leading some to describe this period as one that witnessed not only the deracialization and legalization of immigration processes but also their democratization. Interestingly, despite the prevalence of legal and humanitarian concerns, the period saw the numbers of people forcibly removed from Canadian soil more than triple, from about 3,500 in each of the three five-year periods before 1967 to 11,766 in the five-year period 1967-71.[51]

Legislative Reforms
Between 1967 and 1976, three important reforms were shaped by the challenges raised by legal and humanitarian discourses in the years since Mackenzie King's 1947 statement on immigration: the adoption of the "point system," the *Immigration Appeal Board Act,* and the 1976 *Immigration Act.* Together these reforms are conventionally represented as the "triumph" of liberalism. However, they also indicate the rising prominence of risk and the logic of crime-security in the governance of immigration enforcement, which were not only preserved but also expanded and entrenched. Unlike the explicitly discriminatory logic of national purity that could not possibly be sustained in the face of legal or humanitarian challenges (and indeed in the face of changing economic and labour market needs and changing international migration patterns), risk-based efforts to secure the nation and protect the public are relatively straightforward, apparently objective, and therefore legitimate justifications for the operations of discretionary power and for the coercive practices of immigration penality.

In 1967, the government introduced the new point system that applied the principle of skill over ethnicity in immigrant selection, creating the new category of the desirable "economic migrant": the talented, acquisitive, and (economically) independent prospective citizen. The point system tends to be referred to as an expression of the official rejection of racism and the adoption of the principle of nondiscrimination in the selection of immigrants. Perhaps, however, this development merits only two cheers. Until 1976, the guiding statute was still the racist and exceedingly discriminatory 1952 act, and there is every reason to believe that the introduction of the point system had more to do with pragmatic international and domestic considerations. A racist immigration policy was clearly inconsistent with the general ethos of international human rights and the United Nations. Also, Canada needed more immigrants, and immigration from traditional (white) source countries was declining.[52] Moreover, critics have persuasively argued that less obvious nonlegal discriminatory mechanisms persisted: the "skill" criteria continued to discriminate against immigrants from developing countries, and most of the resources committed to the recruitment of migrants continued to reflect a "preference for British immigrants,"[53] as did the government's placement of foreign visa offices.[54]

As recommended in the Sedgwick Report, the *Immigration Appeal Board Act* created an independent appeal tribunal that had final authority over all deportation decisions subject to judicial review (with leave) to the superior courts on questions of law and jurisdiction. The creation of the new Immigration Appeal Board (IAB) responded directly to the sustained legal critique of (unchecked) ministerial discretion by devolving the final discretionary authority over exclusionary decisions from the minister to the IAB. Unlike the previous, largely ineffective board, the new IAB could hear appeals on both deportation and sponsorship decisions. As well, its jurisdiction was expanded. It could now consider not only legal and factual questions but also humanitarian and compassionate factors (known as the board's "equitable jurisdiction"). The legal paradigm that holds the right to know the case made against you as a requirement of natural justice was also acknowledged, this legislation stipulating in its final form that the board "may, and at the request to the parties of the appeal, shall give reasons for its disposition of the appeal."[55] Under the IAB act, Cabinet retained the discretion to specify the classes of relatives that could appeal a negative sponsorship decision, and, despite the efforts of opposition members, judicial review continued to be denied for those rejected on security grounds.

In 1973, the government announced its intention to carry out a major review of immigration law and policy and to publish its findings in a green paper. In February of 1975, the green paper was tabled in the House of Commons, and twenty-one public hearings were subsequently held across the country by the Joint Committee of the Senate and House of Commons. In July of the same year, the committee submitted its report and recommendations, most of which were incorporated into the *Immigration Act* of 1976.[56]

This act tends to be represented as the culmination of a substantive historical shift in the nature and orientation of Canadian immigration law and policy: from "illiberal" to "liberal." Consider the following glowing summations made by contemporary political scientists: "The *Immigration Act, 1976,* as it is known, constituted the most liberal piece of immigration legislation ever to become law in Canada. The Act showed a positive emphasis and set as immigration priorities, the reunification of families, humanitarian and compassionate treatment of refugees, and the promotion of programs satisfying Canada's economic, social, demographic and cultural goals."[57] Or "The coming into force of the Immigration Act, 1976 on 10 April 1978 ushered in a new era in the history of Canadian immigration law ... The new act was a significant departure from its predecessors."[58] Or, finally, "the 1976 Act marked the beginning of a new, more liberal and more cooperative era in Canadian immigration."[59] There is no question that the 1976 *Immigration Act* responded to and integrated the discursive challenges raised by liberal legality and humanitarianism. However, what is obscured by these readings is that it also and no less centrally entrenched and intensified to an unprecedented degree the guiding logic of crime-security effected through discretion.

The usual view is that the 1976 *Immigration Act* was a liberal triumph over illiberal policies and that whatever injustices persisted were and are also illiberal. However, if liberalism is seen as an active form of government rather than a political doctrine or ideology, then the substantial extension of discretion in matters of national security under the *Immigration Act* is no less liberal than that which came before. Law and discretion are technologies for the dividing practices of a liberal regime that requires that government takes place "at a distance."[60] The use of coercive state powers against individuals, as in the case of the removal of those deemed undesirable and undeserving, must be legitimated, legally, socially, and politically. Legal discourses construct the citizen and to a certain degree the noncitizen as rights-bearing subjects deserving of due process and thereby complicate and legitimate detention and deportation practices. The historically enduring construction of national sovereignty further deflects attention from the coercions at play, and the crime-security nexus is a powerful justification for these enforcement practices previously framed by now illegitimate racist and moralistic logics.

As urged in the 1966 *White Paper on Immigration,* the new inadmissibility provisions of the 1976 *Immigration Act* removed all explicit traces of moral and racial grounds for exclusion, including the long-standing grounds "physically defective persons," "homosexuals," "the insane," and "idiots, imbeciles and morons." The 1976 *Immigration Act* also removed the 1952 prohibition against persons who were convicted of (or who admitted to committing) crimes involving moral turpitude. It replaced "prohibited" categories with "inadmissible classes" and itemized a total of seventeen different grounds on which prospective immigrants should be denied access to or removed from Canada. The breakdown of these seventeen specified grounds is revealing: one dealt with medical inadmissibility of persons due either to the danger posed to public health or safety or to the likelihood (on "reasonable grounds") of causing excessive demands on health or social services;[61] another dealt with economic inadmissibility due to "reasonable grounds" to believe that claimants would be "unable or unwilling to support themselves";[62] yet another dealt with people who were not, in the opinion of an adjudicator, "genuine visitors or immigrants";[63] and one dealt with those entering Canada without the express consent of the minister when they were required to have this consent.[64] The remaining thirteen grounds were entirely devoted to matters of criminality and security.

The inadmissibility provisions were concerned to exclude not only the "threats" posed to the nation by subversion, terrorism, and/or espionage, threats conventionally linked with the guiding logic of "security" as associated with reason of state, but also those posed by organized criminals. Consistent with the forward-looking preoccupations of risk management strategies, the 1976 *Immigration Act* prohibited the entry into Canada of persons "who there are reasonable grounds to believe *will* engage in acts of violence that would or might endanger the lives or safety of persons in Canada or are members of or are likely to participate in the unlawful activities of an organization that is likely to engage in such acts of violence."[65]

These inadmissibility provisions were thus both backward- and forward-looking, concerned with deeds done, deeds likely to have been done in the past, and deeds likely to be done in the future. Similarly, with respect to national security, the 1976 *Immigration Act* referred to "persons who have engaged in or who *there are reasonable grounds to believe are likely to engage in* acts of espionage or subversion against democratic government, institutions or processes, as they are understood in Canada, except persons who, having engaged in such acts have satisfied the Minister that their admission would not be detrimental to the national interest."[66] The act also excluded "persons who there are reasonable grounds to believe will, while in Canada, engage in or instigate the subversion by force of any government."[67] "Subversion," "reasonable grounds," and "democratic government, institutions or processes" were not defined in the act.

An additional extension of discretionary powers in relation to exclusions is provided by the removal of the concept of "domicile" in the 1976 *Immigration Act*. In the 1952 act, noncitizens who had been living in Canada for five years were deemed to have acquired domicile and, with some exceptions, could not be deported. The removal of this protection effectively rendered all noncitizens vulnerable to deportation regardless of how long they had been in Canada.

Of particular interest is the manner in which the 1976 *Immigration Act* dealt with permanent residents deemed to represent a "security risk." The 1910 act had not provided for any appeals against a deportation order. It had instead vested final discretionary authority over admissions and removals in the minister. The 1952 act had created a very limited and largely ineffective Appeal Board that could only review certain deportation decisions and whose decisions could be reversed by the minister. The 1967 *Appeal Board Act* had, for the first time, conferred upon the IAB the authority to stay or quash a deportation order made against a permanent resident on the basis of "all the circumstances of the case." However, this new power was subject to the discretion of the minister and the solicitor general if they agreed to issue a certificate indicating that, based on security and criminal intelligence reports, it would be against the national interest or public good to provide discretionary relief.

The 1976 *Immigration Act* left unchanged the powers of the IAB to hear appeals. Appeal decisions would consider questions of law, fact, mixed law and fact, and compassionate or "equitable" grounds. It continued to limit access to appeal if the minister and the solicitor general issued a jointly signed security certificate. The 1976 *Immigration Act* initially provided for a hearing before a Special Advisory Board in addition to the filing of a certificate in accordance with the recommendation of the 1969 Royal Commission on Security.[68] This board only heard one case before it was eventually replaced by the Security Intelligence Review Committee (SIRC) under the *Canadian Security Intelligence Service Act* of 1984.[69]

On 12 December 2003, the Canada Border Services Agency (CBSA) was created as part of the new Public Safety and Emergency Preparedness portfolio. The CBSA brings together all those engaged in the enforcement of border security, including the Customs program from the Canada Customs and Revenue Agency (CCRA), the Intelligence, Interdiction, and Enforcement program from Citizenship and Immigration Canada (CIC), and the Import Inspection at Ports of Entry program from the Canadian Food Inspection Agency (CFIA). The transfer of the enforcement sections of CIC to the new Border Agency was accompanied by the transfer of the responsibility for immigration enforcement from the minister of immigration to the solicitor general, who also became the deputy prime minister and the minister of public safety and emergency preparedness.[70] One of the contentious consequences of the combining of these two roles is that security certificates will now only require the signature of one minister rather than two.[71]

The conventional reading of the 1976 *Immigration Act* is that it marked the beginning of a new, liberal era in Canadian immigration law and policy. Such a reading focuses on its nondiscriminatory dimensions and enhanced attention to due process while glossing over its extensive discretion- and enforcement-oriented provisions as unproblematic and legitimate attempts to protect the public and secure the nation. From this perspective, the act represents a compelling effort to "balance" freedom and security. The review and analysis offered here of the development of exclusionary immigration law and policy suggest instead that the 1976 *Immigration Act* represents the legalization, formal entrenchment, and expansion of the logics of risk and security, supplemented by criminality concerns and facilitated by the operations of law and discretion.

5
Floods and Frauds

The 1976 *Immigration Act* created a permanent, onshore refugee determination system that at last brought Canadian law and procedure in line with the country's international obligations under the 1951 *Refugee Convention*. However, Canada has always preferred to select its own refugees. It is much more at ease in the business of selective refugee resettlement, sending teams of immigration officers to refugee camps around the world to hand-pick those whom they judge most desirable – those in good health, able to speak English or French, and with marketable skills and high "establishment potential."

No sooner had the Canadian government implemented an onshore refugee determination system than it proceeded vigorously to limit access both to the shore and to the system. In addition to measures that made it more difficult for refugee claimants to get to Canada in the first place, managing the backlog by improving case-processing time, system efficiency, and integrity were guiding preoccupations. This improved management was to be achieved by finding faster and more efficient ways to weed out unfounded, fraudulent, or otherwise inadmissible claims at an earlier stage in the process. During the period under review, enforcement-oriented legal and policy reforms were justified by the need to preserve the integrity of the system, protect the safety of the public, and ensure national security.

This chapter begins with a general discussion of the devaluation of refugee claimants through the mobilization of fraud and criminality concerns in the context of emergent neoliberal governing regimes. I then turn to the major legislative developments of the 1980s and early 1990s, paying particular attention to two themes: the changing discursive formations that governed their development and promotion and the ways that distinctly neoliberal fears about fraud, coupled with increasingly dominant fears about crime and victims, merged to produce the regulatory figure of the "bogus refugee."

Neoliberalism, Fraud, and Deserving Victims

It has not been part of Canada's history to respond generously to the needs of "spontaneous," "self-selected" refugees who arrive at Canada's borders.[1] Both of these designations, commonly used in official discourse, recast the situations facing refugees and the circumstances leading to their arrival in Canada. "Spontaneous" suggests a "natural" and "unconstrained" impulse that arises from internal forces, that is "independent of external agencies; self-acting."[2] Similarly, "self-selected" implies a greater degree of calculation and choice than is permitted to many refugees fleeing persecution. As such, these terms are founded in assumptions that are themselves contrary to the constituent features of a *genuine* refugee: someone forced to leave a country through no personal fault in order to avoid state-sanctioned persecution – *not* voluntary, *no* choice. The implication that the arrival of refugees in Canada has more to do with spontaneous and voluntary decision making than with fear and persecution goes some way toward explaining the relative ease with which refugees are (re)constructed as undeserving, unscrupulous "system abusers."

Two contrasting and often conflicting kinds of risk assessment guide Canadian immigration and refugee decision making as it relates to the admission and exclusion of noncitizens. The first aims to assess and exclude the risks thought to be posed by noncitizens seeking access to Canada: threats to national security, public safety, the integrity and efficiency of the state's administrative systems, and the national economy. However, because of Canada's international humanitarian obligations, it must also assess the risks and dangers that would be faced by individual refugee claimants were they to be returned to their countries of origin. Over the course of the 1980s, the objective to identify and extend protection to those genuinely "at risk" and deserving of protection effectively shifted to identifying and barring entry to or removing the "risky": the bogus, even criminal, refugee claimant. Legal and humanitarian discourses were still important – for the most part, enforcement initiatives continued to be justified in the name of the "truly deserving" – but they were intertwined with and increasingly eclipsed by neoliberal preoccupations with fraud and system abuse and the crime-security nexus.[3]

During the 1980s, the "fraudulent claimant" was constituted as the perpetrator of offences against the state and the tax-paying public. While the deservedness of *genuine* refugees has rarely been questioned, refugee *claimants,* particularly onshore, "self-selected" claimants, were regarded with intense suspicion. The currency of "fraud" discourses in the context of refugee determinations was both guided and strengthened by a more general preoccupation with crime, law and order, and victims emerging in most areas of public law and policy. The rise of law and order programs and the emergence of a more punitive social and political climate in Western industrialized countries has been accompanied by what some have termed "the rise of the victim" as a new ground of citizenship and a guiding rationale for a range of public policies and initiatives.[4] While this preoccupation with victims could theoretically have led to an expansion of sympathy for refugees, it translated instead into citizens at large regarding themselves as potential victims of fraudulent and criminal "system abusers."

These developments do not indicate a change from Liberal to Conservative Party politics, from liberal to illiberal orientations, or from inclusionary to exclusionary ones. Rather, they reflect the more general transitions from welfare liberal to neoliberal regimes of governance and the reconfiguration of the classifications and dividing practices that these transitions bring in tow. The dividing practices of liberal regimes construct historically specific moralized categories of deserving and undeserving that are given practical effect through the operations of discretionary power. In the context of social welfare, the deserving recipients of the state's largesse are acquisitive, independent, law-abiding citizens who have become needy and dependent "through no fault of their own." They are genuine victims of circumstances beyond their control who therefore *deserve* the state's help to get back on their feet again.

Similarly, it is only the genuine refugee who, by virtue of his or her legally defined and confirmed genuine victim status, *deserves* Canada's protection and access to the benefits of Canadian citizenship. In both contexts, the "fraudulent" claimant is the epitome of undeservedness. Add to this a suspicion of criminality and an archetypal neoliberal threat is complete: the fraudulent if not downright criminal refugee or new immigrant who victimizes the state, threatens public safety, and jeopardizes the integrity of the system through false claims of deservedness in the context of either welfare or refugee claims – or both.

Dividing practices construct those deserving of inclusion as well as those to be ushered into zones of exclusion. While welfarist discourses typically highlight inclusion, social responsibility, and collective risk management, exclusion comes into focus more readily under neoliberal modes of rule that highlight accountability, individual responsibility, and individual risk management. While onshore claimants could quite appropriately be constructed as exemplary of independent risk managers who shrewdly weigh costs and benefits and pursue a life free from fear and persecution against all odds, instead they have been constructed as potentially fraudulent, probably criminal, "asylum shoppers" seeking to take advantage of Canada's generosity. There are those who are more widely accepted as deserving claimants, but they tend to be found in camps overseas and are selected according to a variety of criteria that, in addition to their confirmed status as *Refugee Convention* refugees, include an inability to stay where they are or return to their countries of origin, whether there is another country where they could resettle, and an assessment of their "establishment potential" in Canada.

The onshore refugee determination system was put to the test swiftly after it had been created by the 1976 *Immigration Act*. Refugees started arriving in greater numbers and from a wider range of "nontraditional" countries – nonwhite, poor, and noncommunist – than ever before. The spectre of "the backlog" so familiar in neoliberal discourses has governed the operations of the refugee determination system through the 1980s and up to the present day. Neoliberal programs of restraint are typically imposed to redress the inefficiency and economic irresponsibility of the state evidenced by unwieldy backlogs in the administration of social benefits. In the context of refugee determination, efforts to redress the legitimacy crisis associated with the backlog included a variety of initiatives to deflect criticisms of government fiscal and organizational mismanagement and put the blame more squarely on the shoulders of the disingenuous refugee claimants "flooding" Canadian shores. The Canadian government, though apparently ready to admit more refugees than most other developed countries, remained determined to limit their numbers and control their selection. It thus introduced an onshore refugee determination system that was in many ways exemplary in its legal recognition of the rights of refugee claimants, while it simultaneously strove with increasing inventiveness to ensure that as few claimants as possible actually succeeded in reaching Canadian soil to benefit from the onshore system.

National and International Movements of Immigrants and Refugees
After the implementation of the 1976 *Immigration Act,* unprecedented numbers of asylum seekers sought Canada's protection. Between 1963 and 1976, for example, the number of onshore refugee claimants accepted by Canada averaged just 3,600 per year (including lows of 600 in 1971 and 1,400 in 1970 and highs of 10,000 in 1968 and 11,000 in 1976).[5] The number of refugee claims made in Canada rose to 37,730 in 1992, fell sharply to 21,190 in 1993, and then hovered around 25,000 per year until 1999, when they began to climb again. There were 30,880, 37,860, and 42,750 claims respectively in the years 1999, 2000, and 2001.[6] Since then, the numbers have been declining. The number of refugee claims dropped to 33,442 in 2002.[7] In 2003, there were 32,268 refugee claims in Canada, and early figures indicate that the year-end totals for 2004 may drop to 20,000, their lowest level since the 1980s.[8]

The United Nations High Commissioner for Refugees (UNHCR) estimated that in 1980 the number of refugees worldwide was close to 8.5 million. In 1985, this figure increased to approximately 11.8 million. It continued rising until 1992, when it reached just over 17.5 million. Since then, the number of refugees worldwide has been generally decreasing: in 2001, the figure was approximately 12 million; in 2002, 10.4 million.[9]

Refugees outside Canada may be selected and resettled in Canada through government or private sponsorship. In 1977, 7,300 government and privately sponsored refugees were resettled in Canada.[10] Two years later this number jumped to 27,564 and one year later, in 1980, to 40,271. Between 1981 and 1986, a period characterized by a major recession, the number of sponsored refugee admissions dropped significantly, averaging between 15,000 and 20,000 per year. It rose again in the late 1980s, peaking in 1989 at 35,439, and declined steadily since then to 10,179 in 1998 and rising slightly to 11,891 in 2001.[11]

Over the late 1980s and 1990s, the total number of immigrants to Canada reached a high of 256,741 in 1993. In 1996, the number declined to 226,039 and declined further to 174,159 in 1998. It rose again to 227,346 in 2000 and has since remained relatively stable. In 2002, there were 229,091 new immigrants to Canada,[12] and CIC's target for 2003 was between 220,000 and 245,000.[13] As of May 2001, 18.4 percent of the total population in Canada were born outside the country, the highest it has been since 1931.[14] Whereas in the past, most immigrants were likely to have been born in European nations, in the 1990s only 20 percent were born in Europe, while most (58 percent) were born in Asia, including the Middle East, 11 percent in the Caribbean and Central and South America, 8 percent in Africa, and 3 percent in the United States.[15]

The growing number of nonwhite new immigrants and refugees was not parallelled by growing social acceptance. Onshore refugees in particular were the targets of negative representations and attitudes. Refugees were increasingly regarded as a multifaceted threat – a numerical threat to be limited and managed in the name of administrative efficiency, fiscal restraint, and economic growth; a threat to the "integrity" of the system due to fraudulent claims made by unscrupulous, "bogus" refugee claimants; and a threat to national security and public safety posed by criminals and terrorists. Racism and xenophobia inflected much of the public sentiment in these matters. One survey after another reported that during this period Canadians were increasingly hostile toward new immigrants and refugees, in particular toward the visible minorities among them. New immigrants and refugees came to be closely associated with the lack of jobs in Canada, with perceptions of rising crime, and with the perceived decline of social order and cohesion.[16]

Spontaneous Landings, Public Panics, and the Fraudulent Claimant
Throughout the 1980s, the dominant preoccupation of the Employment and Immigration Commission (EIC) was not with the plight of the soaring numbers of refugees worldwide. Rather, what secured their attention was

the growing backlog of onshore refugee claims. In popular and political discourse, this backlog was then and continues to be primarily attributed to fraudulent refugee claims made by "bogus" refugees. The bogus refugee is generally understood to be an economic migrant who, although not covered by the *Refugee Convention,* nonetheless seeks admission to Canada by fraudulently claiming refugee status.

It is unlikely that economic pressures alone were responsible for the increase in refugee claims after the *Singh* decision in 1985.[17] Clearly, the rising number of refugees worldwide during this period explains some of the increase. Also, a 1986 study conducted by the UNHCR confirmed that the level of public and political panic centring on abuses of Western refugee determination systems by so-called bogus refugees was vastly disproportionate to the actual size of the problem. It reported that the number of "manifestly unfounded claims" made in Western countries was no more than 10-15 percent of the total claims made.[18] A study of IRB decisions between 1989 and 1994 carried out by David Matas, a Canadian immigration and refugee lawyer, found that only 38 individuals out of 122,000 processed by the board actually defrauded it.[19] Also revealing is a 1999 UK study of Sikh refugee claimants: "At least some asylum applicants are being unjustly labelled as 'economic migrants,' 'bogus refugees' or 'abusive claimants' and refused asylum to which, by any humane or legal standards, they are fully entitled. They are in danger of being sent back to an environment they rightly fear, of summary detention, torture, 'disappearance' or execution in a 'false encounter.'"[20] Nonetheless, the objective of finding better and more efficient ways to identify and dispose of fraudulent and unfounded claims in order to better control, manage, and ultimately eliminate the refugee backlog was the central focus of the political and legal activity relating to refugees during this period.

As noted, the restrictive and enforcement-oriented measures introduced in the late 1980s continued to be justified by reference to the humanitarian ideals. While on the face of it, the increasingly hard-line, exclusionary emphasis might appear to be inconsistent with such objectives, it is in fact entirely consistent with liberal discourses that categorize deservedness and desirability and that authorize differential treatment on the basis of these categories. The figures of the deserving genuine victim and the desirable citizen exist only in constant and continuous opposition to those constructed as undeserving and undesirable. Over the 1980s, and through the 1990s, the undeserving, undesirable outsider came to be epitomized by the fraudulent, even criminal, "self-selected" refugee claimant.

In the 1980s, the primary association of undesirability and undeservedness with fraud and criminality was forged in the public, political, and legal realms. The importance of humanitarian concerns with regard to deserving victims, in this case the "genuine" refugee, was not in the least inconsistent with or contrary to this discursive development. Moreover, the rising influence of victim discourses that has underpinned law and order reforms in the context of the criminal justice system has similarly bolstered calls for stricter immigration and refugee measures. The argument became that the undeserving and the undesirable must be more rigorously and effectively excluded precisely in order to ensure that genuine and therefore deserving victims may be appropriately protected. Gerry Weiner, minister of state for immigration in 1987, defended the hard-line measures taken by the government in the following terms: "We will not tolerate abuse, either within the system or without, because to do so is to deny protection to those who need it and to undermine this country's long-standing immigration policy itself ... Refugee policy is for refugees. And within the policy, the person who claims refugee status from Canada, must merit it. This must be clearly understood. *Canada's determination system has but one purpose. To distinguish the genuine refugee in need of Canada's help from all other claimants.*"[21]

The adoption of hard-line enforcement-oriented legislative reforms in the late 1980s was further facilitated by the eruption of public and political panics around illegal immigrants and refugees. The initial triggering of this panic came in the spring of 1986 when 155 Tamils from Sri Lanka were found in a boat off the coast of Newfoundland. While the Tamils were initially received with relative compassion and quickly granted landing, subsequent news that they had lied about their route elicited a backlash about "queue jumpers" and Canada's inadequate control of its borders.

The public reaction to that landing was positively cordial when compared with the veritable explosion of xenophobia, racism, and moral outrage fifteen months later following the "spontaneous landing" of a boat carrying 173 Sikhs and one Turkish woman on the East Coast of Canada. As has been carefully argued by several authors, this "Sikh landing" and the public and political reaction to it provided the government with the justification for enforcement-oriented exclusionary reforms.[22] The rhetoric blossomed exponentially. The government was called upon to respond to this newly constructed "refugee crisis" propelled by unscrupulous "queue jumpers," "bogus refugees" (including primarily economic migrants but also a variety of criminal types), and "waves" of naïve and witless migrants taken advantage of by international smugglers. A trickle of 174 refugees was quickly likened to a wave – a comparison that inevitably raised fears about the impending flood.[23]

Queue jumpers, bogus refugees, and cheaters in general offend liberal sensibilities relating to rules, fair play, and order. The provocative analogy of queue jumping was quickly deployed in public and political discussions of the onshore refugee claimant. The ill will toward refugee claimants seen as queue jumpers is compounded when they are also believed to have lied in their efforts to gain admission to Canada and if they are thought likely to pose a criminal threat. The figures of the queue jumper, the bogus refugee, the economic migrant, and the criminal (be they people smugglers or terrorists) were quickly abstracted and generalized as threatening and undeserving, fuelling a nation-wide backlash against immigrants and refugees that was riddled with racism. As acknowledged by then Minister of Employment and Immigration Benoît Bouchard, the increasing hostility to immigrants and refugees was an expression "of a sort of fear" because the new arrivals "are from such places like Asia, whereas in the old days they came from Europe."[24]

The casting of those who land on Canada's shores and claim refugee status as queue jumpers caught on fast despite the reality that, for those hoping to claim refugee status in Canada, there is really no queue to join, let alone jump. The use of this designation is both defamatory and inflammatory. As explained by Julius Grey, the reality is that "most immigrants have to apply for visas *outside* the country, but most refugee status claimants arrive here and then make the claim. The argument against 'queue-jumping' would be somewhat stronger if a queue in fact existed. But most immigration applicants are accepted or refused within a relatively short time. There is no list of people waiting for a 'place' to become vacant. It is therefore difficult to see over whom refugee claimants are 'jumping.'"[25]

Stemming the Flood: The Crackdown on "Bogus" Refugees

Prior to the East Coast arrival of the Sikhs in 1987, the government had already been seeking ways to counteract the impact of the *Singh* decision both by trying to deal with the existing refugee backlog and by further limiting access to Canada's refugee system. It was feared that a general amnesty would open the flood gates to thousands more claims by economic migrants hoping to be granted another amnesty. Nevertheless, a partial amnesty was granted in May 1986. In one fell swoop, it reduced the 21,500 refugee applicant backlog figure by 15,000.[26] However, it was not long before a second backlog developed, and tough talk by immigration officials about cracking down on abusers became louder.

In February 1987, several "administrative measures" were promoted in terms of helping genuine refugees by cracking down on and deterring abusers. Changes in American immigration law a few months prior had made the situation difficult for Central American refugees, in particular those from Guatemala and El Salvador, two countries acknowledged by Canada to produce refugees. The tightening of the US refugee legislation resulted in an increase in the number of Central American refugees seeking protection in Canada. Canada responded by sending claimants from the US back across the border to wait for their hearings.[27] This move was very threatening to Guatemalan and El Salvadoran claimants, who feared with good reason that they would then be returned by American authorities to their home countries. This Canadian approach had the effect of preventing the great bulk of potential Latin American claimants from making onshore refugee claims.

As well, Canada had already imposed visa requirements on travellers from both countries (El Salvador in 1978 and Guatemala in 1984) in spite of the well-documented state-sanctioned political persecution and terror that characterized them. The government also imposed transit visas on ninety-eight countries to prevent potential claimants with the intention of disembarking and claiming refugee status from booking flights that include a transit stopover at a Canadian airport.

The effectiveness of visa requirements as an immigration control mechanism is bolstered when airlines are obliged to return any passenger who does not have the required documents. The new visa requirements entailed this obligation. A further initiative eliminated the granting of automatic admission and the right to stay and work in Canada for up to a year to refugee claimants from eighteen recognized refugee-producing countries. These various restrictive administrative measures shed some light on how the problem of the bogus refugee was deployed and acted upon. The need to deter fraudulent refugees rationalized the adoption of measures that entailed the effect of reducing the number of all onshore refugee claims.

Many critics charged that immigration officials had fuelled and then taken advantage of exaggerated public and political concerns about abuse in order to maintain control over the selection of refugees. As put by the chair of the Refugee Status Advisory Committee (RSAC) in 1987, "There has been an effort ... since 1980, to delegitimize the whole process of refugee determination in our country, to characterize this movement as abusive ... Their view is that anyone who comes to Canada without prior permission of the Canadian government has abused our process."[28] In this view, immigration officials had deliberately created "a sense of crisis, a sense of being inundated by unscrupulous people who see us as patsies."[29]

In May 1987, the government introduced Bill C-55,[30] the *Refugee Reform Bill,* followed swiftly two months later by the *Deterrents and Detention Bill,* Bill C-84.[31] Together they marked a major mobilization of restrictive and enforcement-oriented legal mechanisms to augment the administrative controls just discussed.

Bill C-55, discussed briefly in Chapter 2, created the IRB, a new, two-tiered refugee determination system. This act, though respecting to an unprecedented degree the procedural rights of refugee claimants, simultaneously limited access by claimants to the system itself. Its central justification was that it would preserve the integrity of the refugee determination system "by ensuring the protection of legitimate refugees, while deterring the 'shameful manipulation' of false or abusive claims."[32]

Bill C-55 acted upon the problem of the "bogus refugee" in several ways. It permitted a person to claim refugee status only at the outset of the immigration inquiry; it significantly expanded the grounds for denying eligibility; it permitted the exclusion of claimants deemed to have come from a "safe third country" (the government intending soon to produce a list of such countries); it excluded from making a refugee claim those with a criminal record who had been certified by the minister as a "danger to the public"; and it denied a refugee hearing to any who had been granted refugee status in another country or who had already had a refugee claim rejected in Canada. In addition, those found to be eligible still had to receive a decision from an immigration adjudicator and a refugee board member that their claim had a "credible basis" (as opposed to the previous standard that excluded only "manifestly unfounded" claims). Finally, Bill C-55 placed contentious limits on access to judicial review of negative decisions regarding a claimant's "credible basis" and/or refugee status. Under Bill C-55, claimants did not have the right to appeal to the Federal Court; instead, they were conceded the much more limited right to apply for leave to appeal to the Federal Court.

Bill C-84, the *Deterrents and Detention Bill*, the second major piece of legislation in 1987, marks the serious intrusion of discourses of crime and punishment (deterrence) into immigration enforcement. While Bill C-55 aimed mainly to screen out "system abusers" through the tightening up of eligibility and credibility criteria, Bill C-84, tabled just over a month after the June 1987 "spontaneous" Sikh landing, sought to enhance control of Canada's borders by providing for tough penalties for smugglers and others who assist in the transportation of illegal immigrants. Bill C-84 increased powers of search and seizure for immigration officials; it imposed fines and jail terms for smugglers and transportation companies; and it even provided authorities with the legal right to turn away boats suspected of carrying refugees before they land.[33] Both bills were widely attacked by immigrant and refugee advocates as inhumane and draconian. A representative of Amnesty International, for example, commented that "these measures are designed to keep refugee claimants out of the country as opposed to ensuring that genuine refugee claimants are given protection."[34] Some have argued that the EIC, through willful neglect or intentional mismanagement, contributed to the general panic about system abuse and bogus refugees in order thereby to clear the way for the restrictive measures already discussed.[35]

Canada has never been keen to become a country of first asylum and has been determined to remain as fully as possible a country of resettlement for refugees whom it chooses. In 1983, Senior Immigration Official Raphael Girard, who would later be the principal drafter of Bills C-55 and C-84, argued that the main emphasis of Canada's refugee program should continue to be offshore selection because it favours those who could "best benefit" as opposed to the self-selected, it is responsive to domestic concerns and priorities, it can be easier "managed and controlled," it is amenable to foreign policy objectives, and it does not entail the problems associated with removing unsuccessful claimants.[36]

In the late 1980s, the putative threat posed by "bogus refugees" provided support for the restrictive and exclusionary dimensions of Bills C-55 and C-84. These measures did not facilitate access for genuine refugees, nor did they exclude only those who could not credibly claim to be refugees as defined in the *Refugee Convention*. Rather, they had the effect of limiting the number of all onshore refugee claimants. Still, that these measures were usually justified *in the name of genuine refugees* indicates the continued discursive currency of humanitarian and international legal discourses. The discursive power of the deserving genuine refugee was maintained and fortified only in contradistinction to the increasingly prominent figure of the widely despised, undeserving, and unscrupulous fraudulent claimant. The denigration of the latter was bound up with distinctly neoliberal concerns about the integrity and efficiency of "the system." As clearly articulated by Weiner, then minister of immigration, the thrust of Bill C-55 was to maintain the integrity of Canada's refugee determination system.

Expanding the Threat: Bogus Refugee Meets the Terrorist and the Serious Criminal

So far, this chapter has traced the emergence of the regulatory figure of the "bogus refugee." Fears about such refugees were further heightened by their association with criminals, in this case terrorists. During the 1980s, a major threat to national security was presented and represented by the figure of the international terrorist. Reg Whitaker identifies this development well: "International terrorism is the great *frisson* of the decade, not unlike the great fear of international Communism that gripped the Western world ... in the late 1940s and early 1950s. Terrorism presents, of course, a real threat to security and public safety. But as in the earlier case, there is also much exaggeration about it, much panic, and much talk of extreme measures. There is no shortage of self-proclaimed 'experts' on terrorism prepared to sell their nostrums to a fearful public. And there is no shortage of voices counselling the abandonment of liberal freedoms and the need for stern repressive measures."[37]

The zero-sum opposition of security and freedom characteristic of North American responses to the attacks of 11 September 2001 is thus not new. Nor is the current conflation of security threats with refugee determination.[38] The threat posed by international terrorists that emerged over the 1970s and 1980s became the discursive replacement of the threat previously posed by communists and other ideological subversives during the height of the Cold War. Thus, while the numerical and moral threat posed by bogus refugees provided the primary and immediate justification for increasingly exclusionary and enforcement-oriented measures, the fears sparked by the image of "waves," "floods," or "tides" of bogus or fraudulent claimants were heightened by the associations between bogus refugees and the threatening figures of the terrorist and the "serious" criminal, coming together to pose a new, hybrid risk to the nation and the public.

Several commentators have argued that, immediately upon the arrival of the Sikhs in June 1987, an "orchestrated hysteria" was created by the minister of immigration, the Immigration Commission, and the prime minister to incite public opinion and pave the way for restrictive reforms.[39] "Orchestrated" or not, the Sikhs were linked with terrorism and constructed as serious security threats.[40] Likewise, the Tamils who arrived in 1986 were linked with international criminal and subversive organizations.[41] This linkage of the bogus refugee and the criminal or terrorist threat is clearly made in the following characteristic defence of Bills C-55 and C-84 by Jim Hawkes, then MP for Calgary West: "We need quick decisions if we are going to have a system of law in which protection is offered to legitimate Convention refugees and abusers can be removed quickly and efficiently. In a world of increasing international terrorism there has to be a means of determining and detaining people."[42]

Bill C-84 sought to deal with "spontaneous landings" by acting primarily upon smugglers and transportation companies. However, it also provided some fairly extensive "security-related" changes. First, Bill C-84 excluded anyone certified by the minister of immigration and the solicitor general as a danger to the public due to criminal convictions, this certification not being reviewable. Second, it provided for the detention of undocumented persons upon their arrival in Canada until their identities could be confirmed. This detention, defended on security grounds, was likely above all to affect refugee claimants since they often do not have the required documentation. The bill also provided for the detention at the border of anyone thought by the authorities to pose a security threat. Those thought to be a security threat were likely to be detained for long periods as they became the subjects of a security review procedure requiring that they appear before a Federal Court judge. While anyone who was the subject of such a review could respond to the judge's summary of the case, he or she had no right either to hear or confront the witnesses or to challenge the evidence presented. If the security threat was judged to be real, the bill provided for the exclusion and immediate deportation of the person in question.

What is remarkable about the two acts of 1987 is that they linked the categories of bogus refugees and criminal terrorists into a new, hybrid object of governance constructed as a monumental threat to administrative systems, commerce, government, and the public. This linkage, forged in the 1980s, became increasingly dominant through the 1990s.

In the Name of the "Truly Deserving": Bill C-86

The discursive linkage of fraudulent abuse and criminality became front and centre with the next major piece of immigration legislation, Bill C-86 (1992).[43] Crime discourses and law and order programs, already well established in the context of criminal justice, were mobilized with unprecedented urgency in the context of immigration enforcement. In addition to emphasizing the need to protect Canadians against terrorist outsiders who abuse the system through fraudulent claims, Bill C-86 shaped and was shaped by growing concerns about criminals and victims.

Refugees had already been devalued through the mobilization of fraud discourses. In addition, since the 1976 *Immigration Act,* the undesirable figure of the criminal immigrant or refugee encompassed an ever-widening range of threatening criminal types. They came to include international terrorists seeking to found new bases for terrorist organizations; war criminals, either the "modern-day" or the traditional (Nazi) variety; "serious" criminals with "serious" criminal histories; people smugglers; organized criminals; human rights violators; and dangers to the public. Moreover, not only has the classification of crimes and criminality expanded and transformed, but it has also merged with and indeed reconfigured an expanded conception of national security as exemplified in the unprecedented move in the mid-1990s to expand the working mandate of CSIS to encompass crime and criminals as threats to national security.[44] Similarly, the notion of "system abuse" and the lack of control over the system that allows such abuse to flourish, previously linked with the numerical and moral threat posed by the bogus refugee, have been discursively extended and linked with the threat posed by terrorists and other dangerous criminals. As articulated by Immigration Canada in 1992, "an immigration program that is not properly controlled is vulnerable to abuses by criminals, terrorists and others who might jeopardize the safety and well-being of Canadians. In recent years we have seen the development of more organized, highly professional criminal networks intent on circumventing international and national laws ... As the volumes of people seeking to enter Canada increase, vigilance is needed to ensure that Canadian society is protected from those who are not welcome in our country and who are intent on breaking its laws."[45]

Bill C-86 was presented as part of a new "managerial" approach to immigration made necessary by "growing, unpredictable, and large scale movements of people from one country to another."[46] In promoting the "new framework for the 1990s," the image of "volumes" of internationally displaced, dispossessed, and needy foreigners clamouring at "our" borders is conjured up as a threat to the Canadian state, its administrative systems, and the public. Sheer numbers of global migrants are emphasized in dramatic and ominous fashion: "Some estimates suggest that today, as many as eighty million people – more than three times the entire population of

Canada – are moving from one country to another at any given time."[47] It is also noted that, although the number of refugee claimants has increased exponentially, "the proportion of claimants who are found to be Convention refugees is falling."[48] An observation made in the context of a hard-line piece of British refugee legislation in 1996 may be applied to the Canadian scene: a "culture of disbelief" about the legitimacy of claims to asylum has been effectively created, and "that is the reason for the dramatic decline in the proportion of asylum seekers granted refugee status or exceptional leave to maintain. Those figures are then used to justify the belief that most asylum seekers are 'bogus.'"[49]

As noted earlier, numerous polls and surveys carried out at this time indicated that many Canadians were concerned about the increase in immigration, in particular the increase in nonwhite immigration and refugee admissions.[50] Politicians mobilized these concerns in the promotion of restrictive immigration policies. The merging and exploitation of the fears about refugees, fraud, and criminality are nicely expressed in the following journalistic observation: "Valcourt [then minister of immigration] has used some strong language in comments defending the bill. He's evoked images of millions of refugees from Third World countries fleeing poverty and turmoil, implying that they may soon be clamouring at our door. He's warned that the government needs more power to keep criminals and terrorists out of the country. He's told the story – several times – of a Montreal refugee claimant who filed 14 fake claims in order to cheat welfare."[51] Immigrants and refugees were widely represented as a threat that needed to be contained and controlled. In Valcourt's own words, "Canadians are compassionate and humane, but we don't want to be taken for a ride."[52]

Neoliberal preoccupations with system integrity and efficiency were front and centre in Bill C-86, which promised to reduce significantly the opportunities for "system abusers" and "criminals" by introducing a new, tighter, tougher, and more efficient managerial immigration regime. The predominant policy objectives were to protect system integrity and the Canadian public. And, once again, humanitarian discourses were proffered in support of this "toughening up" of the system: it was necessary to crack down on criminals and system abusers in the name of the genuinely deserving *Convention* refugee: "The proposed changes ... provide for a more streamlined refugee determination system, ensuring that we can help those who *truly need* refuge."[53]

Immigration enforcement had come to be represented and justified as the thin blue line protecting Canadians from the wide-ranging criminal threats lurking just outside the borders. Canadian immigration law and policy emerged in the 1990s as a critical and necessary instrument of crime control to an extent unprecedented in Canadian history.[54]

Bill C-86 radically extended the criminality-based grounds for inadmissibility.[55] It sought to fill perceived gaps in the existing legislation with respect to the inadmissibility of criminals "and others who threaten the security of Canada."[56] Specifically, it aimed to more thoroughly exclude "organized criminals." Existing legislation was deemed inadequate because it did "not directly enable immigration officials to refuse admission to persons who may have no criminal convictions, but who are nevertheless involved in organized crime or other criminal activity, according to foreign police reports or intelligence sources."[57] Bill C-86 therefore expanded the definition of criminal inadmissibility to permit the exclusion of a person when there are "reasonable grounds to believe" that the person was or is a member of an organization "that there are reasonable grounds to believe" is or was engaged in "a pattern of criminal activity planned and organized by a number of persons acting in concert in furtherance of the commission of any offence that may be punishable ... by way of indictment."[58] Moreover, it also allowed for the exclusion of persons where there are "reasonable grounds to believe" that they have committed an "act or omission" outside Canada that would constitute an offence inside Canada. *No conviction is required by this provision.*[59]

Bill C-86 also addressed the perceived weakness of the existing legislation to exclude terrorists, although there was no clear definition of terrorism. Bill C-86 authorized immigration officials to bar entry and/or deport individuals who have engaged in or who, upon "reasonable grounds," are believed may engage in espionage, subversion, and/or terrorism as well as those who are members of an organization that has, or is reasonably believed, may engage in espionage, subversion, terrorism, and/or "other acts of violence that would or might endanger the lives or safety of persons in Canada."[60] Finally, the bill included a new "catch-all" ground for exclusion on security grounds.[61] Even permanent residents could be deported under these provisions.[62]

The act also sanctioned the exclusion of people who are or were "senior members of or senior officials in the service of a government that is or was engaged in terrorism, systematic or gross human rights violations or war crimes or crimes against humanity."[63] The section provided a "general" guide to the definition of "senior members" or "senior officials." This list includes (a) heads of state or government; (b) members of the cabinet or governing council; (c) senior advisors to heads of state, cabinet, or governing council members; (d) senior members of the public service; (e) senior members of the military, intelligence, and/or internal security apparatus; (f) ambassadors and senior diplomatic officials; and (g) members of the judiciary. The list is thus sweeping in its examples but makes it clear that it is not intended to be exhaustive.[64]

In addition to widely extending the criminality provisions of the act, Bill C-86 toughened the provisions and penalties relating to the transportation of illegal migrants to Canada[65] and the smuggling of illegal immigrants into Canada.[66] The bill also included amendments relating to border controls. These provisions gave immigration officers the power to fingerprint and photograph refugee claimants and expanded their powers to search and seize.[67] The latter amendment sanctioned the search of person, luggage, and/ or vehicle *without warrant* when there are "reasonable grounds to believe" that the person has hidden identity documents. The same authorization was given to officers to search "persons seeking to come to Canada who are believed on reasonable grounds to be smugglers, document couriers, and others involved in the illegal entry of persons."[68]

Bill C-86 ushered in a new era in the governance of immigration penality. It broadly defined and acted upon the emergent threat of the criminal immigrant to an unparalleled degree, and it legally entrenched and intensified the coercive powers of immigration officers to enforce the act and police the borders.

As was true for Bills C-55 and C-84, Bill C-86 was greeted with extensive and well-organized criticism from a wide range of critics.[69] Of particular concern to nongovernmental representatives was the revival of the safe third country provision included in Bill C-55 but not yet activated. This provision disallowed refugee claims made by individuals if they had travelled to Canada either directly or indirectly from a country prescribed by the governor-in-council as "safe." A safe third country is one that complies with article 33 of the *Refugee Convention,* which prohibits *refoulement* (the return of people to a place where they would face persecution under the *Refugee Convention*). This provision would exclude refugee claimants from many developing countries who are unable to get direct flights to Canada. The likelihood that the United States would be designated as a safe third country was also a source of concern.

Many warned that the United States is not in fact a "safe" country for many refugees, who, if returned there, could face deportation to countries where they could be at risk of persecution. In December 2002, despite widespread and long-standing opposition, Canada did sign the *Safe Third Country Agreement* with the United States. This agreement, promoted as a way to stop the practice of "asylum shopping," as contributing to "harmonization," and as a means to improve system efficiency, provides that refugees must make their claims in whichever of the two countries they arrive first. People who have relatives in Canada, children, or people who make their claims from within Canada are among those excluded from this provision. It is also therefore likely that this agreement will result in people attempting to get into Canada through more dangerous means in order to make their refugee claims from within the country. These concerns have led some to characterize it as a human rights disaster.[70] In early 2003, the decline in the number of refugee claims made in Canada since 2001 led advocates to argue that the agreement be scrapped.[71]

The safe third country provision, along with most of the other enforcement amendments of Bill C-86, again has the effect of limiting the numbers of refugees able to seek protection in Canada. Its orientation is toward regulating populations and the efficient management of administrative systems rather than protecting refugees. As observed by David Matas, "managing immigration really means, in a refugee protection context, denying protection to people who otherwise might be allowed and entitled to come as refugees. That is indeed the effect of many of the provisions in the bill. They make it more difficult for refugees to seek protection or even to arrive in Canada to make a claim for protection."[72]

Finally, the new legislation eliminated the first-stage credibility and eligibility hearing introduced by Bill C-55 to weed out "system abusers" at an early stage in the process. Interestingly, the number of clearly unfounded "bogus" claims cannot have been readily apparent in these hearings, for 94 percent of refugee claims considered by a first-stage hearing were referred to the CRDD for a full hearing.[73] Bill C-86 gave SIOs the power to rule on refugee eligibility, thus replacing a quasi-judicial process with a bureaucratic one. The government sought to minimize the significance of this expansion of the discretionary power of SIOs by asserting that the eligibility decisions would be made on the basis of a checklist of "facts" (rather than on "matters of judgement") and would therefore be, in its judgment, entirely nondiscretionary.[74]

Thus, it can be seen that the crime-security nexus articulated with neoliberal discourses about fraud, efficiency, and system integrity provided the primary rationale for the enforcement provisions of Bill C-86. The problem of the "bogus refugee" had been legally constructed by and acted upon through Bills C-55 and C-84. It reemerged with Bill C-86 as the more general problem of "system abuse" attributed in large part to a lack of adequate control over the immigration system. This lack of control was in turn linked with what was presented as the more dominant threat of the 1990s: the criminal refugee or immigrant broadly defined. Bill C-86 linked and acted upon these two problems by expanding the exclusionary categories and by sanctioning more enforcement-oriented measures. As summed up by Doug Lewis, the minister of public security in 1993, "with Bill C-86 we introduced a wide range of tools to deal with those who try to abuse our immigration program or violate our laws."[75]

The Creation of the Canadian "Public Security Portfolio" in 1993

In 1993, on the heels of Bill C-86, in one of the more transparent political moves of this period, the Conservative government created a new Public

Security Portfolio. It brought together the EIC, the Royal Canadian Mounted Police (RCMP), the Canadian Security Intelligence Service (CSIS), and the Canada Parole Board into a newly created government department, the Department of Public Security. The first minister of public security, Doug Lewis, explained the logic behind the move by reference to the "global community [that] is awash with people seeking new homes" (again the water metaphor conjuring up a disastrous flood); to the need to "reinforce and defend the integrity of our generous and valuable immigration policy"; to "give extra weight to the issue of enforcement"; to have "more efficient control over the security of our borders"; and to better protect Canadians. In his words, through this consolidation "we can exercise more effective control over entry to Canada; ensure that we better protect all Canadians; and reduce abuse of Canada's generous immigration and refugee programs."[76] Again the discourses of fraud and criminality are linked with guiding concerns about system integrity and legitimacy. According to Lewis, despite "only a tiny percentage" of newcomers who are of concern, the choice is straightforward: "We can either reinforce and defend the integrity of our generous and valuable immigration policy or we can watch public confidence and support for the policy collapse."[77]

This was not a subtle move. Critics charged that then Conservative prime minister Kim Campbell was fanning the populist flames against new immigrants and refugees by "baiting Canadians' fear that immigrants commit a disproportionate amount of crime, and by ... linking the solution to the perceived crime problem with cleaning up the immigration and refugee system."[78] As succinctly stated by Shyla Dutt of the Asian Canadian Caucus, the government had succeeded in "re-focusing public debate away from immigration as an economic and social issue, and [toward immigration] as a security and public safety issue."[79]

By 1992, the hybrid figure of the fraudulent criminal immigrant or refugee represented the archetype of undesirability. This figure was mobilized as evidence of a vulnerable, underpoliced, and poorly managed system open to abuse by criminal and security risks. The victims of the fraudulent and even criminal character of bogus refugees were the integrity of the nation's administrative systems, economic health, and the population at large. In the following chapter, I examine more closely the relations between this discursive redefinition of refugees, from deserving victims to undeserving frauds and criminals, and the more general neoliberal preoccupation with fraud in the area of social services. The effects of these developments on the lives of refugees in Canada will be illustrated by an examination of one particular group of refugees, Somali refugees living in Toronto.

6
Risky Refugees

On the heels of yet another recession in 1993, and in the face of the massive displacement of people globally, it is perhaps not surprising that the issues of welfare and immigration would be considered in relation to each other. Less straightforward is the way in which fears about "welfare fraud" and "bogus refugees" merged with law and order and crime discourses in the mid-1990s. The resulting composite figure of the "bogus refugee on welfare" was mobilized in ways that entailed adverse effects for a number of visible minorities and for noncitizens in particular.[1]

Neither the association of immigration and crime, nor that of immigration and social welfare, is historically unprecedented.[2] Criminality is a flexible category that has been used at different moments in Canadian history to exclude or deport "dangerous foreigners" for various combinations of moral, racial, economic, and ideological reasons. At other times, most notably during the Depression years, the association between immigration and welfare was manifested in dramatic increases in the deportation of the poor and unemployed under the public charge provisions of immigration legislation.[3]

However, while current conditions display some similarities with past configurations, the present juncture is unique. While criminality has always been an exclusionary category, the degree to which it has come to provide *the* guiding rationale for exclusionary immigration law and policy is historically unprecedented. As documented in preceding chapters, during the Cold War, national insecurities fostered an entrenched and sustained preoccupation with national security. Ideological concerns mixed with racial and ethnic prejudices in the development of a Canadian national security apparatus that could deport those deemed dangerous. As the Cold War waned, and as previously acceptable and explicit racial and moral grounds for exclusion were delegitimized, criminality-based exclusions proliferated. Moreover, during the 1970s and 1980s, expanded categories of criminality merged with and reconfigured national security concerns that came to encompass ever-increasing varieties of criminality.

As noted earlier, this crime-security nexus is evidenced most dramatically by the unprecedented inclusion in the mid-1990s of "transnational criminal activity" in the working mandate of the Canadian Security Intelligence Service (CSIS). Whereas terrorism and espionage have traditionally posed the primary "threat" to Canada's national security, with the demise of tra ditional Cold War enemies and fears and in accordance with the increasing dominance of law and order concerns, CSIS maintains that organized transnational crime now poses a similarly serious threat to "various aspects of Canadian national security, law and order, the integrity of government programs and institutions, and the economy."[4] In the 1990s, the figure of the dangerous foreign outsider joined the mix as a threat to be contained and deported. The criminality provisions and related enforcement activities of immigration penality have thus come to occupy hitherto unprecedented dominance in the governance of this domain such that today, as discussed in Chapter 1, it is indeed governed through crime.[5]

It is also the case that, while current constructions of risk and criminality are certainly "raced," there are important differences from past constructions. Whereas immigration exclusions of the past were explicitly racist and justified by discourses of racial purity and biological degeneration, present constructions display the heightened dominance of national classifications (Jamaican drug dealers, Chinese triads, etc.) and are mediated more by cultural stereotypes than by biological typologies. One final development makes the present juncture unique. As detailed in the previous chapter, the threatening figures of the international terrorist and the organized criminal were joined in the 1980s by that of the bogus refugee. The claimant of administrative state benefits (whether of refugee protection or of social services) emerged and has merged with the threatening figure of the criminal foreigner.

At the level of discourse, the developments outlined here can be understood as the incremental but steady redefinition through which the "genuine" and therefore "deserving" victim under international human rights law came to be replaced by the fraudulent, even criminal, "bogus refugee/welfare cheat." The description of Somali refugees as "masters of confusion" found in one report commissioned by the Department of Citizenship and Immigration,[6] rich in Orientalist echoes, would not have been used in the mid-1970s, when immigration and refugee policy was being liberalized, but by 1993-94, it was written down and repeated, in somewhat different language, in the press and among Reform Party politicians.

This chapter begins with a brief review of the rise of neoliberalism as a rationality of rule and the criminalization of certain kinds of fraud. It traces the emergence of the problem of the welfare cheat in Ontario in the early

1990s. It then examines the ways in which the discourses of fraud and abuse converged with law and order discourses in the construction and regulation of the fraudulent criminal refugee. This discursive redefinition of refugees from deserving victims to undeserving abusers and criminals is then considered in relation to its effects on Somali refugees living in Toronto in the mid-1990s.

The Rise of Neoliberalism as a Rationality of Rule

In 1726, Jonathan Swift wrote, "look upon fraud as a crime greater than theft ... for they allege, that care and vigilance, with a very common understanding, may preserve a man's goods from thieves but honesty hath no fence against superior cunning ... Where fraud is permitted or connived at, or hath no law to punish it, the honest dealer is always undone, and the knave gets the advantage."[7] This quotation reemerged in the late 1990s on the web page of the Toronto Police Service "Fraud Squad." By citing it, the police clearly hoped to give an air of timelessness and universality to the historically specific neoliberal campaigns against fraud of the 1990s, campaigns that consistently targeted not the traditional tricksters and confidence men of Swift's time, or for that matter the new practitioners of money laundering and shady international transactions, but those who were formerly, under welfare liberalism, regarded as rights holders, as legitimate claimants upon state services. Alongside the construction of the "bogus refugee," fraud in the context of social welfare services became a major preoccupation. The increasing dominance of the logic of fraud over the late 1980s and 1990s was thus not limited to the domain of immigration and refugee governance. This redefinition of people coming to Canada due to persecution (or wars or dire poverty) was facilitated by a broader shift in governmental rationalities from welfare liberalism to neoliberalism.

Neoliberalism grew in influence as the postwar boom came to a close in the 1970s and high inflation, unemployment, and recession marked the next few decades. Since the 1970s, both the economy and the public discourse have changed dramatically. Neoliberalism seeks to reassert pre-Keynesian classical economic theory. The classical liberal commitment to shrink the size of the state and restore the primacy of market forces has been revived. The welfare state must be retrenched if not completely dismantled since it is wasteful, a hindrance to wealth creation and to the state's ability to compete economically in international markets.[8]

This neoliberal rationality is both a strategy for reducing state expenditures and thus taxes and a moral campaign. The claim is that the welfare state reduced freedom by enforcing financial redistribution from taxpayers to welfare recipients. It has eroded the work ethic and made recipients dependent. It has created a huge public sector that has a vested interest in its perpetuation.[9] All this is viewed as untenable in the face of massive economic global restructuring; instead, "market forces must be liberated, the state downsized and social welfare programs emasculated, so that the state can meet the challenges posed by global restructuring."[10] These adjustments certainly unsettle labour markets, rendering employment more uncertain and insecure. However, these features of the labour market are legitimized as "unavoidable," "normal," even "desirable."[11] A belief in the superiority of the market as a mechanism for organizing society underlies the economic propositions of neoliberal doctrine. State intervention is an impediment to the smooth functioning of the market: "The logic of the doctrine of market superiority requires the state to remove impediments through such measures as reduced expenditures, deregulation, privatization, contracting out, and tightening the rules for unemployment insurance and other social welfare programs."[12]

The complex constellation of rights, services, and financial arrangements known by the misleading monolithic term "the welfare state" has come to seem untenable in the face of new moral insights about "dependency" that Thatcher and Reagan and their organic intellectuals popularized and in relation to the massive economic global restructuring that is pushing states to provide cheaper labour, fewer social benefits, and less business regulation.

Not everyone promoting neoliberal techniques to reduce "dependency" is a right-wing political conservative; neoliberal effects are being achieved all around the globe regardless of the particular local ideology, as can be seen in Tony Blair's New Labour and the related "Third Way" discourse popular in Germany and to a lesser extent in the US. When understood as a way of governing (rather than as an ideology), neoliberalism can be shown to require the constitution of a new subject-citizen, one constructed through appeals to the enterprise, responsibility, and independence of individuals.[13] Liberal doctrines of freedom and limits of power are accompanied by strategies to foster the self-regulating or self-organizing capacities of markets, citizens, and civil society in desired directions.[14]

Neoliberal political rationality does not accept as legitimate any avoidable adult dependency. As discussed in Chapter 1, in contrast to welfare liberalism that tempered the devaluation of dependency by its acknowledgment of its social causes, neoliberalism individualizes and stigmatizes dependency through its reassertion of notions of individual responsibility and enterprise.

The Rise of "the Welfare Cheat" in Ontario
The early 1990s witnessed a distinctly neoliberal campaign to stigmatize all recipients of state social benefits for simply being on benefits. In addition, the suspicion of criminality was added to this general devaluation. In Ontario, the New Democratic Party (NDP), then in power, initially appeared to resist

this new hegemony. Its 1992 report on social assistance in Ontario, *Time for Action*, critically observed that the system had "become infused with value judgements about people, about whether they are considered to be deserving or undeserving of assistance, the authors or the victims of their own impoverished circumstances."[15] At the time of this report, the NDP government played down concerns about fraud and abuse of the system. While it recommended a comprehensive audit system, it was careful to note that this was not because "we believe there is widespread fraud in the [welfare] system. We believe that it is the hallmark of any efficient system to monitor itself."[16]

But just two years later, the same NDP government issued yet another policy paper on social service provision, entitled *Turning Point*.[17] The neo-Keynesian discourse of collective responsibility, entitlement, social justice, and equity, so prominent in the earlier report, is completely absent in the newer document. Competitiveness, independence, individual "talents" (a specifically economic "value-added" term), long-term economic strength, training, incentives and disincentives, the changing global economy, and sound fiscal management are the key terms of *Turning Point*. No longer do notions such as collective responsibility, human dignity, and respect underpin the proposed changes. Rather, the changes are justified by reference to the increasing competitiveness of global economics.[18] Whereas the earlier policy orientation directly challenged neoliberal assumptions that social assistance is a preferred "lifestyle" with the discursive arsenal of Canadian social democracy, the later report repeats the neoliberal wisdom that welfare recipients are "locked in a lifestyle of dependency."[19]

This notion reflects the neoliberal preoccupation with rational choice and cost-benefit analysis as the basis for individual decision making about the distribution of time between labour and leisure. Welfare recipients can thus be seen to "freely choose" to be on welfare. Moreover, the lifestyle trope has the effect of suggesting that people who have come to rely on welfare will do anything, including lying and cheating, to maintain the lifestyle to which they have become accustomed. The ethical focus is thus shifted away from issues of economic redistribution and toward the individual soul of the welfare recipient. Welfare recipients, now under constant suspicion of cheating, have come to be regarded as offending our sense of fairness, our valorization of merit and individual accountability. Cheaters – and by extension all those whose workless life is read as a lazy lifestyle choice – are always already a threat to the system. Cracking down on those who cheat, for example through "snitch lines," is less important as a cost-cutting exercise than as a contribution to the maintenance of the liberal moral universe in which thrift and enterprise must be rewarded and lack of economic success is always under suspicion of laziness. Over the 1990s, fraudulent claims to the state's "generosity," whether in the context of claims for refugee status or claims for social assistance, came to represent the epitome of undeservedness.

It is telling that in Ontario the cutting of social assistance benefits and the crackdown on welfare fraud in 1994 were spearheaded by the New Democratic Party. The Conservatives, then in opposition, found themselves supporting the NDP welfare reform proposals in language that stressed the immorality of joblessness. Mike Harris, later premier of Ontario and champion of the neoliberal "Common Sense Revolution," then stated, "if it truly deals with welfare reform, with removing from the rolls those who are ripping us off, those who are staying home and doing nothing because they want to do nothing, then that will be good enough for me ... It's all those people who can get out of the house, who can do something and are choosing to stay home and do nothing."[20]

In March 1994, Tony Silipo, the Ontario NDP minister of community and social services, announced a major crackdown on welfare fraud. The government hired 270 inspectors to review almost 690,000 welfare cases. It did so while freely admitting that it was motivated less by any data on fraud than by the discursive winds of neoliberal change: "Mr. Silipo said he does not know just how serious a problem welfare fraud is ... [He] said the government is responding in part to a widely held belief that welfare fraud is increasing, even though there is no evidence to back up that belief."[21] Indeed, what evidence did exist at this time placed the level of welfare fraud at less than 3 percent of all claims.[22]

This "crackdown" and the admittedly unsubstantiated "problem" of welfare fraud received massive media coverage. Reporters at the *Toronto Sun*, a conservative daily tabloid, took advantage of the opportunity afforded them by the Ontario NDP by writing such stories as "Living High off the Hog,"[23] "Cheaters Beware,"[24] "Welfare 'Gravy Train' Derailed,"[25] and "Welfare Fraud Deluge."[26] Confidential documents obtained under the *Freedom of Information Act* presented in the legislature in April 1994 did little to diffuse the panic. These documents attributed the "skyrocketing" costs of provincial social assistance to government error in the form of massive overpayments.[27]

The hiring of new inspectors to detect fraud was accompanied by other initiatives that had the effect of stigmatizing all recipients of social benefits and even constructing them as criminals. The NDP also investigated the idea of issuing welfare ID cards to all social assistance recipients and looked into fingerprinting as an antifraud measure.[28] However, these technologies, some of which were borrowed from criminal justice, were deployed differentially. The crackdown on fraud did not target old-age pensioners, tax evaders, or corporate, white-collar criminals; it targeted the poor. In 1995, Premier Harris clarified his position on fraud and system abuse by stating that, "while wealthy citizens who evade taxes are committing a 'regrettable' action, they are nonetheless reacting in accordance with 'human nature' against wasteful government spending."[29] At the time of this provocative pronouncement, his government had just launched a massive crackdown on welfare cheats, which included a toll-free provincial fraud hotline and a 20 percent cut of welfare rates. Opposition members were quick to point out that, in Harris's Ontario, poor people who make fraudulent welfare claims are portrayed and acted upon as crooks, whereas rich people who defraud the government are normalized; they are merely acting in accordance with their inherently acquisitive and independent (and, needless to say, essentially desirable) human nature.[30]

The Merging of Fears about Immigration, Welfare, and Crime

The year 1994 also witnessed much controversy and debate about Canadian immigration and refugee law and policy. The announcement that the federal government was going to maintain immigration levels at 250,000 sparked much criticism. The right-wing, populist, Reform Party of Canada stated that "immigration is still twice what it should be ... [and] demanded an explanation for continued high levels while unemployment continues to soar and Canada's social welfare system is under strain."[31] In its anti-immigration platform, the Reform Party routinely alluded to "rising crime rates, bulging welfare rolls, unemployment and underfinanced social services."[32]

Support for the arguments of anti-immigration advocates was provided by a 1992 report written for the conservative public policy research institute, the C.D. Howe Institute, by Toronto freelance journalist Daniel Stoffman.[33] Stoffman refuted the old federal government's argument that immigrants are an economic asset to the Canadian economy but did not raise the old right-wing spectre of mass unemployment. Arguing that the economic effect of immigration is "neutral," Stoffman focused instead on its putative noneconomic effects such as increasing racial tensions, cultural divides, social disorder, crime, and the overburdening of social services. He argued that immigration should be reduced for these reasons and that the priority should be placed on taking more skilled, highly trained, and educated independent applicants rather than on those accepted for humanitarian reasons.[34]

In February 1994, the government announced that it was not going to reduce immigration levels. However, it did make changes to the intake levels of the different classes of immigrants. Within the overall number of 250,000, there were to be more independent immigrants chosen for their skills and potential contributions to the economy, more family class immigrants, and significantly fewer refugee admissions.[35]

Concerns about welfare were further linked with immigration in the mid-1990s when the provinces and the Department of Immigration expressed concerns over the drain on welfare dollars posed by sponsored immigrants, the vast majority of whom are women and children from Third World countries. The federal government commissioned a series of studies on the economic dimensions of family class immigration. One of the reported findings was that in 1994 at least 10 percent of family class immigrants in the greater Toronto area over the past ten years were on social assistance. In light of these findings, in 1996 the federal minister of citizenship and immigration and the Ontario minister of social services announced regulations designed to protect the welfare system by targeting sponsors who default on their obligations and by limiting sponsorship by those judged likely to be unable to fulfill sponsorship undertakings. The government introduced stricter eligibility requirements and tougher administrative measures that would, for example, enable the federal government to go to court in cases of sponsorship breakdown in order to recover welfare payments on behalf of the province.[36]

Like the crackdown on welfare fraud, these enforcement-oriented measures were adopted in the absence of any evidence that sponsorship defaults were in fact a major problem. Indeed, in maintaining the income cut-off levels, the minister specifically noted that the vast majority of sponsorship undertakings (86 percent) were fulfilled without default.[37]

By the early 1990s, the regulatory figures of the bogus refugee and the welfare cheat were well established in Canadian public and political discourse, and efforts were under way to crack down on both. The increased preoccupation with fraud under neoliberalism facilitated the relatively easy link forged between fraud (system abuse) and criminality that was mobilized against new immigrants and refugees. As discussed in the preceding chapter, over the late 1980s and early 1990s, concerns about fraud, criminality, and public safety joined reconfigured national security concerns as the guiding rationales for a series of tough, enforcement-oriented reforms that aimed to deport "risky" noncitizens deemed to pose a threat to system integrity, national security, and public safety and to refuse refugee claimants who were similarly assessed. Furthermore, as examined in more detail in the following chapter, the outcry in 1994 in Toronto about the fatal shooting of a white woman, Georgina Leimonis, and a white police officer, Todd Baylis, by black men of Caribbean origin was crucial in shaping not only public opinion but even government policy. The ruling Liberals, though historically associated with pro-immigration policies and beneficiaries of most of what is called "the ethnic vote," took advantage of the popular outcry to push through some extremely tough, enforcement-oriented measures, including Bill C-44 in 1995 (the Just Desserts Bill). All of these initiatives worked to further entrench the logic of criminality in the governance of exclusionary immigration law and policy.

The stage was set. The welfare-fraud campaign had made it possible to look at immigrant and refugee claimants as "welfare bums" first and immigrants second because the campaign against welfare fraud was carried out not as a measure to recover revenue but as a moral campaign to scrutinize social benefits claimants and, in general, anyone who might make a claim upon the state. Somewhat independently, the perpetual Canadian worry that there is too much immigration, especially from less desirable parts of the globe, had become linked to existing campaigns for law and order, to get tough on crime, in turn fuelled by local Toronto racism against blacks of Caribbean origin. Refugees and new immigrants became the subjects of new techniques of state scrutiny (e.g., the "danger to the public" provision) as well as of popular outcries similar to those haunting people receiving, or thought to be receiving, social benefits. In a sense, criminality was the common denominator, allowing people to begin a sentence with "immigration policy" and end it with "system abuse" or "welfare fraud." In some cases, the criminality was thought to be overt and violent (Caribbean males were stereotyped in this way); in other cases, the criminality was thought to be devious (Chinese "snakeheads"). Either way moral corruption/criminality was the common ground upon which fears about welfare fraud and immigration system abuse converged.

One of the most troubling aspects of these developments was the near disappearance of concern for the subject of international human rights law, the refugee fleeing persecution. A pervasive culture of disbelief was forged. Refugee claimants have been reconstructed: they are rarely received as deserving victims, regardless of the conditions from which they are fleeing. Instead, they are presented as opportunistic frauds who have "freely chosen" to come to Canada. By virtue of this allegedly free choice, they become "rational" calculators and hence potential system abusers who need to be deterred through clearly laid-out disincentives. While it is generally conceded that *genuine* refugees are deserving of protection and that *genuinely* needy welfare recipients are deserving of assistance, the emphasis has shifted to the *un*deserving and *un*desirable side of the liberal equation. The guiding assumption tends to be that genuinely deserving refugees are not able to make it to Canada to make their claims but are languishing much more helplessly in camps overseas.

Immigration and Crime in Toronto, 1993-95
Federal developments attest to the heightened preoccupation with and the links between new immigrants and refugees, criminality, fraud, and system abuse. Provinces and municipalities were no less animated by the same issues. Indeed, arguably, provinces and municipalities were further motivated by the rising costs borne by provinces and municipalities for social service

provision due to federal cuts in transfer payments. In addition, Greater Toronto has always been extremely vocal on immigration issues due to the large numbers of new immigrants and refugees who live there.

Canadian national and local media, including the *Toronto Sun* tabloid, became obsessed with "foreign dangerous criminals" in the mid-1990s. Typical of the hyperbole deployed in this medium was the following column: "Worst of all the word has gone out to foreign violent criminals that Canada is easy to enter and has a loosely run system that can be 'worked' to frustrate deportation even when caught. Many of these criminals-murderers, drug traffickers, terrorists, pimps, etc., – apply for 'refugee' status and stay on for years. And when they run out of time they simply 'disappear' ... When you see the amount of chronic, large scale unemployment in Canada – with 3 million on the welfare rolls – you have to wonder about the insanity of these new immigration increases."[38]

While the proliferation and tenor of anti-immigration reporting cannot be used as a surrogate measure of what people think, or used to make any positive claims about the scope of popular racism, they still provide insight into the reasons for the heightened public anxiety about and hostility toward immigration and refugee policy (and immigrants and refugees). Media reports also provide insight into the dominant discursive logics that provide the rationales for restrictive and enforcement-oriented policy reforms.

This populist panic had a variety of precedents and enabling conditions, not all of which were located in "right-wing ideology." One of these prior conditions lay in the evolution of immigration policy, which, as pointed out, took a significant, draconian turn in 1994-95 but which had already been evolving in a rightward direction over the 1980s and early 1990s. As described in the previous chapter, the enforcement-oriented legal reforms of this period (Bills C-55 and C-84 in 1987 and Bill C-86 in 1992), as well as a variety of restrictive policy measures, were justified by reference to the need to prevent the "flood" (or "stop the flow" or "stem the tide") of so-called bogus refugees, prevent the admission of foreign criminals, protect national security and the public, and preserve the integrity of Canadian administrative systems.

It is therefore not surprising that in April 1993, when restricted police and immigration documents were leaked to a municipal politician in Toronto, John Papadakis, he used them as "proof" that there was a real connection between immigration and crime: "Canada has a serious problem with foreigners coming into the country and committing violent crimes."[39] Soon after, Papadakis released them at a public forum on crime that he had organized. In attendance at the forum were other municipal politicians and representatives of the Department of Immigration and the police. Its stated purpose was to "focus attention on bogus refugee claimants and illegal immigrants."[40]

The fact that the documents around which Papadakis built his argument were leaked confidential documents only bolstered his resolve. Giving expression to right-wing grumblings about political correctness, system abuse, and popular fears about crime and victimization, Papadakis explained that the leaking of these documents was proof that "law-abiding" citizens are "fed up with government inaction, with having their country abused, with being afraid to walk around at night, with being robbed in their stores, and with being accused of being racist every time they open their mouths to say there's something wrong."[41]

Papadakis emphasized that national security and public safety supersede any privacy laws. The easy slippage between criminality and fraud/system abuse, as well as the general view that *any* government assistance is, in a sense, "criminal," are evidenced in his remark that "crime is crime. When my folks came to Canada in the 1950s they had no help, no handouts."[42] With this statement, Papadakis linked "new" (Third World) immigration to crime and that in turn to welfare fraud.

Papadakis, and his allies in immigration, won official acceptance of the links that they alleged between illegal immigrants and refugee claimants, welfare, and the "crime problem" when the Conservative government created the new "Public Security" portfolio. The message was clear – immigrants and refugees are a threat that needs to be contained and controlled, "a menace that society has to be protected from."[43] Thus, even though Papadakis spoke from a discursive space to the right of mainstream liberalism, his comments were in keeping with the federal agenda. He argued, among other things, that any refugee claimant or new immigrant convicted of a criminal offence should be automatically deported, with no right of appeal.[44] And while the federal government never enacted anything as draconian as this proposal, as will be discussed in the next chapter, criminality was indeed made into a criterion for the deportation of permanent residents without appeal a few months later.

The linkages between immigrants and refugees, crime-security, and "system abuse" in both welfare and immigration departments had national and local dimensions. In Toronto in the mid-1990s, Somalis were one significant group bearing the brunt of this general development.[45] Their experience illustrates the material results of the "demonic" combination of racist discourse, governmental moves to tighten access to permanent resident status, fears about "dependency," law and order programs, and neoliberal moves to restrict claims upon the state.

From "Deserving Victims" to "Masters of Confusion": The Case of Somali Refugees in Canada in the 1990s

Over the 1980s and 1990s, hundreds of thousands of Somalis were forced to flee state-sanctioned persecution in their country. Africa Watch observed that "it is difficult to overstate the Somalia government's brutality towards its own people, or to measure the impact of its murderous policies. Two decades of the Presidency of President Siad Barre have resulted in human rights violations on an unprecedented scale which have devastated the country. Even before the current wars the human rights of Somalis were violated systematically, violently and with absolute impunity."[46] Most ended up in neighbouring countries in refugee camps. However, many who had the resources for international air travel were eventually granted refugee status in Canada and the United States. The Somali community in Toronto began to form in the mid-1970s soon after refugees began to flee the Ethiopian-Somalian war. Thousands more followed over the 1980s and 1990s as conditions within Somalia steadily deteriorated. According to the Somali Immigrant Aid Association, over the 1990s the size of the Somali community in Canada grew from 65,000 to over 90,000.[47] Most were refugees. Between 1995 and 1998, Somalia was among the top ten "source" countries for refugees in Canada.[48]

After arriving in Canada, many Somalis moved to Toronto, where thousands of Somalis live in six high-rise apartments on Dixon Road in Etobicoke, a suburb of Toronto.[49] In the general panic created about the fraudulent and criminal identities and activities of Somali refugees, conditions faced by the Somalis living at Dixon steadily worsened.

Somali Refugees: "Cheats," "Criminals," and "Desert Gypsies"
This emerging community soon became the target of another bundle of leaked government documents. These "secret federal reports" leaked from the Intelligence Unit of the Department of Immigration made their way into the hands of provincial Liberal leader Lyn McLeod in October 1993. The reports, one of which bore the racist and inflammatory title "Desert Gypsy,"[50] were written by a bureaucrat in this Intelligence Unit. The gypsy reference was not idle Orientalist fantasy. As discussed later in this chapter, in 1992 Bill C-86 had already sanctioned the denial of permanent residency status to refugees, as well as the detention of refugee claimants, who lacked official identity documents from their home countries. Many Somalis do not have identity documents such as a birth certificate, not only due to the total breakdown of government machinery in Somalia, but also because many have been traditionally nomadic and have no "place of birth" – something that is fetishized in modern regimes of citizen identification.[51] An examination of IRB and Immigration Appeal Division (IAD) decisions on Somali refugee claims evidences the centrality of "identity" issues in these cases and associated assumptions about "credibility" that frequently result in a negative refugee determination.[52]

The leaked reports alleged that Somalis were engaged in widespread and organized welfare abuse and that the Canadian government was being defrauded of millions of dollars as a result of this abuse.[53] McLeod's interest in the reports was not in the evidence they supplied of the prejudices within the Department of Immigration. Rather, McLeod used them as part of her campaign against welfare fraud. According to the reports, Somali refugees were described as "masters of confusion [who] were importing refugees to systematically pillage our vulnerable and exposed social welfare systems." The report also contained allegations that the money was being used to buy weapons for use by Somali "warlords" in the continuing civil war in Somalia.[54]

These allegations were also reported in a *Vancouver Sun* article in October 1993. This story relied in large part on comments made by an anonymous former immigration investigator whose allegations were reportedly confirmed by similarly anonymous "law-abiding" Somalis. It reported that tens of millions of dollars in welfare money was being fraudulently collected by Somali refugees across Canada and that the practice of "tithing" resulted in a huge percentage of this money being sent back to Somalia to buy weapons for "warlords." The article quotes this former investigator, who, when asked why Somali refugees come to Canada when many of them arrive in the US first, responded that "you can't buy arms in Mogadishu with food stamps,"[55] a comment that once again identified refugees with welfare fraud and criminal activities.

This report was leaked and publicized at the time of Silipo's crackdown on welfare fraud in Ontario. While distancing himself from the specifically racist dimensions of the allegations, Silipo did little to calm the fears about refugees and welfare fraud. He responded that the government was currently investigating allegations that "some refugees are receiving multiple welfare cheques by using false identification."[56] While he observed that some of the statements in the report could incite racism, he did not challenge the validity of its content: "I don't know if the particular report is authentic. I can't tell, but certainly the issue that's raised is an authentic issue."[57]

Just as the more general "welfare cheat" panic was not grounded in any statistical evidence of the actual extent of the problem, this refugee-specific welfare panic was also not substantiated by any numbers. As admitted by Silipo, the government of the day had no estimate on the size of this problem: "I don't think that one can say there is fraud in the millions. I don't think we know that quite honestly ... I think that what we have to do is to make sure we get at whatever level of fraud there is in the system." In fact, according to Silipo, the report in question provided very few cases of fraud, "something like twenty."[58] Moreover, according to a subsequent news story, "the reports make specific reference to only a handful of cases and provide no proof – other than assurances from Somali community 'sources' – that money being bilked from welfare is being sent to warlords in Mogadishu."[59] Thus, while the focus of the allegations was on Somali welfare fraud, this report raised the added dimension of criminality evoked by the reference to welfare payments for weapon purchases in Somalia.[60] Engagement in "systematic" welfare fraud, already socially and politically criminalized, was said to be directly in aid of further "criminal" activities abroad.

This claim, which may have been rooted in nothing more devious than the common immigrant practice of saving up funds to send to one's more unfortunate relatives back home, enabled both federal immigration officials and the provincial Liberal Party to deploy all the force of the existing welfare fraud panic and articulate it with racist myths about "warlords" engaged in "tribal" warfare. The funding of people in Somalia who may or may not have been involved in warfare was then used to construct the Somalis in Canada as a risk to *Canadian security.*

The overall result was to turn Somalis precisely into the negative stereotype of "desert gypsies" – unreliable, shiftless people without home or hearth, living nomadically just like gypsies but roaming the desert rather than the cities of Europe and, like the gypsies, living not by wage labour but through shady financial transactions. The Somalis' use of "confusion and misrepresentation" was said to be "unparalleled except by the gypsies of eastern and western Europe." As described in the usually liberal *Toronto Star,* one federal report claimed that "one Somali interpreter has been quoted as saying that you can believe only 50 percent of what a Somali tells you. My experience tells me that 50 percent is extremely generous."[61]

The leaked document and the allegations it contained received wide coverage in the press. The very identity of Somalis was being recast. Instead of deserving victims of persecution, Somalis were re-presented as unscrupulous and cunning "masters of confusion." The report itself was subsequently discredited in the media, and even the minister of immigration, Sergio Marchi, explicitly distanced himself. However, much damage had been done, resulting in a subsequent meeting of 500 Somalis in Ottawa to discuss their situation and share stories of harassment by neighbours, employers, and strangers.[62]

In 1994, the *Toronto Sun* tracked a number of welfare fraud allegations, taking care to specify both the alleged offender's ethnicity (Somali) and immigration status (refugees or refugee claimants). Headlines were sensational. Even mere "suspicions" of welfare fraud by Somalis were reported at this time: "A Somali refugee claimant is being sought on suspicion that he defrauded an immigration welfare program of $4000 while his claim was being heard."[63] Another article entitled "Somali Woman Shopping for a Country"[64] included a six-inch by eight-inch photograph of the woman in question and her two children, identifying her in uppercase letters as "COLLECTOR." While in the text the woman is later identified as having claimed refugee status, she is first introduced as a "Somali expatriate." This designation, in keeping with the shopping metaphor, undermines the victimization experiences that legally and ethically justify refugee status. On 16 March

1994, the *Toronto Sun* ran another story on the same woman that identified welfare fraud and refugee claims through the clever title "On the Move on the Dole."[65] Once again the woman was identified as Somali but without mention of the disastrous war in her country or her refugee status. This time she was constructed as an affluent consumer of nationalities: a "Somalia-born globetrotter."

This designation was not the *Toronto Sun*'s invention. It speaks to the supposed problem of "asylum shopping," an official concern for some time. Indeed, a major official justification for the safe third country provision of Bill C-86 was to stop asylum shopping. This justification was repeated in 2002 when Canada signed the *Safe Third Country Agreement* with the United States. People who asylum-shop have been, or could have been, granted asylum in a so-called safe third country in which they had been present before arriving in Canada.

Despite the absence of any reliable statistical evidence of the extent of welfare fraud, Minister of Immigration Sergio Marchi announced in March 1994 that "information sharing" measures were being implemented with municipal governments in order to assist in the crackdown already in progress. Once again Marchi announced these initiatives while being cautious about exaggerated reports of the problem: "The problem of welfare abuse by refugee claimants – while worthy of attention and action – should not be exaggerated." He also took the opportunity to distance himself again, as he had in November of 1993, from reports about Somali welfare abuse: "I just don't buy it when there's references in the report that go from individual guilt to a collective community blanket guilt."[66]

The identity of Somalis became indelibly tainted by allegations of welfare abuse, war criminality, and asylum shopping. This devaluation in turn enabled divisions and conflicts within the community to be amplified and taken up by official bodies, with highly detrimental consequences. In 1994, similarly unsubstantiated allegations about the fraudulence and criminality of Somalis surfaced in the local community in Etobicoke. According to Ali Mohamud, at the time an ordinary community member and later executive director of Dejinta Beesha, a Somali settlement services community organization, members of the Somali community were accused of misappropriating government funds that had been allocated to Dejinta Beesha. As with the Somali welfare fraud allegations, these local allegations also linked fraud and criminality. Somalis were accused of redirecting the fraudulently obtained funds to Somalia to support the "war crimes" or local warlords.

This allegation triggered an RCMP investigation. In 1994, members of the RCMP went to Dejinta Beesha to investigate the charges. According to Mohamud, the RCMP were satisfied with the legality of the organization's operations and produced a report indicating that there was "no substance to the allegations."[67] This was not, however, the end of the matter. Less than two years later, the same allegations sparked a second RCMP investigation. Its findings were the same as those in 1994.

The hybrid spectre produced by combining welfare fraud and immigration fraud, coupled with criminality/security concerns, thus converged upon Somalis in a particularly powerful manner, at a time when the community was in any case experiencing a racist backlash from neighbours.

Conflict at Dixon

In July 1993, hundreds of Somali residents demonstrated on Dixon Road in protest of what they described as racist and discriminatory treatment by building management and private security staff. According to press reports and subsequent interviews with Somali and non-Somali residents, this demonstration was triggered by an altercation over a parking infraction between a security guard and a Somali visitor to the building. As the altercation developed, a crowd grew, and the security guard called for reinforcements. A security dog was brought onto the scene by the reinforcements. It was let loose by the guards and soon after bit a Somali woman, who had to be taken to hospital.[68]

Interviews reveal a history of tension and conflict between Somali and non-Somali residents, aggravated by the actions of security personnel. The interviews clearly point to overcrowding as a central variable in the hostilities. They also reveal that, for many non-Somali residents, the problem of overcrowding was exacerbated by the problems posed by Somali residents in particular. Building security personnel were frequently called upon by disgruntled non-Somali residents to take action against Somali residents or visitors whom they regarded as ill behaved, and security frequently dealt with Somali residents in hostile and coercive ways.[69]

Non-Somali residents at Dixon went so far as to describe Somali refugees as "animals" who have no respect for rules or non-Somali residents. They talk too loud, they gather in the courtyard in large groups, they don't control their children, they walk on the grass, they don't hold the door open for non-Somali residents, they monopolize the elevators. "These people were as low as animals could go," an interviewee candidly stated. In keeping with the old stereotypes of Africans as animals, rumours were rife about Somalis defecating and urinating in elevators, rumours whose source remained obscure. Somalis were described as rude, aggressive, impolite, unclean, and uncivilized. Even their sleeping arrangements came under moralistic scrutiny, with one interviewee opining that there should be "no opposite sex kids in the same bedroom. Two of each sex in a bedroom, that's a normal family. A normal family is not a clan." The non-Somali residents tended to assume, without any proof, that all Somalis were collecting welfare. One respondent observed that, while there had always been a racial and ethnic mix at Dixon, prior to the Somali "invasion" everyone had gotten along well. Another respondent observed that "this is a country for humans, and, when you bring animals in from other parts of the world, it takes animals time to adjust ... These people are not working, are on fixed incomes, and are sitting at home."

While many of the complaints of non-Somali residents were not racially specific and referred to problems that clearly stem from overcrowding – rising utility costs, increased noise, increased use of the elevator, and few parking spots – more often than not the identification of these more practical issues was infused with denigrating moral and racial stereotyping.

The nature and degree of the hostilities were no doubt further fuelled by the spectre of the fraudulent and criminal refugee. Doubts were raised about the credibility of Somali claims to refugee status. For many of the non-Somali residents, the Somali residents of Dixon did not fit the dominant construction of the genuine and deserving victim. They did not appear to be grateful to Canada and Canadians for their generous protection. They were "aggressive" and "difficult" rather than compliant. They were wealthier than refugees should be, and, to make matters worse, they "milk the system" by collecting welfare. One respondent, harkening back to the days of "traditional" immigration, observed that "all of a sudden the fad is when refugees come they can afford cars – when I was an immigrant we had to work for many years to afford a car. As a matter of fact, since my husband died, I don't have a car. Refugees are getting free rent and free homes, we're not ... What do we do with our lives? We can't start over." A few of the non-Somali residents interviewed expressed dismay at the way in which Somalis were being represented and treated by non-Somali residents and by security. However, those who disputed the generally racist portrayal of Somalis were outnumbered by those who saw them as uncivilized and lazy.

Non-Somali residents offered a variety of "get tough" recommendations to ease the "problem" at Dixon. These solutions included tighter immigration screening procedures; increased removals ("people should be kicked out of Canada if they misbehave"); limits on the number of people allowed to live in the units; stronger enforcement of the rules; a prohibition on renting to welfare recipients ("get rid of welfare recipients"); facilitating management's access to the units (to "get proof of what's going on"); and distributing the Somali residents more thinly ("even out the population, spread the one dominant culture around so that you don't have a concentration of one group").

While a few non-Somali respondents focused on the lack of understanding and communication between Somalis and non-Somalis, Somali respondents invariably emphasized the importance of encouraging communication and cross-cultural understanding between the two groups. Many advocated holding workshops and seminars to facilitate communication and understanding. Many felt misunderstood, that their identity and experience as refugees were disbelieved, dismissed, or unknown. The vastly different conceptions held by Somali refugees and non-Somali residents of what constitutes a "problem" is emphasized here:

> Some other residents might say there is noise such as the aeroplanes, which are a problem, but when you have stresses like you have, like the problems in Somalia, you don't notice these things as much. People from Somalia had other pressures when they were living in Somalia – people dying, trying to stay alive. People don't understand how hard some of these people have it. A lot of Somali women ... now have no husband, they don't speak much English, they have five or six children. They are in a dream, a trauma. People don't understand. There is a lack of communication. Neighbours don't understand. They think that all of us want government help and want it easy. Many of us want to work and can't find day care. These women are not having it easy, and people don't understand because of language barriers and lack of communication. Not all of us are on welfare.

Finally, in July 1993, Somalis took to the streets to protest their treatment at Dixon. The events that took place and the sentiments that underpinned them cannot in any simple way be explained by overcrowding. Nor can they be reduced to mere cultural difference. The broader context of this preliminary and admittedly sketchy microstudy of Dixon must be considered – a context in which the morally despicable figure of the undeserving fraudulent refugee and the companion figures of the welfare cheat and the criminal foreigner were already well familiar.

Fanning the Flames in the Popular Print Media and the Enforcement Response
In 1995, the same allegations of misappropriation of funds by a Somali settlement agency that had prompted the 1994 RCMP investigation were made by a Somali living in Toronto. This time this allegation and others were given much more publicity than the original ones through a long feature article in the much-read *Toronto Life* magazine written by Daniel Stoffman (author of the anti-immigration report for the C.D. Howe Institute mentioned above).[70]

Stoffman begins by restating what had by then become rather commonplace and inflammatory allegations levelled at the Somali community in Toronto. In bold typeface, the article states that "many" Somalis "are cheating the welfare system" and that "some are probably war criminals." Welfare fraud is but one of the allegations pursued by Stoffman in this article. He also attends, in a manner heavily inflected by rumour and innuendo, to the criminality/fraud-related allegations of corruption and cronyism among government officials in Toronto; of shady, clan-based practices of ripping off the welfare system in order to send money back to Somali warlords; of the presence of Somali war criminals in Canada; and even of Somali consumption of *khat* (see the discussion on page 134).

Stoffman offers that "anyone with dark skin who arrives at the border or an airport without documents and claims to be fleeing Somalia is allowed to apply for the status of a Geneva Convention Refugee." In fact, individuals fleeing persecution are not "allowed" to claim refugee status; they have the "right" to do so under the *Refugee Convention* and domestic legislation. The colour of their skin is not relevant to this right. Moreover, that many do not have government-issued travel documents is hardly surprising given the circumstances of their departure and the absence of a functioning civil authority in Somalia.

Further strengthening the link between Somali refugees and criminality, Stoffman ruminates provocatively about the husband of one of the Somalis whom he interviewed. He poses a series of questions that leads the reader to think of her husband as complicit in the atrocities of the Barre government. He concludes this line of questioning by asking, "Isn't this the sort of abuse that has brought our refugee determination system into disrepute?" Stoffman here transforms what appears to be pure speculation into an allegation of abuse. Even the layout of the article makes its own contribution. It carries bright red enlarged quotations that run across the top and bottom of each page: "The real beneficiaries of the world's most open refugee determination system are the Somali criminals of war"; "Some Somalis think of all governments as the enemy. They call welfare 'shab' – meaning something for nothing."

At the close of the article, Stoffman refers to the stated wish of one of his Somali sources that the Somalis would "disappear," assimilate, adapt to the "Canadian way of life." Canadians are imagined as a homogeneous group, bound by common practices and sensibilities. Somalis are constructed as the problematic, dark-skinned, alien "other" whose practices and sensibilities are, in large part, criminal and fraudulent.

While Stoffman's article outraged many, it clearly fanned the anti-immigrant/refugee flames and provided fuel for the enforcement fire already well under way. Mohamud remembers that Stoffman's article was "very, very damaging to the Somali community and was the starting point for all that followed. It triggered everything. Even some people, some anti-immigrant groups, duplicated and distributed the article, free of charge, in front of the University Avenue Immigration offices."[71]

Shortly after the publication of Stoffman's article, the RCMP was back on the case. They contacted Peter Crosbie of the Family Services Association, an old, reputable agency acting as a trustee for Dejinta Beesha's funds. In Crosbie's judgment, Stoffman's article was a central factor in the RCMP's renewed interest in the Somali agency's financial operations. Indeed, the

RCMP specifically referred to it as well as to another "community-source" in their explanation of their visit. According to Crosbie, a member of the Somali community who was the primary source of the "community-based" information attained by the RCMP had written many letters to politicians and law enforcement authorities restating the allegations.[72] The publication of these allegations in Stoffman's article in August 1995 tweaked the RCMP into action again. However, just as in 1993, no evidence was found of any wrongdoing.

Stoffman's article claimed legitimacy by giving prominence to information derived from the community. It relied extensively on the comments and allegations of a member of the Somali community; indeed, many of Stoffman's arguments and observations were initially raised by one of several Somali voices. Thus, community-based information was the primary source of information for the article, as it had been for the 1994 RCMP investigation and as it was for the 1995 RCMP investigation that followed publication of the article. However, it appears that in all three cases the information derived from the "community" was not only the same substantive information but also likely derived in large part from the same community member.

The RCMP visits to social agencies, while bothersome, were trivial compared to state actions upon certain Somalis around the same time. Corruption and fraud were two of the allegations expressed in Stoffman's piece. War crimes and human rights violations were others. One holiday weekend in 1995, the RCMP conducted several raids on the homes of Somalis in Etobicoke who were suspected, under the 1992 amendments to the 1976 *Immigration Act,* of being "senior members of or senior officials in the service of a government that is or was, in the opinion of the Minister, engaged in terrorism, systematic or gross human rights violations or war crime or crimes against humanity."[73]

Several Somalis who had worked at Somali embassies abroad were arrested, along with some former military officers. Another who had been a chauffeur of a Somali government official was arrested, as was a woman who had been active in the campaign against female genital mutilation.[74] Some of those arrested were subsequently deported, and some left voluntarily.[75] The Canadian state was thus showing that the definition of "senior government members or officials" and the understanding of their involvement in government-sanctioned "crimes against humanity" were extremely flexible.

That the net cast by this section of the 1976 *Immigration Act* is potentially very wide is evident in Immigration Appeal Division (IAD) decisions that have reviewed deportation decisions hinging on this provision. The interpretation and constitutionality of this section remain hotly contested. The act specified that the phrase "senior members of or senior officials in the service of government" means "persons who, by virtue of the position they hold or have held, are or were able to exert a significant influence on the exercise of government power." It goes on to list seven positions that such persons would hold. They include, "without limiting its generality, "heads of state or government," "senior members of the public service," and "ambassadors and senior diplomatic officials."[76]

A central preoccupation of IAD decisions has been whether this list creates a presumption that anyone holding an official title that fits in one of the categories is automatically deemed to have exerted influence on "malevolent" government power or whether the decision must grapple with the actual degree of influence enjoyed. In legal terms, the question frequently raised is whether the above-mentioned sections are "rebuttable": that is, does the person in question have the right to present evidence that contradicts the above-mentioned presumption? Also debated is whether the list is meant to be exhaustive or whether people who held positions not included in the list could still be "caught" by the provision.

The result of these interpretive vagaries is that someone may be deported simply because he or she held one of the enumerated positions (as was held by the majority in *Canada (Minister of Citizenship and Immigration) v. Duale* [1997]); others may have their admission refusal quashed and a new inquiry ordered because, while they did hold one of these positions, their exclusion did not consider whether they *actually* exerted influence on "malevolent" government power (as was held in *Mursal v. Canada (Minister of Citizenship and Immigration)* [1997]); and yet others may be deported because, while they did not hold one of the enumerated positions, they nonetheless are found to have exerted influence on government power (as emphasized in the concurring reasons in *Canada (Minister of Citizenship and Immigration) v. Duale* [1997]).[77] This last scenario sheds light on how a chauffeur or a women's rights activist might be excluded under this provision. As explained in the concurring reasons in the 1997 *Duale* case, in a manner reminiscent of a Le Carré novel, "history is replete with examples of persons such as chauffeurs, secretaries, lovers, butlers, messengers, bodyguards, physicians, barbers and other trustees who were able to exert significant influence over dictators, and thus governments, engaged in gross human rights violations. None of them would fit within the enumerated list of (a) to (g). But in my view, they are 'persons who' ... could nonetheless be caught by the clarification of 'senior officials' set out in (1.1) by virtue of the influential positions they held."[78]

Thus, while the provision is written to apply to "senior" members of government, the fact of working for the government in any capacity can be enough to raise suspicion and trigger enforcement response. This heightens the impact of this provision on those Somalis who did not end up in refugee camps but managed to flee to Canada. Only Somali refugees with substantial resources could do so. They are generally well educated and have considerable work experience. They are also therefore refugees most likely to have occupied at least one and probably many government positions under Barre's twenty-three-year socialist rule. This provision has thus effectively criminalized most of the adult (male) Somali refugees in Canada. As observed by Mohamud,

> That piece of legislation was and still is unfair to the Somali community in Canada. It is well known that Said Barre ruled the country for twenty-three years. The government was the main employer, it was a socialist form of government, no private ownership ... so most people, when you finish university, you were placed in one of the government departments. You go from there, you work here, you work there, you become the head of the section. And since the salaries were so low, people were given some titles in order to get some extra benefit. So to become a director was nothing. People compare it to being a director or a manager in Canada, but you can't compare it ... When people came here as refugees, they told [the authorities] I was the director of that department, I was the member of the government, I did these jobs. And that was held against them. People said if you were in a decision-making position you are a war criminal. Not necessarily that you have committed any crimes against humanity, but the mere fact that you held that position excludes you, makes you a member of an inadmissible group.[79]

After the Stoffman-enhanced panic died down, so did RCMP enforcement activity in the Somali community. As observed by Mohamud, "since that sweep and the subsequent deportations, the RCMP and political interest has died down, and we haven't seen a lot of other deportations under that legislation."

Proof of Identity: Prudence or Prejudice?
In 1992, Bill C-86 effectively assured that the vast majority of Somali refugees in Canada would not be able to become permanent residents. It required that refugees provide "satisfactory" (government-issued) identity documents in order to be granted landed status (permanent residency). The legislation also sanctioned the detention of refugee claimants without official papers. Two large groups of refugees already in Canada bore the brunt of the former requirement, Somalis and Afghanis.

The denial of permanent residency status is a severe blow to those already displaced and disempowered. Without it, refugees who have been found to be "genuine" cannot travel outside Canada, sponsor relatives, or attend university. They are ineligible for many jobs and training programs and cannot obtain a bank loan. The inability to sponsor family members is a particularly painful consequence for many Somalis who had to leave behind close family members when they fled their country.

The anger and frustration felt by Somalis left in legal limbo by this legislation was further heightened by the fact that, just as Bill C-86 took effect, the federal government had taken measures to facilitate the acceptance of 26,000 refugees from the former Yugoslavia. No such measures had been initiated to help Somali refugees, and, if implemented, the safe third country provision would have precisely the opposite effect because of the limited number of direct flights to Canada from Africa, Asia, and Central and South America.

The official response to criticisms of the unequal treatment of different groups of refugees served to further malign and anger Somalis. Bernard Valcourt, then minister of immigration, explained that the Somalis' situation was less compelling because they were "nomads" who didn't want to come to Canada anyway. This remark sparked a protest at Queen's Park in Toronto by Somalis angry at this dismissive official response to their difficult circumstances,[80] As has been noted, the representation of Somalis as nomads was neither isolated nor incidental.

The differential impact of this requirement on Somali refugees was officially acknowledged in 1997 when the government announced measures to deal with undocumented refugees. The minister acknowledged that many refugees from Somalia and Afghanistan "have been unable to obtain proper documentation due to sustained civil war and lack of an effective government authority to issue identity documents."[81] In response to this situation, the government introduced the Undocumented Convention Refugees in Canada Class (UCRCC), which would allow *Convention* refugees from specified countries to become permanent residents five years after a positive refugee board decision.[82]

Many then argued that the waiting period was unfair given that many of the refugees had already waited up to three years to have their claims heard, but the government was not persuaded. The persuasiveness of the humanitarian argument was eclipsed by law and order concerns, by concerns about crime-security and fraud, and by corollary notions of deservedness. The minister's justification for imposing the five-year waiting period is quoted here at length:

I have carefully reviewed all the comments received during the prepublication period. I understand and share the humanitarian concerns expressed by certain organizations, which argued that we should find a more generous solution to the difficult situation that Somali and Afghan refugees are experiencing in Canada. I certainly would respond differently if my only concern was the specific circumstances of the affected communities. As the Minister responsible for immigration to Canada, I must ensure that every effort is made to discern the background and character of applicants for permanent residence. At the same time, the asylum system must not be abused by those who may choose to conceal their identity as Canada continues to be generous to those who really deserve protection.[83]

A year later the minister made the same point even more explicitly: "Because they have no ID, we will not grant these people permanent resident status until they have had time to demonstrate respect for the laws of Canada and for us to detect those who may be guilty of crimes against humanity or acts of terrorism ... The message is clear – fraud will not be tolerated."[84]

In this instance, the crime-security nexus and the spectre of fraud converged and were mobilized in direct opposition to humanitarian concerns. Moreover, this discursive convergence legitimized the use of various coercive and invasive means to "contain the threat." So, for example, in addition to the rather punitive consequences facing Somalis without identity documents who must wait years for family reunification, they may also have to go through expensive DNA testing to prove their family relationships.

Despite the forceful rhetoric that had justified the five-year waiting period, in 1999 the new federal minister of immigration, Elinor Caplan, quietly announced the reduction of the waiting period for application for permanent residence from five years to three years for undocumented *Convention* refugees.[85]

As mentioned earlier, the method of "detection" employed by authorities relies in a central way upon community-based information. As explained by Brian Grant, acting director general of CIC in 1998, this is an important dimension of enforcement practices particularly when identity is an issue:

> We have tried to build flexibility into the system, precisely because you often don't know who they are. They don't have a document. They've come from outside North America so you don't have linkages. The police system may not be reputable in the country they've come from. They will gravitate towards their community and often what happens is that people in the community might recognize them and come forward. You'll often get tip-offs like oh, so-and-so, we know him and he was involved in this. That will often give us the lead we need to follow up on security threats or perhaps criminality.[86]

While community-based information is treated seriously by authorities in the context of enforcement activities, to the degree that it may justify extreme coercive responses, when community-based information is offered as a way of confirming identity for the purpose of obtaining permanent residency, authorities are less willing to act on it. In 1996, prior to the announcement of the five-year waiting period, members of the Somali community announced a legal challenge of the identity document requirement on the ground that it discriminates against their community by requiring "satis-factory identity documents" when none is available. Representatives of the Somali community suggested that, in the absence of documents, and given the relative impossibility of acquiring them, the community's "elders and clergy would verify the authenticity of the claims." They stressed that they share "the federal government's concern that sworn affidavits could be abused to allow criminals and imposters to enter the country" and that Somalis "have no desire to live alongside law-breakers." As evidence of their identity as good self-governing citizens and of their credibility, they ob-served that "the community has already identified 6 members of the former Said Barre regime to the RCMP and CSIS."[87] The reluctance of immigration authorities to give credence to community-based information that favours the refugee claimant stands in stark contrast to their willingness to act upon similarly identity-related community-based information when that infor-mation implies an enforcement response.

On 14 December 2000, Judge Hugessen of the Federal Court of Canada Trial Division issued the "Aden Order."[88] This order responded to the allega-tions of discrimination made by members of the Somali community regard-ing the identity document requirement. The Aden Order provided that, if *Convention* refugees applying for landing are unable to obtain a "satisfac-tory identity document," they may instead provide a sworn declaration at-testing to their identities in addition to either a sworn declaration from "a Canadian citizen, permanent resident, or any other person deemed accept-able in the discretion of the officer" attesting to their identities or "a sworn declaration attesting to the applicant's identity from an official belonging to a credible organization representing nationals of the applicant's country of origin."[89]

In 2002, the House of Commons Standing Committee on Citizenship and Immigration heard submissions on the proposed *IRPA* regulations. In making their arguments for the elimination of the UCRCC, a number of advocacy groups cited the findings of a 2001 assessment of the UCRCC program commissioned by the CIC. Of particular note were its findings that the forcefully stated fraud- and crime-security-based concerns offered by the government as justification for the waiting period had not been borne out: "The delayed landings in the UCRCC program have not revealed any legitimate security or criminality concerns among the persons affected."[90] Critics noted further that the assessment found that only one person in the UCRCC program had in fact been denied landing for reasons of criminality and that the waiting period was really just "passive" time that did "little more than impose additional bureaucratic obstacles on a small section of the Convention Refugee population."[91] After six years of operation, the UCRCC was eliminated, and *IRPA* now allows *Convention* refugees applying for landing to submit sworn declarations attesting to their identities.[92]

The Criminalization of *Khat*

There is one final entry in this constitutional tale. The fact that so many Somali refugees in Canada have been living in legal limbo with no affirmed or protected citizenship status also makes them particularly vulnerable to deportation for reasons of criminality. This reality was further entrenched in 1997 when the Canadian government criminalized the plant *khat* under the new *Controlled Drug and Substances Act (CDSA)*.[93] The *CDSA* was an enforcement-oriented and prohibitionist piece of legislation.[94] It consolidated Canadian drug policy in accordance with international obligations. It repealed the *Narcotic Control Act* and parts 3 and 4 of the *Food and Drugs Act*.[95] The inclusion of *khat* under schedules 3 and 4 of the *CDSA* was justified because it contains cathinone, a "psychoactive ingredient" and sometimes d-amphetamine.[96]

Khat is a plant with stimulant properties that is grown in East Africa and the Arabian peninsula and known to be popular with some members of the Somali community. Chewing *khat* has long occupied a central place in the cultural tradition of male Somalis (a fact duly noted in Stoffman's 1995 article). *Khat* has traditionally been used socially, much like coffee in Western culture. While Ali Mohamud concedes that it may be the cause of some "family conflict" due to its gendered consumption, he notes that the degree of conflict associated with *khat* does not compare with that of alcohol. For example, "if you eat some, you might want to eat some more ... but it doesn't make you want to kill or fight; it's a harmless pastime."[97] Farah Khayre, of Midaynta (Association of Somali Service Agencies), describes *khat* as a mild stimulant consumed in social environments, comparable to coffee.[98]

The American inclusion of cathinone as a schedule 1 narcotic (the most restricted category), alongside heroin and marijuana, took place soon after the posting of US marines in Somalia as a peacekeeping force in the early 1990s. The United States subsequently placed *khat* on its list of proscribed substances and urged other governments to do the same. [99]

Canada followed the American lead. Prior to 1997, the use of *khat* was legal in Canada. It was regulated as an "alien plant" by the Canadian Food and Drug Inspection Agency and could be seized by Canada Customs at the border. However, *khat* had become the focus of enforcement activity before 1997. In 1995, in the midst of the panic surrounding Somali refugees in Canada, Canada Customs had stepped up its enforcement of *khat*-related import violations.[100]

The *CDSA* creates six major offences: possession, trafficking, cultivation, import, export, and prescription shopping. Since 1997, possessing, importing, and trafficking *khat* is a hybrid offence that may be processed summarily or by indictment. If possession is dealt with as a summary offence, the punishment is up to six months in prison and a $1,000 fine for the first offence and twelve months in prison and a $2,000 fine for subsequent offences. If the approach is indictment, the maximum punishment is three years in prison.[101]

The consequences of a conviction for possession of *khat* for an individual who does not have permanent residency status in Canada are potentially extremely serious. At that time, under section 4(2.1) of the 1976 *Immigration Act,* a person found to be a *Convention* refugee loses his or her right to remain in Canada if convicted of an offence under any act of Parliament for which a term of imprisonment of more than six months has been imposed or five years or more may be imposed. For Somalis in Canada without secure citizenship status, a conviction for the possession of *khat* has the real potential to trigger deportation.

Another significant dimension of the *CDSA* is its strongly "prohibitionist" orientation and resultant emphasis on enforcement. The *CDSA* sanctioned increased enforcement powers for those engaged in the "war against drugs." Among other provisions, the act extended the powers of search and seizure. In the 1995 Legal and Constitutional Affairs Standing Committee Hearings on the bill that created the *CDSA* (Bill C-8), Robert Kellerman, a member of the Law Union of Ontario, forcefully criticized the enforcement orientation of the bill from a legal, rights-based perspective. Kellerman argued that the enforcement of drug laws has resulted in the court-sanctioned "erosion of many of our civil liberties," despite the protection of privacy rights afforded by the *Charter.* He noted that "an overwhelming number of searches take place under our drug laws."[102]

The clauses dealing with seizure or forfeiture of property under the act are broad. As observed by Kellerman, "this clause has the danger [that] ... property could be taken away from people who are totally innocent." He explained that "the idea is that the property of drug dealers can be seized. Yet it is so broadly defined that it includes even the seizing of property for the simple offence of possession of marijuana."[103]

Since Somalis make up the vast majority of *khat* consumers in Canada, the consequences of criminalization were limited for the most part to them. And the consequences were severe, involving the mobilization and application of both criminal justice and immigration enforcement systems and sanctions. Soon after the criminalization of *khat,* in the spring of 1998, the police carried out numerous raids on Somali residences on the grounds of suspected *khat*-related offences. Armed with their newly increased powers of search and seizure, officers did both. They confiscated substantial amounts of gold and jewellery without providing receipts, and according to reports they also damaged other items of Somalis' property in the course of the raids: "Police from York Region came to Dixon Road, invaded people's homes, confiscated jewellery and money without explaining anything, in the name of drugs, in the name of *khat. Khat* is a tradition that Somalis chew, and they made it one of the controlled substances. They know that Somalis chew *khat*. And you cannot equate *khat* with other narcotics. So it was one way of criminalizing Somalis."[104]

According to members of the Somali community, the police engaged in unprofessional and downright nasty conduct during these raids: "They wore trench coats, and they had their pistols, and they would come into our homes and destroy everything – break personal property and destroy computers, break everything."[105]

What is both particularly troubling and revealing is that there had been no prior effort to communicate the changes in the law and in enforcement priorities to the Somali community. In a background paper prepared for Senator Pierre Claude Nolin's June 1999 motion to have Canada's Senate conduct a thorough review of Canadian drug law and policy, Diane Riley of the Canadian Foundation for Drug Policy made specific mention of this rather shocking fact. Riley observed that the inclusion of new drug offences under the *CDSA* ensures "that more Canadians than ever ... would be burdened with a criminal record for simple possession (this is already occurring with respect to *khat,* especially among the Somali community who were not even informed of the criminalization of activities related to a previously legal substance)."[106] According to Farah Khayre of Midaynta, "[the law] was passed quietly, not even fully debated in Parliament, no community information was sought, and no outreach to the community for information about this law was made. We just started getting these calls from people who had been arrested or their homes broken into. The wake up call was these calls from our clients."[107]

Kellerman's predictions about the abuses associated with the strict enforcement of drug laws appear to have been accurate. According to reports, homes were searched and property seized of Somalis who had never even used *khat,* let alone sold it.[108] Outraged once again, the Somali community organized a large community meeting to decide how to respond to the criminalization of *khat* and the severe enforcement response that had been executed in the Somali community. Members of the Somali community began preparing to challenge the law in the courts and in the meantime asked police to put an end to the raids of Somali homes.[109]

The perception among the Somali community is that a conviction for *khat* means "that's the end of it, you are gone": "Hundreds and hundreds of Somalis have been wrongfully convicted of drug charges and other minor things, and they were refused to be landed for the reason of criminality."[110] Indeed, even in the absence of actual criminal convictions, the prohibition of *khat* certainly served to further criminalize the Somali community.

These consequences had been anticipated; the government had been warned. During the course of the Standing Committee on Legal and Constitutional Affairs hearings on Bill C-8 (*CDSA*), the consequences of criminalizing *khat* were raised as a particular concern. Perry Kendall, president and CEO of the Addiction Research Foundation (ARF), warned strenuously of the dangers of criminalizing drugs and intensifying enforcement. From a public health harm reduction perspective, Kendall observed that criminalization and tough enforcement have been associated with the magnification of the potential health harms posed by certain substances and that this was a pattern that the criminalization of *khat* could provoke: "We are concerned that, in a tiny way, the same pattern could happen to *khat*, a drug which in plant form is popular in East Africa and the Arabian peninsula and is used by a considerable percentage of some immigrant groups in Canada. Criminalizing this drug as this bill would – and the drug is currently only available in the form of a vegetable – could have the unintentional consequence of encouraging sellers and markets to refine it into a more potent powder whose effects would be potentially more severe than the current use of the vegetable."[111]

Arguably, this "public harm" argument against criminalization held out the most promise to be persuasive in the enforcement-oriented, prohibitionist context of the bill. However, Kendall also raised concerns relating to the discriminatory and inequitable enforcement of drug laws in general and of the criminalization of *khat* in particular: "We are concerned that prohibiting *khat* would create a new form of a dangerous drug and criminalize a whole community in this country."[112]

The warnings were not heeded. The concerns raised regarding the consequences of the criminalization of *khat* were well founded. After it was criminalized, the cost of *khat* rose dramatically: "The effect was immediate and the price went through the roof. The street price of marduuf, a handful-sized bundle of khat, enough for one person to consume for one session, shot from as little as $45 to as much as $80."[113] The criminalization of *khat* effectively did criminalize an entire community, bringing in tow rather dire consequences for Somalis, including police raids, searches, seizures, arrests, and removals. It also had wider implications, as observed by Eugene Oscapella of the Ontario Bar Association:

> The war on drugs allows us to dress our racism and xenophobia in less obvious trappings. In North America, our early drug laws were to a significant degree premised on the vilification of immigrants and people whose skin colour or ethnic culture did not make the grade ... This [still happens]. Canada for example, in 1996, criminalized a stimulant called *"Khat." Khat* is a substance used by some people of African origin. It is not used by white Canadians of European descent to any appreciable extent, if at all ... Why prohibit these recent immigrants to Canada, these people of another culture, another skin colour and another continent – from using a substance that has long been part of their lives?[114]

In the 1990s, the presumption took hold that, rather than being genuinely at risk and truly deserving, refugees who make their claims in Canada are risky – likely fraudulent, unscrupulous, and dangerous opportunists, even criminals. Whereas the undesirable, undeserving other of the past was excluded through the mobilization of explicitly moralistic and racist discourses of national purity or through the justification of national security understood in more narrow, ideological terms, the contemporary undesirable, undeserving foreigner is excluded through the mobilization of the logic of fraud in the merged contexts of refugee determination and welfare provision and by its articulation with increasingly prominent law and order discourses that have entailed effects extending well beyond the criminal courts. The contemporary understanding of national security now encompasses not only the traditional "political" threats posed by subversion and espionage but also, and much more prominently, international terrorism, organized crime, and serious criminals who pose a threat to public safety.

This chapter demonstrates the importance of challenging the traditional academic and policy boundaries that define the domains of immigration, welfare, and crime and details how government as well as populist discourses and actions have crossed these lines in interesting and often dangerous ways. The crime-security nexus, particularly when articulated with the spectre of "welfare fraud," has been used to govern immigration penality in new ways. And "crime" is not a single entity; the violent crime attributed to Jamaican immigrants to Toronto differs markedly, discursively, from the alleged devious activities of Somali "war criminals" and their Canadian supporters. In turn, the spectre of the "dark" alien, so familiar in Canadian immigration history, has had an impact on both the field of criminal justice and the field of welfare provision. These dimensions are not readily apparent from the point of view of official law and policy, and, as this chapter demonstrates, they are not merely abstract but entail concrete, often dire, consequences for those subject to their operations.

7
Discretion, Dangerousness, and National Security

Under the emergent neoliberal regimes of government of the late 1980s and 1990s, law and order programs and discourses of crime merged with those relating to fraud, and concerns about criminal threats were steadily redefined and expanded as threats to "national security." Concurrently, the dominant understanding of national security was itself extended and modified to encompass various forms of criminality. Thus, while criminality and security have each long been exclusionary immigration categories, in the 1990s crime-security emerged as *the* dominant governing rationale for exclusionary Canadian immigration law and policy.

I begin this chapter by returning to the question of discretion and its relation to immigration enforcement, followed by a more detailed discussion of the legal construction and regulation of the "criminal foreigner" through a major and tough piece of legislation, Bill C-44, in 1995.[1] The "danger to the public" provision of this act entailed the broad extension of ministerial discretion to exclude those deemed dangerous by the minister. This reform can be read as a major manifestation of the powerful transition in the governance of immigration penality that has redefined, expanded, and merged criminality and security concerns and has brought both to the fore. I then turn to the laws and policies that govern the deportation of those deemed to be national security threats in relation to Canada's international obligations to refugees. I close the chapter with an examination of the 2002 Supreme Court of Canada *Suresh* judgment, which dealt with these issues, paying particular attention to the centrality of guiding liberal legal oppositions: law/discretion, freedom/security, and liberty/authority.

Discretion is most helpfully regarded, as argued at length in Chapter 3, as a productive activity rather than a residual and latent "space." The context of discretionary power must be taken seriously. Shaped and inflected by the operation of dominant discourses, the exercise of discretionary power under a liberal regime is a central technology in the normative project that constitutes national borders, national identities, and historically specific versions of citizenship and citizens. As already demonstrated, in the context of the policies and practices of immigration penalty, these representations have come to be framed primarily by crime-security, fraud, and victim discourses.

In Western liberal regimes, if discretion is seen to be employed unfairly or unjustly, the problem is attributed to inadequate legal constraints leading to "arbitrariness" and the undermining of procedural fairness and objectivity. Conversely, if law is seen to be too blunt, too general, and unforgiving of individual circumstances, then this problem is mitigated by reference to discretion and the expertise of authorities. Rather than accepting the liberal representation of law/discretion (or freedom/security or liberty/authority) as zero-sum oppositions, law and discretion are here understood as mutually constitutive, intersecting technologies of regulation. The following discussion will highlight their roles in relation to the production and enforcement of "dangers to the public" and "national security threats."

The "Just Desserts" Bill

In April 1994, Georgina Leimonis, a twenty-two-year-old white woman, was shot and killed in Just Desserts, a small café in an affluent neighbourhood in downtown Toronto. Four black men, Lawrence Brown, Gary Francis, O'Neil Grant, and Mark Jones, were charged with her killing. The massive and sensationalist media coverage of this event tended to gloss over the fact that the men had come to Canada as children and that one of them, Mark Jones, was actually born in Trinidad – not Jamaica.[2] In July of the same year, Constable Todd Baylis (also white) was shot and killed by black, Jamaican-born Clinton Gayle, under warrant for deportation at the time of the killing.

These murders, coupled with already heightened tensions between the black community and the police, triggered a massive public panic around the issues of race, crime, and immigration, a panic that the government seized upon and responded to swiftly and on several different fronts. Bill C-44 was first tabled on 15 June 1994 and was passed into law in July 1995. The bill introduced the danger to the public provision (section 70[5]), which sanctioned deportation without appeal of any noncitizen deemed by the minister of citizenship and immigration to represent a danger to the public – even those who are permanent residents or *Convention* refugees and regardless of how long they have resided in Canada. This provision was one of a number of enforcement-oriented measures included in the bill that were designed to facilitate and expedite deportations.[3]

Shortly after Bill C-44 was tabled, on 7 July 1994, Sergio Marchi, minister of citizenship and immigration, announced "Criminals First," a reorientation of Canada's detention and deportation priorities. Soon after, he also announced the creation of the Joint Immigration-RCMP Task Force to assist, among other responsibilities, in tracking down and arresting noncitizens with criminal records wanted for removal. Also in 1994, CIC announced the creation of an Organized Crime Section. Bill C-44 was thus the first of a flurry of government initiatives following the Just Desserts murder that aimed to get tough on "criminal immigrants" – hence its informal reference as the "Just Desserts Bill."

The danger to the public provision provides a powerful example of the guiding influence of the logic of criminality in the governance of immigration enforcement, of the relative dominance of crime-security discourses vis-à-vis those concerning human rights and refugees, of the ways in which discretion works to facilitate the translation of dominant social concerns into exclusionary immigration law and policy, and of discretion's multiple effects vis-à-vis legitimizing and sustaining the coercions of sovereign power under a liberal legal regime.

The strength of the linkage between immigration and criminality evidenced by Bill C-44 must be understood in its historical context. Previously accepted grounds for immigration exclusion had long been delegitimized. Fears about racialized crime, about fraudulent claimants, and about immigration numbers had already become intertwined, and the crime-security nexus and the focus on public safety had been in place long before the murderous events of 1994. Moreover, the force of this preoccupation with getting tough on "criminal foreigners" coincides with a more general contemporary law and order climate evident in many areas of public policy. As nicely put by Carolyn Strange, "in the 1990s, 'get tough' politics have become everyday politics as crime and justice receive unprecedented levels of media coverage. Popular calls for draconian measures against criminals fuel a climate of punitiveness that politicians find irresistible for fear of appearing soft on crime."[4]

As documented in Chapters 5 and 6, the conceptual slippage between criminals, refugees, and "foreigners" more generally is more pronounced today than it has ever been. While the association between criminality and immigration enforcement is not in and of itself a new development, the emergence of crime-security as *the* guiding rationale in the governance of exclusionary immigration laws, policies, and practices is historically unprecedented. Understood in this wider context, Bill C-44, while extreme and troubling, was not surprising. And it did trouble a lot of people. Criticism tended to focus on the radical extension of ministerial discretion sanctioned by section 70(5), the impact of the provision on permanent residents and refugees, as well as the particular impact on Caribbean-born men, especially those born in Jamaica.[5] This provision was eliminated in 2002 under *IRPA*, which continues the zero-sum game by replacing the discretionary dimensions of assessing dangerousness under section 70(5) with the "certainty" of strict legal criteria for the determination of "serious criminality." Under *IRPA*, inadmissibility for the reason of criminality is determined if there has been a conviction in Canada for an offence punishable by a term of at least ten years or for an offence for which a term of more than six months has been imposed.[6] The right of permanent residents or "foreign nationals" to appeal a finding of inadmissibility for the reason of serious criminality is denied if there has been a conviction in Canada for a crime that was punished in Canada by a term of imprisonment of at least two years. No ministerial opinion is now required.[7]

Section 70(5) removed the right of a permanent resident to appeal a deportation order to the Immigration Appeal Division (IAD) in cases where the individual had been convicted of a crime for which the maximum available penalty is ten years or more and who had been deemed by the minister or a delegate to represent a danger to the public. This provision had applied to anyone without the protections afforded by full citizenship, including, as noted, permanent residents and those who had been granted refugee status in Canada but who had not yet become citizens. With the enactment of this bill, those deemed a danger to the public joined those judged to be a threat to the national security as the two groups denied access to the usual deportation appeals process.

The text of the provision relating to the power to deport on grounds of danger to the public read as follows: "No appeal may be made to the Appeal Division by a person described in subsection (1) or paragraph 2(a) or (b) against whom a deportation order or conditional deportation order is made where the Minister is of the opinion that the person constitutes a danger to the public in Canada and the person has been determined by an adjudicator to be (c) a person described in paragraph 27 (1)(d) who has been convicted of an offence under any Act of Parliament for which a term of imprisonment of ten years or more *may* be imposed."[8]

The range of offences covered under this provision was thus very wide, including many nonviolent crimes such as obtaining credit by false pretence, forgery, cattle theft, and trafficking in small amounts of marijuana or other narcotics. Writing in 1996, Arthur Weinreb and Rocco Galati observed that the minister was applying a very wide definition of dangerousness: "Persons who have been convicted of trafficking in small quantities of crack have been found to constitute a danger where there has been no evidence of violence or weapons. Presumably the rationale is that since crack is a dangerous drug, persons who sell it are dangerous."[9] The wording of this provision also allowed a person to be declared a danger to the public even if he or she had actually received a much lighter sentence than the ten years or more. Furthermore, many offences in Canada carry a very wide spread of possible punishments. For example, a conviction for the offence of breaking and entering may result in a sentence ranging from an absolute discharge to life imprisonment. And police routinely overcharge suspects in order to provide more leverage in plea bargains. The use of conviction and sentencing criteria for determining whether someone is a danger to the public is thus an unreliable measure of dangerousness, an unreliability increased by a range of other factors, such as differential enforcement practices and disparities in sentencing.

Policy guidelines set out the likely profile of individuals deemed to be a danger to the public: those who, "as a result of their actions, have caused or might reasonably be expected to have caused death or serious physical or psychological harm to persons and/or significant damage to property. For example, this would normally apply to persons whose offences include violence, narcotics trafficking, sexual abuse, or the use of weapons." In making their determinations of danger, the minister's delegates were advised that "it cannot be emphasized too strongly that it is not simply the commission of an offence that brings into play danger to the public processing."[10] The following factors were therefore also to be considered:

1   The nature of the offence: Did the offence in question involve violence, weapons, or drugs? Was it a "sexual" offence?
2   The circumstances of the offence, its severity, and what led to its commission.
3   The sentence given, as a measure of the severity of the offence.
4   Recidivism: Multiple offences given more weight than single offences.
5   Humanitarian and compassionate considerations.[11]

These guidelines resemble those that guide the release decisions of immigration adjudicators in detention reviews. In deciding whether an individual represents a danger to the public and should therefore remain in detention, adjudicators are similarly advised to give weight to the seriousness of the offences committed and the likelihood of the individual reoffending.[12] Despite this similarity, while adjudicators reviewing detentions regularly form "danger opinions," a decision by an adjudicator that a person should not be released because he or she is likely to pose a danger to the public did not mean that the minister or delegates would also judge the person to pose a danger to the public under section 70(5). Conversely, and more provocatively, a person released from detention because he or she was found not to represent a danger to the public could still have been deported without appeal because the minister did detect a danger to the public. As observed in the 1998 *Guidelines on Detention*, "the Minister's opinion to the effect that a person constitutes a danger to the public is not binding on an adjudicator. The latter's decision must be based on the adjudicator's own analysis and assessment of facts of the case. Therefore, it is possible that an adjudicator could order a person's release from detention although the Minister has issued a 'danger to the public' opinion."[13] Thus, the same person may be deemed to be both a danger to the public and not a danger to the public and may accordingly be ordered both released from detention and deported.

Beyond these policy guidelines, no legally defined standards guide either of these decisions about danger. And, short of an application for leave to appeal to the Federal Court, there were no meaningful procedural safeguards in place. This relative absence of legal standards and safeguards contrasts with the dangerous and long-term offender provisions of the *Criminal Code of Canada (CCC)*, another site on which risk assessments and predictions of dangerousness take place with punitive and coercive consequences.[14] In 1997, the federal government introduced Bill C-55 as part of its stated commitment to crack down on high-risk offenders to enhance public safety.[15] Even with these "get tough" reforms of 1997, the dangerous offender and long-term offender provisions in the *CCC,* unlike the danger to the public provision of section 70(5) of the former *Immigration Act,* at least attempt to provide some guidance on the kind of wrong, the nature and level of apprehended harm, and the magnitude of risk under consideration.[16] The *CCC* provisions detail the requirements relating to the hearing at which the offender is present, expert testimony, criteria that relate to the timing of the application in relation to sentencing, and the right to appeal.[17] In contrast, the only remedial option available to a person deemed a danger to the public under section 70(5) was the much more limited right to *apply* for leave of the Federal Court for judicial review. And, as will be discussed, if granted, this review was confined in scope to errors of law or capricious findings of fact.

As noted in Chapter 1, the move from "dangerousness" to "risk" displaces the individual subject and substitutes whatever characteristics have been identified by the specialists as risk factors.[18] Both the danger to the public provision of the 1976 *Immigration Act* and the dangerous offender provisions of the *CCC* rest upon the widely contested assumption that risk as a "present and future danger" can be predicted with a certain measure of reliability based on the consideration of certain risk factors.[19] However, predictions of dangerousness are notoriously difficult to make, and, even where actuarial risk prediction tools and clinical expertise are employed, there are still high rates of error (false negatives and false positives), as research on parole and preventative detention decision making has confirmed.[20] Nonetheless, under section 70(5), immigration officials with no particular expertise in risk prediction and with the relatively meagre guidance of policy guidelines, regularly made risk-based decisions that entailed dire consequences for those deemed a danger to the public. Furthermore, the "actuarial" nature of risk-prediction tools in the context of criminal justice punishment has itself been questioned by insights regarding the moral content and assumptions of these tools and their conflation of risks and needs.[21]

Indeed, even the actuarialism of insurance practices has been revealed to be much more limited than has been widely assumed.[22]

In addition to the definitional vagueness of the provisions and the absence of procedural safeguards, the discriminatory effects of section 70(5) have been the subject of considerable attention. It has been argued in several cases that this section "breaches s. 15 of the *Canadian Charter of Rights and Freedoms* by creating an unreasonable risk that members of vulnerable groups will be the victims of discrimination by government officials."[23] The "danger opinion" is intimately linked, both in definition and in application, with criminal justice definitions, decisions, and enforcement practices. Studies have repeatedly confirmed the presence of systemic and individual forms of racism and other kinds of discrimination in the administration of justice.[24] For example, in 1995 the Commission on Systemic Racism in the Ontario Criminal Justice System found that blacks are far more likely to be stopped, charged, and imprisoned than whites, a finding confirmed by criminologists.[25] In 2002, a study of Metropolitan Toronto Police arrest data carried out by the *Toronto Star* confirmed again that blacks are treated more harshly by police than whites.[26] In 2003, the Ontario Human Rights Commission released its detailed report on the human costs of racial profiling.[27]

This reality means that the danger to the public provision, resting as it did on the policing and enforcement practices of the criminal justice system, necessarily applied and enforced the individual and systemic racism that traverses that system. This situation is not addressed by *IRPA* provisions relating to "serious criminality" since the decision to exclude continues to rest upon criminal justice enforcement and sentencing practices. Male members of the Jamaican community and blacks continue to be particularly vulnerable to being deemed a danger to the public and as such deported without appeal. Part of this vulnerability stems from the fact that many members of the Jamaican community have not, for a variety of reasons, applied for and received Canadian citizenship (the $200 fee for adults and the $100 fee for children are likely factors here). Other reasons include the racism that has historically inflected Canadian immigration law and policy, the widely discretionary nature of the provision, the racism that is an endemic feature of the administration of criminal justice, and the fact that it was Jamaicans who were associated with the Baylis and Leimonis killings, which led to a racist backlash and precipitated this reform.[28]

The Corruption of Discretion as a Quality of Mercy

The passage of Bill C-44 sparked immediate outrage among community advocates and lawyers working on behalf of new immigrants and refugees. Scholarly critiques of the legislation were also produced. Many regarded this bill as yet another instance of the hardening of hearts regarding immigrants and refugees giving expression to the welfarist/humanitarian liberal view of discretion. As shrewdly observed by eminent Canadian scientist and social activist, Ursula Franklin,

> Discretion has shifted from being a humanitarian quality of mercy directive to being a license to think the worst. Discretion was initially intended to mitigate, to allow the context of an individual case to be of benefit to the recipient, whereas now discretion protects the decision maker's "freedom to choose"; it is today an option that can protect officials from critical questions and accountability. Whereas discretion used to be founded upon an intent to "help," it now justifies doubly harsh decisions. Discretion used to imply "if in doubt, assume the best," and now it means "if in doubt, assume the worst case scenario and act accordingly." This is not the meaning of discretion. The new *Immigration Act* [at the time still in the works in Canada] ought to specify that discretionary power should be used to mitigate.[29]

In this view, discretion is an essentially inclusionary, humanitarian, and desirable quality of mercy. It is represented in its "essence" as a buffer between the universality of law and individualized equity. Its inherent benevolence has been corrupted, and discretionary processes have been hijacked in the name of "getting tough." While certainly discretion provides a protective shield against legal and political scrutiny, historical examples alongside more recent amendments such as Bill C-44 surely exemplify that discretion cannot be said to have any *essential* quality. The idea that the original, "real" meaning of discretion is benevolent and compassionate ignores its multiple and contrary effects. For the sovereign in feudal times, discretion may have been a quality of mercy, but this quality was not linked with humanitarian ideals or notions of equity. The ability to suspend the rule and the capacity to withhold punishment were tied to the display and maintenance of the power of the sovereign. Also, as demonstrated in Chapter 4, the increasing discursive dominance of humanitarian and legal discourses in the postwar period did provide a rationale for a series of significant changes to immigration and refugee law and policy in the 1960s and 1970s. However, even in the context of those decades, humanitarian and legal discourses did not displace or supplant exclusionary ones, nor indeed could they. The guiding concern to protect genuine refugees coexists with, shapes, and is itself shaped by the concern to exclude frauds, criminals, and security threats. Discretion is a central technology of both projects. To regard discretion as essentially inclusionary, humanitarian, and compassionate denies the mutually constitutive relations of inclusions and exclusions, of discretion and law, and obscures the view of discretion as a technology that can be used to achieve diverse governmental objectives with a variety of effects.

"Unfettered" Ministerial Discretion and the Rule of Law

Whereas the humanitarian view regards discretion in terms of compassion, mercy, and equity, the more strictly legal view locates it in a dichotomous relation with law. In this view, as discussed at length in Chapter 3, discretion is a problem only when it is inadequately constrained and guided by legal or legalistic rules to the extent that it threatens the rule of law, procedural fairness, and individual rights. The legal critique of section 70(5) demonstrates the primacy of the legal paradigm and its constituent ideals: "Procedurally, the *Bill C-44* regime provides neither coherent discretionary structure nor adequate checking. There is no notice. There is no hearing of any kind (in fact, the point of the exercise is exactly the opposite – to remove the chance of a hearing) ... At no stage is there a requirement to consult with another executive member ... It is, in its lack of explicative detail and absence of any kind of external involvement in making the decision, much more an exercise in *absolute discretion* ... Ultimately, the process *is pure discretion with no objectifying factors.*"[30] In this view, unchecked discretion is a problem in that it introduces the possibility of disparity, personal prejudice, and political interference in decision making, thereby resulting in arbitrariness. As put by the CBA, "political determinations are unpredictable, inconsistent and risky. Accessibility to the Minister and the Minister's delegate, for all parties involved, may become a significant and unfair factor."[31] Unchecked discretion offends legal principles, most obviously those relating to the rule of law and individual rights. The solution required is more law or lawlike rules.

In this view, the role of the Immigration Appeal Board (IAB) is one of ensuring an appropriate "balance" between public safety and national security, the protection of the legal rights of those subject to negative sponsorship decisions and deportation orders, as well as the assurance that those refugees truly in need of humanitarian protection receive it. Discretion is firmly linked to law in oppositional relation; decision making is a balancing game between rights and risks, freedom and security, law and discretion. Richard Haigh and Jim Smith argue, for example, that the IAB was always concerned to structure and guide its discretion in such a way as to take cognizance of the legal rights of the individual without jeopardizing the state's interest in ensuring public safety. As noted in a 1970 decision of the IAB that expresses a view of Canadian immigration policy at odds with conventional myths, discretion "was not intended [by Parliament] to be applied so widely as to destroy the essentially exclusionary nature of the Immigration Act and its Regulations."[32] In this view, the board was much more likely than the minister to make these exclusionary decisions in accordance with the principles of fundamental justice and fairness free of political interference.[33]

There is a guiding belief in the ability of a system, adequately regulated by law or lawlike rules, to make fair decisions. The CBA echoed these concerns in its 1994 submission on Bill C-44. It was troubled by the fact that "almost every provision of the Bill seeks to diminish the existing rights of individuals within the purview of the *Immigration Act* or regulations." It criticized the procedural dimensions of the ministerial opinion on danger, noting that "removal decisions as rendered by an immigration official rather than an independent tribunal, even on the basis of Ministerial guidelines, may suffer from lack of procedural formality, sufficiency of evidence, inconsistency, and absence of accountability."[34]

Discretion, Exclusion, and Racism
In contrast to both the humanitarian and the legal view, a more radical critique of section 70(5) alleges that it has essentially racist dimensions and applications. Ministerial discretion in this view is regarded as an "instrument of," or less deterministically as a "vehicle for," state-sanctioned racism in immigration exclusions. The sweeping, largely "unchecked" scope for ministerial discretion is seen as facilitating the targeting of black Jamaican males and other racialized groups for deportation. Julian Falconer and Carmen Ellis, for example, have argued that "the unfettered discretion available to the Minister in issuing [danger] opinions opens the door for colour profiling and the targeting of certain groups."[35]

In this approach, it is often unclear whether the discriminatory effects of the legislation are understood to be the result of an intentionally racist state agenda or as unintended negative consequences. Ministerial discretion sanctioned under section 70(5) is variously represented as "opening the door" to racism, "facilitating" racism, or being racist "in purpose and effect." Falconer and Ellis argue that statistics show that "the Immigration Department and its officers are operating under a system of criminal profiling that seems to target black Jamaicans in a manner that defines them more commonly as dangers to the public than any other immigrant population in Ontario, leading to their deportation in record numbers."[36] This rather ambiguous observation (*"seems* to target") is expressed in more definitive terms later: "These statistics bear out that a government initiative has been in place since 1995 to target a specific racial group with the specific aim of cleansing the community of those perceived as a "danger to the public."[37] And, finally, at the end of the paper, the authors refer in no uncertain terms to "the agenda of the state in targeting members of a particular racial community."[38]

The critical race critique of section 70(5) should be welcomed for its attention to historical context and to substantive justice. Moreover, given the close definitional link between the ministerial "danger opinion" and criminal justice enforcement, prosecution, and sentencing, and the ways that criminal justice processes are inflected by systemic and individual forms of racism, the focus on the racist dimensions of section 70(5) is important and compelling. This is all the more true when one takes into account the historical legacy of previously explicit racist ideals and discriminatory laws and policies.[39] While the explicit racism of immigration policy has been delegitimized, arguably it continues to be manifested in, for example, the privileging of certain characteristics in the point system, the selective location of overseas visa offices, and, more recently, interdiction practices and safe third country agreements that will have particularly dire effects on certain groups of predominantly nonwhite refugees.[40]

Nevertheless, while there is no question that racialized borders and identities both shape and are shaped by law and discretion, the approach followed here resists the temptation to explain law, discretion, or constructions of "undesirability" by reference to a single, universal axis of oppression. The operations of immigration penality and the crime-security nexus cannot be reduced to racism. In addition to the effects of the general decline of liberal welfarism and the rise of neoliberal governmentalities, a diverse and intersecting range of historically specific factors has contributed to the development and enforcement of law and policy in this field: from race to gender to ideology to morality; from economics and labour market issues to the exigencies of electoral politics; from shifts in global migration patterns to the rivalries embedded in the Cold War, et cetera. Therefore, while the linkages between criminality, race, and more recently nationality are clearly important in the domain of immigration penality, and while immigration enforcement practices are no doubt raced, they are not exclusively or inevitably so.

Danger, Discretion, and Judicial Review

The danger to the public provision was the subject of much legal argument. Lawyers drew constitutional attention to the excessive "vagueness" of the legal provisions and guidelines, to the lack of adequate procedural safeguards, and to its discriminatory dimensions. Nevertheless, in the 1997 *Williams* case,[41] the Federal Court of Canada (FCC) upheld the overall fairness of the public dangerousness scheme. This decision nicely encapsulates some of the central issues raised in Chapter 3 regarding law/discretion and the policies and practices of immigration enforcement.

In *Williams*, the FCC reemphasized the finding in *Chiarelli*,[42] a case about exclusion on security grounds, that there is no obligation on Parliament to provide any kind of appeal or discretionary relief to people who have violated an essential condition under which they were permitted to remain in Canada. It thus reaffirmed what is perhaps the most enduring of all founding tenets of Canadian sovereignty and Canadian immigration policy – that entering Canada is a privilege and not a right.

Williams held that the deportation of a permanent resident without appeal on the basis of a ministerial opinion on danger does not represent a breach of fundamental justice. Justice Strayer declared that "the substitution of judicial review for a right of appeal, by virtue of the Minister forming his opinion, does not strike me as a serious effect on his rights." The Federal Court refused to entertain the proposition that a ministerial danger opinion is the equivalent of "an arbitrary order issued by a despotic official ordering the random imprisonment or exile of otherwise innocent citizens." In the words of Judge Strayer, "at worst it replaces an appeal on law and facts with judicial review, substitutes the Minister's humanitarian discretion for that of the Appeal Division, and substitutes the possibility of a judicial stay of deportation for the certainty of a statutory stay."

In *Williams*, the defence argued unsuccessfully that section 70(5) was "void for vagueness" under section 7 of the *Charter*. Part of this argument addressed the vagueness and breadth of the policy guidelines relating to the danger opinion. In his decision, Judge Strayer defended their lack of specificity and confirmed the need to preserve the unfettered discretion of the minister, stating that "I would first observe ... that the guidelines are not law, are not binding, and they do not purport to be exhaustive. Indeed if they did purport to be exhaustive the Minister could not so fetter her discretion. I see nothing in the guidelines that is irrelevant to the proper formation of an opinion under subsection (5) (other than perhaps, humanitarian considerations to which the respondent cannot take exception) but they can in no way be seen as a definition of the totality of the considerations of which the Minister could properly take into account."

In *Williams*, the failure of section 70(5) to require the minister to provide reasons for finding that a person constitutes a danger to the public was also challenged. That courts and tribunals should provide reasons for their decisions is a generally accepted principle of fundamental justice. However, in *Williams*, the court did not compel the provision of reasons for the minister's "opinion," arguing that while desirable there is no legal duty to provide reasons particularly if the decision is discretionary and in the absence of a statutory requirement to provide reasons. Moreover, the decision notes that the issuance of reasons was not really "properly raised by this case" because the minister was not making a "determination" about potential dangerousness but merely "forming an opinion." The court thus accepted and gave weight to the government's extension of the minister's discretionary power by distinguishing an opinion from a determination. Nonetheless, the decision goes on to argue that, even if it were properly understood as a "decision," judicial review of discretionary, "subjective" decision making is limited to "grounds such as that the decision-maker acted in bad faith, or erred in law, or acted upon the basis of irrelevant considerations."

Interestingly, this acknowledgment of the limited grounds for the judicial review of discretionary immigration decision making, in this instance the danger opinion, does not figure in the judge's opinion regarding the effects of a danger opinion vis-à-vis the individual's fundamental rights. There is no absolute "statutory" right of noncitizens to appeal to a superior court a deportation order based on a danger opinion. Nor indeed, with a few exceptions, is there a statutory right to appeal any decisions under the act.[43] Rather, there is a "very limited right to commence a judicial review" by applying for leave of the Federal Court Trial Division, and only about 15 percent of cases obtain leave.[44] However, Judge Strayer maintains that the removal of a permanent resident's right to appeal a deportation order to the Immigration Appeal Division of the Immigration and Refugee Board, an independent administrative tribunal, simply substitutes the possibility of judicial review for the certainty of appeal on facts and law.

As noted above, Judge Strayer also addresses the question of the vagueness of the danger opinion provision. He concludes that the provision offers sufficient direction so that the minister and the courts can determine whether the exercise of this discretionary authority is for purposes intended by Parliament. He cautions against using the constitutional doctrine of fairness "to prevent or impede State action in furtherance of valid social objectives" and, reaffirming the role of discretion in the reconciliation of the universality and particularity of liberal legality, adds that "a measure of generality also sometimes allows for greater respect for fundamental rights, since circumstances that would not justify the invalidation of a more precise enactment may be accommodated through the application of a more general one." The primary defence of the "generality" of the provision hinges upon the importance of not impeding the "valid social objectives" pursued by Parliament through the legislation (the exclusion of dangerous and risky noncitizens and the protection of the public) and upon the distinction between law and equity.

The courts subsequently took a different position on the requirement of fairness and the need for government decision makers to provide reasons for discretionary decisions. The groundbreaking case was *Baker v. Canada* in 1999,[45] which held, among other things, that in certain circumstances the provision of written reasons is indeed required by the duty of procedural fairness. This is the case when the decision is of "profound importance" to those affected and is "so critical to their future." Although the focus of the *Baker* decision was a humanitarian and compassionate review, a number of Federal Court decisions have subsequently applied its reasoning to cases involving ministerial danger opinions.[46] What distinguishes several of these is that they involved refugee claimants, people for whom forced removal to their countries of origin could mean returning them to persecution. Moreover, the danger opinion deprives the individual of the right to have a refugee claim determined. In such cases, the danger decision is indeed of "profound importance," and, as was held again in 2000 in *Navarro v. Canada,* written reasons are required by the duty of procedural fairness.[47]

National Security, Refugees, and *Refoulement*

There are obvious reasons to compare the danger opinion process with the security certificate process. Each involves the exercise of broad discretionary powers from which there are only limited appeals, and each can result in the denial of access to refugee claim determination and in detention and deportation even for permanent residents.

In 1984, the *Canadian Security Intelligence Service Act*[48] was proclaimed after considerable debate. This act gave CSIS responsibility over national security issues, a responsibility previously held by the RCMP.[49] The *CSIS Act* also created the Security Intelligence Review Committee (SIRC). SIRC hears individual complaints against CSIS and, until 2002, reviewed the security assessments of permanent residents. All applications for landing and for citizenship go through a security check. Where there is a security concern, CIC will refer the case to CSIS. Under the authority of the *CSIS Act,* CSIS carries out a security assessment and forwards its report to CIC.[50] A "security assessment" is defined in the *CSIS Act* in distinctly moral terms: "an appraisal of the loyalty to Canada and, so far as it relates thereto, the reliability of an individual."[51] Under the 1976 *Immigration Act,* the minister of immigration and the solicitor general issued the security report on a permanent resident to SIRC, which then investigated the report and made a recommendation to Cabinet as to whether a security certificate should be issued.[52] Cabinet could then direct the minister to issue the "security certificate" barring the person's admission to Canada or, should the person already be on Canadian soil, mandating deportation. In the SIRC hearing, the person in question was represented and could make a submission. For national security reasons, this person was not provided with any comprehensive information about the nature of the evidence against him or her.

Under the 1976 *Immigration Act,* nonpermanent residents were denied this SIRC hearing. In their cases, the minister and the solicitor general could file a security certificate, and the person in question could be detained until the certificate was reviewed by a Federal Court judge. As noted earlier, the transfer in 2003 of the enforcement sections of CIC to the new Border Services Agency also transferred the responsibility for immigration enforcement from the minister of immigration to the solicitor general, who also became the deputy prime minister and the minister of public safety and emergency preparedness. This means that the security certificates now require only one signature because the minister responsible is also the solicitor general.[53]

Under *IRPA*, the SIRC hearing is now denied to permanent and nonpermanent residents alike. Both permanent and nonpermanent residents who are the subjects of a security certificate may now be detained.[54] The only remaining difference in the treatment of the two groups is that the reasons for the detention of a permanent resident are subject to judicial review, whereas "foreign nationals" are automatically detained until the Federal Court reviews the certificate.[55]

Both the danger opinion and the security certificate enable the minister to bypass the appeal of a removal to the IAD; both allow for the deportation of permanent residents without this avenue of appeal; and both entail the possibility that a refugee might be forcibly returned to his or her country of origin. Moreover, both processes have been the target of sustained critique, including numerous *Charter* challenges.

The advice provided by CSIS relates directly to the inadmissibility criteria contained in *IRPA*.[56] According to CSIS, the 1992 amendments made to the inadmissibility provisions by Bill C-86, in particular the insertion of explicit prohibitions against terrorists and members of criminal organizations, brought Immigration's inadmissibility provisions into closer alignment with CSIS's definition of threats to the security of Canada, namely and primarily terrorism and espionage as well as organized crime.[57] However, the security provisions of *IRPA*, like those of the former *Immigration Act*, are even more vague and less definitive than those provided in the *CSIS Act*.[58]

The vagueness of the terms "terrorism" and "membership in a terrorist group" was a central issue in the cases of two Kurds from Turkey, Suleyman Goven and Sami Durgun, whom CSIS suspected of being members of a terrorist organization. The two men had been in limbo awaiting immigration status for seven and eleven years respectively. In May 2001, SIRC released its reports on the two cases and came down hard on CSIS. It recommended that CSIS keep tapes of the interviews that it conducts; that more specific definitions of terrorism and membership in a terrorist group be developed and applied; that the individuals being investigated be told in advance of their right to counsel at the interviews; and that CSIS be held accountable for the delays in immigrant processing.[59]

Canada has an obligation under the *Refugee Convention* not to return to the country of origin any refugee whose life or freedom would thereby be threatened there. Article 33(1) of the *Refugee Convention* sets out this prohibition against *refoulement:* "No Contracting State shall expel or return (*"refouler"*) a refugee in any manner whatsoever to the frontiers of territories where his [sic] life or freedom would be threatened on account of his race, religion, nationality or membership of a particular social group or opinion." However, the *Refugee Convention* also sets out an exception to this prohibition in article 33(2): "The benefit of the present provision may not, however, be claimed by a refugee of whom there are reasonable grounds for regarding as a danger to the security of the country in which he [sic] is, or who, having been convicted of a serious crime, constitutes a danger to the community of that country."[60]

The *Refugee Convention* thus permits the expulsion of refugees or refugee claimants for reasons of national security or serious criminality. Article 32 states categorically that "the Contracting States shall not expel a refugee lawfully in their territory save on grounds of national security or public order." Thus, it has been argued that, under international law, refugees lose their right to protection against expulsion, even to a place that presents a threat to life or freedom, if they are deemed to be a danger to the public or a security threat. While the *Refugee Convention* does stipulate in article 32(2) that this exclusionary decision must be made in accordance with "due process of law," exceptions even to this requirement are forgiven if there are "compelling reasons of national security" that require otherwise.[61]

Humanitarian and international legal discourses in the context of refugee determination produce and act upon the figure of the "deserving victim," in this case the *genuine* victim of state-sanctioned persecution, at the same time as they contribute to the production of the undeserving and undesirable outsider, the latter constituted by the intersecting discourses of crime-security and fraud. The right to protection in Canada of an individual found to be a *Convention* refugee (a genuine and therefore "deserving" victim) is unsettled if that person is subsequently deemed to represent a danger to the public or to national security who should therefore be deported. Refugee claimants deemed to be a danger to the public or a threat to national security will lose their right to have their refugee claims heard and may be forcibly deported to a country where they may face persecution, so long as the procedures at play are fair and just. Canada, despite having lobbied for its promulgation, held off signing the 1951 *Refugee Convention* until 1969, long after the vast majority of developed countries had signed it. As noted earlier, this delay was due to the Canadian government's fear that signing the *Refugee Convention* would undermine Canada's ability to deport refugees on security grounds.

In addition to those deemed "serious criminals," *IRPA* provides for the deportation without appeal of noncitizens, including permanent residents, refugees, and refugee claimants using the broad and vague classifications of "organized crime," "terrorism," and "security of Canada." Moreover, the expanded inadmissibility provisions render those found to be "serious criminals," "organized criminals," or "terrorists" ineligible to make a refugee claim and vulnerable to removal.

While the *Refugee Convention* contains exceptions to the prohibition against *refoulement*, the *United Nations Convention against Torture and Other Cruel,*

Inhuman, or Degrading Treatment or Punishment,[62] to which Canada is also a signatory, does not. It entails an absolute prohibition against returning a person to a place "where there are substantial grounds for believing that they will be in danger of being subjected to torture."[63] While *IRPA* does make specific reference to the *Convention against Torture,* it does not respect this absolute prohibition. Under *IRPA,* people who are inadmissible on the ground of serious criminality or security may well be sent back to torture if, in a Pre-Removal Risk Assessment (PRRA), the risks posed to Canada are held to outweigh the risks posed to the person by removal.[64] In January 2002, the Supreme Court of Canada rendered its decision in the *Suresh* case, which centred on these issues, a decision all the more anxiously anticipated as the court's deliberations spanned the September 11th attacks.

The *Suresh* Case (2002)

Manickavasagam Suresh came to Canada from Sri Lanka in 1990 and was found to be a *Convention* refugee by the IRB in 1991. He became the subject of a security certificate in 1995 because of his activities in Canada as a fundraiser for the World Tamil Movement (WTM) and the Federation of Associations of Canadian Tamils. In accordance with the requirements of the former *Immigration Act,* the certificate was reviewed by the Federal Court Trial Division (FCTD), which found it to be fair and reasonable. Justice Teitelbaum of the FCTD rejected arguments that the Liberation Tigers of Tamil Eelam (LTTE) was a national liberation movement whose members were legitimately fighting for their right to self-determination rather than a terrorist group properly understood. Instead, Justice Teitelbaum found that Suresh was a member of the LTTE; that the WTM supports the activities of the LTTE; and that there are reasonable grounds to believe that the LTTE has committed terrorist acts. The security certificate was upheld despite the undisputed fact that Suresh had not directly engaged in any violent activities. Justice Teitelbaum also dismissed concerns about the definitional vagueness of the term "terrorism," stating that, "when one sees a terrorist act, one is able to define the word."[65]

Suresh was subsequently informed that the minister was considering declaring him a danger to the security of Canada under section 53(1)(b) of the former *Immigration Act,* which allowed for the deportation of a refugee on security grounds even if his or her "life or freedom" would be endangered by the return. In response, Suresh submitted numerous documents that evidenced the torture, killing, and disappearance in Sri Lanka of members of the LTTE. While acknowledging that Suresh had no direct involvement in the "terrorist" activities of the LTTE, and that he did face a risk upon his return, the immigration officer who reviewed the case concluded that humanitarian and compassionate considerations were not sufficient to preclude deportation. Without giving Suresh the opportunity to review or respond to the immigration officer's memorandum, and without providing written reasons, the minister subsequently declared him to be a danger to the security of Canada who should be deported.[66]

Suresh then made an unsuccessful application to the Federal Court for judicial review and another to the Federal Court of Appeal. His counsel argued that removing Suresh would contravene the *Convention against Torture* as well as the *Charter*. She also argued once again that the definition of terrorism was unconstitutionally vague; that Suresh's fund-raising activities did not constitute terrorism properly understood; and that Suresh did not represent a threat to Canadian security. The initial decision was upheld on the basis that the protection against torture under the *Convention against Torture* was limited by a nation's right to expel security risks and that fund-raising for "terrorist violence" was not protected under section 2(b) (freedom of expression) or 2(d) (freedom of association) of the *Charter*. With respect to the former, the court held that "those who freely choose to raise funds used to sustain terrorist organizations bear the same guilt and responsibility as those who actually carry out the terrorist acts. Fundraising in the pursuit of terrorist violence must by necessity fall outside the sphere of protected expression." The court also ruled that the definitions of terrorism and danger to the security of Canada were not unconstitutionally vague; that no oral hearing was required to assess the risk of torture upon return; and finally that, while returning a person to torture was a violation of that person's section 7 *Charter* right to life, liberty, and security of person, it was justified under section 2 of the *Charter* because of the "pressing and substantial" objective of preventing Canada from becoming a "haven for terrorists."[67]

This ruling disappointed many. It failed to distinguish between the non-violent fund-raising activities of a national liberation movement and the violent activities of terrorist groups. It did not uphold the absolute prohibition against torture contained in the *Convention against Torture*. It did not acknowledge the need for more specific terminology of the key terms of "danger to the security of Canada," "terrorism," and "membership." More generally, the Federal Court refused to interfere in any substantive way in the realm of ministerial discretion.

The ruling was welcomed by CIC officials, who had warned earlier that "this case will determine whether Canada will become a haven for terrorists,"[68] and by senior members of Canada's security establishment, who had cautioned in the most dramatic fashion that a decision in favour of Suresh would "be devastating for both the security and the reputation of Canada ... Within a very short period of time the message would be communicated to terrorists and spies around the world that Canada can no longer expel them if they arrive here. The decision would attract the worst of the worst."[69] This warning was rivalled by a journalist's assertion that a ruling in favour of Suresh "would strip Canada of its power to deport foreigners considered security threats opening the borders to a rogues gallery of international terrorists and other dangerous criminals."[70]

The case did not end there. Suresh's lawyers were granted leave to appeal the decision to the Supreme Court of Canada (SCC), which released its decision on 11 January 2002.[71] The SCC allowed the appeal and held that Suresh was entitled to a new hearing before the minister on the questions of whether he represented a danger to Canadian security and whether he would face a risk of torture were he deported to Sri Lanka. Following *Baker*, this decision was based on the court's finding that the minister had violated the duty of fairness owed to Suresh once he had established that he would indeed face "a risk of torture or similar abuse" were he to be returned to Sri Lanka. The Supreme Court ruled that the duty of fairness and the principles of fundamental justice require that Suresh be apprised of the case against him, that he be given a chance to respond in writing to the case against him, and that he be provided with written reasons for the decision. In the words of the court, "if the refugee establishes that torture is a real possibility, the Minister must provide the refugee with all the relevant information and advice she intends to rely on, provide the refugee [with] an opportunity to address that evidence in writing, and after considering all the relevant information, issue responsive written reasons. This is the minimum required to meet the duty of fairness and fulfill the requirements of fundamental justice under s. 7 of the *Charter*."[72] Ministerial discretion, the decision states, should conform to the principles of fundamental justice and should generally be exercised in such a way that declines deportation where there is a "substantial risk" of torture. Nevertheless, this deprivation of a refugee's right to life, liberty, and security may be justified if the process is found to be in accordance with the principles of fundamental justice. In light of these principles, the SCC held that section 53(1)(b) does not violate section 7 of the *Charter*.

The Supreme Court thus upheld the duty of fairness and the requirements of fundamental justice, allowed the appeal, and ordered a new hearing without unsettling maximum judicial deference to ministerial discretion. And, as pointed out by Audrey Macklin, the decision to *refoule* is not a singular event: "The path to refouling a refugee is paved with a series of discretionary decisions by the Minister."[73]

In *Suresh*, the Supreme Court held that the courts should not interfere with ministerial discretion so long as ministerial decisions are not "patently unreasonable" and the exercise of discretion is "in conformity with the values of the *Charter*."[74] The Supreme Court even referred to the events of September 11th as further evidence of the importance of preserving maximum ministerial discretion in matters of national security. It quoted an excerpt of a speech made by Lord Hoffman in the House of Lords following the attacks:

I wrote this speech some three months before the recent events in New York and Washington. They are a reminder that in matters of national security, the cost of failure can be high. *This seems to me to underline the need for the judicial arm of government to respect the decisions of ministers of the Crown on the question of whether support for terrorist activities in a foreign country constitutes a threat to national security.* It is not only that the executive has access to special information and expertise in these matters. It is also that such decisions, with serious potential results for the community, require a legitimacy which can be conferred only by entrusting them to persons responsible to the community through the democratic process. If the people are to accept the consequences of such decisions, they must be made by persons whom the people have elected and whom they can remove.[75]

The court's decision in *Suresh* illustrates in clear terms the centrality of the law/discretion dichotomy. So do the powerful legal critiques of the decision, which are similarly framed by the conventional law/discretion binary and the assumption that discretion is a "hole" created by the absence of law. For example, as expressed by Macklin, the task of the judiciary is not only to assure constitutionality on paper "but also to scrutinize the implementation of those laws so that human lives do not fall through the cracks of discretion into a dark space where the law does not reach."[76]

In the *Suresh* decision, the Supreme Court managed to cover a variety of diverse and apparently conflicting positions. It condemned torture. It condemned terrorism. It acknowledged international legal prohibitions against torture and those against deporting to torture. It affirmed the primacy of the Canadian *Charter* (over international instruments) in the context of Canadian decision making relating to torture and deportation to torture.[77] One interpretation of this last achievement is that, by according primacy to the authority of the Canadian *Charter* over international instruments, the SCC reasserted the "sovereign" control over Canadian borders that the *Refugee Convention* undermines. As observed by Macklin, "policing the borders is seen as a matter of national sovereign control, and to the extent that the *UN Convention Relating to the Status of Refugees* shears this power, interpreting the available exceptions to the duty to admit refugees emerges as a site for reclamation of control."[78]

Suresh upheld the duty of fairness and the principles of fundamental justice in the making of deportation to torture decisions in cases where the person in question has established a prima facie case of risk of torture. At the same time as the Supreme Court released its decision in the *Suresh* case, it also released its decision in the *Ahani* case, which related to the same issue of the power of the state to deport to torture on the ground of national security.[79] Unlike Suresh, Ahani was ordered deported on the ground that, because he had not established a prima facie case of risk of torture (as decided by the minister), there was therefore no obligation to accord to him the duty of fairness or principles of fundamental justice.

The United Nations Human Rights Committee (UNHRC) had previously urged Canada, unsuccessfully, to refrain from deporting Ahani until it had reviewed his case. On 25 May 2004, the UNHRC released its view that the deportation of Ahani had violated a number of his rights under the *International Covenant on Civil and Political Rights,* including those protected under article 13 (the right of a noncitizen to present reasons against deportation) and article 7 (the right to protection from torture or cruel treatment). The committee also expressed some concerns regarding Ahani's eight-year detention during the process.[80]

Danger to the public and national security are two justifications for the coercive practices of detention and deportation. Liberal legal concerns about fairness, procedural justice, and the preservation of discretion complicate the ease with which they may be carried out. Thus, as discussed above, while neither criticizing the policy objective of forcibly removing permanent residents who are deemed a danger to the public or a threat to national security, nor questioning the correctness of these designations in individual cases, or even the reliability of the designations themselves, when pressed the superior courts have indicated their concern to ensure that discretion is preserved while the procedures involved remain in accordance with the principles of the rule of law and due process. Macklin reflects on the different outcomes of these two cases in the following terms:

> One cannot but wonder whether rejecting this Middle Eastern man, alleged to be a hired assassin for a brutal Islamist regime, provided a useful counterweight to the relatively favourable outcome for Suresh, whose activities were non-violent and not even unlawful at the relevant time. Permitting an [indirect] fundraiser to remain in Canada is surely less controversial than the prospect of allowing a hired assassin to stay indefinitely because he might be tortured if returned to his country of nationality. What better way to convey an image of transcendent judicial neutrality and perfect balance between liberty and security than a tie score – refugee 1: government 1.[81]

The foregoing extended discussion highlights the centrality of the law/discretion dichotomy in the governance of immigration penality as well as the primacy of the crime-security nexus in this governance. It also demonstrates the way that the complicated social and political issues and debates raised by both *Suresh* and *Ahani* were reframed in legal terms and decided upon according to the dictates and limits of the guiding liberal dichotomies of liberty/authority, freedom/security, and law/discretion.

Legal and humanitarian discourses relating to international human rights, natural justice, and due process gained currency in the 1960s and were officially embedded in the legislation and apparatus of onshore refugee determination and deportation and sponsorship appeals. Humanitarian discourses constituted the figure of the deserving genuine refugee, and legal discourses constructed the refugee as a rights-bearing subject. These developments continue to be influential and underpin an extensive range of political, social, economic, and legal efforts relating to international and national refugee issues. For example, Canada still grants full citizenship to *Convention* refugees, unlike many European countries. It is still widely accepted, even by many of Canada's harshest critics of its "liberal" and "generous" immigration and refugee systems, that Canada has an obligation to provide asylum to genuine refugees (although clearly most would prefer that the Canadian government select them offshore). The enforcement practices that have proliferated in the governance of immigration penality are widely justified "in the name of the truly deserving." And, while government initiatives to get tough on noncitizens deemed to pose a criminal threat to public safety or a security threat to the nation proliferate, liberal legality and its constituent notions of the rule of law, due process, and procedural fairness continue both to complicate these objectives and to legitimize associated coercive practices.

This chapter has argued that the danger to the public provisions contained in Bill C-44 exemplified the centrality of the crime-security nexus in the governance of immigration penality in Canada in the 1990s. It has also demonstrated the importance of discretion in the legal construction and regulation of dangerous criminals and security threats and the degree to which the zero sum relations of law/discretion, rights/risks, and freedom/security are embedded and taken for granted in the liberal legal paradigm.

Over the 1980s and 1990s, new immigrants and refugees were represented and acted upon as risky – as frauds, criminals, and security threats who endanger government systems, public safety, and national security. The next chapter examines the range of enforcement-oriented initiatives that have proliferated over the 1990s in the name of border security, public safety, and system integrity, demonstrating the degree to which immigration enforcement and border security practices are articulated through the language of risk and have become central instruments of national crime control.

8

Criminals First

In just over an hour on the morning of Tuesday, 11 September 2001, the world had changed forever.[1]

While it is often claimed that everything changed after September 11th, that it is a brand-new world, the crime-security nexus coupled with emerging and powerful neoliberal concerns about fraud have guided and justified the promotion and development of extensive enforcement measures for some time. This chapter focuses on the prominent crime-security problems that have emerged over the past decade or so and the range of legal and administrative responses to these threats. It further demonstrates that immigration enforcement and border control have been reshaped under the banner of crime.[2]

"Criminals First": Enforcement Priorities

On 7 July 1994, in response to the Leimonis and Baylis murders in Toronto and the intense public response that they generated, the minister of immigration announced the adoption of the "Criminals First" removal policy. It involved a major reorientation of the priorities of Canada's detention and deportation policies from removing failed refugee claimants to removing criminals. The results of this policy change were significant. In the 1993-94 fiscal year, 15 percent of removals had been for reasons of criminality. In 1995-96, this figure had more than doubled to 37 percent.[3] The following table provides a breakdown of removals from Canada from 1995 to 2002.

In an interesting development, the Metropolitan Police Association initiated a $120 million lawsuit against the government of Canada on behalf of Todd Baylis and his family. In response to a government report claiming that the failure to deport Clinton Gayle was a result of "systemic" failures, the Police Association stated its position succinctly: "Notwithstanding that one of the principal objectives of the *Immigration Act* is to maintain and

Table 8.1

Breakdown of removals from Canada, 1995-2002

Year	Total removals	Failed refugee claimants		Criminals		Others	
2002	8,434	n/a		1,547	(18%)	33 organized crime, security threats, human rights violators	
2001	9,165	n/a		1,804	(20%)	13 organized crime, security threats, human rights violators	
2000	8,636	5,755	(67%)	1,701	(20%)	n/a	
1999	8,311	n/a		n/a		n/a	
1998	8,109	5,095	(63%)	1,791	(22%)	1,223	(15%)
1997	7,968	4,800	(60%)	1,446	(18%)	1,722	(22%)
1996	5,838	2,464	(42%)	1,838	(32%)	1,536	(26%)
1995	4,798	1,597	(32%)	1,756	(37%)	1,495	(31%)
Total	26,713	13,906		6,831		5,976	

Source: Table derived from figures contained in CIC, *Department Performance Reports*, 1999-2003 (Ottawa: Minister of Public Works and Government Services, 1990-2003).

protect the safety and good order of Canadian society, and notwithstanding that Gayle was known to be a commercial drug trafficker, heavily armed and prepared to use his firearm, immigration officials did nothing to carry out the deportation order. As a direct result of government inaction, incompetence, bureaucratic indifference and gross negligence, one of our own was murdered in cold blood. This tragedy will be repeated if we do not hold those responsible, accountable for their actions."[4]

Whereas civil suits have been used by those who believe they were victimized due to the negligence of criminal law enforcement or corrections personnel (although in Canada still a relatively rare event), this resort to a civil suit in the context of immigration enforcement was unprecedented. That it was initiated by the Police Association evidences not only the deep reactions evoked by the killing of fellow police officers but also a sense of betrayal at what was believed by the police to be CIC's lack of commitment to its enforcement role. In addition to indicating the overall associations between immigration and crime, the focus here on accountability, individual responsibility, and government incompetence is clearly consistent with the certain disillusionment with, and even hostility toward, traditional government institutions under emergent neoliberal regimes.

After the shootings, CIC stepped up its enforcement activities. Lucienne Robillard, then minister of immigration, explained in 1998 that, although most removals are *not* for reasons of criminality, the department does "place a special emphasis on finding and removing criminals ... We will not tolerate the presence of people within Canada who threaten or prey upon the Canadian public."[5] Between 1999 and 2001, the number of removals increased from 8,311 to 9,165.[6] The department explained the additional resources required for enforcement activities in the following terms: "The removal of criminals, particularly those who pose a danger to Canadian society (that is, people convicted of more serious offences involving weapons, drugs and violence), takes precedence over all other removals. As criminals are often uncooperative and require escorts during removal, these cases are generally more resource intensive."[7] In 2001, the year of the September 11th attacks, terrorists were added to the mix of dangerous outsiders whose removal is vital in protecting "the integrity of Canada's citizenship, immigration and refugee programs" and "the safety, security and well-being of Canadian society."[8] In 2002, the number of removals dropped slightly to 8,434, of which 1,547 (18 percent) were removed for reasons of criminality.[9]

In 2002, CIC promoted the implementation of *IRPA* as the "first and most important" departmental activity relating to the protection of the health, safety, and security of Canadians. The benefits of *IRPA* as outlined by the department revolve around the identification and removal of dangerous people, including stronger authority to arrest and detain criminals, security risks, and people whose identities are in doubt; broader grounds for barring entry or deporting people for reasons of organized crime; elimination of appeals for dangerous and risky people (for reasons of security, organized crime, human rights violations, or serious criminality) in order to "speed up removals"; barring of refugee claims by the same groups of dangerous and risky people; a streamlined process for removing security threats; and a greater ability to use "sensitive evidence" to bar entry or remove dangerous and risky people.[10]

While *IRPA* does include the protection of refugees as a desirable objective, the government expresses this objective in terms that characteristically rest upon and reproduce the distinction between the deserving, those who are genuinely at risk, and everyone else who is undeserving and risky. Moreover, the protection of genuine refugee claimants at risk is represented as contingent, in the first instance, upon the identification and exclusion of the risky: "Our ability to fulfil Canada's humanitarian and international obligations is determined, in large part, by our capacity to quickly and fairly determine refugee status in a manner that safeguards the security of Canadians and extends our protection only to people in genuine need of it."[11]

Crime Problems and Enforcement Responses

The quest for national security, public safety, and system integrity has generated new legislation, policies, departments, affiliations, networks, and practices dedicated to the eradication or at least minimization and management of different varieties of crime-security threats. Prior to the intensified focus on terrorism that followed the attacks of 11 September 2001, it was organized crime that animated Canada's "partners in security."

Organized Crime

The ten-member Organized Crime Unit (OCU) of CIC was created in 1994 to enforce the organized crime inadmissibility provision of Canadian immigration legislation. Under the former *Immigration Act,* immigration officials already were empowered to refuse admission or remove any individual if there were "reasonable grounds" to believe that he or she has been "engaged in activity that is part of a pattern of criminal activity planned and organized by a number of persons acting in concert in furtherance of the commission of an offence punishable under an Act of Parliament by way of indictment."[12] Under *IRPA,* "transnational crime" such as people smuggling, trafficking in people, or money laundering and inadmissibility for reasons of organized criminality have been added as grounds that deny refugee claim eligibility (alongside serious criminality, violating human rights, and national security grounds).[13]

The OCU's mandate has been to understand organized crime as a global issue, to gather intelligence, to target overseas organized criminal groups, to intercept organized criminals at ports of entry, and to ensure that criminals are removed if found in Canada.[14] In 1998, Michel Gagné, its director, explained that "we don't have to show that the person participated in crime, just that the person is a member of an organized criminal group." Nor need the group be tightly organized; it could be more "loosely structured." In quick recognition of the constitutional implications of this provision, Gagné added that "some people believe the section offends the Charter, but we've never lost a case yet ... When people knowingly associate with criminal groups the burden of proof is on them to show it would not be detrimental to Canada to allow them in."[15] In 1998, the unit boasted that it had developed a databank that contains "the names and aliases of 7,000 suspected criminals, and those of their wives, children and parents,"[16] and information on physical descriptions, criminal activities, and links to criminal organizations.[17] Lists of suspected organized criminals are shared between CIC, the RCMP, CSIS, and international law enforcement agencies such as Interpol. Immigration officers overseas and at ports of entry use this database for screening travellers to Canada. In this work, the OCU cooperates most closely with its "main partner," the RCMP.[18] In addition to its work within Canada and at Canadian ports of entry, the OCU is active overseas.

For example, its officials screen potential immigrant and travel visa applicants. In this capacity, they establish profiles, carry out police checks, and communicate with RCMP headquarters and field intelligence.[19]

By 2001, the Organized Crime Unit of CIC had become one of the six main divisions of the Case Management Branch (CMB) of CIC, whose overall responsibility is to "review and manage contentious, sensitive and high profile cases." The CMB provides expertise on "security, terrorism, organized crime, modern war crimes, criminality/rehabilitation and danger to the public issues."[20] The role of the OCU in the CMB is to acquire an understanding "of the organization and operations of international organized crime, and of specific types of organized crime (such as: Asian, Russian, Caribbean organized crime, Italian Mafia groups, Outlaw Motorcycle gangs and Latin/South American Cartels), with the ultimate goal of ensuring that any inadmissible person is denied an entry visa or removed from Canada." The OCD provides this information to the minister and to immigration officers both in Canada and abroad.[21] As with those developed by CSIS, the profiles developed by the OCU are organized according to nationality and ethnicity, for example profiles of members of Japanese syndicates *(Yakuza)*, Hong Kong triads, and organized crime groups from the former Soviet Union *(vor v sakonye* or thieves-in-law); "officers ... target people who fit the profile of organized criminals: Japanese with missing fingers and tattoos could be *yakuza*; Russians who can't explain their sudden millionaire status and sport tattoos of an eight point star could be 'thieves-in-law.'"[22]

The Organized Crime Unit is one of several immigration-related initiatives over the 1990s that targeted organized crime. For example, in 1997 the Cross Border Crime Forum was established by Canada and the United States to improve the "cooperation and sharing of information" relating to organized crime and other border control issues between Canadian and American customs and immigration authorities.[23] In 1999, the RCMP was given $15 million per year to fight organized crime at the international airports in Vancouver, Montreal, and Toronto. One hundred RCMP officers were devoted to targeting organized criminals seeking entry to Canada.[24] And, as mentioned, in 2002 *IRPA* expanded the organized crime provisions, introduced tough new penalties for human trafficking and people smuggling, and made organized crime a ground for refugee claim ineligibility. These initiatives represent only a small fraction of the national and international enforcement measures introduced during this period targeting organized crime. They include Bill C-95, *An Act to Amend the Criminal Code (Criminal Organizations) and to Amend Other Acts in Consequence*[25] enacted in 1997, which among other things made participation in a criminal organization a criminal offence; Bill C-51, *An Act to Amend the Criminal Code, the Controlled Drugs and Substances Act, and the Corrections and Conditional Release Act*[26] enacted in 1999, which barred those convicted of organized crime offences from early parole; and Bill C-22, the *Proceeds of Crime (Money Laundering) Act*[27] enacted in 2000, which made the reporting of suspicious financial transactions and cross-border movements of currency mandatory.[28] In December 2000, Canada signed the *UN Convention against Transnational Organized Crime* as well as two supplemental protocols: the *Protocol against the Smuggling of Migrants by Land, Sea, and Air* and the *Protocol to Prevent, Suppress, and Punish Trafficking in Persons, Especially Women and Children*.[29] All of these measures were promoted as part of a massive federal government campaign against organized crime both within Canada's borders and internationally.

CSIS and Transnational Crime
In January 1996, CSIS created its Transnational Criminal Activity Unit, signifying the entry of the security service into the realm of criminal activity and evidencing the prominence of the crime-security nexus. According to CSIS, this service was created "as part of a government-wide effort to combat this threat."[30] It proclaimed that the threat posed by organized criminals is monumental: "They attack the very fabric of life in a democratic, law-based society like Canada."[31] This unit distinguishes its work from that of traditional law enforcement agencies by referring to the difference between "technical" and "strategic" intelligence; the police collect "tactical intelligence" that is "short term and operational in nature, geared towards action in the field leading to arrests and prosecutions," while the CSIS unit provides the government with "reliable information and strategic intelligence on the extent and nature of transnational crime in Canada."[32] Strategic intelligence is thus long term and "provides a comprehensive view of a threat environment, assesses the extent of the threat and points out which areas are at risk."[33]

This initiative represents an unprecedented expansion of the working mandate of CSIS, effected without any amendment to its legislated terms of reference. CSIS now monitors transnational organized criminal activity under its existing mandate to "investigate foreign-influenced activities detrimental to Canadian interests" under the *CSIS Act*.[34] CSIS explains this expansion by claiming that globalization has created a world "virtually devoid of national borders," which, it argues, provides vast opportunities for "members of highly sophisticated and organized criminal syndicates to pursue a complex web of lucrative legal and illegal activities worldwide."[35] Whereas terrorism and espionage have traditionally posed the primary threat to Canada's national security, with the demise of traditional Cold War enemies and fears and in accordance with the increasing dominance of law and order concerns, CSIS maintains that transnational crime now poses a similarly serious threat: "Transnational crime threatens various aspects of Canadian national security, law and order, the integrity of government programs and institutions, and the economy."[36] The range of criminality included in the new operational mandate of CSIS is thus wide:[37]

> While still involved at the lower level with drug trafficking, prostitution, loan-sharking, illegal gambling and extortion ... [organized criminals] have expanded their activities to a quasi-corporate level where they are active in large-scale insurance fraud, the depletion of natural resources, environmental crime, migrant smuggling, bank fraud, gasoline tax fraud and corruption. In addition, their frequent use of money earned from their illegal ventures to fund legitimate ones allows them to launder money and earn even more profits. They apply many of their criminal tactics in these legal business operations, never hesitating to use violence or murder to get ahead.[38]

It is reasonable to suggest that CSIS's new mandate issued out of a growing institutional need to reassert its importance in the post-1989 world order in which traditional Cold War foes and fears have become obsolete. National security, previously understood in strict sovereign relation to the political state, now encompasses social and national concerns with "public safety." As CSIS itself notes, "in response to the rise of terrorism worldwide and the demise of the Cold War, CSIS has made public safety its first priority."[39]

Certain forms of criminality have been reconceptualized and acted upon as threats to national security. Conversely, the dominant sovereign conception of "national security" has been radically modified and extended to include governmental concerns over public safety and to therefore encompass certain forms of criminality. As clearly expressed by the Department of National Defence in 2002, "the concept of security has expanded from denoting the safety of the state and protection against military danger to conveying the notion of freedom from fear and focusing on the security of people against a whole range of risks ('human security'). Many transnational criminal activities seem to fit this wider definition."[40] As discussed in Chapter 1, these developments clearly raise the theme of the governmentalization of the state that has entailed the mobilization of "the population" and "the economy" in the justification of the practices of immigration penality and border control. While the traditional threats posed to the "sovereign" political state are still a concern, those posed to the welfare of the population more generally have come to provide the primary justification for policies and practices associated with national security.

The representation of organized crime as a threat to national security thus also signals the emergence of a new conception of "the state." The focus on ideologically based threats to national security, central throughout the Cold War years, was consistent with a conception of the modern liberal state as a sovereign political institution. In contrast, the focus on organized criminal threats to national security constructs the state as primarily concerned to promote the welfare of the population understood in terms of the security of property and the advancement of economic interests.[41] This focus is thus consistent with the processes of governmentalization and with neoliberal priorities, including notably free-market economics but also corollary concerns relating to fraud and system abuse. As articulated by CSIS, organized crime threatens Canadian society in multiple and fundamental ways: "Given that they attack the very fabric of life in a democratic, law-based society like Canada, the illegal actions of transnational crime organizations threaten law and order, directly affecting people's sense of security, trust, order and community – the very underpinnings of Canadian society."[42] They jeopardize the integrity of government programs and institutions through corruption, add to enforcement costs, further burden the criminal justice system, contribute to long-term social costs (including drug dependency and a rise in violent crime), and finally pose "a serious threat to the economic security of the nation" in that its basic activities could "undermine the workings of the free-market economy."[43]

The conflation of national security risks and criminal risks with public safety has multiple effects, including the blurring of boundaries between CSIS and the RCMP, the mandate of the former traditionally limited to national security (understood largely in terms of espionage and subversion) and that of the latter restricted to public safety (understood in terms of criminality). This distinction, a foundational feature of the creation of CSIS under the *CSIS Act* in 1984, has now become quite fuzzy. Officials of each do their best to emphasize "integration and cooperation" while being clear on the continuing distinction between the law enforcement responsibilities of the RCMP and the intelligence-gathering role of CSIS. As articulated by Lawrence MacAulay, solicitor general in 2001, "the RCMP have the lead Federal role for combating crime, but I believe that the increasing threat of transnational crime – notably the illegal traffic of drugs, people and the laundering of money across international boundaries – means that the RCMP and CSIS have to marshal all their resources in a cooperative and integrated fight against these activities."[44]

The global dimension of contemporary crime-security threats is also a persistent theme. As put by the solicitor general of Canada in 1998, "no single person, no single country can stop the daunting flow of transnational crime."[45] The protection of public safety and national security in Canada is today located in relation to a variety of international wars against international risks: the war against organized crime, the war against terrorism, the war against war criminals, the war against people smuggling, and the war against drugs. As mentioned, Canada has worked on a variety of international enforcement initiatives. In 1999, CIC reported that it had developed an "International Enforcement Strategy" to "help in the struggle against criminality, security threats and the worldwide phenomenon of increasing illegal migration." The strategy emphasizes information sharing on these threats, coordinating immigration control activities, and forging "partnership agreements" and "cooperative arrangements" with "affected countries."[46] As put with dramatic flourish in a 2003 legislative guide for the implementation of the *UN Convention against Transnational Crime:*

> When criminals are cosmopolitan, interventions cannot afford to be parochial. When the types of transnational crimes and the number of criminal groups seem to be increasing, no countries are immune ... against sophisticated and harmful offences. When rapid advances in technology and the impressive cross-border mobility of people, capital and commodities are taken advantage of by smart criminals acting either alone or, more dangerously, with additional associates, law enforcement cannot fall behind. When criminals can generate extraordinary profits from their illicit enterprises, move them and hide them from the authorities, the international community falls victim in multiple ways.
>
> Political processes, democratic institutions, social programs, economic development, and human rights are all undermined by the wealth and influence organized criminal groups can exercise. At stake is also the integrity of the financial system, particularly in parts of the world awash with proceeds of crime. Victims and witnesses feel intimidated and doubly victimized, if justice is not done.[47]

The construction of national security itself has also been "transnationalized" – not only in the sense that economic globalization and technological sophistication have unsettled national borders, but also in the sense that domestic measures pursued in the name of national security and public safety are justified to protect both domestic national security and international security. For example, recent measures taken in Canada to crack down on international terrorism in the name of national security have been justified by the need to counter a possible terrorist attack "occurring in" or "originating from" Canada.[48] The construction of Canada as a "safe haven" for dangerous outsiders who pose a threat to the United States is now a constituent feature of contemporary constructions of national security.

Project Sidewinder and the Intangible Triad Menace
In the mid-1990s, Chinese triads came to epitomize this new and monumental threat to Canadian national security. The developments that surrounded the constitution of and responses to this threat exemplify the range of factors, other than the existence of a clear and present danger, that contribute to the emergence of different, racialized crime-security risks. The

first major report about the threat posed by triads, "The New International Criminal and Asian Organized Crime Report," had been circulated in 1992 at the introduction of the enforcement-oriented Bill C-86.[49] A second report was circulated among immigration bureaucrats and RCMP officers while the bill was still being debated (it came into force on 1 January 1993).[50] Among other changes, Bill C-86 included the new provision to exclude people "reasonably" suspected of being organized criminals. According to a newspaper article with the sensational headline "Triad Menace," these reports described the triad menace as an iceberg and triad members as "ruthless, vicious criminals."[51]

It was this putative threat that provided the impetus and justification for Project Sidewinder. In 1995, in the midst of the flurry of enforcement-oriented government initiatives related to immigration and crime described earlier, the joint CSIS-RCMP Project Sidewinder was launched to assess the threat posed to Canadian security by Chinese business "tycoons," Chinese government officials, and members of Chinese crime syndicates called triads.[52] In May 1997, after a year of information gathering, the Project Sidewinder team members (two RCMP and two CSIS officers) completed their draft report, "Chinese Intelligence Services and Triads Financial Links in Canada." The report alleged that Chinese business tycoons and members of Chinese organized crime groups with links to the Chinese government had infiltrated Canadian society, that they were amassing increasing economic and political influence by buying and investing heavily in Canadian companies and by financing Canadian political parties, and that they posed a significant threat to Canada's national security: "China remains one of the greatest ongoing threats to Canada's national security and Canadian industry. There is no longer any doubt that the Chinese Intelligence Service ha[s] been able to gain influence on important sectors of the Canadian economy, including ... real estate, high technology, security and many others. In turn, it gave them access to economic, political and some military intelligence of Canada."[53]

The draft report was to be examined by the Joint Review Board, but before this took place CSIS carried out its own review and promptly shelved it. According to CSIS officials, the draft was a "rumour laced conspiracy theory" with little intelligence value.[54] The director general of CSIS's Requirements, Analysis, and Production Branch explained that the report had been shelved because its findings were "based on innuendo and unsupported by facts."[55] Members of the RCMP, a handful of experts on security and intelligence issues, and a collection of right-wing Alliance politicians were outraged at this blatant disregard for Canada's national security and sovereignty. A series of newspaper articles reported, among other things, that the report was shelved as a result of political interference from the highest level of government for fear of jeopardizing important Canadian economic interests in

China. As put by Michel Juneau, coauthor of the report, "senior managers at CSIS prevented us from completing our job, not because the report was wrong but because they didn't like what we were finding out."[56] The Security Intelligence Review Committee (SIRC) was enlisted to investigate these and other allegations relating to the way in which CSIS handled the Sidewinder report. In brief, the committee found that there was no evidence of political interference. It also found that there was no evidence that the decision to shelve the project had been "premature" or that this decision had "subsequently hobbled the government's ability to deal with emerging threats to the country."[57] SIRC also characterized the report in unforgiving terms: it was "deeply flawed and unpersuasive in almost all respects. Whole sections employ leaps of logic and non-sequiturs to the point of incoherence; the paper is rich with the language of scare-mongering and conspiracy theory. Exemplifying the report's general lack of rigour are gross syntactical, grammatical and spelling errors too numerous to count."[58]

Media coverage and familiar grumblings were tweaked again by the release in 2000 of these results of SIRC's investigation.[59] They were further fuelled by public statements made by Brian McAdam, a former Immigration officer in Hong Kong, and Robert Read, a suspended RCMP officer, about corruption in the Canadian Consulate in Hong Kong that was facilitating the entry of Chinese "criminals" into Canada.[60] According to Michel Juneau, what makes "Red China" such a "grave threat" to Canada, greater perhaps than even the Russians, is that the Chinese are sneakier, more devious, and less likely to leave clues: "With the Russians, you will find a smoking gun ... but not with the Chinese."[61]

Indeed, in a manner reminiscent of the representations of identity-shifting terrorists and devious welfare-cheating Somali war criminals, the deployment of racial/ethnic and cultural stereotypes is again central to the production of this triumvirate threat to Canadian national security. Unscrupulous Chinese business tycoons and triad members enter Canada through the "entrepreneur" or "business" immigration categories, disguise their true intentions, and then begin – with snakelike stealth and cunning – to extend their tentacular grip on Canadian society. Just as the identity of Somali refugees came to be associated with the negative stereotype of "desert gypsies," Chinese immigrants, particularly those making perfectly legal investments in Canada (as indeed has been encouraged by Canadian authorities through the creation of special classes of immigration designed specifically for this purpose), came to be identified as a devious, cunning, and invisible ("intangible") criminal menace. This stereotypical representation is evocatively captured by the words of Sun Tzu in *The Art of War,* which are reproduced in the draft report, as if to invest the stereotype with a degree of legitimacy and an air of truth by reference to the reflections of an ancient yet well-known Chinese military general who has become a widely cited cultural icon, particularly among Western self-help business guides and motivational consultants: "Be so subtle that you are invisible. Be so mysterious that you are intangible. Then you will control your rival's fate."[62]

War Crimes and Crimes against Humanity
Under the *Crimes against Humanity and War Crimes Act* (2000), crimes against humanity are defined as "murder, extermination, enslavement, deportation, imprisonment, torture, sexual violence, persecution or any other inhumane act or omission that is committed against any civilian population or any identifiable group and that, at the time and in the place of its commission, constitutes a crime against humanity according to customary international law or conventional international law or by virtue of its being criminal according to the general principles of law recognized by the community of nations, whether or not it constitutes a contravention of the law in force at the time and in the place of its commission."[63] A war crime is defined as "an act or omission committed during an armed conflict that, at the time and in the place of its commission, constitutes a war crime according to customary international law or conventional international law applicable to armed conflicts, whether or not it constitutes a contravention of the law in force at the time and in the place of its commission."[64] War crimes thus include murder, extermination, enslavement, torture, and any other inhumane act committed against civilians in a widespread or systematic manner.[65] The *Crimes against Humanity and War Crimes Act* includes genocide as a separate prohibited category.[66]

World War Two War Criminals
The question of how to deal with people in Canada who are suspected of war crimes has long been the subject of much attention and controversy. In 1985, the Deschenes Commission of Inquiry on War Criminals produced a list of 883 suspected war criminals in Canada and recommended that the RCMP and the Department of Justice be given the mandate to investigate them. The War Crimes/Immigration and Passport section of the RCMP was set up to assist the commission in its work. In 1987, the government announced that criminal prosecutions and citizenship revocations of suspected war criminals would be pursued and that deportation would be used for individuals who had entered the country through fraud or misrepresentation, and the *Immigration Act, Citizenship Act,* and *Criminal Code of Canada* were amended accordingly. Shortly thereafter, the Crimes against Humanity and War Crimes Unit of the Department of Justice was created, and it continues to be the lead department with respect to World War Two cases.[67]

Between 1987 and 1992, the government began four criminal proceedings against suspected war criminals in Canada, none of which resulted in criminal convictions. The difficulties posed by, for example, dead or inaccessible witnesses, the death of the accused, missing documents, and other procedural rules made it very difficult to secure convictions for alleged crimes that had been committed decades earlier. In addition, in 1994 the Supreme Court ruling in *R. v. Finta* set a high burden of proof for these cases.[68] As a result, in 1995 the government announced a shift in focus, from criminal prosecution to the civil avenues of denaturalization and deportation. This approach allows the government to take action against suspected war criminals in Canada without actually having to prove that the person in question is a war criminal. Instead, under section 10 of the *Citizenship Act*, citizenship may be revoked if it can be proven that "they had entered Canada and/or obtained citizenship through misrepresentation, fraud, or the concealment of material facts."[69] By pursuing administrative as opposed to criminal proceedings against suspected war criminals, cumbersome procedural safeguards of criminal prosecution are side-stepped, making punitive action in the form of revocation and deportation more likely.

The civil approach is criticized by those concerned with the lack of procedural protections for and the possibility of wrongful decisions against those suspected of war criminality. But it is also criticized by those who argue that the failure to prosecute war criminals is not only an affront to the victims and the principles of justice but may even encourage the "rogue's gallery" of war criminals to come and seek "safe haven" in Canada.[70]

The objective of criminal prosecution for war crimes and crimes against humanity persists both in Canada and internationally. In May 1993, the United Nations Security Council created the International Tribunal for the former Yugoslavia, and in November 1994 the International Tribunal for Rwanda was created. In 1998, the *Rome Statute on the International Criminal Court* established the International Criminal Court (ICC), which came into force on 1 July 2002.[71] The ICC is a permanent court set up to try people accused of war crimes, crimes against humanity, and genocide. It will step in only when national authorities are unwilling or unable to prosecute the case themselves. In 2000, to strengthen Canadian criminal law relating to war crimes and crimes against humanity and to implement the *Rome Statute*, Canada passed the above-mentioned *Crimes against Humanity and War Crimes Act*. It created the new offences of genocide, crimes against humanity, war crimes, and breach of responsibility by military commanders and civilian superiors. It also introduced provisions to protect the administration of justice at the ICC and the safety of judges, officials, and witnesses. This act enables Canada to prosecute any individual in Canada for any of these offences regardless of where they took place.[72] In 2002, CIC reported that seventy-two cases had been "identified for possible prosecution."[73]

Modern War Criminals

In 1987, the 1976 *Immigration Act* was amended to include suspected war crimes and crimes against humanity as grounds for inadmissibility, and in 1989 it was amended again to allow for the exclusion of individuals from making a refugee claim if they are suspected on reasonable grounds of having been complicit in crimes against humanity. In 1993, the *Immigration Act* was amended further to exclude individuals who were senior officials in the service of a government that, in the opinion of the minister, engages or has engaged in terrorism, systematic or gross human rights violations, genocide, a war crime, or a crime against humanity.[74] All of these amendments were justified by the need to bring the criminal inadmissibility classes of the *Immigration Act* in line with contemporary international developments resulting in refugee claims being made by people suspected of war crimes and crimes against humanity.

In 1996, the government established a small centralized national unit within the CIC to monitor modern war crime cases. In 1997, the government conducted a review of its war crimes strategy and announced that $46.8 million over three years was to be allocated to the RCMP, the Department of Justice, and CIC to "initiate some 14 new WWII cases, process its existing caseload of modern-day war criminals, improve Canada's ability to prevent new arrivals and ensure the prompt removal of those who managed to enter Canada."[75] Subsequently, a number of initiatives were announced, including the expansion of CIC's Modern War Crimes Unit (from three to sixteen members), the creation of an intelligence unit, the development of an information technologies infrastructure, the establishment of streamlined procedures, and the creation of the Interdepartmental Operations Group to coordinate the war crime activities of the RCMP, the CIC, and the Department of Justice.[76]

The enforcement of war crimes and crimes against humanity exclusions has three main objectives: prevention through refusal of entry to Canada, denial of refugee protection, and removal of those detected within Canada. The number of cases of World War Two war crimes initiated as a result of this multipronged effort to "break the cycle of immunity" and to ensure that Canada "is not and will not become a safe haven for war criminals" is small. The number of allegations of war criminals in Canada investigated since 1995 is 1,673. Only eighteen have resulted in the initiation of revocation and deportation cases. The prosecution of these cases suffered from long delays. Of those concluded at the end of the 2001-2 fiscal year, six of the defendants had passed away during the proceedings, three cases were concluded in favour of the defendants, and six were concluded in favour of the minister of immigration.[77]

The enforcement of war crimes and crimes against humanity exclusions against those suspected of being modern war criminals has produced greater numbers. As a measure of success, in its 2001-2 annual report, Canada's Crimes against Humanity and War Crimes Program reported that, since the creation of the Modern War Crimes Unit in 1996, 2,011 immigrant and visitor cases have been refused overseas. In 2001-2 alone, overseas immigration officers investigated 1,797 cases and refused 445. This number represents a decline from the previous year, during which overseas officers investigated 2,374 cases and refused 644. This decline is explained by CIC by the overall reduction in travellers to Canada after the September 11th attacks. In 2002-3, 2,103 modern war criminal cases were investigated overseas, and 355 individuals were denied entry to Canada. These numbers do not necessarily reflect the numbers of applicants who were actually complicit in war crimes or crimes against humanity. Even putting aside the interpretive vagaries of "complicity" and "reasonable grounds to believe," these numbers include those who were investigated for war crimes or crimes against humanity but who were ultimately refused on other grounds as well as those who withdrew their claims.[78]

Since 11 September 2001, more refugee claimants are being investigated, and this has resulted in more ministerial interventions in refugee claims to exclude those suspected of war criminality or crimes against humanity violations. In 2001-2, CIC intervened in 350 refugee determination cases, up from 227 in 2000-1.[79] Fifty-three claimants were excluded on this basis, up from thirty-five the previous year.[80] In 2002-3, 242 interventions in refugee determination cases were filed by CIC, and seventy-three claimants were excluded from the determination process.[81]

The resort to deportation and revocation proceedings instead of criminal prosecutions has troubled not only those concerned with the civil rights and liberties of suspects accorded fewer protections under civil proceedings but also those who see deportation and revocation as inadequate punishment for the "world's worst criminals ... who have committed the world's most heinous crimes."[82] The question of how to deal with those suspected of war crimes and crimes against humanity raises a host of complicated legal, political, and administrative issues.[83] In addition to the heightened focus on criminality that these developments indicate, of particular interest here is the interchangeability of administrative immigration proceedings and criminal proceedings, of deportation and criminal punishment.

Drug Crimes

As previously discussed, under Canadian immigration legislation, a person may be denied the right to make a refugee claim. Amendments to the *Immigration Act* in 1989 granted the minister (and delegates) the power to intervene in refugee claims if exclusion issues are raised. Under the *Refugee Convention,* persons may be excluded if they have committed a serious nonpolitical crime outside the country of refuge, if they have committed crimes against humanity, or if they have been guilty of acts contrary to the purposes and principles of the United Nations.

Traditionally, none of these provisions was interpreted as extending to drug offences. However, after the introduction of several major UN initiatives relating to international drug trafficking and in light of the three major international drug control treaties,[84] the Toronto CIC Appeals office reported in 1997 that it had begun to successfully argue that "drug traffickers should be denied protection as refugees" because drug trafficking is contrary to the purposes and principles of the United Nations. CIC proudly announced that "drug traffickers are now routinely excluded from protection as refugees."[85] However, in 1998, the Supreme Court of Canada released its controversial decision on this question in *Pushpanathan*.[86] The SCC held that people cannot be denied their refugee hearing because of a conviction for drug trafficking. The court noted that the purpose of article 1F(c) of the *Refugee Convention* "is to exclude those individuals responsible for serious, sustained or systemic violations of fundamental human rights which amount to persecution in a non-war setting." So, notwithstanding the pronouncements of the United Nations,[87] national governments, and the efforts of CIC officials, the SCC held that drug trafficking does not represent a sustained violation of human rights and therefore is not contrary to the purposes and principles of the United Nations.

Nonetheless, individuals may still be barred from making a refugee claim for reasons of "serious criminality" defined in section 36(1) of *IRPA* as (a) a conviction in Canada for a criminal offence for which a sentence of ten years or more may be imposed or for which a term of two years in prison was received, (b) a conviction outside Canada that, were it received in Canada, would result in a prison term of ten years or more, and (c) an act committed outside Canada that, were it committed inside Canada, would be punishable by ten years or more. This category continues to have the potential to encompass and therefore exclude those with convictions for drug offences.

The Metropolis Project and the Production of Knowledge on the "Problem" of Crime and Immigrants

The 1990s witnessed a proliferation of government-sponsored research-oriented initiatives on different issues relating to Canada, immigration, and immigrants. CIC's Metropolis Project is a major, government-initiated, and well-funded site of knowledge production relating to immigration. It is also a distinctly neoliberal technology of government, characterized by the forging and nurturing of "partnerships" and "networks" between "key stakeholders," including formal government institutions, universities, research institutes, think tanks, the private sector, and nongovernmental, community-based organizations. These partners, though funded largely by the federal government, together engage in the production of knowledge and expertise on "critical policy questions, options and program delivery options."[88] The

Metropolis Project is promoted as a necessary response to the reduction in public spending that has "forced governments everywhere to reevaluate their priorities and to seek strategic alliances that would rationalise scarce resources and leverage help from other sectors."[89]

The mandate and goals of Metropolis are exemplary of what Nikolas Rose describes as advanced liberal diagrams of power in which the state is "partner, animator and facilitator for a variety of independent agents and powers and should exercise only limited powers of its own, steering and regulating rather than rowing and providing."[90] As explained by Meyer Burstein, executive head of the project in 1997, it had become apparent to governments that they needed "to build new institutions, to engage a broader spectrum of stakeholders and to create a shared strategic focus."[91] To effectively manage both "the flow of immigrants" and the "consequences of immigration for the host society," Metropolis is founded on the belief that governments *"need to invest more heavily in knowledge."*[92] Its objectives are to "improve public policy by situating knowledge at the core of decision-making. Our goals are to build a unique network of researchers and decision-makers; to create a policy thrust by continually involving governments and stakeholders in project design and problem definition; and to energize the network through conferences, policy forums and extensive informational exchanges."[93] "Centres of Excellence" have been set up by CIC in Montreal, Vancouver, Toronto, and Edmonton. These centres support research carried out by academic and community-based "partners" on settlement and integration issues as they relate to the "host" communities and the immigrants themselves. Metropolis also hosts numerous national and international conferences, workshops, seminars, and "conversations."

As described by Metropolis, "since its beginnings in 1996, the Metropolis Project has created a formidable network of policy professionals and scientific researchers drawn from governments, universities, inter-governmental organizations, think tanks, and non-governmental agencies here in Canada and in over twenty other countries. This network has greatly enlarged the body of knowledge and expertise available to policy and program development experts, has increased sensitivity amongst academics to the needs of government and inter-governmental bodies, and has led to more productive relations with NGOs."[94] Metropolis thus aspires to engage stakeholders "beyond the state" in the production of knowledge for public policy development. As put by Rose, "the complex of actors, powers, institutions and bodies of knowledge that comprise expertise ha[s] come to play a crucial role in establishing the possibility and legitimacy of government. Experts hold out the hope that the problems of government can remove themselves from the disputed terrain of politics and relocate onto the tranquil yet seductive territory of truth."[95]

According to Metropolis, "in the course of struggling to meet new challenges in the area of immigration, it has become apparent that governments need to forge a shared strategic focus and to invest in the creation of knowledge."[96] This aim guided the February 1997 Justice/Immigration Domain Seminar, cosponsored by the Metropolis Project (CIC), the RCMP, the Correctional Service of Canada, the Solicitor General Secretariat, and the federal Department of Justice. Participants included policy officials, academics from the Centres of Excellence, law enforcement officials, NGO representatives, and several "international partners" of Metropolis. The goal was to "determine the state of knowledge regarding immigration and justice, to identify gaps in that knowledge, and to determine where our research efforts should be focused."[97]

In spite of the title, it was the issue of criminality and immigration that became the focus of this two-day seminar. Enforcement – not justice – was the guiding concern. Despite the organizers' explicit rejection of dominant myths and misconceptions about immigrant criminality and the promised rejection of polemic and partisan debate, which tends to approach the issue from the perspective of either "immigrants as victims of crime" or "immigrants as perpetrators of crime," hopes for a new approach were quickly dashed. The dichotomy was not to be unsettled by this seminar; rather, it would be more comprehensively reproduced. Both sides of it, not just one, were to be addressed: "This seminar addressed both aspects of the issue by soliciting input from the enforcement, immigrant and policy-making communities."[98] The conference was accordingly divided into two sessions: "immigrants as participants in crime" and "immigrants as victims of crime." In the first session, seminar participants heard from senior representatives of KPMG Security (a private security company), the Criminal Information Service of Canada (CISC, a national police organization), the Organized Crime Unit of CIC, a Canadian sociologist on the subject of gangs, and a representative from the Dutch Ministry of Justice. In the second session, Canadian academics made presentations on hate crimes, racism in the criminal justice system, and legal pluralism.

The seminar's working groups were similarly structured by the victim/offender opposition. One workshop was designated for and attended by law enforcement personnel only. The other workshops were open to all participants. The result was that few enforcement officials worked with anybody other than other enforcement officials. Another aspect of this seminar was the pervasive tendency to conflate immigration enforcement and criminal justice enforcement. As noted in the executive summary of the seminar, "there has been a general failure to distinguish between immigration enforcement and criminal justice enforcement. While there may be overlapping areas of responsibility, the two systems need to be distinguished from each other."[99] Thus, although there was a stated concern to avoid an us-

and-them approach and to side-step the limits of conventional oppositions and misconceptions, the very organization and structure of the seminar reproduced these assumptions and ultimately reproduced, with the participation and collaboration of a range of diverse nonstate stakeholders and experts, the problem of the criminal immigrant in contradistinction to the immigrant victim.

Good Guys and Bad Guys

The incremental and systematic reconceptualization of immigration penality in terms of crime-security is consistent with the entrenchment of an "enforcement mentality" among frontline immigration officers. This is neither a new nor an uncommon concern. Immigration enforcement consists of five main components: investigation, detention, inquiry, appeals, and removals. In 1996, the Tassé Report had identified the enforcement mentality of the Enforcement Branch of CIC as a serious problem resulting in numerous infringements of people's rights, inappropriate uses of coercion and intimidation, and inhumane practices that are illegal, borderline legal, or merely underhanded. As noted in the report, "removal officers often act as if they believed that all individuals under a removal order were dangerous criminals, liars and dishonest. This leads to bad attitudes and the improper treatment of people."[100] The report recommended a complete overhaul of the CIC Enforcement Branch's code of ethics.[101]

Former frontline immigration officer Lorne Foster observes that "there is no doubt that being on the frontline in the immigration business affects one's view of the human panorama."[102] It is all about good guys and bad guys: "To seasoned immigration officers the matter is clear: you either do the job of enforcement and control or you get out. There is no alternative or in between. For the frontliner, the big tribe always takes precedence over the little tribes ... There are only 'good guys' and 'bad guys.' You do your damnedest to get the good guys in and get the bad guys out ... This good-guy-bad-guy equation on the frontline ... guides immigration officers' conduct beyond explicit rules."[103]

This enforcement mentality results in many questionable practices. Indeed, the Tassé Report was commissioned in response to an incident made public a month earlier. A former police officer and manager of CIC in Winnipeg was accused of falsifying deportation papers to expedite the removal process. Disregarding CIC's advice that the story "did not merit a formal investigation," the RCMP went ahead with its own internal investigation to find out why the case had not been acted upon. The police also initiated a criminal investigation.[104] It was after this incident that the minister appointed Tassé to review removal policies, observing that "it's not an easy job but ... forgery is unacceptable and should never be condoned."[105] Subsequently, two other immigration officers from Mississauga, one of whom was also a manager, were charged with forging a document also to expedite removal.[106]

No charges were laid against the Winnipeg Immigration manager, and in March 1996 the criminal charges against the other two officers were dropped. While initially the Crown had wanted a conditional discharge and community service, one of the officers charged had been promoted while the case was being handled. Because her promotion relocated her to Tokyo, she could not be monitored, and the Crown agreed to drop the criminal charges. Instead, she and her colleague were charged under the 1976 *Immigration Act* with "making a false statement" and were suspended for several days.[107]

Immigration lawyer David Matas describes the enforcement mentality as an organizational and systemic problem that issues in part from the dual purposes of immigration law and policy: "If you look at the Act [it] serves two purposes. It is to allow some people in and to keep other people out ... The department is bicephalous. But the individual people, they only perform one function. There's an admissions side and an enforcement side. The enforcement people develop a group ethic and they tend to support one another, they tend to agree with what they are doing, they attend to trade practices."[108]

In a manner reminiscent of those now fabled days of the Wild West, there are good guys and bad guys, cops and criminals, borders and badges: "The custodial 'feeling' or 'desire' of the frontline immigration officer is to wrestle the bad guy to the ground right at the nation's turnstiles, take him for a spin and send him home ... Despite all the fine print and officialese, seasoned frontline immigration officers are really only concerned with one thing – rooting out the bad guys; everything else is bureaucratic minutiae and 'small potatoes' and not really worth worrying about."[109]

The Temporary Entry Permit

Sovereign power entails not only the violent power to punish but also the power to suspend the rule or to withhold punishment. In the context of immigration, this may involve, for example, ordering a stay of deportation, issuing a permit to allow someone to stay for humanitarian and compassionate reasons, or issuing a temporary entry permit or minister's permit.

This permit, subsumed under *IRPA* by the Temporary Resident Permit provision, overrules any and all exclusionary decisions previously made and allows a person who is legally inadmissible for criminal, health, or technical reasons to enter Canada for a limited period.[110] The permit is subject to revocation at any time. Under the 1976 *Immigration Act,* only designated officers were delegated this ministerial power; under *IRPA,* all immigration officers may issue the permit – except when the reason for inadmissibility is serious criminality, in which case immigration officers make a recommendation to a senior immigration officer, who makes the final decision. CIC officers are cautioned that "decisions to allow criminally inadmissible persons to come into Canada should not be made lightly."[111] With respect to criminal inadmissibility, officers are advised to consider the time elapsed since the sentence was served and whether "the client" is rehabilitated or "might be eligible for rehabilitation."[112]

More specifically, the granting of a temporary permit is a matter of assessing the risk posed by the person in question. Only those presenting an "acceptable risk" – that is, those unlikely to commit future offences – are to be granted a permit. Officers are to assess

- the seriousness of the offence
- the chances of successful settlement without committing further offences
- behavioural factors involved (drugs, alcohol)
- evidence that the person has reformed or rehabilitated
- pattern of criminal behaviour (e.g., was the offence a single event and out of character?)
- completion of all sentences, fines paid or restitution made
- outstanding criminal charges
- restriction of travel following probation or parole
- eligibility for rehabilitation or a pardon
- time elapsed since the offence occurred
- controversy or risk caused by presence of the person in Canada.[113]

As explained by Minister of Immigration Denis Coderre in 2002, "the permits give us the flexibility to respond to people in exceptional circumstances ... That being said, the health, safety and security of Canadians remain our top priority. We carefully consider any risk to Canadians before issuing a permit."[114] Unlike the finding of "humanitarian and compassionate" reasons to suspend the rule, this measure is framed in terms of risk, not relief.

That the temporary entry permit is used to grant entry to criminal offenders, even "serious" ones, suggests that the government's prohibition against foreign criminals in Canada is not the zero tolerance program that it claims to be. The 1997 ministerial report to the House of Commons on the issuance of discretionary entry permits noted that over 4,000 permits had been issued that year. Of those, 1,497 had been issued to people who were otherwise inadmissible for reasons of criminality; 395 of the crimes in question were described as "serious."[115] The right-wing Reform Party of Canada responded by seeking to pass a motion requesting the names, crimes, and countries of origin of these 1,497 people. This tactic elicited much opposition from those concerned about privacy and the possible discriminatory uses of such information. In 1999, the number of minister's permits granted to those seeking entry into Canada as well as those already in Canada jumped to 10,359. Of the 10,192 permits issued to inadmissible people seeking admission to Canada, 195 were issued to people inadmissible on medical grounds, and 7 were issued to people inadmissible for financial reasons. A further 377 were issued to people who had been convicted, inside or outside Canada, of a serious offence punishable by ten years or more in prison, and 1,010 were issued to those convicted inside or outside Canada, or to those for whom there were reasonable grounds to believe that they had been convicted outside Canada, of an indictable offence punishable by less than ten years in prison. The remaining 8,548 permits were issued under a catch-all provision covering those who do not fulfill or comply with any of the conditions or requirements of the act or regulations.[116]

Likely as a result of the controversy engendered by the granting of these permits, in 2000 the overall numbers dropped dramatically to 3,989. However, the number of permits granted to inadmissible people seeking entry to Canada who would be considered "serious" criminals by the government's own definition (convicted of an offence punishable by ten years or more in prison) actually *rose* from 377 to 464. The granting of permits to less serious criminals also rose slightly from 1,010 to 1,088.[117] In 2001, CIC reported success in holding steady the number of minister's permits at 3,994. However, once again, the number of permits granted to those fitting the "serious criminality" category rose from 464 to 606, as did the number of permits issued to those fitting the less serious category of criminality (from 1,088 to 1,178). The justification for granting ministerial permits to "serious criminals" is grounded in nationality and economics, as noted by Coderre: "Most of the permits issued to past serious criminals went to residents of the United States seeking temporary entry into Canada for employment or business, tourism or travelling to and from Alaska."[118] In 2002, the overall number of permits jumped again to 12,630. Some of them were issued under the former 1976 *Immigration Act* and some under *IRPA*. Of this total, 786 were issued to those deemed inadmissible for reasons of serious criminality, and 3,593 were issued to those deemed inadmissible for reasons of less serious criminality. Nine permits were issued to those deemed inadmissible for security reasons, 36 to those deemed inadmissible for human rights violations, 179 to those inadmissible for health reasons, and 21 to those inadmissible for financial reasons.[119]

For the Reform Party and other immigration critics, the issuance of discretionary ministerial permits to "criminals" brings the integrity of the system into question and casts doubt upon the government's true commitment to cracking down on criminals and protecting the public. In 2003, the auditor general's report on risk management was critical of the issuance of these permits due to the negative risks that they occasion and due to perceived inaccuracies in record keeping. While critics regard the issuance of minister's permits to criminals as a threat to public safety or as a weak link in the risk management approaches of contemporary government, from a different angle it indicates the rhetorical quality and discursive power of concerns about criminality and public safety and the myriad of enforcement techniques that they justify. The representation of foreign criminals and criminality, now fuelled further by terrorist forms of criminality, is largely unwavering in its condemnation. The ministerial granting of relief to those deemed inadmissible for reasons of criminality is seemingly inconsistent with that condemnation. It has been seen time and time again that humanitarian notions of mercy or relief are "trumped" by crime-security discourses. The practice of granting temporary entry permits to "criminals" thus indicates a crack in the constructed armour. This quiet, rarely publicized provision concedes that "criminals" are not always undesirable and that zero tolerance prohibitions against criminal immigrants are not as strict as the rhetoric implies. To some extent, the administration of the government's zero tolerance policies demonstrates what has been found in other contexts, such as welfare and the policing of wife assault: efforts to stamp out discretion in the pursuit of zero tolerance programs will inevitably fail. Discretion will always pop up at other locations. Frontline decision making is a complex process involving a diverse range of factors and considerations that extend well beyond the substance of policy provisions. And, indeed, in the case of temporary entry permits, the sovereign discretion to withhold punishment (in this case exclusion from Canada) is delegated to frontline decision makers and is written into the law and policy that they administer.

These discretionary permits are thus consistent with the form of sovereign power employed against undesirable and undeserving noncitizens in the context of contemporary immigration penality. The sovereign power "to decide on the exception"[120] accompanies the power to exact or withhold bodily punishment. Like the sovereign of the premodern and early modern periods, the minister of immigration (and delegated officials) are present "not only as the power exacting the vengeance of the law, but as the power that could suspend both law and vengeance ... [The sovereign] alone must remain master, he alone could wash away the offences committed on his person; although it is true that he delegated to the courts the task of exercising his power to dispense justice, he had not transferred it; he retained it in its entirety and he could suspend the sentence or increase it at will."[121]

Cosmopolitan, mobile, and "smart" criminals not only threaten "international security" and global economic systems but also pose what are regarded as dire national threats – to the security of Canada, the efficiency of the free-market economy, the integrity of state systems, and the health and safety of Canadians.

Despite the magnitude of the threats as they are constructed, measurements and statistics relating to the size of the threats are elusive.[122] The image of the iceberg used in relation to the triad threat is illustrative in this regard; it is evocative of a massive yet largely invisible danger. Indeed, even the apparent absence of the problem is itself used to demonstrate its attendant dangers and as evidence that the enforcement people are doing their jobs well and that they must continue to be supported lest the thin blue line dissolves and crime and disorder reign. The invisibility of the problem may also be explained as evidence that shape-shifting outsiders are getting more crafty at disguising their presence and concealing their identities, making the risks that they pose all the more intangible, unknowable, unpredictable, and hence dangerous.

Serious, dangerous crimes, organized crime, transnational crime, war crimes, crimes against humanity, drug crimes – as the twenty-first century begins, the border is produced and policed as a thin blue line indeed. While there has clearly been an intensification and proliferation of enforcement-oriented measures since September 11th, and while these measures have since received more vigorous public and political support, it is not – as many have proclaimed – a "brand-new world."

The "problem" of crime-security and linked concerns about fraud and victims became the central preoccupation and justification of immigration enforcement policy and practice over the 1990s. Immigration enforcement is now a central and largely taken-for-granted mechanism of national crime control, and immigration penality is indeed "governed through crime." The next chapter examines the diverse and intersecting authorities, networks, modes of power, technologies, and forms of knowledge involved in the quest for border security.

9
Risk-Smart Borders

While the quest for border security has unquestionably intensified since the attacks of September 11th, the pursuit was already well under way before then. The crime security nexus coupled with the spectre of fraud and articulated with the logic of risk has framed this quest and the endless and energetic development of new and better strategies that it inspires.

Whether national borders are viewed as fortified or fading away – or as both depending on the border crosser's relationship with the global economy and on other points of disadvantage – the border itself is largely taken for granted. It is "black-boxed"; its sociotechnological complexity and heterogeneity are obscured. The border is an ongoing accomplishment, yet the processes by which it is continually produced are erased by its apparent self-evidence.

Diverse and intersecting authorities are involved in the production and regulation of the border. They include an array of national and international authorities, government and quasi-government agencies, law enforcement agencies, nongovernment organizations, ethnocultural community-based organizations, legal and human rights agencies, health agencies, private security agencies, and public and private agencies. The print and broadcast media weigh in heavily as well, not only in the general sense of their role in shaping public opinion and the cultural constitution of social anxieties but more specifically because of their practical role in the exposure of individual cases (e.g., of detention or sanctuary) that can result in ministerial interventions. Community members are also enlisted in the regulation of the border through, for example, third-party risk management programs or community policing strategies that hail out desirable and law-abiding community members and engage them as informants.

In addition to this multiplicity of authorities, different modes of power and diverse governing technologies are at play. Many of these technologies evidence the continuing presence of sovereign power through coercive, violent, and bodily punishments and the ways in which the rule and the punishment can be suspended. Others give practical effect to governmental techniques and diverse forms of risk knowledge that shape and are shaped by the endless and endlessly unfulfilled "yearning for security." Put simply, the border is continuously constituted on a variety of sites, through an assemblage of diverse authorities, technologies, forms of knowledge, and modes of power that include but are not limited to legal regimes or the formal institutions of government. As discussed in Chapter 1, this interplay of sovereign and governmental regimes demonstrates the governmentalization of immigration penality.[1]

This chapter begins to pry open the black box of the border by surveying the range of state and nonstate authorities, networks, "partnerships," technologies, and practices engaged in the continual production and enforcement of the border at a variety of territorial and extraterritorial sites, paying close attention to the central place of risk management strategies in this assemblage. The proliferation of efforts to develop and implement national and international risk management strategies indicates the prominence of governmental technologies in the production of borders, the governance of immigration penality, and the regulation of the population. These strategies do not aim to normalize individuals through discipline and the production and use of expert knowledges, nor do they manifest the repressive, negative, and legalistic characteristics of sovereign power. While managing risks is not a new governmental project, the initiatives described here are distinct from the social techniques of risk management characteristic of welfare liberalism that consist of risk pooling across the whole nation-state. In contrast, many of the risk management strategies pursued in this domain are distinctly neoliberal. They map onto a private as opposed to a social version of risk management in that they are characterized by the differentiation of the risk pool through small group risk profiling.[2]

The development and application of risk assessment and management techniques are guiding preoccupations promising that new and better and more innovations will tame uncertainty, control risk, and enhance security. Their inevitable failure to live up to such promises only reenergizes the quest, providing a "perpetual incitement for the incessant improvement of systems, generation of more knowledge, invention of more techniques, all driven by the technological imperative to tame uncertainty and master hazard."[3] In the quest for security, there is an endless need to improve information production and sharing technologies, described by Richard Ericson and Kevin Haggerty in terms of the "insatiable quest ... for inexhaustibly detailed and continuous risk management knowledge."[4] The improvement of existing information technologies, the development of new and better information networks, and the forging and nurturing of diverse partnerships are seen as critical to the pursuit of smart borders: "risk management makes the border smart."[5]

"Partners in Security": From Cops to Communities

"Partners," "integration," "collaboration," "cooperation," "networks" – these are key terms in the domain of border control, as in most domains of governance. The importance of forging, enhancing, and nurturing national and international interagency cooperation, communication, and exchange of information is a long-standing theme that has become even more prominent since September 11th.[6]

The steady expansion and merging of the categories of crime-security and rising concerns about fraud are central to these developments, as is the prominence of the language of risk and the development and implementation of risk management strategies. Also notable is both a broadening of the mandates of, as well as a certain blurring and reconfiguration of the boundaries between, Canada's different "partners in security." As some of the preceding discussion has revealed, they include CIC; CSIS; the Canada Border Services Agency (CBSA), which consists – as of 12 December 2003 – of the customs program of the Canada Customs and Revenue Agency (CCRA), the intelligence, enforcement, and interdiction functions of CIC, and the port of entry passenger and import inspection functions of the Canadian Food Inspection Agency (CFIA); RCMP; Department of Foreign Affairs and International Trade; Department of Defence; municipal, provincial, and national police forces; Interpol; foreign law enforcement authorities and governments (most notably the United States); international organizations; airlines and airports; private security (airports, detention centres, deportations); legal and advocacy groups; and members of religious and ethnic communities.[7] The following discussion reviews a few of these key "partnerships" in more detail.

Law Enforcement

The RCMP Immigration, Passport and Citizenship Program
The RCMP's Immigration, Passport and Citizenship Program (IPC) is responsible for investigating violations of *IRPA*, the *Citizenship Act*, and the *Criminal Code of Canada*. In 2003, the program had approximately 200 regular members posted to seventeen immigration and passport sections across Canada.[8] The mandate of this program is to "work in concert with domestic and foreign agencies at all levels as well as the community at large, to protect and enhance the quality of life through education, prevention and enforcement."[9]

Two guiding concerns of this program are people smuggling and the proliferation of high-quality fraudulent travel and identity documents.[10] These concerns are linked with the threats posed by organized crime and terrorism. IPC is also responsible for the criminal identification, screening, and investigation of *Convention* refugee claimants arriving in Canada in order "to provide information to CIC that members or associates of organized crime groups, terrorists, persons with criminality or war criminals are attempting to enter Canada." All refugee claimants are fingerprinted by CIC immigration centres and officers or by "accredited fingerprint contractors."[11] The RCMP receives and records the fingerprints of all refugee claimants in Canada until the person becomes a citizen (or until the person reaches the age of eighty, as provided under the *Privacy Act*). All fingerprints are now entered into the Automatic Fingerprint Identification System (AFIS), which checks for criminal histories or multiple refugee claims. In 2003, the program reported that the database contains more than three million fingerprints, including more than 250,000 *Convention* refugee fingerprints.[12]

The RCMP warns that, without criminal identification screening of refugee claimants, "Canada potentially could become a haven for the world's most notorious organized crime syndicates and terrorist organizations using the guise of the Convention refugee process to illegally enter Canada. The Canadian elected government officials have a duty to the Canadian public and electorate to keep Canada a sovereign nation and provide Canadians with safe communities and safe homes."[13] Public safety, communities, homes, and national sovereignty are here linked to the threats posed to them by criminals and terrorists in the figure of the fraudulent refugee claimant.

The RCMP Immigration Task Force

With respect to the arrest of persons who are the subject of an immigration warrant, the RCMP responds to requests from CIC to assist in the actual arrest or removal of an individual, where, "in the view of both agencies, the individual poses a danger to the public due to a history of criminality, or who resides in a geographic location known to be hostile to law enforcement personnel."[14] In these matters and indeed in all of their work, members of the program cooperate closely with municipal and provincial police forces: "Metro, Peel, regional police and any others in the area, the O.P.P. – there's real partnerships there."[15]

Until 1994, the RCMP responded as needed to requests from CIC to carry out high-risk arrests on its behalf. However, in the wake of the 1994 murders of Todd Baylis and Georgina Leimonis in Toronto,[16] CIC and the RCMP announced the creation of a "fully dedicated" arrest unit, called the Greater Toronto High Risk Arrest Unit (later called the RCMP/Immigration Task Force [ITF]). These 1994 murders and the hue and cry that ensued provided the impetus for the creation of this unit; while the department had been previously strapped for cash, "after Baylis, suddenly we had a task force *and* ... with existing funds." The official justification for the provision of this service on a permanent basis in Toronto was framed by the need to protect the safety of unarmed CIC enforcement officers responsible for arresting individuals with outstanding deportation orders against them and, related to that, the view that certain areas of the city were known to be traditionally hostile to law enforcement. In 1998, this unit was staffed by twelve regular RCMP members and five CIC investigators. Later a number of officers from the Toronto Police Services Repeat Offender Parole Enforcement (ROPE) were added to the force.[17]

CIC does the initial assessment to determine whether the case is likely to entail a high-risk arrest. If such is the case, it is referred to the ITF. There are two criteria for assessing the risk level of an arrest: whether the crimes committed by the person involved violence and whether the person lives in an area known to be hostile to law enforcement – for example, the area surrounding Jane and Finch in Toronto, home to a large black population.

In 2003, the ITF outlined its objectives "to apprehend persons dangerous to the public or possessing a record of serious criminality, domestic or foreign, who are subject to immigration enforcement action."[18] Or, as summed up by one of the force's officers, "to hunt down those who choose to flee."[19] The ITF usually sends five or six officers to carry out an arrest to lessen the likelihood that the person will attempt to flee or resist.[20] This doesn't always work. In 1999, Glenford Johnson died during an apparent attempt to avoid arrest. Five ITF officers, a security guard, and a trained guard dog forcibly entered Johnson's apartment, where he was inside with his wife. Johnson fled to the balcony and fell to his death. He was not a "career criminal" or a "high risk fugitive" of the sort described by the ITF. He had no criminal record, and his only violation was that he had overstayed his visitor's visa. He also had a valid immigration application for sponsorship under way at the time of his death. In the judgment of immigration lawyer Lorne Waldman, it was "an immense overreaction" and a "terrible tragedy" – made worse by the fact that, if his wife's sponsorship application had been approved, Johnson would have been able to stay in Canada legally.[21]

Other Law Enforcement Links
There are a variety of links between CIC and other law enforcement agencies, including information- and technology-based links (e.g., interconnected databases); institutional links (e.g., co-locating of personnel, joint task forces); and practical, everyday links (e.g., informal communications and practices).

If somebody slated for deportation does not appear for removal as required, a warrant is issued by CIC for that person's arrest. The warrant is entered into the Canadian Police Information System, which can be accessed through the computer of every police officer's vehicle across Canada. Police information contained in this system is also accessible to customs and immigration officers. When the police stop somebody for whatever reason, and that person turns out to be wanted under an immigration warrant, CIC is contacted, and the person is arrested. In 1995, CIC set up the Immigration Warrant Response Centre (IWRC) in partnership with the RCMP and the Canadian Police Information Centre (CPIC). It enables immigration and police officers across Canada to confirm immigration warrants anytime and to arrange for the person under warrant to be taken into custody.[22] The decision to arrest depends on a variety of factors, including whether there is room in the region's detention centre.

Prior to September 11th, the links between CIC and various municipal, provincial, and federal police authorities had already led to the creation of a variety of more local, collaborative enforcement initiatives. They have included those targeting "people smugglers," the "multi-national criminal element" in casinos, suspicious arrivals at airports, illegal land or water border crossers, ports, and marine "vulnerabilities."[23] Predating the above initiatives by nearly three decades is the Combined Forces Special Enforcement Unit (CFSEU) created in the Toronto area in 1977 to "investigate, prosecute, expose, and dismantle organized criminal enterprises." Its mandate is also "to share intelligence with our partners and to cooperate with, and assist other organized crime enforcement units at the national and international levels."[24] Designed to "provide one stop shopping," the unit was originally made up of seventeen officers from the Ontario Provincial Police (OPP), Toronto Police Service, York Regional Police Service, Peel Regional Police Service, and Royal Canadian Mounted Police. In January 1999, it was expanded to sixty-six members, including officers from CIC, CCRA, and the Criminal Intelligence Service of Ontario.[25] In 2002, another CFSEU team was launched in the Golden Horseshoe Area of Ontario.[26]

After September 11th, the RCMP created Integrated National Security Enforcement Teams (INSETs), "multi-agency law enforcement teams" in Toronto, Montreal, Ottawa, and Vancouver. Working closely with their "national and international partners," these teams target the linked threats posed by the criminality, terrorist groups or individuals who pose a threat to national security."[27] In 2003, it was announced that the CFSEUs and INSETs would come together in the new CFSEU/INSET integrated operational centre. This facility will house investigators from eleven different federal, provincial, and municipal partners in security to work collaboratively "on major criminal extremist and organized crime investigations." These partners include the Toronto Police Service; Ontario Provincial Police; Royal Canadian Mounted Police; York, Peel, and Durham Regional Police; CIC; Canada Customs and Revenue Agency; Canadian Security Intelligence Service; federal Department of Justice; provincial Crown Prosecution Service; and provincial Anti-Terrorism Unit, funded by the Ontario Provincial Police.[28] As noted by the RCMP in 2004, "the greatest benefit of the new facility, however, is that partnering agencies will have access to the communication systems and computer databases of all member agencies."[29]

In addition to these formal links, informal networks and communications among the security partners are extensive and critical to their enforcement activities. For example, CIC and CCRA border enforcement officers will routinely communicate with police departments regarding possible criminal concerns relating to noncitizens in Canada. These concerns may relate to well-known events that attract large numbers of those considered to be high-risk groups of people, such as the Friday the 13th Bike Rally in Dover, Ontario, or the Caribana festival in Toronto. Communications may also be more case specific, as when police are given a "heads up" by border officers about certain border crossers who, while technically admissible, have nonetheless raised suspicions or when CIC officers are informed about certain border crossers of concern to law enforcement.[30]

Canada Customs

In addition to the monitoring of the movement of goods and services across the border and the collection of taxes, customs officers carry out the primary inspections of travellers seeking entry to Canada on behalf of CIC. Canada Customs has been through several recent transitions. The Canada Customs and Revenue Agency (CCRA) was created in 1999 with the passage of the *Canada Customs and Revenue Agency Act*.[31] While still accountable to the minister of revenue, the former ministry was vested with a new neoliberal corporate identity, a board of management, and new uniforms. The change was justified by reference to the need to make its operations more streamlined, efficient, accountable, and flexible as "part of the Canadian government's process of modernizing Canada's public service for the new millennium."[32]

As the revenue collection side of the work of customs diminished after the North American Free Trade Agreement (NAFTA) was signed in 1992, it became more common to hear CCRA officers promoted according to their border enforcement activities as the "first line of defence against drugs, contraband, and illegal firearms."[33] In 1997, January 26th was designated International Customs Day as a tribute to "the contribution of the men and women of Canada Customs to the safety of Canada's communities."[34] And the latest move, which joined Canada Customs with CIC enforcement and CFIA inspections in the CBSA, represents at least a formal acknowledgment of the identity shifts and role changes that have characterized the work of Canada Customs over the years, changes that, while under way over the 1990s, were certainly infused with added urgency after the attacks of September 11th.

Also pivotal was the 1991 abduction and murder of Nina de Villiers by Jonathan Yeo, a man with a history of violence against women who was wanted by American authorities and who had crossed the border into Canada. Many argued that this tragedy could have been prevented had customs officers had the power to detain him. In March 1997, then minister of revenue Jane Stewart announced the tabling of legislation that amended the *Customs Act* and the *Criminal Code* to expand the enforcement powers of designated customs officers.[35] The wide and sensational public and political attention that Nina de Villier's murder received, the recommendations of a coroner's jury, and the sustained lobbying efforts of Canadians against Violence Everywhere Advocating Its Termination (CAVEAT), Mothers against Drunk Driving (MADD), and CEUDA (Customs Excise Union Douanes Accise) certainly contributed to the support of this legislation, and in May 1997 *An Act to Amend the Customs Act and the Criminal Code* (Bill C-18) received royal assent.[36] Since then, there has been increasing emphasis on crime control. As expressed by Stewart, "Working with the RCMP and other domestic and international law enforcement agencies, the men and women of Revenue Canada's custom's operations have contributed greatly to keeping our communities and our streets safe."[37]

This reform recognized CCRA officers as the "first response" to criminal and dangerous people seeking entry to Canada. The "First Response" program was introduced in 2000 at selected ports of entry across Canada. It vested designated customs officers with expanded powers to arrest without warrant and to detain individuals suspected of having committed offences under the *Criminal Code*. Designated officers received training on the use of force and on the *Criminal Code* and were equipped with handcuffs, batons, and pepper spray.[38] In 2003, CCRA announced that all customs officers will be trained and designated as having first response capabilities by the end of 2005.[39] This issue is contentious. CEUDA has argued for some time that customs officers should receive more compensation for their work since their law enforcement role has been expanded. In June 2004, customs officers at airports and ports of entry began a series of job actions in protest. A related and also controversial issue that has engaged the CCRA and CEUDA for some time is the Canadian government's refusal to arm frontline CCRA officers.[40]

Communities

Further demonstrating the governmentalization of immigration penality and the rise of neoliberal regimes of government as discussed in Chapter 1, in addition to the kinds of links and partnerships already outlined, Canada Customs has initiated two programs that enlist different communities in the work of border control. The Partners in Protection (PIP) program aims to "secure the flow of low risk, legitimate goods and travellers" across the border by encouraging businesses and organizations to sign "goodwill agreements" that indicate their willingness to work with the CBSA to enhance their security levels.[41] In the effort to align the aspirations of business with those relating to border control, private industry is offered a variety of benefits in return for its goodwill. These include quicker movement of low-risk travellers and goods through customs; better security levels; enhanced reputations for their organizations; better understanding of customs requirements; and better communication between their employees and the CBSA. More generally, the CBSA notes that, "by working together with the CBSA, private industry helps protect Canadian society and facilitates legitimate trade."[42]

The CBSA also maintains a "Border Watch Toll Free Line." Its promotion encourages ordinary community members to call in any "information about suspicious border activity," day or night, no matter how trivial or whether the reported suspicions are "after the fact." While the information provided may be shared with the CBSA's national and international partners in security, the caller's anonymity and confidentiality are assured. While a reward is not guaranteed, it is offered as a possible outcome left to the discretion of the CBSA.[43] Like Crime Stoppers, Border Watch is an example of "governing at a distance" consistent with neoliberalism. Border Watch uses "anonymization," rewards, and promotion (although the last is largely limited to the website) as key techniques to generate distance between authorities and citizens or communities and to avoid the risk of *knowingly* receiving and acting upon information that may have been provided by tainted or "morally spoiled" tipsters.[44]

Immigration enforcement and border control have not been immune to the emergence of the idea of "community policing," which has taken hold in the context of law enforcement across the country. A senior official of the Immigration, Federal, and Foreign Policy Branch of the RCMP expressed the importance of this relatively new mode of policing in no uncertain terms: "In my opinion, community policing is the only way to do immigration work ... Any other way is not successful. You need to get the communities on side." The official explained that the RCMP in general, and its immigration branch in particular, were in transition "from what they call traditional response-based policing to community-based policing."[45] The idea of community policing conjures up a vision of the forging and nurturing of mutually cooperative relationships between communities and the police in such a way as to reconfigure the relationship from one of hierarchy and alienation to one of mutual support and collaborative problem solving and policy design. In this ideal, "the community" is engaged in the setting of priorities and the development of policing policies and strategies, and the police are more accessible, less preoccupied with reactive crime control, and more concerned with problem solving and identifying the "root causes" of disorder through consultation with their "partners" in the community.

Community policing works to constitute "the community," and it engages community members in the active and ongoing regulation of themselves and the community. Community-based health and safety committees, Neighbourhood Watch programs, Crime Stoppers programs, and snitch lines are examples of well-known community policing initiatives. They encourage the active involvement of community members in identifying and reporting not only criminal activities that have taken or are taking place but also merely unfamiliar, suspicious, and risky elements that are perceived to threaten the community and its members.

In the immigration context, community policing works in a similar fashion. The idea is to facilitate "open communication with the RCMP by ethnic communities about people who represent a threat or danger to everyone's well-being."[46] After the barrier between new immigrants, refugees, and the police has been broken down, and new immigrants and refugees have let go of whatever negative views they may have held about state authorities, the RCMP official observed that they are then willing to report on suspected wrongdoers: "We find that, after they've been here a few years and they see what's going on, they're actually quite eager to come forward ... They see a challenge or threat to their lifestyle, and, when people from their country come in and they see they are criminals or war criminals or whatever, they see that as a threat to their own community, so they're really keen, they definitely come forward."[47]

In order to effectively encourage community members to inform on risky members of their community, the RCMP has focused on two particular "angles." The first rests squarely on liberal notions of dessert, increasingly dominant concerns about victims, victimization, public safety, and security: "We're focusing on the angle that, just because you're an immigrant or a refugee, you don't deserve to be ripped off, and we want to know if you are – you don't deserve to be a victim, you don't deserve to be harassed."[48] The RCMP communicates this message in a variety of ways, including using the print and broadcast media of different ethnocultural groups. Here community policing is analogous to a kind of snitch line/Neighbourhood Watch program. Victimization or potential victimization has become the basis of active citizenship. All good citizens or aspiring citizens are at risk due to the presence of unidentified, unknown, and therefore unpredictable dangerous outsiders in their midst. To protect themselves and their community from victimization or other negative consequences, and to be good, active, and responsible citizens, community members need to be energetically involved in policing themselves and their communities by identifying and casting out the risky elements.

The second angle pursued by the RCMP in this process is "the safety issue." This more humanitarian-flavoured rationale points out that, while we may understand why people might want to leave their countries of origin, the safety of those who try to circumvent Canada's immigration laws should not be ignored. Illegal entry is dangerous, and "alien smugglers" have enormous control over people once they have been transported here.[49]

These discourses work to continuously constitute "the community" and to draw out deserving, desirable, law-abiding members of different communities and enlist them in the work of both law and order. Community policing is a technology that literally broadcasts dominant discourses in the work of "hailing out" law-abiding and deserving community members just as it operates to constitute and exclude the undesirable others.[50] In this way, community policing enhances the self-governance of community members in certain desirable directions. As observed by George Pavlich in relation to community mediation, community policing has the effect of "integrat[ing] communities, individuals and selves by ... aligning the personal aspirations of subjects ... with the wider goal of a non-rebellious community of communities."[51]

The CCRA, CIC, RCMP, CSIS, and law enforcement agencies all use informants in their operations. This policing strategy encourages and acts upon community-derived information about the identities of suspected criminals or otherwise risky or dangerous noncitizens. However, this encouragement of community members to be involved in the regulation of their communities is not without exception. There has been, in contrast, an unwillingness to accept as reliable community-derived information about the identities of others to facilitate admission. As discussed in Chapter 7, prior to the Aden Order in 2000, CIC had refused to accept as legitimate any community-derived information verifying the identities of undocumented Somalis applying for landed immigrant status. Affidavits from family members, employers, and/or close friends were explicitly rejected by the government as alternatives to identity documents, as were sworn statements from community elders and clergy. In contrast, government and law enforcement authorities actively encourage and act upon community information when it may lead to enforcement action.

The coincidence of increasingly prominent community-centred regulatory initiatives with neoliberal regimes of governance is not incidental. The quest for community regulation is part of the more general decline of welfare liberalism and social democracies: "The modern, liberal foundations of social welfare states have been fundamentally challenged by a persistent neo-liberalism that seems determined to fracture the social domain and replace it with a particular vision of community that is not incompatible with its enterprise culture."[52]

Through these programs, "community" is not merely acted upon but also continuously constituted as a "sector for government." As put by Nikolas Rose, "community is not simply the territory within which crime is to be controlled, it is itself a *means* of government."[53] Governing *through* community involves the mobilization, enrollment, and deployment of its "vectors and forces" in "novel programmes and techniques which encourage and harness active processes of self-management and identity construction of personal ethics and collective allegiances."[54]

The constitution and mobilization of "communities" in the work of immigration penalty and border control are consistent with the individualization of risk management under neoliberal regimes of rule. In place of social or collective risk management programs of welfare liberalism, individuals and smaller communities assume responsibility for their own risk management. This becomes part of their responsibility and identity as active citizens, what Pat O'Malley calls the "new prudentialism."[55] It contrasts with the dependent and passive citizenry said to be encouraged by welfare liberalism. As observed by Rose, "new modes of neighbourhood participation, local empowerment and engagement of residents in decisions over their own lives will, it is thought, re-activate self-motivation, self-responsibility and self-reliance in the form of active citizenship within a self-governing community."[56]

The United States

Partnerships with US border security and law enforcement agencies are extensive and have been for some time. In 1995, Canada and the United States signed the *Canada United States Accord on Our Shared Border,* committing the two countries to "streamlining and harmonizing border policies and management, expanding cooperation at and beyond the border, and collaborating on common threats outside the United States and Canada."[57] The accord placed considerable emphasis on developing better risk assessment and management strategies on both sides of the border. A variety of Canadian and American border security agencies are involved in the accord's initiatives, including the United States Immigration and Naturalization Service (USINS), Citizenship and Immigration Canada (CIC), the United States Customs Service (USCS), the Canada Customs and Revenue Agency (CCRA), the United States Department of State, and Foreign Affairs and International Trade Canada (DFAIT).[58]

The 1995 accord mandated the implementation of a variety of risk-based initiatives designed to facilitate the movement of low-risk travellers, goods, and services across the border and to enhance enforcement measures directed at those deemed to be high risk. The stated objective was to "simplify, harmonize and modernize customs clearance processes along our common border" in order to "expedite the flow of goods" and "improve the process for exporters, importers and the trading community."[59] This, the rationale holds, will free up time and resources to focus enforcement efforts on high-risk travellers and commercial goods and services. Borders should be "managed" through, for example, increased interdiction efforts; advanced technologies to "facilitate the movement of genuine travellers and to control the movement of illegal migrants"; sharing intelligence data;

harmonizing visa requirements and processes; and enhanced "cooperation and coordination" between the two countries.[60]

Two years later, the 1997 USINS-CIC "Border Vision" agreement more or less reaffirmed these bilateral and multi-agency commitments on a regional level to "develop a joint regional approach to migration through information and intelligence sharing, policy co-ordination, joint overseas operations and border co-operation."[61] CIC sums up the guiding objective by reference to the linked threats of criminals and terrorists but with additional scope provided by the sweeping category of "illegals" and the notably moralistic, anachronistic category of "undesirables": the aim is to improve cooperation between Canada and the United States "all along the migration continuum (overseas, border and interior) to protect the region against both illegal migration and the movement of terrorists, criminals and other undesirables."[62] And again, in 1999, Canada and the United States restated their agreement on these general principles of border cooperation in the Canada-United States Partnership (CUSP).

The two countries have also been cooperating since 1997 through the Canada-US Cross Border Crime Forum. Led by the Canadian solicitor general and the US attorney general, it brings together on an annual basis over 100 senior, national, and provincial/state law enforcement and justice officials from both countries to examine "issues such as the impact of cross-border crimes, telemarketing fraud, money laundering, missing and abducted children, high-tech crime and other emerging issues."[63]

While the quest for security is one that long predates September 11th, the attacks infused existing trends and trajectories with heightened urgency, greatly augmented their popular and political legitimacy, and gave rise to a variety of new and/or improved enforcement measures. For example, other established areas of cooperation between the United States and Canada include the Integrated Border Enforcement Teams (IBETs). These "multi-agency special law enforcement teams" made up of customs, immigration, and law enforcement officers from both countries were developed in 1996 as a way to respond to cross-border crime. After September 11th, the IBET program was expanded, and terrorist threats to national security joined the list of its criminal targets: "The importance of IBETs has been heightened by the new reality of terrorism and the need to enhance border integrity. The model is built on the premise of partnership and on sharing information more effectively to stay one step ahead of criminals and terrorists."[64]

The new CIC Intelligence Branch was created after September 11th to centralize intelligence resources and to provide a "focal point" for sharing information with its "partners in security." This move has been accompanied by the provision of additional resources to improving intelligence gathering, screening, and managing security.[65] This provision began with the December 2001 "security budget," which pledged $7.7 billion over five years to Canada's "security partners" in order to "build personal and economic security by keeping Canadians safe, terrorists out and our borders open and efficient."[66] Among other initiatives, the new funding was used to place more immigration officers at ports of entry in order "to improve the front-end security screening of refugee claimants."[67]

Indeed, much post-September 11th enforcement activity has revolved around the putative threats posed by risky refugees. The framing of refugees and refugee determination in terms of crime-security and fraud, while perhaps more vociferous after September 11th, cannot be explained in any simple way by reference to a racialized public panic triggered by the attacks or by latent or explicit racism – although both were clearly present. Nor, indeed, is the conflation of refugees and security a reasonable reaction to the December 1999 arrest of rejected refugee claimant Ahmed Ressam for his failed attempt to transport explosives across the border for the purpose of bombing the Los Angeles airport and the subsequent arrest of Lucia Garofalo, suspected of assisting Algerian terrorists to get into the United States. The widespread depictions of refugees as terrorists and Canada as their haven simply cannot be explained by these two incidents.

The representation of refugees as risky and the refugee determination process as a security problem long predates both Ressam's arrest and the September 11th attacks. The crime-security nexus and the spectre of fraud have framed this domain for decades. This preexisting discursive formation helps to explain the ease and speed with which the "risky refugee" was mobilized in the wake of September 11th, notwithstanding the absence of any evidence of a direct connection between the attacks of September 11th and any refugee or refugee claimant in Canada.[68] Furthermore, "self-selected" or "spontaneous" refugees have always been a source of considerable discomfort for the Canadian government. As observed in the previous chapter, onshore refugee claimants and international human rights obligations unsettle this conventional touchstone of sovereign territorial control. The association of refugees, crime-security, and fraud has thus made possible the reassertion and reconstitution of national sovereignty; it provides an increasingly rare opportunity to override international commitments in the context of increasingly "global" regimes.[69]

The attacks of September 11th provided the impetus needed to finalize long-standing negotiations with the United States regarding a safe third country exception to the right to apply for refugee status. The Canada-US Safe Third Country Agreement was signed on 5 December 2002. Like so many of the post-September 11th developments, this too was not a new initiative. Canada has had a safe third country provision on the books since 1987, but until the December 2002 agreement with the US it had not been used. This agreement requires refugee claimants to make their claims in the first "safe" country that they reach, and it designates the US as a safe country for refugees. Critics point out that the United States has a much stricter refugee determination system than Canada and that historical and contemporary experiences indicate that the US is safer for some refugee claimants than for others, depending on country of origin and American foreign policy toward that country.

Notwithstanding criticisms that the agreement is "full of loopholes" such as exemptions for people who have family members in Canada, for unaccompanied minors, and for those who might face the death penalty in the US, there is little doubt that this agreement will prevent large numbers of refugees from making their claims in Canada (about a third of refugee claims in Canada are made at the US border). While refugees who travel through the United States to claim refugee status in Canada are to be turned back, refugee claimants who make their claims from within Canada are not covered by the agreement. As with interdiction practices more generally, the agreement is likely to result in people pursuing more dangerous ways to enter Canada in order to make their refugee claims internally.[70]

The 2002 Safe Third Country Agreement was drafted and promoted after the September 11th attacks as part of the Canada-US "Smart Border" plan. The "Joint Statement on Cooperation and Regional Migration Issues" signed on 3 December 2001 by the solicitor general of Canada, the minister of citizenship and immigration, and the attorney general of the United States restated the "mutual interest" of the Canadian and US governments "in protecting our populations, our institutions and economies" and committed each to taking specific actions to "enhance our common security."[71] In addition to the Safe Third Country Agreement, the initiatives laid out in the joint agreement include the expansion of the Integrated Border Enforcement Teams (IBETs); the "reinvigoration" of Project North Star to improve the "communication, coordination and partnerships" between US and Canadian law enforcement agencies, now including CIC as "a full partner"; the insertion of a Canadian presence on the US Terrorist Tracking Task Force; the coordination of visa policies between the two countries; the creation of Joint Passenger Analysis Units at international airports staffed by officers of both countries; the increased number of immigration control officers overseas as part of the focus on prevention and interdiction; and the development of common biometric identifiers to "enhance security and allow control authorities to quickly identify those who require greater scrutiny."[72]

The Canada-US Action Plan for Creating a Secure and Smart Border itemizes thirty security-related objectives of the two countries. These objectives repeat those discussed above and add others, such as the development of a permanent resident identity card; the resumption and expansion of pre-clearance programs for low-risk travellers; enhanced security screening for refugee claimants; and the development of compatible databases for information sharing.[73]

Since the September 11th attacks, criticisms of the "porous" nature of the Canada-US border, the lax qualities of its refugee determination system, and the problems that this poses for American national security have been reinvigorated. Initially, this construction of Canada as a "safe haven" fuelled calls for the creation of a North American "security perimeter" or "a perimeter of control" (to create, some said, "Fortress North America"). The idea is that, by keeping "undesirables" off the continent, there will be no need to interfere with the free flow of goods and services within the continent. As expressed by Ontario's industry and business leaders, "economic and security interests are best guaranteed by a security perimeter approach. Effective enforcement at the North American perimeter and the border would ease the movement of low-risk goods, services and people, while freeing up resources to focus on high-risk security matters."[74] The contentious idea of a perimeter and its implications for Canadian sovereignty was soon toned down to the more comforting notion of a "zone of confidence" that "builds on the trust and extensive cooperation that already exist between the U.S. and Canada."[75] Three years later, the talk tends to focus on the soothing – even musical – idea of "harmonization."

Canada and the US have been engaged in different aspects of harmonization for some time. For example, safe third country discussions have gone on since Bill C-55 was introduced in 1987. Efforts to align Canadian and American visa requirements have been ongoing, and the two countries have long been exploring ways to make border crossing more "seamless" for low-risk importers, exporters, traders, and businesspeople. Most of the joint measures undertaken by Canada and the United States are centrally concerned with interdiction.

Interdiction

> The frozen body of a suspected stowaway was found on a plane at Pearson International airport early this morning. Police were called to Terminal 3 shortly after midnight when maintenance workers found the body of a man in his mid-30s in a compartment above the left rear landing gear of a Skyservice airplane.[76]

Stepping up efforts to prevent inadmissible, undocumented, or improperly documented people from reaching Canada is particularly troubling. For legitimate and compelling reasons that relate to their experience of persecution and the circumstances of their departure, refugees often do not have government-issued documentation. Overseas interdiction measures put refugees at risk by making it more difficult for them to flee the country in which they face persecution.[77] Furthermore, interdiction forces migrants and asylum seekers to pursue increasingly dangerous means of entering the destination country, often with tragic results. Many lives have been lost on overloaded ships, in containers on freighters, on rickety rafts, in train cars, in overcrowded, overheated, oxygen-deprived tractor trailers, and in airplane wheel wells. As evidenced by the efforts to prohibit alcohol in the 1920s, or by contemporary prohibitions against the sex trade, the enforcement of interdiction measures is more likely to redirect the undesired activity in more covert and unsafe directions than to eradicate it. As conceded by Brian Grant, director of program management at CIC, "if we could prevent everyone from stepping on an airplane, I suspect you would have boats arriving on the coast. People will try to get here no matter which way."[78] The series of arrivals in the summer of 1999 of 599 people on four boats from Fujian, China, on the West Coast of Canada is surely such an example.

Interdiction increases the demand for commercial migrant transportation operations – people smuggling. Yet it is the effect, rather than the cause, that is the focus of government action. The problem of people smuggling has been linked not to the sustained efforts of Western nations to fortify their territorial borders through more restrictive immigration legislation and tougher enforcement practices, but to the threat posed by the ubiquitous activities of organized crime.

The past few decades have witnessed Western governments stepping up measures to prevent inadmissible or improperly or undocumented people from reaching their borders – interdiction.[79] As put by CIC, "border control begins overseas"[80] – a catchphrase that darkly but appropriately turns on its head the usual dictum that "charity begins at home." Interdiction clearly displays the ways in which the border is constituted and policed at sites other than the geopolitical space of the border. A major strategy since the 1980s, interdiction has received more attention since September 11th. This policy priority depends upon forging and strengthening connections with international law enforcement authorities, governments, and national and international airlines and airports. It is heavily reliant on the development and improvement of "hard" technologies, such as fraud-resistant identity cards, document scanning, and information-sharing technologies, as well as "soft" technologies, including a range of innovations in social practices.

Overseas immigration screening is a key interdiction mechanism. CIC cooperates with the RCMP Immigration Branch to screen out inadmissible applicants before they are able to board a plane headed to Canada. As explained by a senior CIC policy official, "for us, a tremendous emphasis is placed on trying to screen out inadmissible persons before they get here, because we know that once they get here, they've got full access to our courts, and they can delay proceeding for a long period of time."[81] And, as put most succinctly by Lucienne Robillard, minister of citizenship and immigration in 1997, "the most important thing is to prevent these people from coming to Canada."[82]

In addition to the screening activities of overseas immigration control officers (now called immigration integrity officers), a host of diverse technologies is used in interdiction efforts: "short stop operations" at foreign airports for temporary blitzes to stop improperly documented people from boarding planes; fraudulent document detection training for inland and overseas immigration officers and airline personnel; visa requirements; target profiling; disembarkation checks; fraud-resistant identity cards; and document-scanning technologies.[83]

Carrier sanctions for transporting improperly documented people are a long-standing interdiction technology – one that enlists airlines and airline personnel in the work of immigration enforcement. Airlines are fined if they permit improperly documented people to board a flight to Canada, but as an inducement to secure their cooperation these fines are reduced if the transport company agrees to sign a memorandum of understanding (MOU) with CIC. By signing the MOU, transport companies agree to screen all travel documents, make use of technological document-screening aids, train their personnel in fraud detection, provide information to immigration officers about passengers (identity, itinerary), make photocopies of travel documents, and even communicate in advance names of passengers whose travel documents are real but who are suspected will destroy them before arriving in Canada. Transport companies are also empowered to seize temporarily the documents in question.[84] As a consequence of these efforts, CIC reports that the number of undocumented passengers arriving on Canadian shores has declined, while there has been an overall increase since 1996 in the interception of improperly documented passengers, from just under 5,000 in 1996 to over 6,000 in 1999,[85] to just under 8,000 in 2001.[86] In 2002, the number of interceptions decreased to 6,167, a decline that, according to the CIC, is due to improved enforcement measures and international cooperation.[87]

Risk-Smart Borders

Managing well in the face of uncertainty.

Risk – and the need to manage it – are facts of life.

We all manage risk intuitively when we make day-to-day decisions in the face of uncertainty about the future ... When making choices, the government's challenge is to strike the right balance in order to maximize potential benefits and minimize negative consequences.[88]

Multiple Borders and Risk Management

Interdiction is embedded in the language of risk and is a key component of the current pursuit of "smart borders." The objectives of the interdiction-oriented "Multiple Borders Approach" that is part of the Joint Canada-US Immigration Risk Management Framework[89] are "to keep the Canada-U.S. border open to legitimate travellers and goods, and to identify and intercept illegal and undesirable travellers as far away from North America as possible. The strategy proposes to broaden border control away from the shared land border with the US to the many, more effective, 'borders' that a traveller will pass through before reaching North America."[90] Similarly, the Risk Management Framework aims to "keep inadmissible and potentially harmful individuals as far away from North America as possible" by identifying risk "at all points of entry along the travel continuum, assessing the degree of threat and matching it with the appropriate level of control."[91] CIC notes that its efforts are concentrated on the "early identification of inadmissible travelers who pose a threat to North American society."[92] In 2003, the Multiple Borders Risk Management Framework was established. To effectively "manage access to Canada," CIC "aims to base its strategies on timely and reliable information and intelligence, supported by effective information-sharing, sound risk management, effective tools and staff development, and strategic domestic and international partnerships ... [and] it aims to use new technologies as much as possible."[93]

These initiatives work to disconnect "the border" from its conventional geopolitical usage, from its sovereign and territorial lineage, and from its physical location. Instead, the border is redefined as any point at which the identity of a traveller can be verified and his or her risk assessed. The border is here reconstituted as a spatial and temporal *process,* the "travel continuum," and is embedded in and articulated through the logic of risk. The production and sharing of information, particularly as they relate to questions of identity, are essential to this reconstitution.

Advanced Passenger Information and Passenger Name Recognition Systems (API/PNR)

The introduction and implementation of the Advanced Passenger Information and Passenger Name Recognition Systems (API/PNR) are promoted in association with the above-mentioned Multiple Borders and Risk Management Framework. Privacy concerns notwithstanding, under *IRPA* CIC can require airlines to provide specific information on international flight passengers. API/PNR allows for the identification, collection, and storage of information about airline passengers entering Canada from abroad. API includes information on a traveller that is collected by airlines at the time of check-in. Passenger name records include the information contained in a traveller's reservation and travel itinerary. According to the CBSA, this information "is used to identify passengers for further examination on arrival, and to conduct ongoing analysis of data for identification of potential future threats relating to the customs mandate."[94] The idea is that "Passenger Analysis Units" set up at Canadian airports will identify high-risk travellers before they arrive. Officials in Canada can run the information through the available criminality data banks to see "whether we get a hit either in terms of criminality or a security concern ... so we can know who's getting off the plane."[95] According to CIC, this technology will help to identify "criminals and security threats earlier in the travel continuum."[96] On 7 October 2002, the CCRA implemented the Passenger Information System (PAXIS) at eight international airports across Canada (Vancouver, Winnipeg, Edmonton, Calgary, Toronto, Ottawa, Dorval, and Halifax).[97] Canada and the United States have subsequently developed Joint Passenger Analysis Units (JPAUs), which include officers from the CCRA, United States Customs Service (USCS), CIC, and the United States Immigration and Naturalization Service (USINS). These agencies have agreed to share API/PNR records on high-risk travellers identified using a "jointly developed risk scoring mechanism."[98] JPAU teams will target high-risk passengers, "with a primary focus on anti-terrorism and national security related issues which may include other criminal activity, contraband enforcement, human smuggling and trafficking, etc."[99]

Alternative Inspection Systems and Pre-Clearance for Low-Risk Travellers

Canada, alongside the United States, strives for "smart borders." As observed by Canada Customs, "New border initiatives include speeding up the implementation of pre-screening and pre-clearance programs to expedite the movement of frequent low-risk travellers and cargo, and the introduction of state-of-the-art detection equipment to intercept individuals with a high or unknown risk. Technological initiatives are increasingly being seen as effective tools to balance the needs of facilitation and security."[100] CCRA explains that it has always had to balance its responsibility in "facilitating trade, travel and tourism" with that of "maintaining a strong and credible enforcement role."[101] As early as 1995, CCRA (then Revenue Canada) had implemented a smart border strategy "based on effective risk management, which allows for the speedy clearance of low-risk people and goods while at the same time keeping out undesirable merchandise and people."[102]

Under the 1995 Shared Border Accord, a number of pre-clearance border-crossing programs (Passenger Accelerated Service Systems – PASS) designed to speed up customs clearance for low-risk travellers and focus attention on high-risk travellers were initiated by Canada and the United States, including CANPASS-Highway (in the US known as PORTPASS Dedicated Commuter Lanes [DCL]) and CANPASS-Air (in the US known as INSPASS).[103] The goal is "a hassle-free border for honest travellers and businesses, and a brick wall for those who try to smuggle illegal weapons, drugs or break other laws at the border."[104]

The NEXUS program that replaced CANPASS-Highway in November 2000 was launched by the CCRA, CIC, USCS, and USINS.[105] It, too, is a pre-clearance risk-based program, but unlike CANPASS and INSPASS programs NEXUS is fully "harmonized." It includes "common eligibility requirements, a common sanctions regime, a joint enrolment process, a common card, and a single application form and instruction process."[106] There is one centralized application process for American and Canadian applicants. CIC is able to carry out "full criminality checks," using both Canadian and American databases, and applicants must not have criminal convictions in either country. Members of NEXUS are issued a photo identification card and have access to a dedicated commuter lane.[107]

Only low-risk border crossers, including anyone who is not high risk, are eligible for NEXUS. High-risk border crossers are those who

- are inadmissible to Canada or the US under applicable immigration laws
- provide false or incomplete information on your application
- have been convicted of a criminal offence in any country for which you have not received a pardon
- have been found in violation of customs or immigration law or
- fail to meet other requirements of the NEXUS program.[108]

Similarly, the Fast and Secure Trade program (FAST) is a harmonized border-crossing program for commercial shipments that allows preapproved companies using preapproved carriers and registered drivers to cross more quickly into either Canada or the United States.

Biometrics
Biometrics are central to the pursuit and promotion of smart borders. Biometric technologies have applications in the risk-based pre-clearance programs. In addition to the photo ID card, imagined biometric solutions include hand geometry technology to be used by INSPASS at selected American and Canadian airports;[109] fingerprint-scanning technology to be used by NEXUS at Canadian ports of entry; and iris-scanning "kiosks" to be used by CANPASS-Air at selected Canadian airports. Digital face recognition technologies have been used in Canada – first in casinos – and then in airports.[110] As already mentioned, document-scanning technologies are being explored and developed. While not new, the fingerprint and the photograph are critical devices in the identification and tracking work of the security partners now

facilitated by the Automated Fingerprint Information System (AFIS), described above.

In the United States, the "US Visitor and Immigrant Status Indication Technology" (US VISIT) is a massive, smart border initiative that uses a biometric-intensive system to track the arrival and departure of nearly every foreign visitor to the United States. Under this system, all visitors from countries without visa waiver status have their travel documents scanned, their left and right index fingers scanned, and their faces photographed. Upon entry and exit, their identities are verified, and their name and fingerprint information is checked against watch lists to search for terrorist connections, criminal violations, or past visa violations.[111] Canada and the United States have agreed to develop common standards for biometrics and to use compatible technology to read them.[112] Biometric capabilities are also seen as essential to the development of new, fraud-resistant identity cards and passports.

Identity Cards

Identity documents are a key technology for making up citizens and governing populations. They also work to reconstitute "states' control over bounded territories and [enhance] ... their embrace of populations."[113]

Not long after September 11th, then Immigration Minister Denis Coderre floated the idea of a high-tech national identity card for all Canadians: "Do we agree to use technology in a friendly way?" The idea was widely criticized as a threat to privacy ("relentless tracking"); as emblematic of a police state ("your papers please"); as extremely costly ($3-5 billion); and as an ineffective security tool ("there is no technology that cannot be compromised or subverted").[114] The idea of an identity card for all citizens was subsequently trimmed down to a plan to issue identity cards for permanent residents.

In the name of border security, public safety, and fraud, Canada proceeded to develop an identity card with "state of the art security features" for Canadian permanent residents.[115] It has a laser-engraved photograph and signature, a description of physical characteristics, and an optical stripe containing all the details from the individual's permanent resident application.[116] In 2004, the cost for the "Maple Leaf" card was fifty dollars. In response to concerns that the card is an unacceptable invasion of the privacy of permanent residents, that its contents exceed that which is required for a passport application, and that it might be used for purposes other than a travel document, CIC explains that "this encrypted information will only be accessible to authorized officials (such as immigration officers) as required to confirm the status of the cardholder. The card cannot be used to monitor the activities or track the movement of the cardholder; this will protect the cardholder's privacy."[117] Notwithstanding such reassurances, critics charge that the "Maple Leaf" card does subject permanent residents to increased monitoring and control and serves to confirm and reproduce the devaluation of permanent residents vis-à-vis citizens. It is unlikely that critics concerned about the differential treatment of permanent residents were happy with Minister Coderre's announcement in July 2003 that all Canadian citizens will be issued identity cards by 2005, and these too will be equipped with "biometric security safeguards."[118] John Torpey explains further that, "ultimately, passports and identity documents reveal a massive illiberality, a presumption of their bearers' guilt ... when called upon to identify themselves. The use of such documents by states indicates their fundamental suspicion that people will lie about who or what they are and that some independent means of confirming these matters must be available if states are to monopolize the legal means of movement and thus sustain themselves as going concerns."[119]

Profiling

Many technologies of border control and immigration penality are borrowed from (or shared with) the field of criminal justice – including the coercive use of body restraints such as handcuffs and shackles, detention, and deportation, but also a variety of surveillance technologies, fingerprinting, and photographing. Profiling is another key tool in the work of Canada's partners in security.

In contrast to the social and legal prohibition against the collection and publication of race and crime statistics in Canada, there is no official prohibition against the identification of the nationality and/or ethnicity of organized criminals and other threats to national security. Indeed, such threats are explicitly organized *according to* nationality and ethnicity (with the exception of the category of "major outlaw motorcycle gangs"). For example, in 2003 CSIS reported that there were approximately eighteen active transnational criminal organizations "represented" in Canada, including "Asian triads, Colombian cartels, Japanese *yakuza*, Jamaican posses, Mafia groups from the USA, Calabria and Sicily, Russian/Eastern European *mafiyas*, Nigerian crime groups and major outlaw motorcycle gangs. In recent years, a great deal of media attention has been paid to Russian/Eastern European based organizations."[120]

While a matter of considerable debate, target profiles of high-risk border crossers are a key technology of border governance. For example, the RCMP continues its traditional "response-based" policing strategy of checking and monitoring flight arrivals. In their efforts to identify criminals as they disembark, the RCMP, in cooperation with CIC and CCRA, develop and use risk profiles. They are generated through monitoring and observing trends. As explained in 1998 by a senior RCMP official, "for example, Air Canada flights from Singapore are starting to transport an increasing number of undocumented passengers ... obviously noticed by customs and immigration ... If this continues, it becomes a trend; then authorities become interested in that flight, they can be there at the terminal to wait for the plane to disembark, and then they develop individual person profiles or 'target profiles.' So you may be looking for a male, Asian, eighteen to thirty-five years old, well-dressed, new shoes, no luggage. You can hone it down that far." According to this RCMP official, target profiles differ depending on the ethnic and/or national origin of the criminal in question, and they do not change much over time: "You may have a profile from Asia, say Singapore, you may have another from Sri Lanka or another from Somalia or another from Russia or Israel. They are generally male; if they are female, it is likely for prostitution."[121]

There is a fine and much disputed line that distinguishes target profiling from racial profiling. The latter is "the use of race, religion, or ethnicity either as the sole reason, or as one factor among many, in a decision to detain or arrest an individual, or to subject an individual to further investigation. Whether used as the sole factor, or one factor among many, profiling allows race, religion, or ethnicity to play a determinative factor in investigative decisions."[122] It has generated much debate, and the practice is usually officially denied by both law enforcement and border authorities.

In 1999, Selwyn Pieters filed a complaint against the CCRA with the Canadian Human Rights Commission that alleged that he had been racially discriminated against by customs officers, who had singled him out and searched only his bags on a train carrying seventy people; he was the only black person on the train. The Canadian Human Rights Commission referred the complaint to the Canadian Human Rights Tribunal. Canada Customs subsequently settled with Pieters out of court. As a result of this important case, CCRA agreed to implement new rules on inspections and searches that require officers to explain to travellers why they are being searched, it agreed to implement new antiracism training for its officers, and it agreed to carry out a study to see if customs officers practise racial profiling in their decision making.[123] As of 2004, these agreements had yet to be fulfilled.

Since September 11th, the issue of racial profiling has reached new heights as widespread concerns have been raised regarding the targeting of Muslims, people of Arab descent, and Middle Eastern nationals. In Canada, these concerns peaked when an internal bulletin was leaked shortly after September 11th suggesting that Canada Customs officers were being directed to intensify the questioning of men who had spent time in any of sixteen named Muslim countries. Officials confirmed that customs officers were checking country of origin but denied that this amounted to racial profiling. Instead, the practice was deemed a part of risk assessment in which officers must use "all the tools we have."[124] Concerns about racial profiling were also raised by Canada's antiterrorist legislation introduced in December 2001 and in the United States by a range of sweeping post-September 11th enforcement measures, including the National Security Entry-Exit Registration System (NSEERS), which requires "nonimmigrant aliens" in the US to register with the INS, provide an address, submit photographs and fingerprints, and repeat this process on an annual basis.[125] NSEERS gives the US attorney general the discretion "to require such information from the natives of any foreign state, or any class or group of aliens."[126] In November 2002, the INS and Department of Justice announced that nonstatus male visitors over sixteen years of age from eighteen named countries were required to register. The first group consisted of noncitizens from Iran, Iraq, Libya, Sudan, or Syria (countries officially designated as "state sponsors of terrorism"). The second group consisted of citizens of Afghanistan, Algeria, Bahrain, Eritrea, Lebanon, Morocco, North Korea, Oman, Qatar, Somalia, Tunisia, United Arab Emirates, and Yemen. In December 2003, Pakistani and Saudi Arabian citizens were added to the list.[127] These announcements led thousands of noncitizens, many of whom were from Pakistan, to flee the US to claim refugee status in Canada.[128] As a result of the policy of "direct backs," refugee claimants were sent back to the US to await an appointment with CIC to process their claims. According to refugee agencies in the US and Canada, when the nonstatus claimants are returned to the US, the men are detained, families are split up, and detention release bonds are set very high.[129]

A range of diverse technologies governs the border in the name of public safety and security. As noted in Chapter 1, dangerousness is constituted by criminality and by the unpredictable and therefore unmanageable risks linked with "unknowability."[130] Many of the technologies and practices that operate in the context of the border aim to govern uncertainty, to know the unknowable. Fingerprinting and photographing, information sharing, identity cards, biometric identification systems, document-scanning technologies, advanced surveillance technologies, advanced passenger lists, pre-clearance programs, profiling – all represent efforts to contain and manage risk and dangers through more and better technologies of "knowing."

A vast array of "security partners" is energetically involved in a range of initiatives designed to manage risk, control the border, and protect public safety and national security in the face of the threats posed by ever-increasing varieties of criminals and criminality. These threats are held to require vigilant, imaginative, and sophisticated policing by a range of national and international agencies, by increasingly indistinguishable customs, immigration, and law enforcement officers, as well as a variety of private agents, who employ a range of hard and soft technologies to identify, assess, and contain the risks posed by criminal and otherwise threatening outsiders.

This preliminary peek into the black box of the border points to the ways that it is continuously constituted at a variety of locations through the operations of different modes of power, authorities, and technologies. Contemporary efforts to secure the border suggest rather extensive relations between borders, risk knowledges, and risk management strategies and do appear to evidence the significance and pervasiveness of risk as a way of thinking about and acting upon the world of which so many social scientists have become interested. Many of the technologies contemplated, developed, and used in border governance are indeed framed and promoted by reference to the need to better predict, identify, and manage risk – as captured by the objective of the risk-smart border.

The auditor general of Canada defines risk as "the uncertainty that surrounds future events and outcomes."[131] Risk management tends to be associated with scientific, expert, and objective probability calculations and predictions. The policies and justifications of contemporary practices of border control and immigration penalty do indicate the prominence of risk management knowledges and technologies. However, in contrast to the "neutral and objective" definition of risk management provided by the auditor general, in the context of border control, risk knowledges and technologies display powerful and intensely moralized associations.

The foregoing should not be read, however, as evidencing the advent of an all-encompassing, fully functioning risk society. While the discussion clearly indicates the prominence of the logic of risk and risk management strategies in the development and promotion of government programs, the degree to which they have been implemented, the extent and ways in which they are used, whether they "work" and how they differ from former practices all remain questions for further empirical investigation.

Moreover, it is not all about risk. Whether in the form of detention, deportation, body restraints, search and seizure, or arrest, border control technologies also manifest the brute and bodily coercions of sovereign power that are connected to the defence of territory. The capacity of the minister "to suspend the rule in a state of exception" – to allow entry in cases where the rules dictate refusal of entry or to allow someone to stay where the rules dictate removal – also evidences the persistence of sovereign power in this domain.[132] The practices of community policing add to border governance normalizing technologies. Many instances thus reveal the coexistence, even codependence, of these different governing regimes and technologies. As proposed by Randy Lippert in the context of the international refugee regime, "the onset of advanced liberalism and a new emphasis on risk in this regime and governmentality more generally have not replaced sovereignty.

Rather governmentality and sovereignty can be understood as mutually constitutive and complementary in particular contexts. In this instance, sovereign intervention may take over where advanced liberal governance and the new fixation on risk ... leave off."[133]

10
Conclusion

"Before the Law"

Before the law sits a gatekeeper. To this gatekeeper comes a man from the country who asks to gain entry into the law. But the gatekeeper says that he cannot grant him entry at the moment. The man thinks about it and then asks if he will be allowed to come in later on. "It is possible," says the gatekeeper, "but not now." At the moment the gate to the law stands open, as always, and the gatekeeper walks to the side, so the man bends over in order to see through the gate into the inside. When the gatekeeper notices that, he laughs and says: "If it tempts you so much, try it in spite of my prohibition. But take note: I am powerful. And I am only the most lowly gatekeeper. But from room to room stand gatekeepers, each more powerful than the other. I can't endure even one glimpse of the third." The man from the country has not expected such difficulties: the law should always be accessible for everyone, he thinks, but as he now looks more closely at the gatekeeper in his fur coat, at his large pointed nose and his long, thin, black Tartar's beard, he decides that it would be better to wait until he gets permission to go inside. The gatekeeper gives him a stool and allows him to sit down at the side in front of the gate. There he sits for days and years. He makes many attempts to be let in, and he wears the gatekeeper out with his requests ... Finally his eyesight grows weak, and he does not know whether things are really darker around him or whether his eyes are merely deceiving him. But he recognizes now in the darkness an illumination which breaks inextinguishably out of the gateway to the law. Now he no longer has much time to live. Before his death he gathers in his head all his experiences of the entire time up into one question which he has not yet put to the gatekeeper. He waves to him, since he can no longer lift up his stiffening body. The gatekeeper has to bend way down to him, for the great difference has changed things to the disadvantage of the man. "What do you still want to know, then?" asks the gatekeeper. "You are insatiable." "Everyone strives after the law," says the man, "so how is that in these many years no one except me has requested entry?" The gatekeeper sees that the man is already dying and, in order to reach his diminishing sense of hearing, he shouts at him, "Here no one else can gain entry, since this entrance was assigned only to you. I'm going now to close it."[1]

Like the man from the countryside in this Kafka tale, refugee claimant Michael Akhimien, who died in custody at the Celebrity Inn detention centre, sought inclusion under the law. Like the man from the countryside, his access was repeatedly denied. And like that man, he died on the doorstep – in the liminal space of detention. In a real and tragic way, Akhimien was the victim of the culture of fear and disbelief that took hold in most fields of public policy over the last few decades of the twentieth century.

The crime-security nexus, coupled with the spectre of fraud embedded in neoliberal mentalities, has facilitated and justified the energetic pursuit of enforcement-oriented laws, policies and practices, bureaucratic initiatives, partnerships and networks, and technological innovations in the domain of border security and immigration penalty. Primary among those who have suffered the dire effects of these developments are refugee claimants, the folk devils of the late twentieth and early twenty-first centuries.

In this book's examination of the discursive formations and technologies of power that have been deployed around detention and deportation in Canada since the Second World War, a number of central and overlapping themes have emerged: the centrality of discretion to the domain of immigration penalty in systems of liberal rule; the relationship of immigration penalty with transitions from welfare liberal to neoliberal regimes of rule; the coexistence of and intersections between sovereign and governmental modes of power, in particular the centrality of risk discourses and risk management strategies, in relation to the development, promotion, and justification of the policies and programs of immigration penalty and border control; the predominance of crime and punishment in the promotion and development of immigration penalty such that it has come to be governed *through* crime; and, finally, "the border" not as merely a negative instrument of exclusion but as a heterogeneous and "artful" accomplishment that contributes to the production of citizens and national identities and the regulation of the population.

Law, Liberalism, and Discretion

The practices of immigration penalty are accomplished in part through the interaction of law and discretion. As I argued in Chapter 3, the conventional view of law/discretion as an oppositional binary serves to obscure the violent material conditions of detention and deportation and both sets and limits the parameters of interrogation and imagined policy reforms. It also renders invisible the work that discretion does as an active mode of governance in the context of liberal rule.

Canadian immigration penalty, like the domain of social welfare, rests upon and continuously reproduces the distinctions between "deserving" and "undeserving" noncitizens. As constituted in the discourses around the development of refugee law and policy during the period under review, the deserving noncitizen is determined to be a genuine victim of state-sanctioned persecution under the provisions of the *Refugee Convention* as they are applied under Canadian immigration legislation, and the archetypal undeserving noncitizen is the onshore refugee claimant presumed to be a fraudulent system abuser and a crime-security threat. The international legal status of the refugee claimant as a rights-bearing subject has largely been overshadowed by the cultural construction of the onshore refugee claimant as a poser of risks. It is the undeserving "risky" refugee claimant rather than the deserving refugee who is today the primary focus of legal, political, and social attention.

Discretion is a central technology in the drawing of these moralized distinctions that construct the identities of both undesirable and desirable citizens and that justify the operations of coercive sovereign power against those who are ushered into zones of exclusion – detained and deported. The mechanism of discretion enables and legitimizes these coercive processes in ways that minimize their offence to, and which thereby sustain, the liberal legal paradigm. In this respect, discretion works to deflect the legitimacy crises that would arise from the clash between the use of coercive force and prevailing liberal democratic values.[2]

Discretion carves out a domain of freedom that reconciles the gap between law and equity, between formal equality and individualized justice. It mitigates and sustains the apparent contradiction between the universality (of principles, ideals, rules, standards) and the particularity (of cases, local practices, contexts) of liberal legality. Law and discretion in this sense are mutually constitutive. This view of discretion echoes Peter Fitzpatrick's observations regarding the law and modern administration: "It is because of the particularistic and pervasive powers of administration that the rule of law can be maintained in its aspects of universality and equality and seen as marking out fields for free action."[3] Moreover, discretion both constitutes and is constituted by liberal notions of individual autonomy in conjunction with liberal legal notions of the rule of law. Discretion produces the figure of the essentially autonomous and free-thinking subject; it is the legal expression of autonomy, the central trope of liberalism.

Rather than viewing it as the unruly shadow of law that allows for the expression of individual agency and the making of choices within boundaries set by legal constraints, discretion is more fruitfully regarded as a productive form of power in modern systems of liberal rule.

From Welfare Liberal to Neoliberal Rule

The universalizing logic of welfare liberalism and the primacy that it accords to the objective of fostering social solidarity have been increasingly unsettled by a neoliberal rationality, the integral elements of which include a belief in the efficiency of markets, the importance of accountability, individual liberty, enterprise, responsibility, independence, and the virtues of the noninterventionist state. Welfare regimes have been criticized for fostering a culture of dependency and passive citizenship. Under neoliberalism, citizenship must be active and energetic. In the place of social solidarity, social citizenship, and social responsibility, neoliberalism carves out a sphere of freedom "where autonomous agents make their decisions, pursue their preferences and seek to maximize the quality of their lives." The political subject of neoliberalism should not be defined by "the receipt of public largesse"; rather, citizenship is to be manifested "in the energetic pursuit of personal fulfillment and the incessant calculations that are to enable this to be achieved."[4]

Neoliberal political rationality does not accept as legitimate any "avoidable" adult dependency. Unlike welfarism, which tempered the liberal commitment to "independence" through an acknowledgment of social causes and collective social responsibility, neoliberalism brings independence, individual responsibility, and enterprise back to the fore. Independence is still fundamentally associated with waged labour and is valorized as a desirable personal quality, and dependency signifies not only lack of paid employment but also "has been inflated into a behavioural syndrome and made to seem more contemptible."[5] People who receive welfare are increasingly stigmatized; they are not independent, enterprising, or responsible. Constructed partly through the discursive denigration of the "lazy" welfare recipient, the neoliberal individual is always self-reliant; dependency and other forms of "neediness" are always suspect.

As Linda Gordon and Nancy Fraser have argued from a slightly different perspective, while liberal welfarism tempered the liberal commitment to independence with an understanding that not all adults could or should be literally independent, neoliberalism regards independence as a universal norm: "Whereas industrial usage had cast some forms of dependency as natural and proper, postindustrial usage figures all forms as avoidable and blameworthy."[6]

While refugee claimants could conceivably be received as enterprising, self-motivated, rational choice makers and managers of their own and their families' risks, instead they tend to be painted with the same neoliberal brush that has cast welfare recipients as dependent and passive claimants on the state's largesse. Furthermore, there is an assumption that genuinely deserving refugees are languishing in camps overseas and that those who are sufficiently enterprising, resourceful, and self-motivated to make it to Canada to make their refugee claims are less "needy" and therefore less likely to be genuinely deserving. Several conflicting assumptions thus converge on refugee claimants and complicate their identities and situations. First, genuine refugees are expected to be dependent, passive, and needy, and those who do not fit this profile are widely assumed to be fraudulently trying to take unfair advantage of the system and likely to be disguising criminal identities and intentions. Second, the dependency and neediness of refugee claimants are at the same time the sources of stigmatization and even criminalization under neoliberalism, which valorizes enterprise and independence. And third, the enterprise, resourcefulness, and risk management capacities of refugees who manage to escape their dire circumstances to make their claims in Canada tend not to be valorized but read as a lack of deservedness.

Neoliberalism is also preoccupied with economic efficiency, good management, and system integrity. The spectre of fraud and its corollary – system abuse – represent a formidable threat to these touchstones of good neoliberal government, made all the worse when considered in relation to the already much maligned distribution of administrative social benefits. Chapters 4 through 6 examined the emergence of these heightened concerns about fraud and system abuse that neoliberalism has brought in tow. I detailed the emergence and conflation of the problems of the "bogus refugee" and the "welfare cheat" and the way in which these linked threats, framed by the crime-security nexus and the spectre of fraud, were supplemented by increasingly dominant law and order programs and produced a powerful new, hybrid threat – the fraudulent criminal refugee. By 2004, criminality-security and fraud had become the true triad threat to national security, public safety, and system integrity.

Concerns about fraud and system abuse are thus consistent with the general decline of welfare liberalism and the rise of more individualistic modes of neoliberal governance. Neoliberalism, premised as it is upon notions of individual responsibility, accountability, autonomy, and rational choice, has a distinctly punitive edge. Recipients of state benefits, whether in the form of social services or refugee status, have become immediately suspect. While criminalization is not necessarily consistent with neoliberal strategies of governing, implying as it does increased costs of criminal justice administration and support for state-administered carceral institutions, the language of deterrence, individual responsibility, and accountability is indeed consistent with neoliberal preoccupations. Moreover, neoliberalism urges a much smaller role for the formal institutions of government; the use of coercion and force in the maintenance of law and order is one of the last remaining domains of legitimate, though clearly not uncontested, state authority. Neoliberal regimes of government are characterized by a certain distrust of and even hostility toward traditional state institutions. The heightened public and political preoccupation with victims expresses this distrust and underpins calls for increasingly punitive law and order reforms. The logic of deterrence, in the context of immigration, just as in the context of criminal justice or social welfare, further justifies an enforcement-oriented, get tough, law and order response to whatever threat is posed. By increasing the costs of coming to Canada through punitive crackdowns, ever-tougher legislation, more rigorous enforcement, interdiction initiatives, and increased sanctions, the rational but criminally inclined outsider will be dissuaded from choosing to come to Canada.

The Coexistence of Governmental and Sovereign Modes of Power
The nature and place of risk technologies and risk management strategies in the government of Western liberal democratic societies have attracted considerable scholarly attention from diverse disciplines and perspectives. While there are a range of views and many areas of debate, there is wide agreement around the general proposition that the concept of risk has become increasingly prominent in most spheres of social relations.[7]

The domain of immigration penality and border control certainly displays governmental risk management preoccupations and strategies. Nowhere is this perhaps more obvious than in relation to the redefinition and the displacement of the refugee as the deserving subject of international human rights law. As noted above, in the transitions from welfare liberalism to neoliberalism, the claimant of administrative state benefits, whether of social welfare or of refugee protection, has become always and already suspect. The liberal legal conception of refugees as "rights-bearing" individuals and the related humanitarian conception of refugees as "deserving victims" have been steadily unsettled and supplanted by a view of refugee *claimants* as posing various risks to the nation and the public.

Into the 1950s, the discourses that constituted the dangers that underpinned Canadian immigration penality were moralistic, ideological, and discriminatory. These dangers have largely been supplanted by threats constituted through crime-security and fraud discourses articulated through the language of risk. Official priorities are directed at the detection, detention, and deportation of the risky onshore refugee claimant rather than identifying and extending protection to refugees at risk. It is not that the objective of protecting genuine refugees has disappeared or that the corollary objective of excluding the risky was not previously present; rather, the humanitarian objective and the international legal obligation to protect refugees have come to be represented as a residual effect that is contingent in the first instance on the identification and exclusion of those who pose risks.

As demonstrated in Chapter 9, a key feature of the quest for border security is the preoccupation with and seemingly endless pursuit of more and better, advanced and enhanced, risk management technologies. Such technologies, epitomized in the domain of immigration penality by the objective of "risk-smart borders," reproduce the idea that scientific expertise can be harnessed, that chance can be tamed, the unknowable known, and the worst predicted and prevented. The impossibility of taming chance and thus the inevitable failures of risk management technologies only fuel the quest for the development of even better technologies. By virtue of its inevitable failures, the quest for security regenerates the insecurities that propel it.

As explained by Nikolas Rose, the aim of risk management technologies is to "act pre-emptively upon potentially problematic zones, to structure them in such a way as to reduce the likelihood of undesirable events or conduct occurring, and to increase the likelihood of these type[s] of events and activities that are desired."[8] Risk technologies and calculations are not solely a matter for the state. Communities, individuals, businesses are all expected to assume responsibility for the management of risks.[9] The construction and mobilization of "the community" and individuals in the risk-based policies and practices of immigration penality (e.g., through third-party liability programs, border watch, community policing, informants, etc.) are thus consistent with the individualized ethos of neoliberalism and the new logics of risk that fracture the social sphere "into a multitude of diverse pockets, zones, folds of riskiness."[10]

Risk is not distinct from morality. Not only are risk classifications themselves constituted by moral considerations, but they are also used in the moralized processes of the dividing practices that categorize the deserving and undeserving and the desirable and undesirable. Furthermore, the language of risk is effective in providing a "veneer of objectivity" to moral judgments and opinions. There is an important difference between the "neutral and objective" foundations of risk theory and probability calculations and the political and public deployment of the concept of risk. While the view of risk assessment as a scientific, neutral, and objective tool of analysis enhances its political power, the persuasive cultural currency of risk-based justifications has little to do with science; as observed by Mary Douglas, "the risk that is a central concept for our policy debates has not got much to do with probability calculations. The original connection is only indicated by arm-waving in the direction of science. The word *risk* now means danger; *high risk* means a lot of danger."[11] From this perspective, risk is used to "protect individuals from predatory institutions or to protect institutions from predatory individuals."[12]

More research is required to investigate on a local level the heterogeneity of the authorities, technologies, and modes of power at play in the micro operations of the border. In addition to contributing to the opening of the "black box" of the border and revealing the complexity of border governance, this research will allow for more grounded reflections on how the logic of risk and risk management technologies are manifested in local, everyday practices. To what extent do they "work"? How does risk intersect with other modes of governance? What kinds of risk knowledges are applied? Is risk simply a new way of talking about the same old moralistic exclusions based on raced, classed, gendered, sexualized, nationalized, and ideological constructions of danger? As observed by Mariana Valverde, "the rise of risk literature is insightful, but in drawing attention to the modernizing, risk-management aspects of contemporary regulation it systematically underrates the persistence of moralizing techniques that are not efficient from the point of view of managing populations or maximizing health but which are nevertheless qualitatively and quantitatively significant."[13]

Moreover, immigration penalty and border control are not all about risk. As noted in Chapter 1, detention and deportation lie at the crossroads of governmentality and sovereignty. Immigration detention is a liminal space where coercive and bodily modes of sovereign modes of power predominate. No governmental efforts are needed to reform, discipline, or normalize those who are detained. The coercive and bodily practices of detention and deportation are perhaps the most powerful indications that sovereign power is not merely a "fiction" or an "archaic residue of the past." Also suggestive are the sovereign capacity to suspend the rule in a state of exception[14] and, as expressed by Foucault, "to suspend both law and vengeance."[15] Clearly, detention and deportation continue to display an affinity for spectacle and are still tied to the territoriality of the nation-state. Yet, as this study reveals, even at this site, there is an intermingling of different authorities and technologies that reveals the coexistence of sovereign and governmental technologies.

Furthermore, no longer are the justifications for detention and deportation grounded exclusively in law or sovereign aims. Rather, they are commonly grounded in the governmental objectives of the welfare of the population and the economy now articulated largely through discourses that prioritize public safety, system integrity, and national security. As noted by William Walters, detention and deportation "are directed not primarily towards augmenting the power and glory of the sovereign, but to promoting the ends of the population. But conversely, the promotion of the population will be used to advance the sovereign power of the state."[16] Detention and deportation may also be understood in terms of the international "police" of populations: that is, as administrative ways of delivering unruly subjects to their proper sovereigns (or substitutions, as in the case of safe third country provisions) in the name of order and tranquillity.[17] Detention and deportation are constitutive practices that work not only to constitute citizens and noncitizens, regulate the population, maintain order, and bolster the sovereign authority of the expelling nation, but they also play a key role in the reconstitution and reconfiguration of citizenship and sovereignties in the global context.

In short, this study of detention and deportation points to the coexistence and intermingling of different modes of power, technologies, authorities, networks, and forms of knowledge in the domain of immigration penality and border control.

Governing through Crime

While criminality has always been an exclusionary immigration category, the extent to which it has come to provide *the* guiding rationale for the policies and practices of immigration penality and border control is historically unprecedented. In the 1960s and early 1970s, dominant racist and morally charged national "purity" discourses were contested by human rights and legal discourses. The logic of national security that was firmly in place when the 1976 *Immigration Act* was adopted encompassed the more traditional Cold War concerns about threats to the Canadian political state posed by political subversives, terrorists, and those engaging in espionage. While the 1976 *Immigration Act* articulated existing concerns about organized crime, since then the logic of "security" has been increasingly linked with that of criminality and, supplemented by concerns about fraud, has underpinned and justified the steady intensification, specification, and in some cases redefinition of a wide range of new exotic and "true" threats such as those posed by organized criminals, international terrorists, domestic political terrorists, war criminals (traditional and modern day), persons connected with regimes that have perpetrated wide-scale human rights abuses, and dangerous or "serious" criminals. As discussed in Chapter 8, the heightened dominance of the crime-security nexus and the reconfiguration and expansion of "security" to encompass public safety and criminality as well as traditional political threats were epitomized by the expansion in the 1990s of the working mandate of the Canadian Security Intelligence Service (CSIS) to include transnational crime.

This trend toward governing through crime is part of a more general crisis in governance ushered in by the decline of welfarist modes of governance. The contemporary preoccupation with crime and punishment is consistent with emergent neoliberal technologies of governing that emphasize the law and order functions of state authority and the importance of responsibility, accountability, and individual (as opposed to collective, socialized) risk management. Governing through crime is "a way of imposing this model of governance on the population."[18] Detention and deportation are understood as practices of penality that operate against noncitizens: "The prison and penality more generally have become crucial elements in the government of insecurity ... The poor, the dispossessed, the unemployed and the recipients of benefits are increasingly 'governed through crime.'"[19] This study attends to the effects of governing through crime on yet another marginalized group, refugees.

Governing through crime is accompanied by its corollary, governing through victimization. Victimhood has become a new basis for claims to citizenship. As nicely put by Alison Young, "crime ... is a great leveller. It provides a sense of community ... But our belonging comes not from the fact that we are all criminals, but rather from the shared fact of victimization. It is through our victimage that we come to belong to the social body. To be a victim is to be a citizen."[20] The victim has come to take on a more representative character whose experience is taken to be common and collective rather than isolated and unique. In the field of criminal justice policy making, the "new political imperative is that victims must be protected, their voices must be heard, their memories honoured, their anger expressed, their fears addressed."[21] However, while this heightened sensitivity to victims might have entailed increased compassion for refugees, instead it has underpinned the rise of discourses that construct the state and the public, not the refugee, as the victim.

Under a liberal regime of government, the application of coercive powers against autonomous and free subjects, even noncitizen subjects, must be carefully justified and administered. While broadly discretionary, explicitly racist, moral, or ideological exclusions are clearly antithetical to liberal legal ideals of natural justice and formal equality, exclusions that aim to protect national security, public safety, and system integrity from crime-security threats are widely accepted as unproblematic and legitimate justifications. Articulated largely through the language of risk and given effect through the operations of discretion, they are continuously constituted as neutral, objective, even scientific bases for national exclusions.

In the present day, crime-security has become the central occasion for the production, reproduction, and enforcement of borders: "Where crime is located, the border can be strengthened. As crime is deemed continually to take new forms, new borders come into crisis, requiring reinforcement and vigilance."[22] The linked threats posed by frauds, criminals, and security risks, threats often represented in the form of the folk devils who are refugee claimants, provide a guiding rationale for border security just as they simultaneously reconstitute border insecurities.

These are not exceptional circumstances. Interdiction is an objective pursued with determination throughout the West. This retrenchment in the name of security, public safety, and border integrity has made it more and more difficult and dangerous for those fleeing persecution, war, famine, and poverty to make a new home in a safe place.

This study encourages in preliminary fashion a conception of the border as an ongoing and artful accomplishment. The border is creatively constituted and reconstituted through the operation of multiple and intersecting authorities, practices, technologies, forms of knowledge, and governing regimes that include but are not limited to legal processes and the formal institutions of government. Central among these are the practices of immigration detention and deportation. They represent a zone of exclusion for noncitizens deemed undeserving and undesirable. As observed by Rose, "it appears as if outside the communities of inclusion exists an array of micro-sectors, micro-cultures of non-citizens, failed citizens, anti-citizens, consisting of those who are unable or unwilling to enterprise their lives, or manage their own risk, incapable of exercising responsible self government, attached either to no moral community or to a community of anti-morality."[23]

Yet the practices of immigration penality and border control that culminate in the expulsion of noncitizens through the violent and bodily technologies of detention and deportation are not only negative and coercive but also productive. Just as detention and deportation contribute to the shaping of borders, so too borders "make up" identities and citizens and regulate populations by classifying and filtering those seeking entry to Canada and by searching out and removing the undesirables who get through. Border control and immigration penality constantly reproduce the border and historically specific configurations of the desirable citizen and national identity.

In this book, I have examined the less visible dimensions and effects of detention and deportation, immigration penality, and border control. I have sought to make visible the connections between what might appear to be rather disparate concerns – immigration, detention and deportation, criminal justice, refugee claimants, welfare recipients, law, discretion, human rights, crime, security, fraud, and risk – and to trace these connections in relation to the more general transitions from welfare liberal to neoliberal rationalities of rule. In so doing, I hope to contribute to the unsettling of taken-for-granted assumptions about detention and deportation, immigration, refugees, and the range and representation of risks, dangers, and uncertainties that shape the border, reproduce border insecurity, and enmesh borders in security.

Appendix
Canadian Immigration Ministries
(1949-2004)

1949-66	Ministry of Citizenship and Immigration
1966-77	Ministry of Manpower and Immigration
1977-93	Employment and Immigration Commission
1993-94	Ministry of Public Security
1994-2004	Ministry of Citizenship and Immigration

Notes

Chapter 1: Overview and Orientations

1 This concept was developed by Jonathan Simon in "Governing through Crime," in *The Crime Conundrum: Essays on Criminal Justice,* ed. Lawrence M. Friedman and George Fisher (New York: Westview Press, 1997), 171-89.
2 A distinction offered by William Walters in "Mapping Schengenland: Denaturalizing the Border," *Environment and Planning D: Society and Space* 20 (2002): 569.
3 John Pratt, "Dangerousness and Modern Society," in *Dangerous Offenders: Punishment and Social Order* (London: Routledge, 2000), 39.
4 Walters, "Mapping Schengenland," 570.
5 *Immigration Act,* S.C. 1976-77, c. 52, s. 1 [hereafter 1976 *Immigration Act*].
6 *Immigration and Refugee Protection Act,* S.C. 2001, c. 27 [hereafter *IRPA*].
7 *An Act to Amend the Criminal Code, the Official Secrets Act, the Canada Evidence Act, the Proceeds of Crime (Money Laundering) Act, and Other Acts, and to Enact Measures Respecting the Registration of Charities, in Order to Combat Terrorism,* S.C. 2001, c. 41 [hereafter *Anti-Terrorism Act*].
8 Department of Justice Canada, "Royal Assent of Bill C-36: The Anti-Terrorism Act," *Backgrounder* 18 December 2001. For an excellent collection of essays dealing with different aspects of the Anti-Terrorism Act, see Ronald J. Daniels, Patrick Macklem, and Kent Roach, eds., *The Security of Freedom: Essays on Canada's Anti-Terrorism Bill* (Toronto: University of Toronto Press, 2001).
9 These and related developments are examined in more detail in Chapter 9.
10 This raises the broader issue of the law/discretion binary explored in Chapter 3. For critiques of Bill C-11, see Amnesty International, "The Immigration and Refugee Protection Act: It Is Faster but Is It Fairer for All Genuine Refugees?" news release, AI Index: AMR 20/C02/00, 7 April 2000; Canadian Council for Refugees (CCR), "New Immigration Bill Reduces Newcomer Rights," news release, 14 March 2001; Sharryn Aiken, Centre for Refugee Studies, "Comments on Bill C-11 Related to National Security and Terrorism," submission to the House of Commons Standing Committee on Citizenship and Immigration, 26 March 2001; Canadian Bar Association (CBA), "New Bill Is 'Unfair' to Immigrants Says CBA's Immigration Section," news release, 21 February 2001.
11 Amnesty International, "The Immigration and Refugee Protection Act," 7 April 2000. This issue is taken up in Chapter 7.
12 CIC, "Caplan Tables New Immigration and Refugee Protection Act," news release, 6 April 2000.
13 *Convention Implementing the Schengen Agreement of 14 June 1985 between the Governments of the States of the Benelux Economic Union, the Federal Republic of Germany, and the French Republic on the Gradual Abolition of Checks at Their Common Borders,* 19 June 1990. The member states in July 2003 were Austria, Belgium, Denmark, France, Finland, Germany, Greece, Iceland, Italy, Luxembourg, the Netherlands, Norway, Portugal, Spain, and Sweden. The United Kingdom and Ireland are not members.

14 *Convention Determining the State Responsible for Examining Applications for Asylum Lodged in One of the Member States of the European Communities* (Dublin Convention), European Union governments, 15 June 1990, J.O. C 254 , 19/08/1997, 1.
15 All EU countries are considered safe third countries. In general terms, this means that refugees must make their claims in the first EU country in which they arrive – they are ineligible to make a refugee claim if they travel through a safe third country first. On 5 December 2002, Canada and the United States signed their Safe Third Country Agreement. It is discussed in more detail in Chapter 9.
16 German Embassy in London, "Foreigners in Germany and Europe Compared: Foreigners in the Federal Republic of Germany," June 2002, http://www.german-embassy.org.uk/foreign.html.
17 US Committee for Refugees, "Country Report: Germany," *World Wide Refugee Information,* 2002, http://www.refugees.org/.
18 US Committee for Refugees, "Country Report: France," *World Wide Refugee Information,* 2002, http://www.refugees.org/.
19 Ibid.
20 Refugee Council On-Line, "UK Asylum Law and Process," http://www.refugeecouncil.org.uk/infocentre/.
21 For additional information on each of these legislative reforms and a wide range of related issues, see Refugee Council On-Line, http://www.refugeecouncil.org.uk/infocentre/.
22 *Asylum and Immigration (Treatment of Claimants etc.) Bill,* Bill 5, 53/3, 2003-2004 Sess., (Royal Assent 22 July 2004). UK Home Office, "Reforming the System – Asylum and Immigration Bill Gets Royal Assent," press release, 22 July 2004, http://www.ind.homeoffice.gov.uk/.
23 "EU Rejects Asylum Camps Plan," *Guardian Unlimited,* 20 June 2003, http://politics.guardian.co.uk/. See also Amnesty International, "Unlawful and Unworkable: Amnesty International's View on Proposals for Extra-Territorial Processing of Refugee Claims," June 2003, http://www.amnesty-eu.org/.
24 "Europe's Asylum Policy Shameful, Says UN: Britain to Push for Launch of Pilot Scheme in East Africa," *Guardian Unlimited,* 20 June 2003, http://politics.guardian.co.uk/.
25 Ibid. This brief review of Western European developments is by no means comprehensive. Switzerland, Finland, Denmark, and Italy have also introduced new and restrictive immigration reforms; indeed, one of the primary focuses of the EU Commission is to find ways to improve border control and curb "clandestine immigration" to all member countries.
26 Amnesty International, "Australia-Pacific: Offending Human Dignity – the 'Pacific Solution,'" AI Index: ASA 12/009/2002, 25 August 2002.
27 US Committee for Refugees, "Country Report: Australia," *World Wide Refugee Information,* 2002, http://www.refugees.org/.
28 Ibid.
29 Australian detention facilities, and the country's immigration and border control policies in general, have been widely and repeatedly criticized by national and international human rights groups. See Amnesty International Report 2003, "Australia," http://web.amnesty.org/report2003/.
30 United States Department of Justice, Bureau of Citizenship and Immigration Services, "Illegal Immigration Reform and Immigrant Responsibility Act: Summary," fact sheet, http://www.immigration.gov/graphics/publicaffairs/factsheets/948.html.
31 US Committee for Refugees, "Country Report: United States," *World Wide Refugee Information,* 2002, http://www.refugees.org/.
32 Ibid.
33 For a review of developments in the United States, see Michael Welch, *Detained: Immigration Laws and the Expanding I.N.S. Jail Complex* (Philadelphia: Temple University Press, 2003).
34 US Committee for Refugees, "Country Report: United States," 2002. In June 2004, the Supreme Court affirmed the legal rights of detainees to challenge their detention in a court of law. "The Supreme Court: The President: In Classic Check and Balance, Court Shows Bush It Also Has Wartime Powers," *New York Times* 29 June 2004.
35 US Committee for Refugees, "Country Report: United States," 2002.

36 There is a large literature that examines the proliferation of enforcement measures and the fortification of territorial borders in the North American context. See, for example, Peter Andreas, "Borderless Economy, Barricaded Border," *NACLA Report on the Americas* 33, 3 (1999): 14-21; Peter Andreas and Timothy Snyder, eds., *The Wall around the West: State Borders and Immigration Controls in North America and Europe* (Boston: Rowman and Littlefield, 2000); Stephen E. Flynn, "Beyond Border Control," *Foreign Affairs* 79, 6 (2000): 57-68; Patrick Fitzgerald, "Repelling Borders," *New Statesman and Society* 8 (1995): 16-17; and Josiah Heyman, "Why Interdiction? Immigration Control at the United States-Mexico Border," *Regional Studies* 33, 7 (1999): 619-30.

37 John Torpey, "Coming and Going: On the State Monopolization of the Legitimate Means of Movement," *Sociological Theory* 16, 3 (1998): 239-59.

38 William Walters, "Deportation, Expulsion, and the International Police of Aliens," *Citizenship Studies* 6, 3 (2002): 282.

39 CIC, "Overview of Bill C-31, *The Immigration and Refugee Protection Act,*" 6 June 2000: 2.

40 Michel Foucault, *Discipline and Punish: The Birth of the Prison*, trans. Alan Sheridan (New York: Vintage Books 1979 [1977]), 25.

41 Alan Hunt and Gary Wickham, *Foucault and Law: Toward a Sociology of Law as Governance* (London: Pluto Press, 1994), 7.

42 Mitchell Dean, *Governmentality: Power and Rule in Modern Society* (London: Sage Publications, 1999), 29.

43 Michel Foucault, "Truth and Power," interview with Foucault, in Paul Rabinow, ed., *The Foucault Reader* (New York: Pantheon Books, 1984), 64.

44 Nikolas Rose, *Powers of Freedom: Reframing Political Thought* (Cambridge: Cambridge University Press, 1999), 3.

45 Nikolas Rose and Peter Miller, "Political Power beyond the State: Problematics of Government," *British Journal of Sociology* 43, 2 (1992): 175.

46 Perhaps as a result of this analytical predisposition toward regulatory apparatuses beyond "the state," as well as a guiding focus on the myriad ways in which citizens are regulated, relatively little attention has been paid until recently in the governmentality literature to the domain of migration. See, for example, Marianne Constable, "Sovereignty and Governmentality in Modern American Immigration Law," *Studies in Law, Politics, and Society* 13 (1993): 249-71; Randy Lippert, "Governing Refugees: The Relevance of Governmentality to Understanding the International Refugee Regime," *Alternatives* 24 (1999): 295-328; Walters, "Deportation, Expulsion, and the International Police of Aliens," 2002; Walters, Wendy Warner and William Walters, eds., *Global Govermentality: Governing International Spaces* (London: Routledge, 2004); "Mapping Schengenland," 2002; Didier Bigo, "Security and Immigration: A Critique of the Governmentality of Unease," *Alternatives* 27 (2002): 63-92; and Lydia Morris, "Governing at a Distance: The Elaboration of Controls in British Immigration," *International Migration Review* 32, 4 (1998): 949-73.

47 Foucault, *Discipline and Punish*, 194.

48 Among the most significant are Didier Bigo, "The European Internal Security Field: Stakes and Rivalries in a Newly Developing Area of Police Intervention," in Malcolm Anderson and Monica den Boer, eds., *Policing across National Boundaries* (London: Pinter Press, 1994), 161-71; Ayse Ceyhan and Anastassia Tsoukala, "The Securitization of Migration in Western Societies: Ambivalent Discourses and Policies," *Alternatives* 27 (2002): 21-39; Jef Huysmans, "Migrants as a Security Problem: Dangers of 'Securitizing' Societal Issues," in Robert Miles and Dietrich Thränhardt, eds., *Migration and European Integration: The Dynamics of Inclusion and Exclusion* (London: Pinter Publishers, 1995), 53-72; Ole Waever et al., *Identity, Migration, and the New Security Agenda in Europe* (London: Pinter Publishers, 1993); Ole Waever, "Securitization and Desecuritization," in Ronnie D. Lipschutz, ed., *On Security* (New York: Columbia University Press, 1995), 46-86; and Barry Buzan, Ole Waever, and Jaap de Wilde, *Security: A New Framework for Analysis* (Boulder: Lynne Rienner Publishers, 1998).

49 The "black box" is a central metaphor of Actor Network Theory. See Bruno Latour, *Science in Action* (Cambridge, MA: Harvard University Press, 1987); and Michael Callon and John Law, "After the Individual in Society: Lessons on Collectivity from Science, Technology, and Society," *Canadian Journal of Sociology* 22, 2 (1997): 165-82.

50 Franz Kafka, "In the Penal Colony," in *The Great Short Works of Franz Kafka*, trans. Joachim Neugroschel (New York: Scribner Paperback, 1995), 197-98.

51 Nikolas Rose and Mariana Valverde, "Governed by Law?" *Social and Legal Studies* 7, 4 (1998): 547. The relationship between the role and place of different modes of power has been the subject of lively scholarly debate. See, for example, Kevin Stenson, "Beyond Histories of the Present," *Economy and Society* 27, 4 (1998): 333-52; Frank Pearce and Steve Tombs, "Foucault, Governmentality, and Marxism," *Social and Legal Studies* 7, 4 (1998): 567-75; Alan Hunt, "Foucault's Expulsion of Law: Toward a Retrieval," *Law and Social Inquiry* 17, 2 (1992): 1-38; and Barbara Hudson, "Punishment and Governance," *Social and Legal Studies* 7, 4 (1998): 553-59.

52 Foucault, *Discipline and Punish*, 49.

53 Ibid., 53.

54 Carl Schmitt, *Political Theology: Four Chapters on the Concept of Sovereignty* (Cambridge, MA: MIT Press, 1988). See also Giorgio Agamben, *Homo Sacer: Sovereign Power and Bare Life* (Stanford: Stanford University Press, 1998).

55 Agamben, *Homo Sacer*, 174.

56 Ibid., 32.

57 I am borrowing the concept of "zones of exclusion" from Nikolas Rose. See *Powers of Freedom*, 258.

58 Sovereign power as it appears in the governmentality and related literature is generally undertheorized. There are, however, important exceptions. Outstanding among them are Schmitt, *Political Theology*; Agamben, *Homo Sacer*; Jenny Edkins, "Sovereign Power, Zones of Indistinction, and the Camp," *Alternatives* 25 (2000): 3-25; Mitchell Dean, "Liberal Government and Authoritarianism," *Economy and Society* 31 (2002): 37-61; Michael Dillon, "Sovereignty and Governmentality: 'From the Problematics of the "New World Order" to the Ethical Problematic of the World Order,'" *Alternatives* 20 (1995): 323-68; and Randy Lippert, "Sanctuary Practices, Rationalities, and Sovereignties," *Alternatives: Global, Local, Political* 29, 5 (2004): 535-55.

59 Michel Foucault, "Governmentality," in Graham Burchell, Colin Gordon, and Peter Miller, eds., *The Foucault Effect: Studies in Governmentality with Two Lectures by and an Interview with Michel Foucault* (Chicago: University of Chicago Press, 1991), 87-104.

60 Rose, *Powers of Freedom*, 23.

61 Jonathan Simon, "Ghosts of the Disciplinary Machine: Lee Harvey Oswald, Life History, and the Truth of Crime," *Yale Law Review* 10, 1 (1998): 81.

62 Rose, *Powers of Freedom*, 23.

63 Hunt and Wickham, *Foucault and Law*, 20.

64 Foucault, "Governmentality," 91.

65 Ibid., 95.

66 Dean, *Governmentality*, 105.

67 Foucault, "Governmentality," 100.

68 Ibid., 92.

69 Dean, *Governmentality*, 20.

70 Foucault, "Governmentality," 102-3.

71 Rose and Miller, "Political Power beyond the State," 189.

72 Dean, *Governmentality*, 21.

73 Jonathan Simon makes a similar point in "Refugees in a Carceral Age: The Rebirth of Immigration Prisons in the US," *Public Culture* 10, 3 (1998): 577-606.

74 CIC, "Lessons Learned: 1999 Marine Arrivals in British Columbia," final report, August 2002, http://www.cic.gc.ca/english/research/evaluation/marine.html#detention.

75 Walters, "Deportation, Expulsion, and the International Police of Aliens," 277.

76 For an examination of related developments, see Gallya Lahav, "Migration and Security: The Role of Non-State Actors and Civil Liberties in Liberal Democracies," paper prepared for the Second Coordination Meeting on International Migration, Population Division, Department of Economic and Social Affairs, United Nations Secretariat, New York, 15-16 October 2003; and Janet A. Gilboy, "Implications of 'Third Party' Involvement in Enforcement: The INS, Illegal Travelers, and International Airlines," *Law and Society Review* 31, 3 (1997): 505-29.

77   Walters, "Deportation, Expulsion, and the International Police of Aliens," 278.
78   Rose and Miller, "Political Power beyond the State," 175.
79   Rose, *Powers of Freedom*, 52.
80   Rose and Miller, "Political Power beyond the State," 180.
81   Stenson, "Beyond Histories of the Present," 341.
82   Or perhaps of the older lineage of police as argued by Walters in "Deportation, Expulsion, and the Police of Aliens." Walters proposes that the administrative, rather than the juridical, early rationalizations of deportation reveal that at its inception deportation belongs to the older lineage of police regulation. Like police regulation, Walters proposes that deportation is an administrative process that works "to protect and sustain public order and tranquility, akin to the removal of a nuisance" (281).
83   See Rose and Valverde, "Governed by Law?"
84   Rose, *Powers of Freedom*, 24.
85   George Pavlich, *Justice Fragmented: Mediating Community Disputes under Postmodern Conditions* (London: Routledge, 1996), 136.
86   See Alan Hunt, *Explorations in Law and Society: Toward a Constitutive Theory of Law* (New York: Routledge, 1993).
87   Nikolas Rose, "Beyond the Public/Private Division: Law, Power, and the Family," in Peter Fitzpatrick and Alan Hunt, eds., *Critical Legal Studies* (Oxford: Blackwell, 1987), 66.
88   Pavlich, *Justice Fragmented*, 155.
89   Pavlich and Fitzpatrick develop a similar argument in relation to "informal" domains of justice that lie "outside" law. See Pavlich, *Justice Fragmented;* and Peter Fitzpatrick, "The Rise and Rise of Informalism," in Roger Matthews, ed., *Informal Justice?* (London: Sage, 1988), 178-98.
90   Alan Hunt, *Governing Morals: A Social History of Moral Regulation* (Cambridge: Cambridge University Press, 1999), 6-7.
91   Foucault's concept of "dividing practices" is applied and developed by Hunt in *Governing Morals*.
92   Rose, *Powers of Freedom*, 181.
93   For more extensive discussions, see Rose, *Powers of Freedom;* and Rose and Miller, "Political Powers beyond the State," 1992.
94   Ibid., 192.
95   Ibid., 196.
96   The use of the term "neoliberalism" is not a straightforward matter in the governmentality literature. Rose in particular has distinguished between neoliberalism as a set of historically specific formulas of liberal government and advanced liberalism as a broad "diagram of power" that includes but extends beyond neoliberal rationality. This new diagram of power is not simply a "return" to classical liberalism but involves the restructuring of social government along economic lines. See Rose, *Powers of Freedom*, 141-42. I defer to Pat O'Malley's observation on this issue: "It is vital to note that for most governmentality work in this domain, the terms neoliberal and advanced liberal have become coextensive." Pat O'Malley, "Genealogy, Systematisation, and Résistance in 'Advanced Liberalism,'" in Gary Wickham and George Pavlich, eds., *Rethinking Law, Society, and Governance: Foucault's Bequest* (Oxford: Hart Publishing, 2001), 15.
97   Rose, *Powers of Freedom*, 142.
98   Ibid.
99   Ibid., 261.
100   Jacques Donzelot, "The Mobilization of Society," in *The Foucault Effect*, 45.
101   Rose, *Powers of Freedom*, 260.
102   Ulrich Beck, *Risk Society: Towards a New Modernity* (London: Sage Publications, 1992); Ulrich Beck, *World Risk Society* (Cambridge: Polity Press-Blackwell Publishers, 1999); Ulrich Beck, *The Brave New World of Work* (Cambridge: Polity Press-Blackwell Publishers, 2000).
103   Pat O'Malley, "Introduction: Configurations of Risk," *Economy and Society* 29, 4 (2000): 457.
104   Beck, *Risk Society*, 34.
105   See, for example, Robert Castel, "From Dangerousness to Risk," in *The Foucault Effect*, 281-98; Daniel Defert, "Popular Life and Insurance Technology," in *The Foucault Effect*, 211-33; Richard V. Ericson and Kevin D. Haggerty, *Policing the Risk Society* (Toronto: University of

Toronto Press, 1997); François Ewald, "Risk and Insurance," in *The Foucault Effect,* 197-210; Jonathan Simon, "The Emergence of a Risk Society: Insurance, Law, and the State," *Socialist Review* 95 (1987): 61-89; Pat O'Malley, "Uncertain Subjects: Risks, Liberalism, and Contract," *Economy and Society* 29, 4 (2000): 460-84; Tom Baker and Jonathan Simon, eds., *Embracing Risk: The Changing Culture of Insurance and Responsibility* (Chicago: University of Chicago Press, 2002); Ian Hacking, *The Taming of Chance* (Cambridge: Cambridge University Press, 1990); Richard Ericson and Aaron Doyle, eds., *Risk and Morality* (Toronto: University of Toronto Press, 2003; and Pat O'Malley, *Uncertainty and Goverment* (London: Glasshouse Press, 2004).

106 See, for example, Jonathan Simon and Malcolm Feeley, "True Crime: The New Penology and Public Discourse on Crime," in Thomas Blomberg and Stanley Cohen, eds., *Punishment and Social Control* (New York: Aldine de Gruyter, 1995), 147-80; Malcolm Feeley and Jonathan Simon, "The New Penology: Notes on the Emerging Strategy for Corrections and Its Implications," *Criminology* 30 (1992): 449-74; Malcolm Feeley and Jonathan Simon, "Actuarial Justice: The Emerging New Criminal Law," in David Nelken, ed., *The Futures of Criminology* (London: Sage, 1994), 173-201; and Pat O'Malley, ed., *Crime and the Risk Society,* International Library of Criminology, Criminal Justice, and Penology (Australia: Ashgate Dartmouth, 1998).

107 Castel, "From Dangerousness to Risk," in *The Foucault Effect,* 287.

108 The multiplicity of risk knowledges in relation to legal processes is examined by Mariana Valverde, Ron Levi, and Dawn Moore in "Legal Knowledges of Risks," report to the Law Commission of Canada, presented at the Joint Session of the Canadian Association of Law Teachers and Canadian Law and Society Association, Halifax, 2 June 2003. See also Mariana Valverde, *Law's Dream of a Common Knowledge* (Princeton: Princeton University Press, 2003).

109 Simon, "Governing through Crime," 174.

110 Rose, *Powers of Freedom,* 259.

111 Ibid., 271.

Chapter 2: Detention at the Celebrity Inn

1 Hereafter Celebrity or the Celebrity Inn. As this book neared completion, the Celebrity Inn was closed and in 2004 the CIC opened a new detention centre in a different, but also aptly named, airport motel – the Heritage Inn.

2 Unless otherwise indicated, the details relating to the death of Akhimien are drawn from the deputation presented on 22 October 1997 by Akhimien's lawyer, Chile Eboe Osuji, to the Inter-American Commission on Human Rights during the commission's on-site visit to Canada (20-22 October 1997). The commission produced a final report in 2000 on refugees and human rights in Canada entitled "Report on the Situation of Human Rights of Asylum Seekers within the Canadian Refugee Determination System," February 2000.

3 Confusion about Akhimien's identity played a part in the decision to detain him. Indeed, the coroner's report names him as Michael Deno.

4 Quoted in *Now Magazine,* "Guards Ignore a Dying Man's Cry for Help," 27 June-3 July 1996: 20.

5 Ibid.

6 Ibid.

7 Ontario Ministry of the Solicitor General, Chief Coroner, "Verdict and Recommendations Arising out of the Inquest into the Death of Michael Deno," 7 June 1996. Akhimien's death was also documented by Amnesty International in its 1997 *Human Rights Report.*

8 *Coroners Act,* R.S.B.C. 1996, c. 72.

9 Ibid.

10 United Nations Committee against Torture, *Decisions of the Committee against Torture under Article 22 of the Convention against Torture and Other Cruel, Inhuman, or Degrading Treatment or Punishment,* Twenty-First Session. Communication No. 67/1997: Canada. 17/11/98. CAT/C/21/D/67/1997. (Jurisprudence).

11 Rose, *Powers of Freedom,* 34.

12 Ibid.

13 A resemblance observed by Dan O'Connor in conversation.

14 Michel Foucault, *Madness and Civilization: A History of Insanity in the Age of Reason* (New York: Random House, 1965), 11.

230Notes to pages 26-31

15 Ibid.
16 Ibid., 40.
17 Agamben, *Homo Sacer.*
18 Rose, *Powers of Freedom,* 258.
19 This chapter is a revised version of my article "Sovereign Power, Carceral Conditions, and Penal Practices: Detention and Deportation in Canada." It is reprinted from *Studies in Law, Politics, and Society* 23 (2001): 45-78. © Elsevier Publications, 2001.
20 *Globe and Mail,* 28 December 1995.
21 Michael Welch, "Questioning the Utility and Fairness of Immigration and Naturalization Service Detention," *Journal of Contemporary Criminal Justice* 13, 1 (1997): 42. See also Welch, *Detained.*
22 Celebrity Budget Inn publicity brochure, 1998.
23 Enforcement detention officer (EDO) interview, 3 February 2000.
24 Joan Simalchik, "Is This Canada? A Report on Refugee Detention in the Celebrity Inn Immigration Holding Centre," prepared for the Toronto Refugee Affairs Council Detention Committee, January 1998, 13.
25 House of Commons, Standing Committee on Citizenship and Immigration, Transcripts of Hearings on Removal and Detention (October 1997 to May 1998) Pursuant to Standing Order 108 (2), 31 March 1998, Ottawa, 22 April 1998, 20 [hereafter House of Commons Standing Committee Hearings, transcripts].
26 EDO interview, 3 February 2000. This observation and, unless indicated otherwise, the several quotations in the following paragraphs are from this interview. In *IRPA*, it is noted that the detention of minors should only take place as a "last resort" (s. 60).
27 Interview with TRAC case worker, 3 February 2000.
28 *Immigration Act* (s. 80.1 and s. 103).
29 Immigration and Refugee Board (IRB), Guidelines of the Chairperson of the Immigration and Refugee Board, *Powers of Adjudicators to Order Detention: Chairperson's Guidelines Issued Pursuant to Section 65(4) of the Immigration Act* (Ottawa: Immigration and Refugee Board, effective 12 March 1998) [hereafter IRB *Guidelines on Detention*].
30 *Immigration Act* (s. 103.1). The inadmissible classes are covered by sections 33-43 of the *IRPA* (formerly s. 19 of the 1976 *Immigration Act*).
31 *IRPA,* ss. 54-60.
32 Detailed departmental guidelines on detention under *IRPA* are found in CIC, Chapter ENF 20, "Detention," *Immigration Manual,* http://www.cic.gc.ca/manuals-guides/english/enf/enf20e.pdf.
33 *Sahin v. Canada (Minister of Citizenship and Immigration),* [1995] 1 F.C. 214 (T.D.).
34 *Canadian Charter of Rights and Freedoms,* Part I of the *Constitution Act, 1982,* being Schedule B to the *Canada Act, 1982* (U.K.), 1982, c. 11 [hereafter the *Charter*]. In *Singh v. Canada (Minister of Employment and Immigration),* [1985] 1 S.C.R. 177, 17 D.L.R. (4th) 422, the SCC ruled that the *Charter* applies equally to all on Canadian soil, citizens and noncitizens alike.
35 IRB, *Guidelines on Detention,* 3.
36 CIC, *Detention Policy.*
37 *Kidane, Derar v. Canada (Minister of Citizenship and Immigration)* (F.C.T.D., no. IMM-2044-96), Jerome, 11 July 1997.
38 CIC, "National Standards and Monitoring Plan for the Regulation and Operation of CIC's Detention Centres," draft, 5 February 1998.
39 *UNHCR Guidelines on Detention of Asylum Seekers,* PRL 5.3, 29 January 1996.
40 United Nations High Commissioner for Human Rights, *United Nations Body of Principles for the Protection of All People under Any Form of Detention or Imprisonment,* adopted by General Assembly Resolution 43/173 of 9 December 1988.
41 United Nations High Commissioner for Human Rights, *Standard Minimum Rules for the Treatment of Prisoners,* adopted by the First United Nations Congress on the Prevention of Crime and the Treatment of Offenders, Geneva, 1955, and approved by the Economic and Social Council by its resolutions 663 C (XXIV) of 31 July 1957 and 2076 (LXII) of 13 May 1977.

42 CIC, *Department Performance Report for the Period Ending March 31st, 2002* (Ottawa: Minister of Public Works and Government Services, 2002).

43 The question of discretion is taken up in detail in Chapter 3. I have explored the relations between law, discretionary power, and the administration of the Canadian *Immigration Act* in more detail in "Dunking the Doughnut: Law, Discretionary Power, and the Administration of the Canadian *Immigration Act*," *Social and Legal Studies* 8, 2 (1999): 199-226.

44 On 12 December 2003, the customs program of the CCRA joined the new Canada Border Services Agency (CBSA) as part of the new Public Safety and Emergency Preparedness portfolio. The CBSA brings together all those engaged in the enforcement of border security, including the customs program from the Canada Customs and Revenue Agency (CCRA), the intelligence, interdiction, and enforcement program from Citizenship and Immigration Canada (CIC), and the import inspection at ports of entry program from the Canadian Food Inspection Agency (CFIA). As a result, the CCRA has been renamed the Canada Revenue Agency (CRA).

45 IRB, *Guidelines on Detention*.

46 Ibid. *IRPA* (ss. 54-62).

47 EDO interview, 3 February 2000.

48 John Stanton and Wayne Madsen, "The Caligulan American Justice System: U.N. Intervention Is Necessary," *Online Journal*, Centre for Research on Globalization (CRG), 8 March 2002, http://www.globalresearch.ca/articles/STA203A.html.

49 Quoted in Aziz Choudry, "The Paydirt of Paranoia," *ZNet Commentary*, 20 February 2003, http://www.zmag.org/sustainers/content/2003-02/20choudry.cfm.

50 GEO Group (formerly Wackenhut Corrections Corporation), "Chairman's Welcome," http://www.wcc-corrections.com.

51 GEO Group, "Fast Facts about GEO," http://www.wcc-corrections.com/facts.asp/.

52 GEO Group, "History," http://www.careerbuilder.com/JobSeeker/Companies/CompanyDetails.aspx?HHName=geogroup&cbRecursionCnt=1&cbsid=b06527a774174b80a23389328d0ac2b8-143484426-xm-2.

53 GEO Group (formerly Wackenhut Corrections Corporation), "Deliver Global Services," 2002. http://www.wcc-corrections.com.

54 For a review of the issues and debates relating to privatization and criminal justice, see, for example, Michael Reisig and Travis Pratt, "The Ethics of Correctional Privatization: A Critical Examination of the Delegation of Coercive Authority," *Prison Journal* 80, 2 (2000): 210-23; Paul Thompson, "Private Prison Partnerships in Criminal Justice," *New Economy* 7, 3 (2000): 150-55; and Todd Clear and Natasha Frost, "Private Prisons," *Criminology and Public Policy* 1, 3 (2002): 425-27.

55 GEO Group, "Advantages of Working with Us," http://www.wcc-corrections.com/advantages.asp/.

56 "Canada Sends Deportees Home Aboard 'Con Air,'" *Globe and Mail*, 20 January 1999.

57 Ibid.

58 "Activists Slam Private Deportations," *Globe and Mail*, 22 February 2001. See also "Resolutions," December 2000, http://www.web.net/%7Eccr/resd00.htm; and "Resolutions," May 2001, http://www.web.net/%7Eccr/resm01.html.

59 CIC, *Performance Report for the Period Ending March 31, 2003* (Ottawa: Minister of Public Works and Government Services, 2003).

60 "Deportation Plan Saves Feds Money," *Calgary Sun*, 16 May 2004.

61 EDO interview, 3 February 2000.

62 Ibid.

63 Chief Coroner, "Verdict and Recommendations."

64 CIC, Detention and Removals, *Mississauga Holding Centre Post Orders*, 29 February 1996, s. 2.06. In February 2000, a new edition of the Celebrity's *Post Orders* was soon to be released.

65 EDO interview, 3 February 2000.

66 CIC, *Post Orders*, s. 12.

67 Ibid., ss. 11.08, 11.13, 11.20.

68 EDO interview, 3 February 2000.

69 Alison Young, *Imagining Crime* (London: Sage Publications, 1996), 72.

70 "Con Air Is an Airline with a Difference," *Globe and Mail,* 20 January 1999.
71 House of Commons Standing Committee Hearings, transcripts, 23 April 1998, 3.
72 "Why do they treat us like criminals?" is perhaps the question I heard most frequently during my time at Celebrity. Of particular concern to the detainees was the use of hand-cuffs on mothers in front of their children. This concern, also voiced during the 1997-98 hearings, was responded to in the subsequent edition of the CIC *Post Orders,* which bans this practice. EDO interview, 3 February 2000.
73 Section 11 of the *Post Orders* details transportation procedures.
74 Ibid., s. 4.
75 CIC, Immigration Holding Centre, Mississauga, *Rules for Detainees,* 1998.
76 CIC, *Post Orders,* s. 8.
77 Ibid., s. 9.
78 The relevant sections of the *Criminal Code of Canada* are set out in section 17 of the *Post Orders*: s. 25 ("Protection of Persons Acting under Authority"); s. 26 ("Excessive Force"); s. 34 ("Self Defence against Unprovoked Attack"); s. 37(1) ("Preventing Assault"); and s. 17.05 ("Rescue or Permitting Escape").
79 EDO interview, 3 February 2000.
80 CIC, *Rules for Detainees.*
81 Interview with TRAC case worker, 3 February 2000.
82 Ibid.
83 Ibid.
84 CIC, *Post Orders,* s. 15.01.
85 Ibid., s. 15.02.
86 Simalchik, "Is This Canada?"
87 CIC, *Post Orders,* s. 8.20.
88 CIC, *Post Orders,* 1996: s. 7.01
89 Ibid., s. 7.08.
90 EDO interview, 3 February 2000.
91 EDO interview, 21 February 2000.
92 Ibid.
93 CIC, *Post Orders,* s. 10.03.
94 Ibid., s. 10.01.
95 House of Commons Standing Committee Hearings, transcripts, 22 April 1998, 4.
96 See Chapter 7 for discussions of these events.
97 CIC Enforcement Branch, Ontario Region, "Ontario Region Jail Day Histories," 1997.
98 Ibid.
99 CIC, *Department Performance Report for the Period Ending March 31st, 1998* (Ottawa: Minister of Public Works and Government Services, 1998). In this report, CIC provides two different numbers of those detained in 2002-3: in the text 7,080 and in the table 7,968.
100 CIC Public Affairs, "Response to Information Request," 24 March 1997.
101 CIC, *Department Performance Report for the Period Ending March 31st, 2001* (Ottawa: Minister of Public Works and Government Services, 2001).
102 Ibid.
103 CIC, *Department Performance Report for the Period Ending March 31st, 2002* (Ottawa: Minister of Public Works and Government Services, 2002). In this report, CIC provides two different numbers of those detained in 2002-3: in the text 141,307 and in the table 141,202.
104 CIC, *Department Performance Report for the Period Ending March 31st, 2003* (Ottawa: Minister of Public Works and Government Services, 2003). In this report, CIC provides two different numbers of those detained in 2002-3: in the text 11,503 and in the table 11,494.
105 Security certificates are issued by the minister of citizenship and immigration and the solicitor general of Canada under section 77 of the *IRPA* (formerly s. 39 of the 1976 *Immigration Act*). The issuance of security certificates is explored further in Chapter 7.
106 CCR, "Detention Statistics 2002," 6 March 2003. CIC produces a weekly "detention snap-shot" of the numbers of people in detention on a particular day. The CCR produces a summary of detention statistics derived from CIC's numbers. All of the above figures are provided in this source. http://www.web.net/~ccr/detentionstats2002.html.

107 CCR, "Detention Statistics: 2003 Year to Date," 1 April 2003, http://www.web.net/~ccr/detentionstatscurrent.html.
108 EDO interview, 3 February 2000.
109 Ibid.
110 CIC, Detention and Removals Unit, "Month End Statistical Report," 3 February 2000.
111 Interview with TRAC case worker, 3 February 2000.
112 EDO interview, 3 February 2000.
113 Ibid.
114 House of Commons Standing Committee Hearings, transcripts, 22 April 1998, 5.
115 Ibid., 27 November 1997, 15.
116 Simalchik, "Is This Canada?" 23.
117 Ibid.
118 EDO interview, 3 February 2000. This definition was also provided in the House of Commons Standing Committee Hearings, transcripts, 21 October 1997, 24. However, CIC's definition of the official length of a "long-term detention" is variable. CIC, Ontario Region, "Long Term Detention Statistics," 30 June 1997, defines "long-term" as "over 60 days." Also, in the 1997-98 CIC Standing Committee Hearings, a "long-term detention" was defined by Paul Thibault, executive director of the Adjudication Division of CIC as "over 90 days." House of Commons Standing Committee Hearings, transcripts, 31 March 1998, 3.
119 These dangers to the public have been so found by an adjudicator. This finding does not necessarily mean that the minister has declared them to be a "danger to the public" under section 70(5) of the *Immigration Act*. This latter provision is examined in detail in Chapter 7.
120 House of Commons Standing Committee Hearings, transcripts, 21 October 1997, 24.
121 CIC, "Long Term Detention Statistics." The variable definition of "long-term" detentions complicates the statistics. The numbers quoted here are based on the thirty-day definition.
122 Ibid. These statistics were submitted to the CIC Standing Committee on 26 March 1998.
123 House of Commons Standing Committee Hearings, transcripts, 31 March 1998, 3. CIC points out that the two main reasons for long-term detentions are similar in both criminal cases and noncriminal cases: lack of detainee cooperation in securing the necessary travel documents and noncooperation of the country of origin.
124 Parkdale Legal Services, "Memorandum re: Metro West Detention Centre Hunger Strike by Immigration Detainees," 22 July 1997.
125 CIC officials at Celebrity report that one of their major frustrations stems from the inappropriate fit of the physical facility and the nature and length of the detentions. EDO interview, 3 February 2000. Furthermore, law and policy dictate that people should not be detained if there is no end to the detention in sight through either release or removal (see the discussion in Chapter 3). There are nonetheless many long-term detentions at Celebrity.
126 CIC, Detention and Removals Unit, "Month End Statistical Report," 3 February 2000.
127 Simalchik, "Is This Canada?" 24.
128 House of Commons Standing Committee Hearings, transcripts, 31 March 1998, 3.
129 EDO interview, 3 February 2000.
130 House of Commons Standing Committee Hearings, transcripts, 18 February 1998, 10.
131 *IRPA* s. 581(d).
132 House of Commons Standing Committee Hearings, transcripts, 25 March 1998, 20.
133 Foucault, *Discipline and Punish,* 37-40.
134 The detailed information in this paragraph is from CIC Public Affairs, "Response to Information Request," 1997.
135 House of Commons Standing Committee Hearings, transcripts, 21 October 1997, 23.
136 EDO interview, 3 February 2000.
137 Ibid.
138 Ibid.
139 Doris Meissner, Commissioner, Immigration and Naturalization Service, Department of Justice, Testimony before the Subcommittee on Immigration Committee on the Judiciary, US Senate, "Concerning INS Reform: Detention Issues," 16 September 1998, http://www.fas.org/irp/congress/1998_hr/98091631_llt.html.

140 Ibid.
141 United States Government, *A Blueprint for New Beginnings: A Responsible Budget for America's Priorities* (Washington, DC: US Government Printing Office, 10 July 2001), 85.
142 Welch, "Questioning the Utility and Fairness of Immigration and Naturalization Service Detention," 44.
143 Meissner, "Concerning INS Reform."
144 Ibid.
145 *IRPA* s. 55.
146 Department of Finance Canada, "More Resources for Detention, Removals, and Refugee Determination," in *Budget 2001: Enhancing Security for Canadians* (Ottawa: Public Works and Government Services Canada, 2001), 16. http://www.fin.gc.ca/budget01/pdf/bksece.pdf.
147 "Canada Plans to Detain Unidentified New Arrivals," *Globe and Mail*, 28 November 2002.
148 "Ottawa Eyes 'Super Jail' for Risky Migrants," *National Post*, 3 January 2003.
149 EDO interview, 3 February 2000.
150 "New Detention Centre for Foreigners Being Readied in Toronto," *CBC News Online*, 29 December 2003, http://www.cbc.ca/stories/2003/12/29/detention_centre031229.
151 Foucault, *Discipline and Punish*, 24.

Chapter 3: Reframing Discretion

1 Ronald Dworkin, *Taking Rights Seriously* (Cambridge, MA: Harvard University Press, 1977), 77. See also Ronald Dworkin, "Judicial Discretion," *Journal of Philosophy* 60, 21 (1963): 624-38.
2 Dworkin sought to complicate and challenge this view by proposing that, even where there are no explicit laws or rules that govern a decision, the constraining reach of the legal principles of the rule of law extends to cover the exercise of discretion. Therefore, he argues, there is really no such thing as "absolute" or "unfettered" discretion. Judicial decision making is always constrained by legal principles. Despite this departure, Dworkin's conception of discretion still rests upon its binary opposition to law, the only difference being the expansive way in which he defines "law."
3 An American exception to the general lacuna of social science and sociolegal approaches to discretion in the field of immigration is Janet A. Gilboy, "Deciding Who Gets In: Decision-Making by Immigration Inspectors," *Law and Society Review* 25, 3 (1991): 571-99; and Janet A. Gilboy, "Penetrability of Administrative Systems: Political 'Casework' and Immigration Inspections," *Law and Society Review* 26, 2 (1992): 273-313. For legal scholarship on detention issues, see, for example, Paula Hurwitz, "The New Detention Provisions of the Immigration Act: Can They Withstand a Charter Challenge?" *University of Toronto Faculty of Law Review* 47, 2 (1989): 587-606; Ron Poulton and Barbara Jackman, "Detention of Asylum Seekers: The Canadian Perspective," in Jane Hughes and Fabrice Liebaut, eds., *Detention of Asylum Seekers in Europe: Analysis and Perspectives* (The Hague: Martinus Nijoff Publishers, 1998), 113-23; and Steve Foster, "Immigration Detention," *Journal of Law and Social Policy* 8 (1992): 107-41.
4 This chapter is a revised version of my earlier article "Dunking the Doughnut: Discretionary Power, Law, and the Administration of the Canadian *Immigration Act*," *Social and Legal Studies* 8, 2 (1999): 199-226. © Sage Publications 1999.
5 Philip Anizman, ed., *A Catalogue of Discretionary Powers in the Revised Statutes of Canada, 1970* (Ottawa: Law Reform Commission of Canada, 1975), Preface.
6 *Dictionary of the English Language*, 2nd unabridged ed. (New York: Random House, 1987), 563.
7 Ibid., 107.
8 Albert Venn Dicey, *Introduction to the Study of the Law of the Constitution* (London: Macmillan, 1985 [1915]).
9 See, in particular, *Discretionary Justice: A Preliminary Inquiry* (Bâton Rouge: Louisiana State University Press, 1969).
10 Ibid., 55.
11 Ibid., 367.
12 An important contribution was made in 1986 by D.J. Galligan in his substantial study of legal discretion. Galligan criticized Davis for, among other things, his failure to include

any consideration of policy making in his study of discretion. Galligan argued that policy making is "the very heart of the discretionary process." Dennis James Galligan, *Discretionary Powers: A Legal Study of Official Discretion* (Oxford: Clarendon Press, 1986), 110.

13 For alternative approaches to discretion that do not resort to humanistic and rule-based conceptions of action, see, for example, Clifford Shearing and Richard Ericson, "Culture as Figurative Action," *British Journal of Sociology* 42, 4 (1991): 481-506; Peter Manning, "'Big Bang' Decisions: Notes on a Naturalistic Approach," in Keith Hawkins, ed., *The Uses of Discretion* (Oxford: Clarendon Press, 1992), 249-85; Robert Emerson and Blair Paley, "Organizational Horizons and Complaint Filing," in Hawkins, ed., *The Uses of Discretion*, 231-48; Peter Fitzpatrick, *The Mythology of Modern Law* (London: Routledge, 1992); Keith Hawkins, *Law as Last Resort: Prosecution Decision-Making in a Regulatory Agency* (Oxford: Oxford University Press, 2002); and Gilboy, "Penetrability of Administrative Systems," 273-313.

14 Davis, *Discretionary Justice*, 4.

15 Beverly McLachlin, "Rules and Discretion in the Governance of Canada," *Saskatchewan Law Review* 56 (1992): 168.

16 Keith Hawkins, "The Use of Legal Discretion: Perspectives from Law and Social Science," in Hawkins, ed., *The Uses of Discretion*, 19-20.

17 Robert Goodin, "Welfare, Rights, and Discretion," *Oxford Journal of Legal Studies* 6, 1 (1986): 250.

18 Pat O'Malley, "Risk and Responsibility," in Andrew Barry, Thomas Osborne, and Nikolas Rose, eds., *Foucault and Political Reason: Liberalism, Neo-Liberalism, and Rationalities of Government* (Chicago: University of Chicago Press, 1996); Rose, *Powers of Freedom*; Nikolas Rose, "Inventiveness in Politics," *Economy and Society* 28, 3 (1999): 467-93.

19 Alan Hunt neatly applies Foucault's concept of "dividing practices" in his study of moral regulation, *Governing Morals*, 6.

20 For discussions of the universality and particularity of liberal legality, see Fitzpatrick, "The Rise and Rise of Informalism," and Pavlich, *Justice Fragmented*.

21 Fitzpatrick, *The Mythology of Modern Law*, 154. See also Fitzpatrick, "The Rise and Rise of Informalism."

22 Nicola Lacey, "The Jurisprudence of Discretion: Escaping the Legal Paradigm," in Hawkins, ed., *The Uses of Discretion*, 294.

23 Ibid., 362.

24 For legal works that deal with discretion and immigration decision making more generally, see, for example, Phillip Bryden, "Fundamental Justice and Family Class Immigration," *University of Toronto Law Journal* 41 (1991): 484-532; Ann Dobson-Mack, "Independent Immigrant Selection Criteria and Equality Rights: Discretion, Discrimination, and Due Process," *Les Cahiers de droit* 34, 2 (1993): 549-72; Michael Heyman, "Judicial Review of Discretionary Immigration Decision-Making," *San Diego Law Review* 31 (1994): 861-910; and Lorne Sossin, "The Rule of Policy: Baker and the Impact of Judicial Review on Administrative Discretion," in D. Dyzenhaus et al., eds., *The Unity of Public Law* (London: Hart, 2004), 87-112.

25 House of Commons Standing Committee Hearings, transcripts, 18 March 1998, 25.

26 *Canada (Minister of Employment and Immigration) v. Chiarelli*, [1992] 1 S.C.R. 711.

27 For a good legal examination of sovereignty and immigration law, see Russell Cohen, "Fundamental (in)Justice: The Deportation of Long-Term Residents from Canada," *Osgoode Hall Law Journal* 32, 3 (1994): 457-80.

28 Jonathan Xavier Inda and Renato Rosaldo, "A World in Motion," in Jonathan Xavier Inda and Renato Rosaldo, eds., *The Anthropology of Globalization: A Reader* (Malden, MA: Blackwell, 2002), 1-12.

29 Jennifer Hyndman and Margaret Walters Roberts, "Transnational Migration and Nation: Burmese Refugees in Vancouver," unpublished paper (December 1998): 4. See also James Clifford, "Diasporas," *Cultural Anthropology* 9, 3 (1994): 302-38.

30 See, for example, James Holsten and Arjun Appadurai, "Cities and Citizenship," *Public Culture* 8, 2 (1996): 187-204; Saskia Sassen, *Losing Control: Sovereignty in an Age of Globalization* (New York: Columbia University Press, 1996); Saskia Sassen, *Global Networks, Linked Cities* (London: Routledge, 2002); and Engin Isin, ed., *Democracy, Citizenship, and the Global City* (London: Routledge, 2000).

31   For a legal philosophical examination of liberalism, sovereignty, and refugee determination, see Catherine Dauvergne, "Amorality and Humanitarianism in Immigration Law," *Osgoode Hall Law Journal* 37, 3 (1999): 597-623.

32   *Immigration Act* s. 3(j).

33   *IRPA* s. 3(2)(h).

34   IRB *Guidelines on Detention,* 2.

35   Bryden, "Fundamental Justice and Family Class Immigration," 484.

36   Jeff G. Cowan, "Recent Developments in Judicial Review," in Garry J. Smith, ed., *Charter of Rights and Administrative Law 1983-1984* (Toronto: Carswell Legal Publications, 1983), 33.

37   Ibid., 32.

38   Colin R. Singer, CBA, National Citizenship and Immigration Law Section, "Key Concerns Respecting Bill C-31, Immigration and Refugee Protection Act," speaking notes, National Congress of Italian-Canadians, Montreal, 10 June 2000.

39   *IRPA* s. 64(1).

40   *IRPA* s. 64(2). A review of the *Criminal Code of Canada* indicates that the most common hybrid offences, such as assault, dangerous driving, and impaired driving, are five-year indictable offences. Property offences such as theft, possession, and mischief under $5,000 are two-year indictable offences. Offences such as theft, possession, and mischief over $5,000, as well as assault, dangerous driving, and impaired driving with bodily harm, are all ten-year indictable offences.

41   Singer, "Key Concerns Respecting Bill C-31."

42   *IRPA* s. 72(1).

43   Michael Greene, Chair, National Citizenship and Immigration Law Section, "Letter to Parliamentary Committee on Citizenship and Immigration and MPs," 2 March 2001.

44   Interview with senior immigration official, Ottawa, 23 April 1998.

45   CIC, *Detention Policy.* In the same year, the IRB also released its *Guidelines on Detention.*

46   CIC, *Citizenship and Immigration Detention Policy.*

47   CIC, *Immigration Manual,* Chapter ENF 20 s. 5(2), "Departmental Policy, General" (October 2002).

48   Interview with senior immigration official, Ottawa, 23 April 1998.

49   CIC, *Immigration Manual* (emphasis added).

50   Interview with senior immigration official, Ottawa, 23 April 1998.

51   Interview with former immigration adjudicator, Ottawa, 24 April 1998.

52   As quoted from the *Globe and Mail,* in Lorne Foster, *Turnstile Immigration: Social Order and Social Justice in Canada* (Toronto: Thompson Educational Publishing, 1998), 64.

53   Canada Employment and Immigration Union, Public Service Alliance of Canada, "Presentation to the House of Commons Standing Committee on Citizenship and Immigration," 25 March 1998, 2.

54   Legislative Review Advisory Group (LRAG), *Not Just Numbers: A Canadian Framework for Future Immigration* (Ottawa: Ministry of Public Works and Government Services, 1997).

55   CIC, *Building on a Strong Foundation for the 21st Century: New Directions for Immigration and Refugee Policy and Legislation* (Ottawa: Minister of Public Works and Government Services Canada, 1998).

56   LRAG, *Not Just Numbers,* 13.

57   Ibid., 104.

58   "Overhaul in Works for Refugee System: Coderre Proposes Dismantling Hearing Board: Skeptics Question Whether Changes Would End Backlog," *Globe and Mail,* 20 March 2003.

59   *An Act to Amend the Immigration Act, 1976, and to Amend Other Acts in Consequence Thereof (the Refugee Reform Bill),* S.C. 1988, c. 36.

60   *Singh v. Canada.*

61   Ibid., 456-63.

62   LRAG, *Not Just Numbers,* 84.

63   Angus Reid Group, *Multiculturalism and Canadians: Attitude Study 1991* (Ottawa: Multiculturalism and Citizenship Canada, 1991). See also Angus Reid Group, "National

Angus Reid/Southam News Poll: Racial Tensions and Law Enforcement in Canada," news release, 3 June 1992.

64 Robert Holton and Michael Lanphier, "Public Opinion, Immigration, and Refugees," in Howard Adelman et al., eds., *Immigration and Refugee Policy: Australia and Canada Compared* (Toronto: University of Toronto Press, 1994), 125-48.

65 Ipsos-Reid Group/Globe and Mail/CTV poll on Canadian attitudes toward immigrants and immigration, 22 November 1999, http://www.ipsos-reid.com/search/pdf/media/pr991122%5F1.pdf. Similar findings had also been reported in August 1999: Ipsos-Reid, "Canadians Split on Illegal Immigration Issue," 31 August 1999, http://www.ipsos-reid.com/search/pdf/media/pr990831%5F1.pdf.

66 Ipsos-Reid, "Canadians and Immigration," 6 May 2000, http://www.ipsos-reid.com/search/pdf/media/mr000506.pdf.

67 "The Image of the 'Canadian Mosaic' as a Benevolent Tapestry of Different Cultures and Religions Is Being Strongly Challenged by a New Poll that Shows Strong Support for Keeping Muslim Immigrants out of the Country," *Ottawa Citizen,* 20 December 2002.

68 The various polls have been analyzed extensively. See, for example, Andrew Parkin, "Attitudes toward Immigration Unchanged," *Opinion Canada,* Centre for Research and Information Canada (CRIC), 4, 34 (26 September 2002), http://cric.ca/en_html/opinion/opv4n34.html; Andrew Parkin, "Reacting to Terrorism: A Review of Canadian Public Opinion," *Opinion Canada* 3, 36 (25 October 2001), http://www.cric.ca/en_html/opinion/opv3n36.html#flle; Chris Baker, "Canada after September 11th: A Public Opinion Perspective," Environics Research Group, http://www.robarts.yorku.ca/pdf/cw_conf_baker.pdf; and Canadian Press/Leger Marketing, "Canadians and Immigration," 18 March 2002, http://www.legermarketing.com/documents/spclm/020318eng.pdf.

69 "Globus: International Affairs Poll," Associated Press poll conducted by Ipsos-Public Affairs, interview dates 7-17 May 2004, http://www.ipsos-na.com/news/pdf/media/mr040527-2tbzz.pdf.

70 For a discussion of these seemingly contradictory developments, see Michael Mandel, *The Charter of Rights and the Legalization of Politics in Canada* (Toronto: Wall and Thompson, 1989), 172-83.

71 Arthur Weinreb and Rocco Galati, *The Criminal Lawyer's Guide to Immigration and Citizenship Law* (Aurora: Canada Law Book, 1996), 3. See also Pearl Eliadis, "The Swing from Singh," *Immigration Law Reporter* 26 (1995): 130.

72 *Dehghani v. Canada (Minister of Employment and Immigration),* [1993] 1 S.C.R. 1053.

73 Weinreb and Galati, *Criminal Lawyer's Guide,* 3.

74 House of Commons Standing Committee Hearings, transcripts, 29 April 1998, 23.

75 House of Commons Standing Committee on Citizenship and Immigration, "Immigration Detention and Removals: Report of the Standing Committee on Citizenship and Immigration," Ottawa, June 1998, http://www.parl.gc.ca/InfoComDoc/36/1/CITI/Studies/Reports/citirp01-e.htm.

76 House of Commons Standing Committee on Citizenship and Immigration, "Refugee Protection and Border Security: Striking a Balance," Ottawa, March 2000, http://www.parl.gc.ca/InfoComDoc/36/2/CIMM/Studies/Reports/cimm02-e.htm.

77 Ibid., 2.

78 House of Commons Standing Committee on Citizenship and Immigration, "Hands across the Border: Working Together at Our Shared Border and Abroad to Ensure Safety, Security, and Efficiency," Ottawa, December 2001, http://www.parl.gc.ca/InfoComDoc/37/1/CIMM/Studies/Reports/cimm03rp/03-covi-e.htm.

79 CIC, "Government Response to the Report 'Hands across the Border: Working Together at Our Shared Border and Abroad to Ensure Safety and Security and Efficiency,'" Ottawa, May 2002, http://www.cic.gc.ca/english/pub/hab.html.

80 *Dictionary of the English Language.*

81 Toronto Refugee Affairs Council (TRAC), "Brief to the Government of Canada about Recommendations by the Legislative Review Committee," March 1998.

82 David Matas, "Immigration Removals: A Submission to the House of Commons Standing Committee on Citizenship and Immigration," 1998, 23. Many briefs to the 1997-98 House of Commons Standing Committee argued the same point, including Mary Jo Leddy, *Comments on Detentions and Removals: Brief to the Standing Committee on Citizenship and Removals* (Toronto: Romero House, 1998), 3; and Amnesty International, "Brief to the Parliamentary Standing Committee on Citizenship and Immigration," 1998, 2.

83 See Irving Abella and Harold Troper, *None Is Too Many: Canada and the Jews of Europe 1933-1948* (Toronto: Lester and Orpen Dennys, 1982).

84 The literature on discrimination in the domain of Canadian immigration is extensive and often excellent. See, for example, Donald Avery, *Reluctant Host: Canada's Response to Immigrant Workers: 1896-1994* (Toronto: McClelland and Stewart, 1995); Agnes Calliste, "Race, Gender, and Canadian Immigration Policy: Blacks from the Caribbean, 1900-1932," *Journal of Canadian Studies* 28, 4 (1993): 131-48; Ian Dowbiggin, "Keeping This Young Country Sane: C.K. Clarke, Immigration Restriction, and Canadian Psychiatry, 1890-1925," *Canadian Historical Review* 76, 4 (1995): 598-627; Lisa Jakubowski, "'Managing' Immigration: Immigration, Racism, Ethnic Selectivity, and the Law," in Elizabeth Comack et al., eds., *Locating Law: Race/Class/Gender Connections* (Halifax: Fernwood, 1999), 98-124; Alan Simmons, "Racism and Immigration Policy," in *Racism and Social Inequality in* Canada v. Satzewich (Toronto: Thompson Educational Publishing, 1998), 87-114; Mariana Valverde, *The Age of Light, Soap, and Water: Moral Reform in English Canada, 1885-1925* (Toronto: McClelland and Stewart, 1993); and Victor Satzewich, ed., *Deconstructing a Nation: Immigration, Multiculturalism, and Racism in 90s Canada* (Halifax: Fernwood Publishing, 1992).

85 Barbara Roberts, *Whence They Came: Deportation from 1900-1935* (Ottawa: University of Ottawa Press, 1988).

86 For a collection of articles that examines this issue, see Mariana Valverde, Linda Macleod, and Kirsten Johnson, eds., *Wife Assault and the Criminal Justice System* (Toronto: Centre of Criminology, University of Toronto, 1995). For a study of the impact of these policies on new immigrant and refugee battered women, see my essay in the same collection entitled "New Immigrant and Refugee Battered Women: The Intersection of Immigration and Criminal Justice Policy."

87 Canadian Bar Association, National Citizenship and Immigration Law Section, "Submission on *Immigration and Refugee Protection Regulations* Parts 1-17," January 2002, http://www.cba.org/pdf/2002-01-31_immigration.pdf. These concerns were also expressed by the Canadian Council for Refugees (CCR) in "Comments on Proposed *Immigration and Refugee Protection Regulations,* Parts 1-17, Published in the Canada Gazette, Part I, 15 December 2001," 13 February 2002, http://www.web.net/~ccr/ccrcomments1-17c-11.htm.

Chapter 4: From Purity to Security

1 Neither this chapter nor indeed this book aims to present a "total history" or an exhaustive analysis of Canadian immigration law, policy, and practice. Readers may wish to consult the rich literature on the development of Canadian immigration and refugee law and policy. See, for example, Ninette Kelley and Michael Trebilcock, *The Making of the Mosaic: A History of Canadian Immigration Policy* (Toronto: University of Toronto Press, 1998); Gerald Dirks, *Controversy and Complexity: Canadian Immigration Policy during the 1980s* (Montreal: McGill-Queen's University Press, 1995); Gerald Dirks, *Canada's Refugee Policy: Indifference or Opportunism?* (Montreal: McGill-Queen's University Press, 1977); Freda Hawkins, *Canada and Immigration: Public Policy and Public Concern* (Montreal: McGill-Queen's University Press, 1972); Avery, *Reluctant Host;* Donald Avery, *"Dangerous Foreigners": European Immigrant Workers and Labour Radicalism in Canada, 1896-1932* (Toronto: McClelland and Stewart, 1979); and Reg Whitaker, *Double Standard: The Secret History of Canadian Immigration* (Toronto: Lester and Orpen Dennys, 1987).

2 As outlined in Chapter 1, welfare liberalism is understood here as a way of governing rather than as a political philosophy or ideology. The decline of welfare liberalism – the "death of the social" – and the rise of neoliberal governance have been amply discussed by governmentality scholars in general terms. This approach is distinct from conventional political science analyses of Canadian policy, political values, and public philosophy.

3   See, for example, Roberts, *Whence They Came;* Avery, *Reluctant Host;* and Avery, *"Dangerous Foreigners."*
4   Prime Minister Mackenzie King, in House of Commons *Debates*, 1 May 1947, quoted in Kelley and Trebilcock, *The Making of the Mosaic*, 312.
5   While the phrase "absorptive capacity" continues to be bandied about, immigration law and policy are more often cast as "long-term" plans rather than the "tap on, tap off," approach entailed by the notion of absorptive capacity.
6   The logic of national purity was not simply about racial purity. See Valverde's examination of the various relations between race, gender, morality, and class in the discursive construction of "purity" in early English Canada, *The Age of Light, Soap, and Water.*
7   *Immigration Act,* R.S.C. 1952, c. 325, s. 61.
8   Ibid.
9   *Immigration Act,* S.C. 1910, c. 27, s. 38(c).
10 Noteworthy (CCF member) reading letter from Harris, in House of Commons *Debates* (1953): 4351-52, quoted in Kelley and Trebilcock, *The Making of the Mosaic*, 325.
11 *Immigration Act,* R.S.C. 1952, c. 325 (s. 5, "Prohibited Classes").
12 See Philip Girard, "From Subversion to Liberation: Homosexuals and the Immigration Act, 1952-1977," *Canadian Journal of Law and Society* 2 (1987): 1-27; Gary Kinsman, "Constructing Gay Men and Lesbians as National Security Risks, 1950-1970," in Gary Kinsman, Dieter K. Buse, and Mercedes Steedman, eds., *Whose National Security? Canadian State Surveillance and the Creation of Enemies* (Toronto: Between the Lines, 2000), 143-53; Daniel Robinson and David Kimmel, "The Queer Career of Homosexual Security Vetting in Cold War Canada," *Canadian Historical Review* 75, 3 (1994): 319-45; and Gary Kinsman, "'Character Weakness' and 'Fruit Machines': Towards an Analysis of the Anti-Homosexual Security Campaign in the Canadian Civil Service," *Labour/Le Travail* 35 (1995): 133-62.
13 Girard, "From Subversion to Liberation."
14 Whitaker describes the absence of any official opposition to the clause prohibiting homosexuals and how it "was rushed through parliament with no discussion whatsoever." Whitaker, *Double Standard*, 37.
15 *Immigration Act,* R.S.C. 1952, c. 325, s. 39. The 1952 act defined and entrenched the legal concept of "domicile" for the purposes of immigration policy. Domicile, defined as a five-year period of residency in Canada, effectively served as a protection against deportation for noncitizens. This "protection" was eliminated from the 1976 legislation.
16 Frank N. Marrocco and Henry M. Goslett, *The 1996 Annotated Immigration Act of Canada* (Toronto: Carswell, 1995), 213. (In their comments on *Canada [Minister of Employment and Immigration] v. Chiarelli,* [1992] 1 S.C.R. 711.)
17 Whitaker, *Double Standard*, 204.
18 There is extensive scholarship that addresses the subject of Canadian national security. See, in particular, Brian Gorlick, "The Exclusion of 'Security Risks' as a Form of Immigration Control: Law and Process in Canada-1," *Immigration and Nationality Law and Practice* 5, 3 (1991): 76-82; Brian Gorlick, "The Exclusion of 'Security Risks' as a Form of Immigration Control: Law and Process in Canada-2," *Immigration and Nationality Law and Practice* 5, 4 (1991): 109-15; Reg Whitaker, "Refugees: The Security Dimension," *Citizenship Studies* 2, 3 (1998): 413-34; Reg Whitaker, "Security and Intelligence in the Post-Cold War World," in Ralph Miliband and Leo Panitch, eds., *Socialist Register 1992: New World Order?* (London/New York: The Merlin Press/Monthly Review Press, 1992), 111-30; Reg Whitaker, "Designing a Balance between Freedom and Security," in Joseph F. Fletcher, ed., *Ideas in Action: Essays on Politics and Law in Honour of Peter Russell* (Toronto: University of Toronto Press, 1999), 126-49; Alvin Finkel, "Canadian Immigration Policy and the Cold War, 1945-80," *Journal of Canadian Studies* 21 (1986): 53-70; and Peter Hanks and John D. McCamus, eds., *National Security: Surveillance and Accountability in a Democratic Society* (Cowansville: Les Éditions Yvon Blais, 1989).
19 Whitaker, *Double Standard*, 35.
20 The criticisms of the 1952 security provisions bear a striking resemblance to contemporary criticisms of the "danger to the public" provisions ushered in with Bill C-44 in 1995, discussed in Chapter 6.

21 Rose, *Governing through Freedom.*
22 Kelley and Trebilcock, *The Making of the Mosaic,* 345.
23 Hawkins, *Canada and Immigration,* 160.
24 Avery, *Reluctant Host,* 178.
25 Hawkins, *Canada and Immigration,* 103.
26 Ibid.
27 Ibid., 110.
28 Ibid.
29 House of Commons *Debates,* vol. 2 (1955): 1165, quoted in Hawkins, *Canada and Immigration,* 110.
30 Kelley and Trebilcock, *The Making of the Mosaic,* 328.
31 Hawkins, *Canada and Immigration,* 126.
32 Kelley and Trebilcock, *The Making of the Mosaic,* 333.
33 Hawkins, *Canada and Immigration,* 126.
34 Ibid., 127.
35 Department of Citizenship and Immigration, Joseph Sedgwick, *Report on Immigration,* Part I (Ottawa: 1965), 18.
36 Ibid., 148.
37 Ibid., 18.
38 For a detailed discussion of the Sedgwick Report and its recommendations, see Hawkins, *Canada and Immigration,* 145-50.
39 Manpower and Immigration, *White Paper on Immigration* (Ottawa: Queen's Printer, 1966).
40 This view was strongly opposed by representatives of industry and labour, who argued that the selection of "skilled" over "unskilled" immigrants would "hamper frontier development" and that there was still a need for unskilled immigrants. Hawkins, *Canada and Immigration,* 162.
41 *White Paper,* 35.
42 United Nations, *Convention Relating to the Status of Refugees,* 28 July 1951, 189 U.N.T.S. 150, arts. 32-33, Can. T.S. 1969/6 (entered into force 22 April 1954, accession by Canada 2 September 1969) [hereafter the *Refugee Convention*].
43 Whitaker, *Double Standard,* 53. This issue is taken up again in Chapter 7.
44 *White Paper,* 16.
45 Ibid., 25 (emphasis added).
46 Castel, "From Dangerousness to Risk," in *The Foucault Effect,* 281.
47 Whitaker, *Double Standard,* 204.
48 Ibid.
49 *White Paper,* 24-25.
50 The processes and procedures relating to security screening were the focus of increasing political and public attention through the 1960s, but legal discourses did little to affect existing procedures until the mid-1980s. For more detailed discussion of the specifics of these debates and developments, see Whitaker, *Double Standard.*
51 Kelley and Trebilcock, *The Making of the Mosaic,* 348.
52 Ibid., 351.
53 Lisa Marie Jakubowski, *Immigration and the Legalization of Racism* (Halifax: Fernwood Publishing, 1997), 19.
54 Kelley and Trebilcock, *The Making of the Mosaic,* 351.
55 Ibid., 163.
56 *Immigration Act,* S.C. 1976, c. 52.
57 Dirks, *Controversy and Complexity,* 14.
58 Kelley and Trebilcock, *The Making of the Mosaic,* 390.
59 Hawkins, *Canada and Immigration,* xv.
60 Rose and Miller, "Political Power beyond the State," 173-205.
61 S. 19(1)(a).
62 S. 19(1)(b).
63 S. 19(1)(h).

64 S. 19(1)(i).
65 S. 19(1)(g).
66 S. 19(1)(d).
67 S. 19(1)(f).
68 Past recommendations by the 1969 royal commission to create a Security Review Board to take over responsibility for security and criminal intelligence screening from the RCMP had been met with fierce opposition from the RCMP. For a full discussion of this issue and the debates surrounding it, see Whitaker, *Double Standard.*
69 *Canadian Security Intelligence Service Act,* R.S.C. 1985, c. C-23 [hereafter *CSIS Act*].
70 Government of Canada, Privy Council Office, Order in Council *Public Service Rearrangement and Transfer of Duties Act* P.C. 2003-2063, 12 December 2003.
71 CCR, "New Security Certificate Rules Further Reduce Rights," press release, 26 January 2004, http://www.web.net/~ccr/relcert.htm.

Chapter 5: Floods and Frauds

1   It would be misleading to give the impression that Canada had taken no humanitarian action with respect to refugees prior to 1976. However, its actions were largely reactive and ad hoc. Canada had resisted the creation of a permanent refugee determination system for onshore claimants until 1976, having preferred to maintain control over which "humanitarian" refugee needs should get priority.
2   *Dictionary of the English Language.*
3   The categories of fraudulence and criminality have also been linked in the domain of social services. This important development will be examined in detail in Chapter 6.
4   See, for example, David Garland, *The Culture of Control: Crime and Social Order in Contemporary Society* (Chicago: University of Chicago Press, 2001); Austin Sarat, *When the State Kills: Capital Punishment and the American Condition* (Princeton: Princeton University Press, 2001); and Young, *Imagining Crime.* The rise of the victim is the corollary of the emergent trend of governing through crime first examined by Simon in "Governing through Crime."
5   Kelley and Trebilcock, *The Making of the Mosaic,* 347.
6   UNHCR, "Number of Asylum Applications Submitted in 30 Industrialized Countries, 1992-2001," 31 May 2002.
7   UNHCR, Population Data Unit, Geneva, "Asylum Applications Lodged in Industrialized Countries: Levels and Trends, 2000-2002," March 2003. See also "Canada: Refugee Claims Plummet in 2002," *Toronto Star,* 10 January 2003.
8   "Fewer Refugees Seeking Asylum inside Canada: Claims Fall by 35%," *National Post,* 18 June 2004. There is some variability in these numbers depending on the source. They should therefore be read as approximate rather than absolute figures.
9   UNHCR, "Refugees by Numbers," 2003 (table).
10 Kelley and Trebilcock, *The Making of the Mosaic,* 347.
11 Numbers compiled and made available by Canadian Council for Refugees (based on CIC statistics), "Immigration to Canada 1979-2001," http://www.web.net/~ccr/statland.htm.
12 CIC, "Facts and Figures, Immigration Overview: Immigration Historical Perspective (1860-2002)," 2002, http://www.cic.gc.ca/english/pub/facts2002/immigration/immigration_1.html.
13 CIC, "Minister Tables Annual Report to Parliament on Immigration," news release, 30 October 2002, http://www.cic.gc.ca/english/press/02/0237-pre.html.
14 Statistics Canada, "Census of Population: Immigration, Birthplace, and Birthplace of Parents, Citizenship, Ethnic Origin, Visible Minorities, and Aboriginal Peoples," *Daily,* 21 January 2003, http://www.statcan.ca/Daily/English/030121/d030121a.htm.
15 Ibid.
16 For a comprehensive examination of Canadian public opinion at this time, see Holton and Lanphier, "Public Opinion, Immigration, and Refugees." See the discussion in Chapter 3 on the findings of public opinion polls and surveys over the 1990s and the first few years of the twenty-first century.
17 See the discussion in Chapter 3.

18   Victor Malarek, *Haven's Gate: Canada's Immigration Fiasco* (Toronto: Macmillan, 1987), 97.
19   "Tales of Refugee Fraud Not True, Lawyer Says," *Vancouver Sun,* 16 March 1995. For an excellent discussion of the range of problematic constructions and determinations of credibility in refugee decision making that contribute to the legal constitution of the bogus refugee, see David Matas, "The Credibility of Refugee Claimants," *Immigration Law Reporter* 21 (1994): 134-54.
20   Duncan Forrest, "A Study of 95 Sikh Refugees Seeking Asylum in UK," *Lives under Threat,* Medical Foundation for Care of Victims of Torture, 1999, http://www.sikhreview.org/june2000/human2.htm.
21   Gerry Weiner, "Canada's Refugee Policy," in Alan Nash, ed., and John P. Humphrey, *rapporteur, Human Rights and Refugees under International Law: Proceedings of a Conference Held in Montreal November 29-December 2, 1987* (Halifax: Institute for Research on Public Policy, 1988), 237-38 (emphasis added).
22   See, for example, the discussions in Kelley and Trebilcock, *The Making of the Mosaic;* Avery, *Reluctant Host;* Mandel, *The Charter of Rights and the Legalization of Politics in Canada;* Foster, *Turnstile Immigration;* and Nash and Humphrey, *Human Rights and Refugees under International Law.*
23   Similar reactions followed the 1999 summer boat arrivals of 599 Chinese nationals on the West Coast discussed in Chapter 1. For an examination of media representations of the Chinese migrants in British Columbia, see Minelle Mahtani and Alison Mountz, "Immigration to British Columbia: Media Representation and Public Opinion," Research on Immigration and Integration in the Metropolis, Working Paper Series 02-15, August 2002.
24   Quoted in Malarek, *Haven's Gate,* 75.
25   Julius Grey, "Refugee Status in Canada," in Nash and Humphrey, *Human Rights and Refugees under International Law,* 306.
26   Mandel, *The Charter of Rights and the Legalization of Politics in Canada,* 176.
27   For a fuller discussion, see Kelley and Trebilcock, *The Making of the Mosaic;* Whitaker, *Double Standard;* and Dirks, *Canada's Refugee Policy.* In 2003, the practice of "direct backs" to the United States was revived, again causing much concern among refugee advocates.
28   Malarek, *Haven's Gate,* 121.
29   Ibid.
30   *An Act to Amend the Immigration Act, 1976, and to Amend Other Acts in Consequence Thereof (the Refugee Reform Bill),* S.C. 1988, c. 36.
31   *An Act to Amend the Immigration Act, 1976, and to Amend Other Acts in Consequence Thereof (the Refugee Deterrents and Detention Bill),* S.C. 1988, c. 35.
32   Weiner, House of Commons *Debates,* 18 June 1987, 7329, quoted in Kelley and Trebilcock, *The Making of the Mosaic,* 416.
33   A provision that was later dropped in light of the prime minister's claim at the time of the Sikhs' arrival that Canada was not "in the business of turning away refugees and we never will under this government." Quoted in Kelley and Trebilcock, *The Making of the Mosaic,* 417.
34   Ibid., 124.
35   Barbara Jackman, "Canada's Refugee Crisis: Planned Mismanagement," in Nash and Humphrey, *Human Rights and Refugees under International Law,* 321-26.
36   Howard Adelman, "Canadian Refugee Policy in the Post-War Period," in Howard Adelman, ed., *Refugee Policy: Canada and the United States* (Toronto: York Lanes Press, 1991), 200.
37   Whitaker, *Double Standard,* 300.
38   During 1986, there were two major government initiatives on terrorism. In both, the refugee determination system was identified as a security problem, as were various "terrorist prone" ethnic groups, including Sikhs. Ibid.
39   See Jackman, "Canada's Refugee Crisis," and Dan Heap, "Panel of Canadian Parliamentarians," in Nash and Humphrey, *Human Rights and Refugees under International Law,* 321-26 and 253-66.
40   Jackman, "Canada's Refugee Crisis," 322-23.
41   Avery, *Reluctant Host,* 221.

42 Jim Hawkes, "Panel of Canadian Parliamentarians," in Nash and Humphrey, *Human Rights and Refugees under International Law,* 255.
43 *An Act to Amend the Immigration Act, 1976, and to Amend Other Acts in Consequence Thereof,* S.C. 1992, c. 49.
44 This and related developments are taken up in Chapters 7 and 8.
45 Manpower and Immigration, *Managing Immigration: A Framework for the 1990s* (Ottawa: Supply and Services Canada, 1992), 7-8.
46 Ibid., 3.
47 Ibid., 4.
48 Ibid.
49 "Asylum for Torture Victims," *Guardian,* 29 April 1996.
50 See Holton and Lanphier, "Public Opinion, Immigration, and Refugees," in Adelman et al., eds., *Immigration and Refugee Policy.*
51 "Complicated, Confusing, and Controversial," *Citizen Valley,* 23 November 1992.
52 "Legislation Would Tell Immigrants Where to Live," *Toronto Star,* 17 June 1992.
53 Employment and Immigration Canada, *Explaining the New Immigration Bill,* "Preface" (emphasis added).
54 With respect to its recruitment and resettlement aspirations, Bill C-86 was primarily supported by economic arguments. It sought to enhance the responsiveness of immigration law and policy to the "economic and labour force needs of Canada." For example, as put by the government, investors must be accepted "without limits" for their contributions to the economy. Bill C-86 also made much of the government's humanitarian objective of family unification, arguably hoping to tap into the increased influence of fundamentally conservative and traditional "family values" evident in the broader social and political context. Employment and Immigration Canada, *Explaining the New Immigration Bill.*
55 Bill C-86 also extended the grounds for medical inadmissibility. While not directly relevant to the current analysis, the risks posed by the "diseased" immigrant (tuberculosis, HIV and AIDS, SARS) are once again gaining prominence in the domain of immigration penality.
56 Sections 19 and 27 of the 1976 *Immigration Act.*
57 Employment and Immigration Canada, *Explaining the Immigration Bill,* section 2: "Protecting Society," 3.
58 S. 19, c. 2.
59 S. 19, c. 1(ii).
60 Ss. 19(e)(f)(g).
61 S. 19(k).
62 In the parliamentary committee hearings on the bill, Alan Borovoy of the Canadian Civil Liberties Association described these amendments as sanctioning "deportation by clairvoyance." Quoted in Kelley and Trebilcock, *The Making of the Mosaic,* 431.
63 S. 19(1).
64 As discussed in Chapter 6, in the 1990s this provision was used against members of the Somali community living in Toronto.
65 Ss. 85, 86, 89.1, 91.1, 92, 92.1, 93, 97.1.
66 Ss. 94.1, 94.2, 102.01(1).
67 S. 110.
68 Employment and Immigration Canada, *Explaining the New Immigration Bill,* section 2: "Protecting Society," subsection 3: "Controls at the Border," 12.
69 For a more detailed discussion of the nature and range of nongovernmental criticisms, see Avery, *Reluctant Host,* 225-29; Kelley and Trebilcock, *The Making of the Mosaic,* 424-27; and Jakubowski, *Immigration and the Legalization of Racism,* 81-89.
70 Some critics refer to the agreement as the "None Is Too Many" agreement. For a review of the major concerns, see CCR, "Comments to the Standing Committee on Citizenship and Immigration on the Proposed Safe Third Country Regulations," 14 November 2002, http://www.web.net/~ccr/s3cregscommentsstandcomm.html. Related developments after September 11th are taken up in Chapter 8.

71 CCR, "Reduction in Refugee Levels Must Trigger Reversal of Anti-Refugee Measures," 13 January 2003, http://www.web.net/~ccr/numbersrelease.html.
72 Quoted in Jakubowski, *Immigration and the Legalization of Racism,* 79.
73 Ibid., 81.
74 This checklist denies claimants access to the refugee determination system on one of five grounds: (a) prior recognition of refugee status in another country; (b) coming to Canada directly from or through a prescribed safe third country; (c) repeat claims; (d) have already been determined in Canada or by a visa officer abroad to be a *Convention* refugee; or (e) "undesirable persons – criminal and security risks." Employment and Immigration Canada, *Explaining the New Immigration Bill,* section 3: "The New Refugee Determination System," subsection 1: "Access to the Refugee Determination System," 2.
75 Department of the Solicitor General of Canada, "Notes for an Address by the Honourable Doug Lewis, P.C., M.P., Minister of Public Security," 9 August 1993.
76 Ibid.
77 Ibid.
78 Titch Dharamsi, "'Fighting for Inclusion': Fighting for the Anti-Immigrant Vote," *Metro World,* October 1993: 29.
79 Ibid., 7.

Chapter 6: Risky Refugees
1 This chapter is a revised version of "From Deserving Victims to 'Masters of Confusion': Redefining Refugees in the 1990s," coauthored with Mariana Valverde, which originally appeared in the *Canadian Journal of Sociology* 27, 2 (2002): 135-61. It has been reprinted with the permission of *CJS.*
2 These linkages have been well documented elsewhere. See, for example, Avery, *Dangerous Foreigners,* and Avery, *Reluctant Host;* Roberts, *Whence They Came;* and Kelley and Trebilcock, *The Making of the Mosaic.*
3 Roberts, *Whence They Came;* James Struthers, *No Fault of Their Own: Unemployment and the Canadian Welfare State, 1914-1941* (Toronto: University of Toronto Press, 1983).
4 CSIS, "Transnational Criminal Activity," http://www.csis-scrs.gc.ca/eng/backgrnd/back10_e.html. I examine the crime-related activities of CSIS in more detail in Chapter 8.
5 Simon, "Governing through Crime."
6 "They Believed the Hype," *This Magazine* 28, 5 (December 1995): 29.
7 Jonathan Swift, *Gulliver's Travels,* quoted on the 1999 web page of the Toronto Police Service Fraud Squad.
8 Andrew Johnson et al., eds., *Continuities and Discontinuities: The Political Economy of Social Welfare and Labour Market Policy in Canada* (Toronto: University of Toronto Press, 1994), 3-4.
9 See, in Johnson et al., eds., *Continuities and Discontinuities,* Philip Resnick, "Neo-Conservatism and Beyond," 25-35; Robert Mullaly, "Social Welfare and the New Right: A Class Mobilization Perspective," 76-94; and Leon Muszynski, "Defending the Welfare State and Labour Market Policy," 306-26.
10 Johnson et al., *Continuities and Discontinuities,* 4.
11 Ibid.
12 Ibid., 7.
13 O'Malley, "Risk and Responsibility"; Rose, *Powers of Freedom.*
14 Nikolas Rose, "Government Authority and Expertise in Advanced Liberalism," *Economy and Society* 22, 3 (1993): 283-99. See also Graham Burchell, "Liberal Government and Techniques of the Self," *Economy and Society* 22, 3 (1993): 268-82.
15 Government of Ontario, *Time for Action* (Toronto: Government Printer, 1992), 47.
16 Ibid., 171.
17 Government of Ontario, *Turning Point* (Toronto: Government Printer, 1993).
18 Ibid., 2.
19 Ibid., 9.
20 "Welfare Cuts May Come Swiftly," *Toronto Star,* 22 March 1994.
21 "Ontario Takes Tough Stand on Welfare Cheats," *Globe and Mail,* 29 March 1994.

22 "Welfare Bashing," *Toronto Star,* 3 April 1994.
23 *Toronto Sun,* 18 March 1994.
24 *Toronto Sun,* 28 March 1994.
25 *Toronto Sun,* 14 April 1994.
26 *Saturday Sun,* 19 February 1994.
27 "247 Million Was Overpaid on Welfare, Liberals Charge," *Toronto Star,* 14 April 1994.
28 "Double Duty for Photo ID Cards," *Toronto Sun,* 21 April 1994; "No Fingerprints, Please, We're Canadian," *Globe and Mail,* 7 March 1994.
29 "Tories Accused of Double Standard on Fraud: Welfare Cheats Face Courts as 'Crooks' While Tax Evaders Get Sympathy for Being 'Human' Liberals Charge," *Globe and Mail,* 16 November 1995.
30 Ibid.
31 "Liberals Open Canada's Door to 250,000 Immigrants in 1994," *Toronto Star,* 3 February 1994.
32 "Nose to Nose on Immigration," *Toronto Star,* 5 February 1994.
33 "Towards a More Realistic Immigration Policy for Canada," *Backgrounder,* C.D. Howe Institute, June 1993. See also "Putting a Price on Immigration," *Globe and Mail,* 11 February 1994.
34 Stottman's book, *Who Gets In: What's Wrong with Canada's Immigration Policy – and How to Fix It* (Toronto: Macfarlane, Walter, and Ross, 2002), continues in the same general vein as he takes aim at "political correctness," "multiculturalism," high immigration levels (particularly for the poor and poorly educated), the refugee determination system (too lax), and refugee claimants (most are frauds).
35 In 1994, approximately 45 percent of immigrants were to be accepted under the family class category, 44 percent were to be selected on the basis of the point system for skills and business credentials, and 11 percent were to be accepted as refugees fleeing persecution. "Nose to Nose on Immigration," *Toronto Star,* 5 February 1994.
36 CIC, "Canada and Ontario Cooperate to Protect the Welfare System," news release, June 1996; CIC, "Minister Lucienne Robillard Maintains Income Cut-Offs for Family Class Sponsorships," news release, 18 March 1997.
37 CIC, "Minister Lucienne Robillard," ibid.
38 "Immigrant Boost Is Insanity," *Toronto Sun,* 4 February 1994.
39 "Use of Leaked Data Called Irresponsible," *Globe and Mail,* 30 April 1993.
40 "Probe into Leak on Refugees Sought," *Globe and Mail,* 29 April 1993.
41 Ibid.
42 Ibid.
43 "Shifting New Ministry Seen as Fanning Flames of Racism," *Globe and Mail,* 13 July 1993.
44 "Probe into Leak on Refugees Sought," *Globe and Mail,* 29 April 1993.
45 However, other groups also feel the effects of these developments. For example, members of the Sri Lankan community felt the effects of widely covered concerns about the links between youth gangs, fund-raising, and the Tamil Tigers – a group widely characterized as a terrorist group rather than as a national liberation movement struggling for independence. This preoccupation has resurfaced through the years, most recently in July 2003 with the publication of a Mackenzie Institute Report. "10,000 Terrorists in Canada: Report Think-Tank Says Most Live Peacefully, but Could Be Activated at Any Time," *Ottawa Citizen,* 9 July 2003. Members of the Chinese community were affected by sustained concerns with and coverage of "triads" (examined in more detail in Chapter 8). Members of the large Sikh community in Canada were widely construed as "foreign violent criminals" after the Air India crash in 1985, and people from the Middle East and South Asia continue to feel the effects of the sustained and recently reenergized preoccupation with international terrorists, discussed further in Chapter 9. My focus here is on Somalis because during 1994-95 they were the most visibly targeted group, but this is not to claim that other communities did not suffer in similar ways.
46 Africa Watch, *Somalia: A Government at War with Its Own People* (New York: Africa Watch Committee, 1990), 1.

47   Somali Immigrant Aid Association, background information, http://webhome.idirect.com/~siao/background.html.
48   CIC, *Canada – A Welcoming Land,* annual immigration plan, tabled in October 1998 (Ottawa: Minister of Public Works and Government Services Canada, 1998).
49   Hereafter referred to as Dixon.
50   This title gives blatant expression to the increasing prejudice against traditionally nomadic people over this period. This prejudicial theme, as will be seen, resurfaces in the context of the Somalis and peaked in reaction to the arrival of Roma people from the Czech Republic in 1997. See CBC TV News in Review, "Gypsies in Canada: The Promised Land," *Resource Guide On-Line,* December 1997, http://www.tv.cbc.ca/newsinreview/dec97/gypsies/.
51   See John Torpey, *The Invention of the Passport* (Cambridge: Cambridge University Press, 2000).
52   For a discussion of "credibility" in relation to refugee claimants in Canada, see Matas, "The Credibility of Refugee Claimants." Somalis have also noted that citizenship and immigration officials as well as welfare officials routinely complain that most male Somalis have the same name (various combinations of Ali and Mohamed are in fact very common), thus facilitating immigration and welfare fraud. Of course, many ethnic groups have varied naming practices, but only in some instances is this read as facilitating lying and criminality.
53   "Minister Unveils Steps to Curb Welfare Abuse," *Toronto Star,* 10 March 1994.
54   "Refugees Accused of Fraud," *Globe and Mail,* 28 October 1993.
55   "Mounties Probe Somali Welfare Scam," *Vancouver Sun,* 21 October 1993.
56   "Refugees Accused of Fraud," *Globe and Mail,* 28 October 1993.
57   Ibid.
58   Ibid.
59   "Minister Unveils Steps to Curb Welfare Abuse," *Toronto Star,* 10 March 1994.
60   Bill C-86, it will be recalled, had criminalized (through its inadmissibility and removal provisions) any activities of individuals that could be linked with terrorism, organized crime, or support of groups, governments, or organizations that use violence and/or engage in human rights violations.
61   "Report's Tone Called Racist," *Toronto Star,* 29 October 1993.
62   "They Believed the Hype," *This Magazine* 28, 5 (December 1995): 30.
63   "4Gs Welfare Payout Probed," *Toronto Sun,* 21 February 1994.
64   *Toronto Sun,* 11 March 1994.
65   "On the Move on the Dole," *Toronto Sun,* 16 March 1994.
66   "Minister Unveils Steps to Curb Welfare Abuse," *Toronto Star,* 10 March 1994.
67   Interview with Ali Mohamud, Executive Director, Dejinta Beesha (Somali Multiservice Centre), 13 January 2000.
68   I am grateful to Kelly Grover for sharing her data with me. The interviews that she carried out with the residents of Dixon were used in her master's thesis, "The Social Organization of a High-Rise Neighbourhood: The Influence of Race, Culture, Economic Class, and Tenure on the Community Sentiments of Kingsview Park," School of Urban and Regional Planning, Queen's University, June 1995.
69   Ibid. All subsequent quotations of and observations about the residents of Dixon are drawn from the transcripts of the interviews carried out by Kelly Grover.
70   Daniel Stoffman, "Dispatch from Dixon," *Toronto Life,* August 1995. The various quotations from Stoffman in the next few paragraphs are all from this article.
71   Interview with Ali Mohamud, 13 January 2000.
72   Interview with Peter Crosbie, Director, Client Service Division, Family Service Association of Metropolitan Toronto, 14 January 2000.
73   *Immigration Act,* s. 19(1)(1), now s. 35(1)(b) under the *IRPA.*
74   Interview with Maggie Redmonds, 6 May 1999.
75   Interview with Ali Mohamud, 13 January 2000, and with Maggie Redmonds, 6 May 1999.
76   Ibid.
77   For judicial perspectives on these and other issues relating to the application of section 19(1)(1) and 19(1.1), see *Canada (Minister of Citizenship and Immigration) v. Duale,* [1997]

I.A.D.D. No. 278, 39 Imm. L.R. (2d) 105, No. T95-06875; *Mursal v. Canada (Minister of Citizenship and Immigration,* [1997] I.A.D.D. No. 455, No. M96-08958; *St-Amand v. Canada (Minister of Citizenship and Immigration),* [1995] I.A.D.D. No. 819, No. M94-07317; *Elmi v. M.C.I. (Minister of Citizenship and Immigration),* [1996] I.A.D.D. No. 840, No. M95-06832; and *Adam v. Canada (Minister of Citizenship and Immigration) M.C.I.,* [1996] I.A.D.D. No. 839 (QL), No. T95-05027.

78 *Canada (Minister of Citizenship and Immigration) v. Duale* [1997].
79 Interview with Ali Mohamud, 13 January 2000.
80 "Valcourt's Remarks Spark Protest," *Toronto Star,* 16 August 1992.
81 CIC, "Lucienne Robillard Announces the Introduction of the Undocumented *Convention* Refugees in Canada Class," news release, Ottawa, January 1995.
82 For in-depth discussion of refugees and the issue of identification documents, see Andrew Brouwer, "What's in a Name: Identity Documents and *Convention* Refugees," Caledon Institute for Social Policy, Ottawa, 1999; Guy S. Goodwin-Gill and Judith Kumin, "Refugees in Limbo and Canada's International Obligations," Caledon Institute of Social Policy, Ottawa, 2000; and Sherene Razack, "Simple Logic: Race, the Identity Documents Rule, and the Story of a Nation Besieged and Betrayed," *Journal of Law and Social Policy* 15 (2000): 183-211.
83 CIC, "Lucienne Robillard Announces the Introduction of the Undocumented *Convention* Refugees in Canada Class."
84 CIC, "Minister Robillard Announces Measures for Refugees Lacking ID to Become Permanent Residents," news release, 13 November 1996.
85 CIC, "Fact Sheet for Undocumented *Convention* Refugees in Canada Class (UCRCC)," 30 December 1999.
86 House of Commons Standing Committee Hearings, Transcripts, 19 February 1998, 10-11.
87 "Refugees to Challenge Immigration Act, Somali Group Alleges Discrimination," *Globe and Mail,* 6 February 1996.
88 Hussein Jama Aden, Fadumo Guire Ali, Fosiya Riyale, Aden Moallimaden, Abdulaziz Mohamed Abdi, Mohamed Ali Abdi, Sharmarke Mohamed Saleh, Amina Nuri Jama Hassan, Ali Haji Mohamed, Madina Mohammed Hassan, Mariam Abdullah Dirie (Plaintiffs) and Her Majesty the Queen, Federal Court of Canada Trial Division, Order, Docket IMM500/501-96, 14 December 2000.
89 Ibid.
90 The Getting Landed Project "Protecting the Unprotected" Submission to the House of Commons Standing Committee on Citizenship and Immigration with Respect to the Proposed Regulations under the Immigration and Refugee Protection Act, 14 February 2002, http://www.cpj.ca/getting_landed/docs/brief0202.pdf; see also The Maytree Foundation, "Brief to the Standing Committee on Citizenship and Immigration Regarding Proposed Immigration and Refugee Protection Regulations," 31 January 2002, http://www.maytree.com/HTMLFiles/RegulationsBrief.htm; and CCR, "Comments on Proposed Immigration and Refugee Protection Regulations."
91 Quoted in Maytree Foundation, "Brief to the Standing Committee," 8.
92 *Immigration and Refugee Protection Regulations,* S.O.R./2002-227.
93 *Controlled Drug and Substances Act,* S.C. 1996, c. 19.
94 Diane Riley, "Drugs and Drug Policy in Canada: A Brief Review and Commentary," Canadian Foundation for Drug Policy, November 1998, http://www.cfdp.ca/sen8ex1.htm.
95 Diane Riley, "Drugs and Drug Policy in Canada" (a study prepared for Senator Pierre Claude Nolin as a background document for his June 1999 motion to have Canada's Senate conduct a thorough review of Canadian drug law and policy), Canadian Foundation for Drug Policy, 1999, http://www.parl.gc.ca/36/2/parlbus/commbus/senate/com-e/ille-e/rep-e/rep-nov98-e.htm.
96 Ibid.
97 Interview with Ali Mohamud, 13 January 2000.
98 Farah Khayre, Midaynta, Association of Somali Service Agencies, interview quoted in Amber Nasrulla, "*Khat:* Harmless Stimulant or Addictive Drug?" *Journal of Addiction and Mental Health* (now *CrossCurrents*) 3, 3 (2000): 5.

99 Jacob Sullum, "Voodoo Social Policy: Exorcising the Twin Demons, Guns and Drugs," *Reason Magazine* 26, 5 (1994): 26-31, http://reason.com/9410/fe.sullum.shtml; Jacob Sullum, "Khat Calls," *Reason Magazine* 24, 10 (1993): 42-44.

100 "Khat on a Hot Fed List," *NOW* 8-14 August 1996: 19-20; "Six Britons Charged in *Qat* Seizure," *Globe and Mail*, 11 November 1995.

101 Riley, "Drugs and Drug Policy in Canada."

102 Robert Kellerman, Law Union of Ontario, submission to Standing Committee on Legal and Constitutional Affairs, transcripts, 13 December 1995.

103 Ibid.

104 Interview with Ali Mohamud, 13 January 2000.

105 Ibid. See also Dave Borden, "Somali-Canadian Community under Attack by *Khat* Enforcers," *Week On-Line DRC Net*, 21 May 1999, http://www.stopthedrugwar.org/chronicle/091/index.shtml.

106 Riley, "Drugs and Drug Policy in Canada."

107 Farah Khayre, quoted in Borden, "Somali-Canadian Community under Attack by *Khat* Enforcers."

108 Interview with Ali Mohamud, 13 January 2000.

109 Borden, "Somali-Canadian Community under Attack by *Khat* Enforcers."

110 Interview with Ali Mohamud, 13 January 2000.

111 Perry Kendall, President and CEO of the Addiction Research Foundation, submission to the Standing Committee on Legal and Constitutional Affairs hearings on Bill C-8 (*CDSA*), evidence, 13 December 1995.

112 Ibid.

113 Khadigia Ali, community health worker at the Rexdale Community Health Centre (RCHC) in Toronto, quoted in Nasrulla, *"Khat:* Harmless Stimulant or Addictive Drug?"

114 Eugene Oscapella, Ontario Bar Association, "The War on Drugs and the Crime Control Industry: 'Profiteers and Prohibition,'" notes for an address to the International Society for the Reform of Criminal Law conference, Drugs, Criminal Justice, and Social Policy, St. Michael, Barbados, 11 August 1998.

Chapter 7: Discretion, Dangerousness, and National Security

1 *An Act to Amend the Immigration Act and the Citizenship Act and to Make a Consequential Amendment to the Customs Act,* S.C. 1995, c. 15 [hereafter Bill C-44]. Royal assent was received on 15 June 1995, and it came into force 10 July 1995.

2 As the trial was subsequently slowed by allegations of racism and illegalities, the case was referred to as the "justice deserted" case. "Just Desserts Case a Mess, Judge Reveals," *Globe and Mail*, 11 November 1998. The charges against Mark Jones were dropped, O'Neil Grant was eventually acquitted, Lawrence Brown was sentenced to life for first-degree murder, and Gary Francis was sentenced to fifteen years for manslaughter.

3 Including the expansion of the circumstances under which deportation orders are issued and the extension of the powers of immigration officers to arrest and search and seize. CIC, *CIC Update* 8 (1997): 1-2; see also CBA, National Immigration Law Section, *Submission on Bill C-44* (November 1994): 1-2.

4 Carolyn Strange, ed., *Qualities of Mercy: Justice, Punishment, and Discretion* (Vancouver: UBC Press, 1996), 14.

5 Julian Falconer and Carmen Ellis, "Colour Profiling: The Ultimate Just Desserts," paper presented at the American Bar Association meeting, August 1998, 21. See also African Canadian Legal Clinic, "Brief to the Legislative Review Secretariat, Citizenship and Immigration Canada, re: *Building a Strong Foundation for the 21st Century: New Directions for Immigration and Refugee Policy and Legislation* 1998," http://www.aclc.net/submissions/immigration_refugee_policy.html.

6 *IRPA,* s. 36(1)(a).

7 Ibid., ss. 64(1) and 64(2).

8 *Immigration Act,* s. 70(5) (emphasis added).

9 Weinreb and Galati, *The Criminal Lawyer's Guide,* 57.

10 As outlined in *Gonzalez v. Canada (Minister of Citizenship and Immigration),* [2000] 4 F.C. D33, IMM-2333-99, IMM-2334-99 (Appendix D).

11 Ibid.
12 IRB, *Guidelines on Detention,* 7. R246 of the *Immigration and Refugee Protection Regulations* details the factors that must be considered in assessing whether someone should be detained because he or she is a danger to the public. These are also laid out in section 5.6 of the CIC manual *ENF20 Detention,* http://www.cic.gc.ca/manuals-guides/english/enf/enf20e.pdf.
13 IRB, *Guidelines on Detention,* 16, n. 33. The equivalent of this caution under *IRPA* is found in section 5.6 of the CIC manual *ENF20 Detention.* No ministerial opinion is required.
14 *Criminal Code of Canada,* R.S.C. 1985, c. C-46, ss. 752-61.
15 *An Act to Amend the Criminal Code (High Risk Offenders), the Corrections and Conditional Release Act, the Criminal Records Act, the Prisons and Reformatories Act, and the Department of the Solicitor General Act* 1997, S.C. 1997, c. 17. The amendments created a new category of "long-term offender" that targets sex offenders; authorized the imposition of a peace bond with conditions on "high-risk" offenders; eliminated the judge's discretion to impose a fixed-term sentence on someone found to be a dangerous offender; replaced the requirement of the testimony of two psychiatrists with that of only one expert at the dangerous offender hearing; and lengthened the time before a dangerous offender can apply for parole from three years to seven years
16 For a detailed comparison of the immigration "danger to the public" provision and the pre-1997 *Criminal Code* "dangerous offender" legislation, see Bryan Schwartz, "Factum: The Preventative Function of Section 15 of the Charter and the Danger Certificate System," *Manitoba Law Journal* 27 (1999): 115-39. For a legal critique of amendments introduced through Bill C-55, see Irwin Koziebrocki and Peter Copeland, "Bill C-55: 'High-Risk Offender' Amendments to the Criminal Code Submissions to the Standing Committee on Justice and Legal Affairs, on Behalf of the Criminal Lawyers' Association," *Criminal Lawyers' Association Newsletter* 18, 3 (1997).
17 Prior to Bill C-55, a dangerous offender application had to be made in advance of sentencing. Bill C-55 allows an application to be made under certain circumstances up to six months after sentencing.
18 See Castel, "From Dangerousness to Risk."
19 See Robert Menzies, Dorothy Chunn, and Christopher Webster, "Risky Business: The Classification of Dangerous People in the Canadian Carceral Enterprise," in Kevin R.E. McCormick and Livy A. Visano, eds., *Canadian Penology: Advanced Perspectives and Research* (Toronto: Canadian Scholars Press, 1992), 61-94.
20 See, for example, Michael Louis Corrado, "Punishment and the Wild Beast of Prey: The Problem of Preventive Detention," *Journal of Criminal Law and Criminology* 86 (1996): 778-81; Canadian Association of Elizabeth Fry Societies, "The Risky Business of Risk Assessment," 2001, http://www.elizabethfry.ca/risky/Contents.html.
21 See Kelly Hannah-Moffat, "Criminogenic Need and the Transformative Risk Subject: Hybridizations of Risk/Need in Penality," *Punishment and Society* 7, 1 (2002): 29-51.
22 Ericson and Doyle, *Uncertain Business.*
23 Schwartz, "Factum," 115.
24 See, for example, Commission on Systemic Racism in the Ontario Criminal Justice System, *Report of the Commission on Systemic Racism in the Ontario Criminal Justice System,* Ontario, 1995; Royal Commission on the Donald Marshall Jr. Inquiry, *Discrimination against Blacks in Nova Scotia: The Investigation of the Criminal Justice System,* Halifax, 1989; and Janet C. Mosher, *Discrimination and Denial: Systemic Racism in Ontario's Legal and Criminal Justice Systems, 1892-1961* (Toronto: University of Toronto Press, 1998).
25 See, for example, Scot Wortley, "Justice for All? Race and Perceptions of Bias in the Ontario Criminal Justice System – a Toronto Survey," *Canadian Journal of Criminology* 38, 4 (1996): 439-67.
26 "Race and Crime Special Series," *Toronto Star,* 19-27 October 2002.
27 Ontario Human Rights Commission, "Paying the Price: The Human Cost of Racial Profiling Inquiry Report," 31 October 2003, http://www.ohrc.on.ca/english/consultations/racial-profiling-report.shtml.
28 See Schwartz, "Factum."
29 Ursula Franklin in conversation, January 1999.

30 Richard Haigh and Jim Smith, "Return of the Chancellor's Foot? Discretion in Permanent Resident Deportation Appeals under the *Immigration Act*," *Osgoode Hall Law Journal* 36, 1 (1998): 283 (emphasis added).
31 CBA, "Submission on Bill C-44," 6.
32 *Chirwa v. Canada (Minister of Manpower and Immigration)* (1970), 4 I.A.C. 338 (I.A.B.).
33 These objections to the use of "unchecked" ministerial discretion echo those asserted by those who called for the drastic curtailment of ministerial discretion to exclude under the 1952 act, discussed in Chapter 3.
34 CBA, "Submission on Bill C-44," 4.
35 Falconer and Ellis, "Colour Profiling," 21.
36 Ibid., 23.
37 Ibid., 24.
38 Ibid., 26.
39 In addition to the significant literature that addresses the racism in the Canadian immigration domain reviewed in earlier chapters, there is an important literature that examines the racism inherent in postcolonial regimes. See, for example, John Gabriel, *Racism, Culture, and Markets* (London: Routledge, 1994); Robert Young, *Hybridity in Theory, Culture, and Race* (London: Routledge, 1995); Edward Said, *Orientalism* (New York: Vintage Books, 1979); Etienne Balibar and Immanuel Wallerstein, eds., *Race, Nation, Class: Ambiguous Ethnicities* (London: Verso, 1994); Homi Bhabha, "The Other Question: Difference, Discrimination, and the Discourse of Colonialism," in Russell Ferguson et al., eds., *Out There: Marginalization and Contemporary Cultures* (New York: New Museum of Contemporary Art, 1990); Peter Fitzpatrick, ed., *Nationalism, Racism, and the Rule of Law* (Brookfield: Dartmouth Publishing Company, 1995); Benedict Anderson, *Imagined Communities* (London: Verso, 1983); and Paul Gilroy, *There Ain't No Black in the Union Jack: The Cultural Politics of Race and Nation* (Chicago: University of Chicago Press, 1987).
40 For reviews of the ways in which systemic racism pervades contemporary Canadian immigration and refugee policies, see CCR, "Report on Systemic Racism and Discrimination in Canadian Refugee and Immigration Policies," prepared for the UN World Conference against Racism, Racial Discrimination, Xenophobia, and Related Intolerance, 1 November 2000, http://www.web.net/~ccr/antiracrep.htm; African Canadian Legal Clinic, "Brief to the Legislative Review Secretariat"; and African Canadian Legal Clinic, "Promoting Full Participation and Reversing the Tide of Criminalization and Expulsion," report prepared for the UN conference Eliminating Racism: Linking Local and Global Strategies for Change, Immigration, and Refugee Issues, Durban, South Africa, 31 August-7 September 2001, http://www.aclc.net/un_conference/report10.html. See also Sunera Thobani, "Closing Ranks: Racism and Sexism in Canada's Immigration Policy," *Race and Class* 41, 1 (2000): 35-55.
41 J.A. Strayer, reasons for judgment, *Williams v. Canada (Minister of Citizenship and Immigration),* [1997] 2 F.C. 646. The quotations in the next several paragraphs are from this judgment.
42 *Canada (Minister of Employment and Immigration) v. Chiarelli.*
43 See Weinreb and Galati, *The Criminal Lawyer's Guide,* 16.
44 Ibid.
45 *Baker v. Canada (Minister of Citizenship and Immigration),* [1999] 2 S.C.R. 817.
46 See, for example, *Bhagwandass v. Canada (Minister of Citizenship and Immigration),* [2000] 1 F.C. 619 (T.D.); *Andino v. Canada (Minister of Citizenship and Immigration),* [2001] 1 F.C. 70 (T.D.); *Gonzalez v. Canada (Minister of Citizenship and Immigration).*
47 *Navarro v. Canada (Minister of Citizenship and Immigration),* [2001] 1 F.C. D17.
48 *Canadian Security Intelligence Service Act,* R.S.C. 1985, c. C-23 [hereafter *CSIS Act*].
49 Although Whitaker points out that the majority of those who took over this responsibility for CSIS were former members of the RCMP. Whitaker, *Double Standard,* 282-83.
50 *CSIS Act,* ss. 14 and 15.
51 Ibid., s. 1.
52 *Immigration Act,* ss. 39-40.

53 Order in Council 2003-2063, 12 December 2003.

54 *IRPA*, ss. 81-83.

55 For a review of the development of national security provisions in Canadian immigration law and their impact on refugees, see Sharryn Aiken, "Manufacturing 'Terrorists': Refugees, National Security, and Canadian Law (Part One)," *Refuge* 19, 3 (2000): 116-33; Sharryn Aiken, "Manufacturing 'Terrorists': Refugees, National Security, and Canadian Law (Part Two)," *Refuge* 19, 3 (2001): 54-73; and Sharryn Aiken, "Of Gods and Monsters: National Security and Canadian Refugee Policy," *Revue québécoise de droit international* 14, 1 (2001): 18-36.

56 *IRPA*, ss. 33-43 (formerly s. 19[1] of the *Immigration Act*).

57 CSIS, "Operational Programs: Security Screening," updated September 2002, http://www.csis-scrs.gc.ca/eng/operat/ss_e.html. The complete threat definitions are found in section 2(a)(b)(c)(d) of the *CSIS Act*.

58 Aiken, "Manufacturing 'Terrorists' (Part One)"; Aiken, "Manufacturing 'Terrorists' (Part Two)."

59 "Review Slams CSIS Treatment of Refugees," *Globe and Mail*, 11 May 2001. SIRC has been critical of CSIS on previous occasions. See, for example, SIRC, *Annual Report 1997-1998: An Operational Audit of CSIS Activities* (Ottawa: Minister of Supply and Services Canada, 1998), http://www.sirc-csars.gc.ca/annual/1997-1998/intro_e html; and SIRC, *Annual Report 1999-2000: An Operational Audit of CSIS Activities* (Ottawa: Minister of Supply and Services Canada, 2000), http://www.sirc-csars.gc.ca/annual/1999-2000/intro_e.html.

60 United Nations, *Refugee Convention*.

61 Ibid.

62 United Nations, *Convention against Torture and Other Cruel, Inhuman, or Degrading Treatment or Punishment*, 1984, 1465 U.N.T.S. 85 (CAT) (adopted 10 December 1984, entered into force 26 June 1987) [hereafter the *Convention against Torture*].

63 Ibid.

64 *IRPA*, ss. 112-16, *Immigration and Refugee Protection Regulations*, R160-174.

65 *Re Suresh* (1997), 140 F.T.R. 88 (F.C.T.D.).

66 The review of developments in the *Suresh* case provided in this paragraph and the next is drawn from *Suresh v. Canada (Minister of Citizenship and Immigration)*, [2002] 1 S.C.R. 3, 2002 SCC 1.

67 *Suresh v. Canada (Minister of Citizenship and Immigration)*, [2000] 2 F.C. 592 (C.A.).

68 Quoted in "Refugees' Case Has Developed into Showdown of Ideologies," *National Post*, 21 May 2001.

69 Alistair Hensler, former assistant director of CSIS, quoted in "On Trial: Right to Deport Terrorists," *National Post*, 21 May 2001.

70 Ibid.

71 *Suresh v. Canada* (2002). For detailed legal analyses of the *Suresh* case, see Aiken, "Manufacturing 'Terrorists' (Part Two)"; and Audrey Macklin, "Mr. Suresh and the Evil Twin," *Refuge* 20, 4 (2002): 15-22.

72 *Suresh v. Canada* (2002).

73 Macklin, "Mr. Suresh and the Evil Twin," 18.

74 *Suresh v. Canada* (2002).

75 Ibid.

76 Macklin, "Mr. Suresh and the Evil Twin," 21.

77 The decision reaffirmed that "Canadian law and international norms reject deportation to torture," *Suresh v. Canada* (2002). It cites Canadian *Charter* protection against cruel and unusual punishment (s. 12) and notes the supporting though secondary importance of international prohibitions against deportations to torture as contained in the *Convention against Torture* and the *International Covenant on Civil and Political Rights*, GA Res. 217 A (III), U.N. Doc. A/810, at 71, 999 U.N.T.S. 171 (entered into force 23 March 1976), both of which Canada has ratified. In so doing, it rejected the earlier judgment that article 33(2) of the *Refugee Convention* sanctions all security-related deportations to torture.

78 Macklin, "Mr. Suresh and the Evil Twin," 18.

79 *Ahani v. Canada (Minister of Citizenship and Immigration)*, [2002] 1 S.C.R. 72.
80 UNHRC, "Views," CCPR/C/80/D/1051/2002, 25 May 2004.
81 Macklin, "Mr. Suresh and the Evil Twin," 21.

Chapter 8: Criminals First

1 "When Our World Changed Forever," special report on terrorism in the United States, *Observer*, 16 September 2001.
2 Borrowed from Jonathan Simon, "Governing through Crime."
3 CIC, Public Affairs, "Response to Information Request."
4 Paul Walters, "Baylis/Leone Lawsuit against Federal Immigration Now in Full Swing," *Metropolitan Police Association Bulletin*, 1997.
5 House of Commons Standing Committee Hearings, transcripts, 29 April 1998, 5.
6 See Table 8.1.
7 CIC, *Performance Report*, 2002.
8 CIC, *Performance Report*, 2001.
9 CIC, *Performance Report*, 2003.
10 CIC, *Report on Plans and Priorities: 2002-2003* (Ottawa: Minister of Public Works and Services, 2002), http://www.cic.gc.ca/english/pub/rpp2002/.
11 Ibid.
12 *Immigration Act*, s. 19(1).
13 *IRPA*, s. 37.
14 Michel Gagné, Director, Organized Crime Unit, CIC, "CIC Strategy to Combat Organized Crime," paper presented at the Metropolis Justice/Immigration Domain Seminar, 27-28 February 1997, Ottawa.
15 "Canada Shuts the Door on Criminals," *National Post*, 21 November 1998.
16 Ibid.
17 Gagné, "CIC Strategy to Combat Organized Crime."
18 Ibid.
19 Ibid.
20 In addition to the Organized Crime Division, CMB includes the Case Review Division, which has three sections that review sensitive cases that do not involve organized crime, security, or modern war crimes (danger to the public and rehabilitation cases [criminality], other high-profile cases, and contentious citizenship cases); Security Review Division; Modern War Crimes Directorate; Litigation Management; and Service Line Support. For more information, see http://infosource.gc.ca/Info_1/pdf/VOLUME1chap046_eng.pdf.
21 Ibid.
22 Gagné, "CIC Strategy to Combat Organized Crime."
23 Department of Justice, "Federal Action against Organized Crime," September 2000, http://canada.justice.gc.ca/en/news/nr/2000/doc_25605.html.
24 Ibid.
25 *An Act to Amend the Criminal Code (Criminal Organizations) and to Amend Other Acts in Consequence*, S.C. 1997, c. 23.
26 *An Act to Amend the Criminal Code, the Controlled Drugs and Substances Act, and the Corrections and Conditional Release Act*, S.C. 1999, c. 5.
27 *Proceeds of Crime (Money Laundering) and Terrorist Financing Act*, S.C. 2000, c. 17.
28 Department of Justice, "Federal Action against Organized Crime."
29 Department of Justice, "Canada Signs UN Convention against Transnational Organized Crime and Optional Protocols," Ottawa, 15 December 2000.
30 CSIS, "The Public Reports," November 1996, http://www.csis-scrs.gc.ca/eng/publicrp/pub1996_e.html#8. All CSIS public reports (1991-2002) are available at http://www.csis-scrs.gc.ca/eng/publicrp/pubreps_e.html.
31 CSIS, "Transnational Criminal Activity."
32 Ibid.
33 Ibid.
34 *CSIS Act*, ss. 12 and 2(b). CSIS, "Transnational Criminal Activity."
35 CSIS, "Transnational Criminal Activity."

36 Ibid.
37 CSIS, "The CSIS Mandate," amended August 2001, http://www.csis-scrs.gc.ca/eng/backgrnd/back1_e.html.
38 CSIS, "Transnational Criminal Activity."
39 CSIS, "The CSIS Mandate."
40 Department of National Defence, "Transnational Crime: The Next Big Threat?" 23 December 2002, http://www.forces.gc.ca/admpol/eng/doc/strat_2001/sa01_26_e.htm.
41 Indeed, the seriousness of the problem is often flagged by reference to the cost of transnational criminal activity, though rarely with solid evidence. For example, in 2003, CSIS cites UN estimates suggesting that the cost of transnational criminal activity in developed states constitutes 2 percent of annual gross national product (GNP). Based on this estimate, CSIS observes that "the *potential* transnational crime-related losses for Canada in 1995 *would have been* about $14.8 billion, based on a GNP of $742 billion. Figures like this led the 1998 G8 summit in the UK to label transnational criminal activity one of the three major challenges facing the world today." CSIS, "Transnational Criminal Activity" (emphasis added). There are no real figures provided in this rationale. Similarly, the 1998 solicitor general's report entitled "Organized Crime Impact Study" reported that "economic crime, like securities and telemarketing fraud, costs Canadians *at least* $5 billion per year. Smuggling people into Canada accounts for *8,000 to 16,000* illegal immigrants each year. Counterfeit products *may* cost Canadians *over $1 billion* per year, and money laundered in Canada *may range from $5 [to] $17 billion each year.*" Department of the Solicitor General of Canada, "Major Study on Organized Crime Confirms Need for National Strategy Solicitor General Andy Scott Tells Chiefs of Police," news release, 24 August 1998 (emphasis added), http://www.sgc.gc.ca/publications/news/19980824_e.asp/.
42 CSIS, "Transnational Criminal Activity."
43 Ibid.
44 Solicitor General MacAuley, quoted in CSIS, "Transnational Criminal Activity."
45 CSIS, "Transnational Criminal Activity."
46 Minister of Public Works and Government Services Canada, *Department Performance Report for the Period Ending March 31, 1999* (Ottawa: Canadian Government Publishing, 1999).
47 International Centre for Criminal Law Reform and Criminal Justice Policy et al., "Legislative Guide for the Implementation of the United Nations Convention against Transnational Organized Crime," March 2003, http://www.icclr.law.ubc.ca/Publications/Reports/TOCLegisguide_English.pdf.
48 CSIS, "Director's Speaking Notes: Appearance Before the Standing Committee on Justice and Human Rights," 3 December 2002, http://www.csis-scrs.gc.ca/eng/miscdocs/director20021203_e.html.
49 "Triad Menace," *Globe and Mail*, 10 October 1993.
50 United States Senate Committee on Governmental Affairs, Permanent Subcommittee on Investigations, *The New International Criminal and Asian Organized Crime: Report* (Washington, DC: US Government Printing Office, 1992).
51 "Triad Menace."
52 "The Trouble with CSIS," *Globe and Mail*, 15 December 1999.
53 Quoted in Nathanson Centre for the Study of Organized Crime, "Chinese Organized Crime," *Organized Crime in Canada: A Quarterly Summary of Recent Events, July to September 2000*, http://www.yorku.ca/nathanson/CurrentEvents/Jul-Sept2000.htm#Chinese.
54 "The Trouble with CSIS."
55 Security Intelligence Review Committee, *Annual Report 1999-2000*, http://www.sirc-csars.gc.ca/annual/1999-2000/intro_e.html.
56 "Mounties Believe CSIS Dulled Chinese Spy Threat," *Globe and Mail*, 16 July 2001. For additional coverage, see "Spy Probe of China Was Aborted: Project Examined Beijing's Role in Canadian Business and Politics," *Globe and Mail*, 30 September 1999; "Triad Probe Still Needed Mountie Declares," *Globe and Mail*, 23 October 1999; and "CSIS Destroys Controversial Asian Crime Report," *Globe and Mail*, 6 October 1999.
57 SIRC, *Annual Report 1999-2000*, 3.
58 Ibid., 6.

59 See, for example, James D. Harder, "Canada Targeted by China Agents," *Insight Magazine,* 18 December 2000, http://www.telusplanet.net/public/mozuz/crime/lemieszewski20001129. html; "The Sidewinder Scandal: A Leaked Report Makes Explosive Allegations about Links between the Liberals and Chinese Agents," *Report,* 6 November 2000, http://www. telusplanet.net/public/mozuz/crime/lemieszewski20001102.html#bottom(9); "The Side-winder Secrets," *Globe and Mail,* 29 April 2000; and "Ex-Spy Takes on CSIS Review Body," *Globe and Mail,* 24 October 2000.

60 "Further Details Revealed about Hong Kong 'Scam,'" *Edmonton Journal,* 10 September 1999.

61 Harder, "Canada Targeted by China Agents."

62 Sun Tzu, *The Art of War* (c. 509 BC), quoted in RCMP-CSIS Joint Review Committee, "Chinese Intelligence Services and Triads Financial Links in Canada," 24 June 1997, http://www.jrnyquist.com/sidewinder.htm.

63 *Crimes against Humanity and War Crimes Act,* S.C. 2000, c. 24.

64 Ibid.

65 Department of Justice, "Canada's War Crimes Strategy," *Backgrounder,* Ottawa, 2002, http://canada.justice.gc.ca/en/news/nr/2000/doc_25439.html.

66 *Crimes against Humanity and War Crimes Act.*

67 CIC, "Canada's Crimes against Humanity and War Crimes Program," *Fifth Annual Report 2001-2002,* 2002, Appendix A, *Backgrounder,* http://www.cic.gc.ca/english/pub/war2002/section07.html.

68 *R. v. Finta,* [1994] 1 S.C.R. 701, (1994) 165 N.R. 1.

69 CIC, "Canada's Crimes against Humanity and War Crimes Program."

70 See, for example, David Matas, "The Struggle for Justice: Nazi War Criminals in Canada," *From Immigration to Integration: The Canadian Jewish Experience: A Millennium Edition,* Institute for International Affairs, B'nai Brith Canada, 2000, http://www.bnaibrith.ca/institute/millennium/millennium00.html.

71 *Rome Statute on the International Criminal Court,* UN Doc. A/Comf.183/9, 17 July 1998.

72 CIC, *Canada's War Crimes Program Annual Report 1999-2000* (Legislative Initiatives), http://www.cic.gc.ca/english/pdf/pub/war2000e.pdf.

73 CIC, "Canada's Crimes against Humanity and War Crimes Program."

74 Now covered by section 35(1)(b) of *IRPA.* This provision was used against members of the Somali community in Toronto in the mid-1990s, as discussed in Chapter 6. In 2002, eight countries had been designated as regimes that engage or have engaged in war crimes, crimes against humanity, genocide, or other gross or systematic human rights violations: the Bosnian Serb regime between March 1992 and October 1996; the Siad Barré regime in Somalia between 1969 and 1991; the military governments in Haiti between 1971 and 1986, 1991 and 1994, except the period August-December 1993; the regimes of Afghanistan between 1978 and 1992; the governments of Ahmed Hassan Al-Bakr and Saddam Hussein in power since 1968; the government of Rwanda under President Habyarimana between October 1990 and April 1994 and the interim government between April and July 1994; the governments of the Federal Republic of Yugoslavia and the Republic of Serbia (Milosevic) between February 1998 and October 2000; and the Taliban regime in Afghanistan from 1996 on. CIC, "Canada's Crimes against Humanity and War Crimes Program," Appendix E: "Designated Regimes," 2002, http://www.cic.gc.ca/english/pub/war2002/section11.html.

75 Department of Justice, "Canada's War Crimes Strategy."

76 CIC, "Canada's Crimes against Humanity and War Crimes Program," Appendix E.

77 Ibid. Appendix G, "World War Two Cases: Litigation Overview," is available at http://www.cic.gc.ca/english/pub/war2002/section13.html.

78 The report speculates provocatively that applicants withdrew their applications "in the face of questions concerning their background." CIC, "Canada's Crimes against Humanity and War Crimes Program," *Fifth Annual Report, 2001-2002,* http://www.cic.gc.ca/english/pub/war2002/section04.html.

79 Ibid. At the time of the 2001-2 report, the majority of these cases had not yet been concluded.

80 CIC, *Canada's War Crimes Program Annual Report 2000-2001,* http://www.cic.gc.ca/english/pub/war2001.html#policy.
81 CIC, "Backgrounder," *Canada's War Crimes Program Annual Report 2002-2003,* http://canada.justice.gc.ca/en/news/fs/2004/doc_31174.html.
82 Matas, "The Struggle for Justice."
83 This overview only scratches the surface of the developments and debates related to this issue.
84 United Nations, *Single Convention on Narcotic Drugs,* 1961; United Nations, *Convention on Psychotropic Substances,* 1971; United Nations, *Convention against the Illicit Traffic in Narcotic Drugs and Psychotropic Substances,* 1988.
85 CIC, *CIC Update,* 1997, 2-3.
86 *Pushpanathan v. Canada (Minister of Citizenship and Immigration),* [1998] 1 S.C.R. 982.
87 Between 1996 and 1998, there were no fewer than twenty-four UN drug-related resolutions made by the General Assembly of the United Nations, its Economic and Social Council (ECOSOC), and the Commission on Narcotic Drugs (CND). UN activity in this area has since increased; in 2001 and 2002, the number of drug-related UN resolutions rose to forty-five. United Nations, Office on Drugs and Crime, *Resolutions and Decisions,* http://www.unodc.org/unodc/resolutions.html.
88 Metropolis Canada, "What Is Metropolis," http://canada.metropolis.net/index_e.html.
89 Ibid.
90 Rose, *Powers of Freedom,* 323-24.
91 Meyer Burstein, Executive Head, Metropolis Project, CIC, letter to Justice-Immigration Domain Seminar participants, 27 January 1997.
92 Ibid.
93 Ibid.
94 Metropolis Canada, "The Metropolis Conversation Series: Backgrounder," http://canada.metropolis.net/events/conversation/backgrounder.htm.
95 Rose, *Powers of Freedom,* 188.
96 Metropolis Canada, "Justice-Immigration Domain Seminar: Preface," http://canada.metropolis.net/events/justdom/justdomrep_e.html#PREFACE.
97 Ibid.
98 Ibid.
99 Metropolis Project, "Report on Justice/Immigration Domain Seminar," unpublished document, Ottawa, 27-28 February 1997, http://canada.metropolis.net/events/justdom/justdomrep_e_html.
100 Robert Tassé, "Removals: Processes and People in Transition," report prepared for CIC, February 1996, 28.
101 Ibid.
102 Foster, *Turnstile Immigration,* 24.
103 Ibid., 30.
104 CBC, *The National,* transcript from 6 September 1995.
105 "RCMP Probe Forgery: Deportation Staff to Be Questioned," *Globe and Mail,* 10 October 1995.
106 Ibid.
107 "Officials Receive Absolute Discharge," *Globe and Mail,* 27 March 1996.
108 David Matas, House of Commons Standing Committee Hearings, 25 March 1998, 15.
109 Foster, *Turnstile Immigration,* 30.
110 *IRPA,* s. 24.
111 CIC, "Temporary Residence Permits," *Inland Processing Manual,* IP 1, s. 14, 2003, http://www.cic.gc.ca/manuals-guides/english/ip/ip01e.pdf.
112 Ibid.
113 CIC, *Inland Processing Manual,* IP 1, s. 14.1.
114 CIC, "Coderre Tables Minister's Report on Minister's Permits," news release, 30 April 2002.
115 House of Commons Standing Committee Hearings, 11 June 1998, 6.
116 CIC, *Annual Report to Parliament on Minister's Permits Issued in 1999,* 2000, http://www.cic.gc.ca/english/pub/permits1999.html.

117   CIC, *Annual Report to Parliament on Minister's Permits Issued in 2000,* 2001, http://www.cic.gc.ca/english/pub/permits2000.html.
118   CIC, "Coderre Tables Minister's Report on Minister's Permits."
119   CIC, *Annual Report to Parliament on Immigration 2003,* 2003, http://www.cic.gc.ca/english/pub/immigration2003.html#table9.
120   Schmitt, *Political Theology.* See also Agamben, *Homo Sacer;* and Mitchell Dean, "Always Look on the Dark Side: Politics and the Meaning of Life," *Proceedings of the 2000 Conference of the Australasian Political Studies Association,* October 2000, http://apsa2000.anu.edu.au/confpapers/Downloadingpapers.htm.
121   Foucault, *Discipline and Punish,* 53.
122   For an examination of the governance of organized crime in Canada and the difficulties associated with its measurement, see James Sheptycki, "The Governance of Organized Crime in Canada," *Canadian Journal of Sociology* 28, 4 (2003): 489-516.

Chapter 9: Risk-Smart Borders

1   For an elaboration of this theme in the context of community mediation, see Pavlich, *Justice Fragmented.*
2   See Ericson and Doyle, *Uncertain Business.*
3   Rose, *Powers of Freedom,* 260.
4   Ericson and Haggerty, *The Risk Society,* 85.
5   As asserted in a presentation by the Borders Task Force, Privy Council Office, "Forum on Enabling Secure Trade," 25 February 2003, http://www.its-sti.gc.ca/en/presentations/Panel%201-1%20-%20Ben%20Roswell%20-%20English.ppt.
6   In relation to the processes of "securitization" in Europe, Bigo refers to such networks as an "archipelago of police." Didier Bigo, "L'Archipel des polices," *Le Monde diplomatique,* October 1996: 9, http://www.monde-diplomatique.fr/1996/10/BIGO/7302.html; Didier Bigo, "When Two Become One: Internal and External Securitisations in Europe," in Morton Kelstrop and Michael Williams, eds., *International Relations Theory and the Politics of European Integration* (London: Routledge, 2000), 171-204.
7   The "welfare cheat" and related fears about "system abuse" provide key occasions for "partnerships." One notable example was addressed in the SCC decision in *Smith v. Canada (Attorney General),* [2001] 3 S.C.R. 902, which upheld the Canada Customs practice of sharing information relating to individual travellers with Unemployment Insurance officials. Links with public health agencies are also important. While the primary disease threats have changed over the years, the spectre of the "diseased" foreigner has long been a feature of the immigration domain. This figure, whether suffering from HIV or AIDS, tuberculosis, or more recently SARS, threatens not only public health but also public health systems by causing "excessive demand on health or social services." *IRPA,* s. 38(c).
8   RCMP, Federal Services Immigration and Passport Program, http://www3.sympatico.ca/mp.kitchener/main.html.
9   Ibid.
10   RCMP, Immigration, Federal, and Foreign Policy Branch, "Background on the RCMP Immigration and Passport National Enforcement Program," Submission to the Citizenship and Immigration Standing Committee Hearings, April 1998.
11   Ibid.
12   RCMP, Immigration, Passport and Citizenship Enforcement Program.
13   Ibid.
14   RCMP, submission to CIC Standing Committee Hearings.
15   Interview with senior policy official, RCMP, Immigration, Federal, and Foreign Policy Branch, Ottawa, 23 April 1998. Unless otherwise indicated, quotations that follow in the next few pages are derived from this interview.
16   See discussion of Bill C-44 in Chapter 7.
17   RCMP, "UK Fugitive Arrested in Toronto," news release, 15 November 2002, http://www.rcmp-grc.gc.ca/on/press/2002/2002_nov_15_e.html.
18   RCMP, Immigration Task Force, "Mission Statement," http://www.rcmp-grc.gc.ca/itf.

19 CBC News, "Immigration Task Force," *Disclosure,* 27 November 2001, http://www.cbc.ca/disclosure/archives/archives_government.html.

20 Ibid.

21 CBC News, "Glenford Johnson," *Disclosure,* 27 November 2001, http://www.cbc.ca/disclosure/archives/archives_government.html.

22 CIC, *CIC Update* (1997): 4.

23 Ibid., 2.

24 Combined Special Forces Unit, "What Do We Do?" http://www.cfseu.org/sitewhatwedo.htm.

25 Ibid.

26 RCMP, "Organized Crime Faces New Threat in Ontario's Golden Horseshoe," news release, 30 May 2002, http://www.rcmp-grc.gc.ca/on/press/2002/2002_may_30_e.htm.

27 RCMP, "Integrated National Security Enforcement Teams (INSET), National Security Investigation Section (NSIS)," http://www.rcmp-grc.gc.ca/security/insets_e.htm.

28 RCMP, "Combined Forces Special Enforcement/Integrated National Security Enforcement Teams Open New Operational Centre," news release, 11 February 2003, http://www.cfseu.org/news30.htm.

29 "On the World Stage," *RCMP Gazette* 65, 1 (2004), http://www.rcmp.ca/gazette/vo15_no1_e.htm.

30 Interview with constable, Ontario Region Police Department, 4 June 1999.

31 [1999] c. 17 (Bill C-43).

32 CCRA, "National Revenue Minister Marks Day One of the Canada Customs and Revenue Agency," news release, 1 November 1999.

33 Ibid.

34 Revenue Canada, "Customs Officers Recognized for Role in Keeping Streets Safe," press release, 24 January 1997. Transitions in the development and promotion of Canada Customs are bumpy, complicated, and ongoing. The present discussion does not begin to convey the heterogeneity and complexity of the processes at play.

35 Ibid.

36 *An Act to Amend the Customs Act and the Criminal Code,* S.C. 1998, c. 7.

37 Revenue Canada, "Customs Officers Recognized for Role in Keeping Streets Safe."

38 Revenue Canada, "Law Gives Customs Officers Expanded Powers under the Criminal Code," press release, 13 May 1998.

39 Customs and Excise Union, "Officer Powers Update," *CEUDA National Headlines,* 25 March 2003, http://www.ceuda.psac.com/english/english.html.

40 CEUDA, "Customs Workers Protest at Pearson International Airport," press release, 25 June 2004, http://www.ceuda.psac.com/english/publications/releases/2004/jun%2025%202004%20TOR.html.

41 CBSA, "Partners in Protection," *Fact Sheet,* January 2004, http://www.cbsa-asfc.gc.ca/newsroom/factsheets/2004/0124partners-e.html.

42 Ibid.

43 CBSA, General Information and Services, "Border Watch Toll Free Line," http://www.cbsa-asfc.gc.ca/general/enforcement/partners/line-e.html.

44 Thanks to Randy Lippert for this observation. See his "Policing Property and Moral Risk through Promotions, Anonymization, and Rewards: Crime Stoppers Revisited," *Social and Legal Studies* 11 (2000): 475-502.

45 Interview with senior policy official, RCMP, Immigration, Federal, and Foreign Policy Branch, Ottawa, 23 April 1998.

46 Ibid.

47 Ibid.

48 Ibid.

49 Ibid.

50 Readers will recall the nature of "community-derived" information used against the Somali community discussed in Chapter 6.

51 Pavlich, *Justice Fragmented,* 130. See also Kevin Stenson, "Community Policing as Governmental Technology," *Economy and Society* 27, 4 (1993): 373-89.

52   Ibid., 13-14. See also Colin Gordon, "Governmental Rationality: An Introduction," in *The Foucault Effect,* 41-46.
53   Rose, *Powers of Freedom,* 250.
54   Ibid., 176.
55   Pat O'Malley, "Risk, Power, and Crime Prevention," *Economy and Society* 21, 3 (1992): 252-75; Pat O'Malley, "Risk and Responsibility," 189-208.
56   Rose, *Powers of Freedom,* 249.
57   CIC, *Canada-United States Accord on Our Shared Border: Update 2000,* http://www.cic.gc.ca/english/pub/border2000/border2000.html.
58   Ibid.
59   Ibid.
60   Ibid.
61   Department of Foreign Affairs and International Trade, "Canada-U.S. Immigration Cooperation," http://www.dfait-maeci.gc.ca/can-am/menu-en.asp?act=v&mid=1&cat=10&did=1679#THE%20BORDER.
62   CIC, *Performance Report,* 1999.
63   Department of Justice, "Federal Action against Organized Crime."
64   RCMP, "Canada/US Integrated Border Enforcement Teams," http://www.rcmp.ca/security/ibets_e.htm.
65   CIC, *Performance Report,* 2002.
66   Department of Finance, Budget 2001: Enhancing Security for Canadians, 16.
67   CIC, *Performance Report,* 2002.
68   For discussions of the association between refugees and security issues in the wake of September 11th, see Macklin, "Borderline Security"; Reg Whitaker, "Refugee Policy after September 11th: Not Much New," *Refuge* 20, 4 (2002): 29-33; Howard Adelman, "Refugees and Border Security: Post September 11th," *Refuge* 20, 4 (2002): 5-14; Aiken, "Manufacturing 'Terrorists' (Part One)"; and Aiken, "Manufacturing 'Terrorists' (Part Two)."
69   Macklin, "Mr. Suresh and the Evil Twin."
70   This brief discussion only scratches the surface of the issues and concerns raised by the Safe Third Country Agreement. Dubbed by some as the "None Is Too Many" agreement, it was widely opposed by, for example, the CCR, Amnesty International, Canadian Ecumenical Justice Initiatives (KAIROS), and the Ontario Council for Agencies Serving Immigrants (OCASI). For more comprehensive discussions, see, for example, CCR, "Responding to Questions about the 'None Is Too Many' Agreement," news release, 10 June 2002, http://www.web.net/%7Eccr/safethirdccr.html; Amnesty International, "Are Canadians Prepared to Forcibly Return People to a Country Which ... ," news release, 20 June 2002; Adelman, "Refugees and Border Security"; CBA, "Letter –Immigration and Refugee Protection Regulations," letter, 20 November 2002, http://www.cba.org/cba/news/2002%5releases/2002-11-21-immigrationletter.asp/.
71   Solicitor General of Canada, "Canada/United States: Meeting our Security Challenges," *Joint Statement on Cooperation on Border Security and Regional Migration Issues,* 3 December 2001.
72   Ibid.
73   Department of Foreign Affairs, "The Smart Border Declaration: Building a Smart Border for the 21st Century on the Foundation of a North American Zone of Confidence," 12 December 2001.
74   Government of Ontario, "Roundtable on Border Issues: Report on the Industry Leaders Roundtable on Border Issues," 2 November 2001.
75   Ibid.
76   "Stowaway Found Dead on Pearson Flight," *Toronto Star,* 11 January 2003.
77   A recent collection of essays adds to the substantial literature on this topic: Edward Newman and Joannes van Selm, eds., *Refugees and Forced Displacement: International Security, Human Vulnerability, and the State* (Tokyo: United Nations University Press, 2003).
78   CIC, Standing Committee Hearings, transcripts, 18 February 1998, 27.
79   For a discussion of the range of interdiction measures taken by Western countries to "maximize the output" and "minimize the input" of refugee claimants, see François Crépeau,

"International Cooperation on the Interdiction of Asylum Seekers: A Global Perspective," in Canadian Council for Refugees, *Interdicting Refugees* (Montreal: CCR, 1998), 7-22.

80 CIC, *Performance Report,* 2002.

81 Gerry Campbell, Assistant Deputy Minister, Operations, CIC, submission to Citizenship and Immigration Standing Committee Hearings, 21 October 1997, 19.

82 CIC, House of Commons Standing Committee Hearings, 18 November 1997, 29.

83 In 1999-2000, CIC tested a new electronic document-scanning technology to be used prior to boarding and upon disembarkation. Any inconsistencies would identify those without valid papers. CIC reported that the technology was "promising," but there were some "technical difficulties," leading to more testing and evaluating of different scanning technologies. CIC, *Performance Report,* 2002.

84 Crépeau, "International Cooperation on Interdiction of Asylum Seekers."

85 CIC, *Performance Report,* 1999.

86 CIC, *Performance Report,* 2001.

87 CIC, *Performance Report,* 2002.

88 Office of the Auditor General, "2003 Report of the Auditor General" ("A Message from the Auditor General"), April 2003, http://www.oag-bvg.gc.ca/domino/reports.nsf/html/20030400ce.html.

89 CIC, *Performance Report,* 2002.

90 Office of the Auditor General of Canada, "2003 Report of the Auditor General" (Chapter 5), April 2003, http://www.oag-bvg.gc.ca/domino/reports.nsf/html/20030405ce.html.

91 CIC, *Performance Report,* 2002.

92 Ibid.

93 CIC, *Report on Plans and Priorities 2003-2004* (Ottawa: Miniter of Public Works and Government Services Canada, 2003).

94 CBSA, "Advance Passenger Information/Passenger Name Record," *Fact Sheet,* July 2003, http://www.cbsa-asfc.gc.ca/newsroom/factsheets/2003/july/july_api_pnr-e.html

95 CIC, Standing Committee Hearings, transcripts, 18 February 1998, 20.

96 CIC, *Performance Report,* 2002.

97 Senate Standing Committee on National Security and Defence, "The Myth of Security at Canada's Airports" ("Recommendations: Security Improvements"), January 2003, http://www.parl.gc.ca/37/2/parlbus/commbus/senate/Com-e/defe-e/rep-e/rep05jan03part2-e.htm.

98 Government of Canada, "Smart Border Action Plan Status Report," 3 October 2003, http://www.canadianembassy.org/border/status-en.asp/.

99 Senate Standing Committee, "The Myth of Security at Canada's Airports."

100 CCRA, "The Smart Border: Security and Protection," presented to the Air Transport Association of Canada, 15 May 2002, http://www.atac.ca/home/Andrea_Spry.ppt.

101 Revenue Canada, "Customs Officers to Be Given Added Responsibilities," press release, 13 March 1997.

102 Ibid.

103 Revenue Canada, "RC4062/CANPASS – Airport," Memorandum on CANPASS, 1998.

104 Ibid.

105 CCRA, "Highlights of the NEXUS Program," October 2002, http://www.cbsa-asfc.gc.ca/newsroom/factsheets/2004/0301nexus-e.html.

106 CIC, *Canada-United States Accord on Our Shared Border Update 2000.*

107 CCRA, "Highlights of the NEXUS Program."

108 CCRA, NEXUS Information and Application Form RC4209(E) Rev. 03/06, http://www.cbsa-asfc.gc.ca/E/pub/cp/rc4209/.

109 Standing Committee on Citizenship and Immigration, "Hands across the Border."

110 "Surveillance Technologies Nibble at Offline Privacy," *Toronto Star,* 5 March 2001.

111 "Fingerprints to Be Required for U.S. Visas," *Globe and Mail,* 20 May 2003; US Department of Homeland Security, "US-VISIT Program," *Fact Sheet,* 19 May 2003, http://www.dhs.gov/dhspublic/display?theme=43&content=736&print=true; US Department of Homeland Security, "US Will Connect Biometric Data on Foreign Visitors: Automated System to Stop Terrorists from Entering Country," *Fact Sheet,* 19 May 2003, http://usinfo.state.gov/topical/pol/terror/texts/03051904.htm.

112 Government of Canada, "Smart Border Action Plan Status Report."
113 Torpey, "Coming and Going," 9.
114 Canadian Press, "High-Tech ID Card Would Cost Billions, Wouldn't Work: Privacy Watchdog," 18 March 2003.
115 CIC, "About the Permanent Resident Card," http://www.cic.gc.ca/english/pr-card/prc-about.html.
116 Ibid.
117 Ibid.
118 "Expect National ID Card by 2005, Coderre Says," *Updates,* 13 July 2003, http://www.ctv.ca/servlet/ArticleNews/story/CTVNews/1058106889051_26///?hub=Canada.
119 Ibid., 13.
120 CSIS, "Transnational Criminal Activity."
121 This seems to contradict Brian Grant, the director of Program Management at CIC, who denied that CIC targeted flights from high-risk countries and claimed that disembarkation checks were carried out "at random." CIC, Standing Committee Hearings, 5 February 1998, 31.
122 Kent Roach and Sujit Choudry, "Racial and Ethnic Profiling: Statutory Discretion, Constitutional Remedies, and Democratic Accountability," *Osgoode Hall Law Journal* 41, 1 (2003): 2-3.
123 Canadian Human Rights Commission, "Tribunal Will Hear Discrimination Complaint against Canada Customs," press release, 23 May 2001; "New Rules for Customs Officers after Human Rights Complaint," *CBC News,* 6 February 2002; Donald H. Oliver, "Racial Discrimination," *Debates of the Senate* 1st Session, 36th Parliament, 139, 92 (5 March 2002): 2297-98; and Jason Gondziola, "Racial Profiling 101," *Alternatives for a Different World* 7, 5 (2003), http://www.alternatives.ca/article306.html.
124 "Customs Officials Will Do Whatever It Takes – Even Target Males with Links to Certain Muslim Countries – to Keep the Terrorists out of Canada, the Federal Minister Responsible Says," *Blue Line News Week: A Weekly Chronicle of News for the Canadian Law Enforcement Community,* 28 September 2001, http://collection.nlc-bnc.ca/100/201/300/blue_line_news/2001/06.39.pdf.
125 US Department of Justice, "Attorney General's Remarks: Implementation of NSEERS," 7 November 2002, http://www.usdoj.gov/ag/speeches/2002/110702agremarksnseers_niagarafalls.htm.
126 US Department of State, International Information Programs, "Pakistani, Saudi Vistors Now Required to Register with INS: Revised Notice Adds Two Countries to 18 Previously Listed," 18 December 2002, http://usinfo.state.gov/regional/nea/sasia/ins/texts.htm.
127 Ibid.
128 "Pakistanis Flocking to Canada," *Globe and Mail,* 15 March 2003.
129 Ibid.
130 Pratt, "Dangerousness and Modern Society," 39.
131 Office of the Auditor General of Canada, "2003 Report of the Auditor General" (Introduction), 2003, http://www.oag-bvg.gc.ca/domino/reports.nsf/html/20030401ce.html#ch1hd3b.
132 Schmitt, *Political Theology.* Lippert examines this feature of sovereign power in relation to sanctuary practices in Canada. See Lippert, "Sanctuary Practices, Rationalities, and Sovereignties."
133 Randy Lippert, "Governing Refugees: The Relevance of Governmentality to Understanding the International Refugee Regime," *Alternatives* 24 (1999): 324.

Chapter 10: Conclusion

1 Franz Kafka, "Before the Law," trans. Ian Johnston (Malaspina University-College, BC, 2003), http://www.mala.bc.ca/~johnstoi/kafka/beforethelaw/htm.
2 Pavlich makes this observation in relation to legal informalism in *Justice Fragmented,* 85.
3 Fitzpatrick, *The Mythology of Modern Law,* 154.
4 Rose and Miller, "Political Power beyond the State," 200-1.
5 Nancy Fraser and Linda Gordon, "A Genealogy of *Dependency:* Tracing a Keyword of the U.S. Welfare State," *Signs* 19, 2 (1994): 328.

6 Ibid., 323.
7 See Ericson and Doyle, eds., *Risk and Morality*.
8 Rose, *Powers of Freedom*, 237.
9 Ibid., 247.
10 Ibid., 160.
11 Mary Douglas, *Risk and Blame: Essays in Cultural Theory* (London: Routledge, 1992), 24.
12 Ibid., 26.
13 Valverde, *Diseases of the Will*, 153.
14 Dean, "Always Look on the Dark Side," 6.
15 Foucault, *Discipline and Punish*, 53.
16 Walters, "Deportation, Expulsion, and the International Police of Aliens," 278.
17 Ibid.
18 Simon, "Governing through Crime," 178.
19 Rose, *Powers of Freedom*, 271.
20 Young, *Imagining Crime*, 55.
21 Garland, *The Culture of Control*, 11.
22 Young, *Imagining Crime*, 12-13.
23 Rose, *Powers of Freedom*, 257.

Bibliography

Canadian Legal Cases

Adam v. Canada (Minister of Citizenship and Immigration), [1996] I.A.D.D. No. 839 (QL), No. T95-05027.

Aden, Hussein Jama, Fadumo Guire Ali, Fosiya Riyale, Aden Moallimaden, Abdulaziz Mohamed Abdi, Mohamed Ali Abdi, Sharmarke Mohamed Saleh, Amina Nuri Jama Hassan, Ali Haji Mohamed, Madina Mohammed Hassan, Mariam Abdullah Dirie v. Her Majesty the Queen (14 December 2000), F.C.T.D. IMM500/501-96; online at Citizens for Public Justice http://www.cpj.ca/getting_landed/docs/aden.pdf.

Ahani v. Canada (Minister of Citizenship and Immigration), [2002] 1 S.C.R. 72.

Andino v. Canada (Minister of Citizenship and Immigration), [2001] 1 F.C. 70 (T.D.).

Baker v. Canada (Minister of Citizenship and Immigration), [1999] 2 S.C.R. 817.

Bhagwandass v. Canada (Minister of Citizenship and Immigration), [2000] 1 F.C. 619 (T.D.).

Canada (Minister of Employment and Immigration) v. Chiarelli, [1992] 1 S.C.R. 711.

Canada (Minister of Citizenship and Immigration) v. Duale, [1997] I.A.D.D. No. 278, 39 Imm. L.R. (2d) 105, No. T95-06875.

Chirwa v. Canada (Minister of Manpower and Immigration) (1970), 4 I.A.C. 338 (I.A.B.).

Dehghani v. Canada (Minister of Employment and Immigration), [1993] 1 S.C.R. 1053.

Elmi v. M.C.I. (Minister of Citizenship and Immigration), [1996] I.A.D. No. 840, No. M95-06832.

Gana v. Canada (Minister of Manpower and Immigration), [1970] S.C.R. 699, 13 D.L.R. (3d) 699.

Gonzalez v. Canada (Minister of Citizenship and Immigration), [2000] 4 F.C. D33, IMM-2333-99, IMM-2334-99.

Kidane, Derar v. Canada (Minister of Citizenship and Immigration) (F.C.T.D., no. IMM-2044-96), Jerome, 11 July 1997.

Mursal v. Canada (Minister of Citizenship and Immigration), [1997] I.A.D.D. No. 455, No. M96-08958.

Navarro v. Canada (Minister of Citizenship and Immigration), [2001] 1 F.C. D17.

Pushpanathan v. Canada (Minister of Citizenship and Immigration), [1998] 1 S.C.R. 982.

R. v. Finta, [1994] 1 S.C.R. 701, (1994) 165 N.R. 1.

Re Suresh (1997), 140 F.T.R. 88 (F.C.T.D.).

Sahin v. Canada (Minister of Citizenship and Immigration), [1995] 1 F.C. 214 (T.D.).

Singh v. Canada (Minister of Employment and Immigration), [1985] 1 S.C.R. 177, 17 D.L.R. (4th) 422.

Smith v. Canada (Attorney General), [2001] 3 S.C.R. 902.

St-Amand v. Canada (Minister of Citizenship and Immigration), [1995] I.A.D.D. No. 819, No. M94-07317.

Suresh v. Canada (Minister of Citizenship and Immigration), [2000] 2 F.C. 592 (C.A.).

Suresh v. Canada (Minister of Citizenship and Immigration), [2002] 1 S.C.R. 3, 2002 SCC 1.

Williams v. Canada (Minister of Citizenship and Immigration), [1997] 2 F.C. 646.

Canadian Statutes

Canada Customs and Revenue Agency Act, S.C. 1999, c. 17.
Canadian Charter of Rights and Freedoms, Part I of the *Constitution Act, 1982*, being Schedule B to the *Canada Act 1982* (U.K.), 1982, c. 11.
Canadian Security Intelligence Service Act, R.S.C. 1985, c. C-23.
Controlled Drugs and Substances Act, S.C. 1996, c. 19.
Coroners Act, R.S.B.C. 1996, c. 72.
Crimes against Humanity and War Crimes Act, S.C. 2000, c. 24.
Criminal Code of Canada, R.S.C. 1985, c. C-46.
An Act to Amend the Criminal Code (Criminal Organizations) and to Amend Other Acts in Consequence, S.C. 1997, c. 23.
An Act to Amend the Criminal Code, the Controlled Drugs and Substances Act, and the Corrections and Conditional Release Act, S.C. 1999, c. 5.
An Act to Amend the Criminal Code (High Risk Offenders), the Corrections and Conditional Release Act, the Criminal Records Act, the Prisons and Reformatories Act, and the Department of the Solicitor General Act, S.C. 1997, c. 17.
An Act to Amend the Criminal Code, the Official Secrets Act, the Canada Evidence Act, the Proceeds of Crime (Money Laundering) Act, and Other Acts, and to Enact Measures Respecting the Registration of Charities, in Order to Combat Terrorism, S.C. 2001, c. 41.
An Act to Amend the Customs Act and the Criminal Code, S.C. 1998, c. 7.
Immigration Act, S.C. 1910, c. 27.
Immigration Act, R.S.C. 1952, c. 325.
Immigration Act, S.C. 1976-77, c. 52.
An Act to Amend the Immigration Act, 1976, and to Amend Other Acts in Consequence Thereof, S.C. 1992, c. 49.
An Act to Amend the Immigration Act, 1976, and to Amend Other Acts in Consequence Thereof (the Refugee Deterrents and Detention Bill), S.C. 1988, c. 35.
An Act to Amend the Immigration Act, 1976, and to Amend Other Acts in Consequence Thereof (the Refugee Reform Bill), S.C. 1988, c. 36.
An Act to Amend the Immigration Act and the Citizenship Act and to Make a Consequential Amendment to the Customs Act, S.C. 1995, c. 15.
Immigration and Refugee Protection Act, S.C. 2001, c. 27.
Immigration and Refugee Protection Regulations, S.O.R./2002-227.
Proceeds of Crime (Money Laundering) and Terrorist Financing Act, S.C. 2000, c. 17.

Australia, Europe, and United States Statutes

Asylum and Immigration Act (U.K.), 1996, c. 49.
Asylum and Immigration Appeals Act (U.K.), 1993, c. 23.
Asylum and Immigration (Treatment of Claimants etc.) Bill, Bill 5, 53/3, 2003-2004 Sess. (Royal Assent 22 July 2004).
Illegal Immigration Reform and Immigrant Responsibility Act of 1996, Pub. L. No. 104-208, 110 Stat. 3009.
Immigration and Asylum Act (U.K.), 1999, c. 33.
Migration Act 1958 (Cth.).
Migration Regulations 1994 (Cth.).
Nationality, Immigration, and Asylum Act (U.K.), 2002, c. 41.
Uniting and Strengthening America by Providing Appropriate Tools Required to Intercept and Obstruct Terrorism Act (USA PATRIOT Act) of 2001, Pub. L. No. 107-56, 115 Stat. 272.

International Legal and Other Documents

Body of Principles for the Protection of All Persons under Any Form of Detention or Imprisonment, GA Res. 43/173, UN GAOR, 76th Plen. Mtg., UN Doc. A/RES/43/173 (1988).
Convention against the Illicit Traffic in Narcotic Drugs and Psychotropic Substances, 1988, E/CONF. 82/15, Corr. 1 and Corr. 2 (entered into force 11 November 1990).
Convention against Torture and Other Cruel, Inhuman or Degrading Treatment or Punishment, 1984, 1465 U.N.T.S. 85 (CAT) (adopted 10 December 1984, entered into force 26 June 1987).

Convention Determining the State Responsible for Examining Applications for Asylum Lodged in One of the Member States of the European Communities (Dublin Convention), European Union governments, 15 June 1990, J.O. C 254, 19/08/1997, 1.

Convention Implementing the Schengen Agreement of 14 June 1985 between the Governments of the States of the Benelux Economic Union, the Federal Republic of Germany, and the French Republic on the Gradual Abolition of Checks at Their Common Borders, 19 June 1990, J.O. L 239, 22/09/2000, 19.

Convention on Psychotropic Substances, 1971, 1019 U.N.T.S. 175 (entered into force 16 August 1976).

Convention Relating to the Status of Refugees, 28 July 1951, 189 U.N.T.S. 150, arts. 32-33, Can. T.S. 1969 No. 6 (entered into force 22 April 1954, accession by Canada 2 September 1969).

International Centre for Criminal Law Reform and Criminal Justice Policy and the United Nations Centre for International Crime Prevention (with the Financial Support of the Department of Justice Canada, Department of Solicitor General Canada, and the Human Security Program of the Department of Foreign Affairs and International Trade of Canada). "Legislative Guide for the Implementation of the United Nations Convention against Transnational Organized Crime." Vancouver. Revised March 2003. http://www.icclr.law.ubc.ca/Publications/Reports/TOCLegisguide_English.pdf.

International Covenant on Civil and Political Rights, GA Res. 217A(III), 1948, UN Doc. A/810, at 71. 999 U.N.T.S. 171 (entered into force 23 March 1976).

Optional Protocol to the International Covenant on Civil and Political Rights, GA Res. 2200A (XXI), 21 UN GAOR Supp. No. 16 at 59, UN Doc. A/6316 (1966), 999 U.N.T.S. 302 (entered into force 23 March 1976).

Protocol Relating to the Status of Refugees, 1967, 606 U.N.T.S. 267.

Rome Statute on the International Criminal Court, UN Doc. A/Comf.183/9 (1998).

Single Convention on Narcotic Drugs, 1961, 520 U.N.T.S. 151 (entered into force 13 December 1964).

Standard Minimum Rules for the Treatment of Prisoners. Adopted 30 August 1955 by the First United Nations Congress on the Prevention of Crime and the Treatment of Offenders, U.N. Doc. A/CONF/611, annex I; and approved by the Economic and Social Council, ESC Res. 663C(XXIV), UN ESCOR Supp. No. 1, UN Doc. E/3048 (1957), and amended by ESC Res. 2076(LXII), UN ESCOR Supp. No. 1, UN Doc. E/5988 (1977).

United Nations Committee against Torture. *Decisions of the Committee against Torture under Article 22 of the Convention against Torture and Other Cruel, Inhuman, or Degrading Treatment or Punishment,* 21st Sess., Communication No. 67/1997: Canada, CAT/C/21/D/67/1997 (17 November 1998).

United Nations Economic and Social Council, Commission on Crime Prevention and Criminal Justice. *The Impact of Organized Criminal Activities upon Society at Large: A Report of the Secretary General.* January 1993. Presented at the Second Session, Vienna, 13-23 April 1993.

United Nations High Commissioner for Refugees. "Asylum Applications Lodged in Industrialized Countries: Levels and Trends, 2000-2002." Geneva: Population Data Unit, March 2003.

–. *Collection of International Instruments Concerning Refugees.* Geneva: UN, 1988.

–. "Comments on Bill C-11, *An Act Respecting Immigration to Canada and the Granting of Refugee Protection to Persons Who Are Displaced, Persecuted, or in Danger.*" Revised 5 March 2001. http://www.web.net/~ccr/c11hcr.PDF.

–. *Handbook on Procedures and Criteria for Determining Refugee Status under the 1951 Convention and the 1967 Protocol Relating to the Status of Refugees.* Geneva: UN, 1988. http://www.ceuda.psac.com/english/publications.

–. "Number of Asylum Applications Submitted in 30 Industrialized Countries, 1992-2001." Revised 31 May 2002. http://www.eza.at/download/opendoc.pdf.

–. "Refugees by Numbers." Revised 2003. http://www.unhcr.org.uk/info/briefings/statistics/documents/numb2003.pdf.

–. *UNHCR Guidelines on Detention of Asylum Seekers,* PRL 5.3, 29 January 1996. http://www.rcmvs.org/investigacion/Asylum.htm.

United Nations Human Rights Committee. Eightieth Session, 15 March – 2 April, 2004. International Covenant on Civil and Political Rights. "Views" Communication No. 1051/2002. CCPR/C/80/D/1051/2002. 25 May 2004. http://www.ohchr.org/tbru/ccpr/Ahani_v_Canada.pdf.

United Nations, Office on Drugs and Crime. *Resolutions and Decisions.* http://www.unodc.org/unodc/resolutions.html.

Canadian Government Publications and Other Documents

Canada Border Services Agency (CBSA). "Advance Passenger Information/Passenger Name Record." Fact sheet. Revised July 2003. http://www.cbsa-asfc.gc.ca/newsroom/factsheets/.

–. CBSA General Information and Services, "Border Watch Toll Free Line." http://www.cbsa-asfc.gc.ca/general/enforcement/partners/line-e.html.

–. "Partners in Protection." Fact sheet. Revised January 2004. http://www.cbsa-asfc.gc.ca/newsroom/factsheets/.

Canada Customs and Revenue Agency (CCRA). "Highlights of the NEXUS Program." Revised October 2002. http://www.cbsa-asfc.gc.ca/newsroom/factsheets/.

–. "National Revenue Minister Marks Day One of the Canada Customs and Revenue Agency." News release. Ottawa, 1 November 1999.

–. NEXUS Information and Application Form RC4209 (E) Rev. 03/06. http://www.cbsa-asfc.gc.ca/E/pub/cp/rc4209/.

–. "The Smart Border: Security and Protection." Presentation to the Air Transport Association of Canada, 15 May 2002. http://www.atac.ca/home/Andrea_Spry.ppt.

Canada Employment and Immigration Union, Public Service Alliance of Canada. "Presentation to the House of Commons Standing Committee on Citizenship and Immigration." 25 March 1998.

Canadian Human Rights Commission (CHRC). "Tribunal Will Hear Discrimination Complaint against Canada Customs." Press release. Ottawa, 23 May 2001.

Canadian Security Intelligence Service. "Director's Speaking Notes: Appearance before the Standing Committee on Justice and Human Rights." Revised 3 December 2002. http://www.csis-scrs.gc.ca/eng/miscdocs/director20021203_e.html.

–. "Operational Programs: Security Screening." Revised September 2002. http://www.csis-scrs.gc.ca/eng/operat/ss_e.html.

–. "The Public Reports." Revised November 1996. http://www.csis-scrs.gc.ca/eng/publicrp/.

–. "The CSIS Mandate." Revised August 2001. http://www.csis-scrs.gc.ca/eng/backgrnd/back1_e.html.

–. "Transnational Criminal Activity." Revised March 2003. http://www.csis-scrs.gc.ca/eng/backgrnd/back10_e.html.

Citizenship and Immigration Canada. *Annual Report to Parliament on Immigration 2003.* Ottawa: Minister of Public Works and Government Services Canada, 2003. http://www.cic.gc.ca/english/pub.

–. *Annual Report to Parliament on Minister's Permits Issued in 1999.* Ottawa: Minister of Public Works and Government Services Canada, 2000. http://www.cic.gc.ca/english/pub/permits1999.html.

–. *Annual Report to Parliament on Minister's Permits Issued in 2000.* Ottawa: Minister of Public Works and Government Services Canada, 2001. http://www.cic.gc.ca/english/pub/permits2000.html.

–. "About the Permanent Resident Card." http://www.cic.gc.ca/english/pr-card/prc-about.html.

–. "Backgrounder: Annual War Crimes Report 2002-2003" (Activities in the Fiscal Year 2001-2). http://canada.justice.gc.ca/en/news/.

–. *Building on a Strong Foundation for the 21st Century: New Directions for Immigration and Refugee Policy and Legislation.* Ottawa: Minister of Public Works and Government Services Canada, 1998.

–. "Canada: A Welcoming Land." Annual Immigration Plan, tabled October 1998. Ottawa: Minister of Public Works and Government Services, 1998.

–. "Canada and Ontario Cooperate to Protect Welfare System." News release. Ottawa, 29 March 1995.

–. "Canada and Ontario Cooperate to Protect the Welfare System." News release. Ottawa, June 1996.

–. "Canada–United States Accord on Our Shared Border: Update 2000." http://www.cic.gc.ca/english/pub/border2000/border2000.html.

–. "Canada's Crimes against Humanity and War Crimes Program. Fifth Annual Report 2001-2002." http://www.cic.gc.ca/english/pub/war2002/index.html.

–. "Canada's War Crimes Program Annual Report 1999-2000" (Legislative Initiatives), 2000. http://www.cic.gc.ca/english/pdf/pub/war2000e.pdf.

–. "Canada's War Crimes Program Annual Report 2000-2001" (Activities in the Fiscal Year 2000-1). http://www.cic.gc.ca/english/pub/war2001.html#policy.

–. "Caplan Tables New Immigration and Refugee Protection Act." News release. Ottawa: 6 April 2000.

–. *CIC Update*, No. 8. Ottawa, April 1997.

–. *Citizenship and Immigration Detention Policy* (draft). 1996.

–. "Coderre Tables Minister's Report on Minister's Permits." News release. Ottawa, 30 April 2002.

–. *Department Performance Report for the Period Ending March 31st, 1998*. Ottawa: Minister of Public Works and Government Services, 1998.

–. *Department Performance Report for the Period Ending March 31, 1999*. Ottawa: Canadian Government Publishing, 1999.

–. *Department Performance Report for the Period Ending March 31, 2000*. Ottawa: Canadian Government Publishing, 2000.

–. *Department Performance Report for the Period Ending March 31st, 2001*. Ottawa: Minister of Public Works and Government Services, 2001.

–. *Department Performance Report for the Period Ending March 31st, 2002*. Ottawa: Minister of Public Works and Government Services, 2002.

–. "Detention and Removals." *Mississauga Immigration Holding Centre Post Orders*. 29 February 1996.

–. "Detention Policy." October 1998. Unpublished policy guidelines document.

–. "Fact Sheet for Undocumented *Convention* Refugees in Canada Class (UCRCC)." 30 December 1999.

–. "Facts and Figures, Immigration Overview: Immigration Historical Perspective (1860-2002)." 2002. http://www.cic.gc.ca/english/pub/facts2002/immigration/immigration_1.html.

–. "Government Response to the Report 'Hands across the Border: Working Together at Our Shared Border and Abroad to Ensure Safety and Security and Efficiency.'" Ottawa, May 2002. http://www.cic.gc.ca/english/pub/hab.html.

–. *Immigration Manual,* Chapter ENF 20, s. 5(2), "Departmental Policy, General." October 2002. http://www.cic.gc.ca/manuals-guides/.

–. Inland Processing Manual 1 (IP1), s. 14. 2003. http://www.cic.gc.ca/manuals-guides/.

–. "Lessons Learned: 1999 Marine Arrivals in British Columbia." Final report, August 2002. http://www.cic.gc.ca/english/research/evaluation/.

–. "Minister Lucienne Robillard Maintains Income Cut-Offs for Family Class Sponsorships." News release. 18 March 1997.

–. "Minister Robillard Announces Measures for Refugees Lacking ID to Become Permanent Residents." News release. Ottawa, 13 November 1996.

–. "Minister Robillard Announces the Introduction of the Undocumented Convention Refugees in Canada Class." News release. Ottawa, January 1995.

–. "Minister Tables Annual Report to Parliament on Immigration." News release. Ottawa, 30 October 2002. http://www.cic.gc.ca/english/press/02/0237-pre.html.

–. *National Standards and Monitoring Plan for the Regulation and Operation of CIC's Detention Centres* (draft). 5 February 1998.

–. "Overview of Bill C-31, *The Immigration and Refugee Protection Act*." Ottawa: 6 June 2000.

–. *Performance Report for the Period Ending March 31, 2003*. Ottawa: Minister of Public Works and Government Services, 2003.

–. *Report on Plans and Priorities: 2002-2003*. Ottawa: Minister of Public Works and Government Services, 2002. http://www.cic.gc.ca/english/pub/rpp2002/.

–. Detention and Removals Unit. "Month End Statistical Report." 3 February 2000.
–. Immigration Holding Centre, Mississauga. "Rules for Detainees." 1998.
–. Metropolis Project. "Report on the Justice/Immigration Domain Seminar." Ottawa, 27-28 February 1997. http://canada.metropolis.net/events/justdom/justdomrep_e_html.
–. Michel Gagné, Director, Organized Crime Unit, CIC. Paper presented at the Metropolis Justice/Immigration Domain Seminar, Ottawa, 27-28 February 1997.
–. Ontario Region. "Long Term Detention Statistics." 30 June 1997. Unpublished document.
–. Ontario Region, Enforcement Branch. "Ontario Region Jail Day Histories." 1997. Unpublished document.
–. Ontario Region, Public Affairs. "Information for Persons Detained." 1998. Unpublished document.
–. Public Affairs. "Removal Statistics for Ontario and Canada, 1993-1997." 1998. Unpublished document.
–. Public Affairs. "Response to Information Request." 24 March 1997.
–. Roger Tassé. "Removals: Processes and People in Transition." Ottawa: CIC, February 1996. Unpublished document.
Customs Excise Union Douanes Accise. "Customs Workers Protest at Pearson International Airport." Press release. Revised 25 June 2004. http://www.ceuda.psac.com/english/publications/releases/2004/jun%2025%202004%20TOR.html.
–. "Officer Powers Update." CEUDA National Headlines. Revised 25 March 2003. http://www.ceuda.psac.com/english/english.html.
Department of Citizenship and Immigration, and Joseph Sedgwick. Report on Immigration. Part I. Ottawa, 1965.
Department of Finance. "More Resources for Detention, Removals, and Refugee Determination" in Budget 2001: Enhancing Security for Canadians, 16. Ottawa: Public Works and Government Services Canada, 2001. http://www.fin.gc.ca/budget01/pdf/bksece.pdf.
Department of Foreign Affairs and International Trade. "Canada-U.S. Immigration Cooperation." http://www.dfalt-maeci.gc.ca/can-am/menu-en.asp?act=v&mid=1&cat=10&did=1679#THE percent20BORDER.
–. "The Smart Border Declaration: Building a Smart Border for the 21st Century on the Foundation of a North American Zone of Confidence." Ottawa, 12 December 2001.
Department of Justice. "Canada Signs UN Convention against Transnational Organized Crime and Optional Protocols." News release. Ottawa, 15 December 2000. http://canada.justice.gc.ca/en/news.
–. "Canada's War Crimes Strategy." Ottawa, 2002. http://canada.justice.gc.ca/en/news/.
–. "Federal Action against Organized Crime." September 2000. http://canada.justice.gc.ca/en/news/nr/2000/doc_25605.html.
–. "Royal Assent of Bill C-36: The Anti-Terrorism Act." Backgrounder. 18 December 2001. http://canada.justice.gc.ca/en/news.
Department of National Defence. "Transnational Crime: The Next Big Threat?" 23 December 2002. http://www.forces.gc.ca/admpol/eng/doc/strat_2001/sa01_26_e.htm.
Department of the Solicitor General of Canada. "Canada/United States: Meeting Our Security Challenges." Joint Statement on Cooperation on Border Security and Regional Migration Issues. Detroit/Ottawa, 3 December 2001. http://www.cic.gc.ca/english/press/01/0126-pre.html.
–. "Major Study on Organized Crime Confirms Need for National Strategy Solicitor General Andy Scott Tells Chiefs of Police." News release. Ottawa, 24 August 1998. http://www.psepc-sppcc.gc.ca/publications/news/19980824_e.asp/.
–. "Notes for an Address by the Honourable Doug Lewis, PC, MP, Minister of Public Security." 9 August 1993.
Employment and Immigration Canada. Explaining the New Immigration Bill. Ottawa: Policy and Program Development, Employment and Immigration Canada, 1992.
House of Commons Standing Committee on Citizenship and Immigration. Transcripts of Hearings on Removal and Detention Pursuant to Standing Order 108 (2), 31 March 1998. Ottawa, October 1997–May 1998.
–. "Hands across the Border: Working Together at Our Shared Border and Abroad to Ensure Safety, Security, and Efficiency. Report of the Standing Committee on Citizenship and

Immigration." December 2001. http://www.parl.gc.ca/InfoComDoc/37/1/CIMM/Studies/Reports/cimm03rp/03-covi-e.htm.

–. "Immigration, Detention, and Removal: Report of the Standing Committee on Citizenship and Immigration." June 1998. http://www.parl.gc.ca/InfoComDoc/36/1/CITI/Studies/Reports/citirp01-e.htm.

–. "Refugee Protection and Border Security: Striking a Balance." Ottawa, March 2000. http://www.parl.gc.ca/InfoComDoc/36/2/CIMM/Studies/Reports/cimm02-e.htm.

Immigration and Refugee Board (IRB). *Powers of Adjudicators to Order Detention: Chairperson's Guidelines Issued Pursuant to Section 65(4) of the Immigration Act.* Ottawa: Immigration and Refugee Board, 12 March 1998.

Info Source Depository Services Program. "Citizenship and Immigration Canada: Organization, Centralized Service Delivery, and Corporate Services" in *Sources of Federal Government Information 2001-2002.* Treasury Board of Canada Secretariat. Ottawa: Communication Canada, 1996-2002. http://infosource.gc.ca/Info_1/pdf/VOLUME1chap046_eng.pdf.

–. "Smart Border Action Plan Status Report." 3 October 2003. http://www.canadianembassy.org/border/status-en.asp/.

–. Privy Council Office, Borders Taskforce. "Forum on Enabling Secure Trade." 25 February 2003. http://www.its-sti.gc.ca/en/presentations/Panel%201-1%20-%20Ben%20Roswell%20-%20English.ppt.

–. Privy Council Office, Order in Council. *Public Service Rearrangement and Transfer of Duties Act.* P.C. 2003-2063. 12 December 2003.

Legislative Review Advisory Group. *Not Just Numbers: A Canadian Framework for Future Immigration.* Ottawa: Minister of Public Works and Government Services, 1997.

Manpower and Immigration. *White Paper on Immigration.* Ottawa: Queen's Printer, 1966.

–. *Managing Immigration: A Framework for the 1990s.* Ottawa: Supply and Services Canada, 1992.

Office of the Auditor General of Canada. "April 2003 Report of the Auditor General." Ottawa, 2003. http://www.oag-bvg.gc.ca/.

Ontario. "Round Table on Border Issues: Report on the Industry Leaders Roundtable on Border Issues." Toronto, 2 November 2001. Unpublished document.

–. *Time for Action.* Toronto: Government Printer, 1992.

–. *Turning Point.* Toronto: Government Printer, 1993.

Ontario Human Rights Commission. "Paying the Price: The Human Cost of Racial Profiling Inquiry Report." 31 October 2003. http://www.ohrc.on.ca/english/consultations/racial-profiling-report.shtml.

Ontario Ministry of the Solicitor General, Chief Coroner. "Verdict and Recommendations Arising Out of the Inquest into the Death of Michael Deno." 7 June 1996. Unpublished document.

Revenue Canada. "Customs Officers Recognized for Role in Keeping Streets Safe." Press release. Ottawa, 24 January 1997.

–. "Customs Officers to Be Given Added Responsibilities." Press release. Windsor, ON, 13 March 1997.

–. "Law Gives Customs Officers Expanded Powers under the Criminal Code." Press release. Ottawa, 13 May 1998.

–. "RC4062/CANPASS – Airport." Memorandum on CANPASS. 16 July 1998.

Royal Canadian Mounted Police/Canadian Security Intelligence Service. "Canada/US Integrated Border Enforcement Teams." http://www.rcmp.ca/security/ibets_e.htm content.

–. "Chinese Intelligence Services and Triads Financial Links in Canada." *Report: As Posted by Canada's Independent Newsmagazine,* 24 June 1997. http://report.ca/webonly/sidewinder.html. In July 2004, posted at http://www.jrnyquist.com/sidewinder.htm.

–. "Combined Forces Special Enforcement/Integrated National Security Enforcement Teams Open New Operational Centre." News release. 11 February 2003. http://www.cfseu.org/news30.htm.

–. "Federal Services Immigration and Passport Program." http://www3.sympatico.ca/mp.kitchener/main.html.

–. "Immigration, Passport and Citizenship Enforcement Program." http://www.rcmp-grc.gc.ca/html/imm_e.htm.

–. "Integrated National Security Enforcement Teams (INSET) National Security Investigation Section (NSIS)." http://www.rcmp-grc.gc.ca/security/insets_e.htm.

–. "On the World Stage." *RCMP Gazette* 65, 1 (2004). http://www.rcmp.ca/gazette/vo15_no1_e.htm.

–. "UK Fugitive Arrested in Toronto." News release. 15 November 2002. http://www.rcmprc.gc.ca/on/press/2002/2002_nov_15_e.htm.

–. Greater Toronto Area Combined Special Forces Unit. "What Do We Do?" http://xtreme10-60.aci.on.ca/cfseu/who.htm.

–. Immigration, Federal and Foreign Policy Branch. "Background on the RCMP Immigration and Passport National Enforcement Program." Submission to the Citizenship and Immigration Standing Committee hearings, April 1998.

–. Immigration Taskforce, Toronto. "Mission Statement." http://www.rcmp-grc.org/itf.htm.

Security Intelligence Review Committee. *Annual Report 1997-1998: An Operational Audit of CSIS Activities*. Ottawa: Minister of Supply and Services Canada, 1998. http://www.sirc-csars.gc.ca/annual/.

–. *Annual Report 1999-2000: An Operational Audit of CSIS Activities*. Ottawa: Minister of Supply and Services Canada, 2000. http://www.sirc-csars.gc.ca/annual/.

–. *Annual Report 2000-2001: An Operational Audit of the Canadian Security Intelligence Service*. Ottawa: Public Works and Government Services Canada, 2001. http://www.sirc-csars.gc.ca/annual/.

Senate. "Racial Discrimination." *Debates of the Senate*, 1st Session, 36th Parliament, 139, 92 (5 March 2002): 2297-98.

Senate Standing Committee on National Security and Defence. "The Myth of Security at Canada's Airports." 2nd Session, 37th Parliament, January 2003. ("Recommendations: Security Improvements"). http://www.parl.gc.ca/37/2/parlbus/commbus/senate/Com-e/defe-e/rep-e/rep05jan03part2-e.htm.

Statistics Canada. "Census of Population: Immigration, Birthplace, and Birthplace of Parents, Citizenship, Ethnic Origin, Visible Minorities, and Aboriginal Peoples." *The Daily*, 21 January 2003. http://www.statcan.ca/Daily/English/030121/d030121a.htm.

United Kingdom and United States Government Publications and Other Documents

United Kingdom. Home Office. "Reforming the System: Asylum and Immigration Bill Gets Royal Assent." Press release. 22 July 2004. http://www.ind.homeoffice.gov.uk/ind/en/home/news/press_releases/reforming_the_system.html.

United States. Department of Homeland Security. "US Will Connect Biometric Data on Foreign Visitors: Automated System to Stop Terrorists from Entering Country." Fact sheet. 19 May 2003. http://usinfo.state.gov/topical/pol/terror/texts/03051904.htm.

–. "US-VISIT Program." Fact sheet. 19 May 2003. http://www.dhs.gov/dhspublic/display?theme=43&content=736&print=true.

United States. Department of Justice, Bureau of Citizenship and Immigration Services. "Illegal Immigration Reform and Immigrant Responsibility Act: Summary." Fact sheet. http://www.immigration.gov/graphics/publicaffairs/factsheets/948.html.

–. "Attorney General's Remarks: Implementation of NSEERS." Niagara Falls, NY, 7 November 2002. http://www.usdoj.gov/ag/speeches/2002/110702agremarksnseers_niagarafalls.htm.

United States. Department of State, International Information Programs. "Pakistani, Saudi Vistors Now Required to Register with INS. Revised Notice Adds Two Countries to 18 Previously Listed." 18 December 2002. http://usinfo.state.gov/regional/nea/sasia/ins/texts.htm.

United States. Executive Office of the President. *A Blueprint for New Beginnings: A Responsible Budget for America's Priorities*. Washington, DC: US Government Printing Office, 2001.

United States. Senate Committee on Governmental Affairs. *The New International Criminal and Asian Organized Crime: Report*. Report by Permanent Subcommittee on Investigations. Washington, DC: US Government Printing Office, 1992.

Articles and Books

Abella, Irving, and Harold Troper. *None Is Too Many: Canada and the Jews of Europe 1933-1948*. Toronto: Lester and Orpen Dennys, 1982.

Adelman, Howard. "Canadian Refugee Policy in the Post-War Period." In Howard Adelman, ed., *Refugee Policy: Canada and the United States*, 172-223. Toronto: York Lanes Press, 1991.

–, ed. *Refugee Policy: Canada and the United States*. Toronto: York Lanes Press, 1991.

Adelman, Howard, Allan Borowski, Meyer Burstein, and Lois Foster, eds. *Immigration and Refugee Policy: Canada and Australia Compared*. 2 vols. Toronto: University of Toronto Press, 1994.

–. "Refugees and Border Security: Post September 11th." *Refuge* 20, 4 (2002): 5-14.

Africa Watch. *Somalia: A Government at War with Its Own People*. New York: Africa Watch Committee, 1990.

African Canadian Legal Clinic. "Brief to the Legislative Review Secretariat Citizenship and Immigration Canada re: *Building a Strong Foundation for the 21st Century: New Directions for Immigration and Refugee Policy and Legislation*." http://www.aclc.net/submissions/immigration_refugee_policy.html.

–. "Promoting Full Participation and Reversing the Tide of Criminalization and Expulsion." Report prepared for the UN conference Eliminating Racism: Linking Local and Global Strategies for Change, Immigration, and Refugee Issues, Durban, South Africa, 31 August-7 September 2001. http://www.aclc.net/un_conference/report10.html.

Agamben, Giorgio. *Homo Sacer: Sovereign Power and Bare Life*. Stanford: Stanford University Press, 1998.

Aiken, Sharryn. "Comments on Bill C-11 Related to National Security and Terrorism." Centre for Refugee Studies submission to the House of Commons Standing Committee on Citizenship and Immigration, 26 March 2001.

–. "Of Gods and Monsters: National Security and Canadian Refugee Policy." *Revue québécoise de droit international* 14, 1 (2001): 8-36.

–. "Manufacturing 'Terrorists': Refugees, National Security, and Canadian Law (Part One)." *Refuge* 19, 3 (2000): 116-33.

–. "Manufacturing 'Terrorists': Refugees, National Security, and Canadian Law (Part Two)." *Refuge* 19, 3 (2001): 54-73.

Alliance Party of Canada. "Alliance Calls for Closer Cooperation with US in War on Terror, Free Trade." News release, 15 December 2002.

Amnesty International. *Annual Human Rights Report*. New York: Amnesty International USA, 1997.

–. "Are Canadians Prepared to Forcibly Return People to a Country Which ... " News release, 20 June 2002.

–. "Australia." http://web.amnesty.org/report2003/aus-summary-eng.

–. "Australia-Pacific: Offending Human Dignity – the 'Pacific Solution.'" AI Index: ASA 12/009/2002, 25 August 2002.

–. "Brief to the Parliamentary Standing Committee on Citizenship and Immigration." 1998.

–. "The Immigration and Refugee Protection Act: It Is Faster but Is It Fairer for Refugees?" News release, AI Index: AMR 20/C02/00, 7 April 2000.

–. "Unlawful and Unworkable: Amnesty International's View on Proposals for Extra-Territorial Processing of Refugee Claims." June 2003. http://www.amnesty-eu.org/.

Anderson, Benedict. *Imagined Communities*. London: Verso, 1983.

Andreas, Peter. "Borderless Economy, Barricaded Border." *NACLA Report on the Americas* 33, 3 (1999): 14-21.

–. "The Escalation of U.S. Immigration Control in the Post-NAFTA Era." *Political Science Quarterly* 113, 4 (1998-99): 591-615.

Andreas, Peter, and Timothy Snyder, eds. *The Wall around the West: State Borders and Immigration Controls in North America and Europe*. Boston: Rowman and Littlefield, 2000.

Angus Reid Group. *Multiculturalism and Canadians: Attitude Study 1991* (National survey report). Ottawa: Multiculturalism and Citizenship Canada, 1991.

–. "National Angus Reid/Southam News Poll: Racial Tensions and Law Enforcement in Canada." News release, 3 June 1992.

Anizman, Philip, ed. *A Catalogue of Discretionary Powers in the Revised Statutes of Canada, 1970.* Ottawa: Law Reform Commission of Canada, 1975.

Avery, Donald. *"Dangerous Foreigners": European Immigrant Workers and Labour Radicalism in Canada, 1896-1932.* Toronto: McClelland and Stewart, 1979.

–. *Reluctant Host: Canada's Response to Immigrant Workers: 1896-1994.* Toronto: McClelland and Stewart, 1995.

Baker, Chris. "Canada after September 11th: A Public Opinion Perspective." Environics Research Group, http://www.robarts.yorku.ca/pdf/cw_conf_baker.pdf.

Baker, Tom, and Jonathan Simon, eds. *Embracing Risk: The Changing Culture of Insurance and Responsibility.* Chicago: University of Chicago Press, 2002.

Balibar, Etienne, and Immanuel Wallerstein, eds. *Race, Nation, Class: Ambiguous Ethnicities.* London: Verso, 1994.

Barsky, Robert F. *Constructing a Productive Other.* Amsterdam and Philadelphia: John Benjamins Publishing Company, 1994.

–. *Arguing and Justifying: Assessing the Convention Refugee's Choice of Moment, Motive, and Host Country.* Aldershot: Ashgate, 2000.

Beck, Ulrich. *The Brave New World of Work.* Cambridge: Polity Press-Blackwell Publishers, 2000.

. *Risk Society: Towards a New Modernity.* London: Sage Publications, 1992.

–. *World Risk Society.* Cambridge: Polity Press-Blackwell Publishers, 1999.

Bhabha, Homi. "Of Mimicry and Men: The Ambivalence of Colonial Discourse." In James Donald and Stuart Hall, eds., *Politics and Ideology.* 85-92. Milton Keynes: Open University Press, 1986.

–. "The Other Question: Difference, Discrimination, and the Discourse of Colonialism." In Russell Ferguson, Martha Gever, Trinh Minh-ha, and Cornel West, eds., *Out There: Marginalization and Contemporary Cultures.* 203-20. New York: New Museum of Contemporary Art, 1990.

Bigo, Didier. "L'Archipel des polices." *Le Monde diplomatique,* October 1996. http://www.monde-diplomatique.fr/1996/10/BIGO/7302.html.

–. "The European Internal Security Field: Stakes and Rivalries in a Newly Developing Area of Police Intervention." In Malcolm Anderson and Monica den Boer, eds., *Policing across National Boundaries,* 161-73. London: Pinter, 1994.

–. "Security and Immigration: A Critique of the Governmentality of Unease." *Alternatives* 27 (2002): 63-92.

–. "When Two Become One: Internal and External Securitisations in Europe." In Morton Kelstrop and Michael Williams, eds., *International Relations Theory and the Politics of European Integration,* 171-204. London: Routledge, 2000.

Borowski, Allan, and Derrick Thomas. "Immigration and Crime." In Howard Adelman, Allan Borowski, Meyer Burstein, and Lois Foster, eds., *Immigration and Refugee Policy: Australia and Canada Compared,* vol. 2, 631-52. Toronto: University of Toronto Press, 1994.

Brouwer, Andrew. "What's in a Name: Identity Documents and Convention Refugees." Caledon Institute for Social Policy, Ottawa, 1999.

Bryden, Phillip L. "Fundamental Justice and Family Class Immigration." *University of Toronto Law Journal* 41 (1991): 484-532.

Burchell, Graham. "Liberal Government and Techniques of the Self." *Economy and Society* 22, 3 (1992): 268-82.

Burchell, Graham, Colin Gordon, and Peter Miller, eds. *The Foucault Effect: Studies in Governmentality with Two Lectures by and an Interview with Michel Foucault.* Chicago: University of Chicago Press, 1991.

Burstein, Meyer (Executive Head, Metropolis Project, CIC). Letter to Justice-Immigration Domain Seminar participants, 27 January 1997.

Buzan, Barry, Ole Waever, and Jaap de Wilde. *Security: A New Framework for Analysis.* Boulder: Lynne Rienner, 1998.

Calliste, Agnes. "Race, Gender, and Canadian Immigration Policy: Blacks from the Caribbean, 1900-1932." *Journal of Canadian Studies* 28, 4 (1993): 131-48.

Callon, Michel, and John Law. "After the Individual in Society: Lessons on Collectivity from Science, Technology, and Society." *Canadian Journal of Sociology* 22, 2 (1997): 165-82.

Campbell, Gerry (Assistant Deputy Minister, Operations, CIC). Submission to Citizenship and Immigration Standing Committee Hearings, 21 October 1997, 19.

Canadian Association of Elizabeth Fry Societies. "The Risky Business of Risk Assessment." 2001. http://www.elizabethfry.ca/risky/Contents.html.

Canadian Bar Association. National Citizenship and Immigration Law Section. "Comments on Proposed *Immigration and Refugee Protection Regulations,* Parts 1-17, Published in the *Canada Gazette,* Part I, 15 December 2001." 13 February 2002. http://www.web.net/~ccr/ccrcomments1-17c-11.htm.

–. "Comments to the Standing Committee on Citizenship and Immigration on the Proposed Safe Third Country Regulations." 14 November 2002. http://www.web.net/~ccr/s3cregscommentsstandcomm.html.

–. "Detention Statistics 2002." 6 March 2003. http://www.web.net/~ccr/detentionstats2002.html.

–. "Detention Statistics: 2003 Year to Date." 1 April 2003. http://www.web.net/~ccr/detentionstatscurrent.html.

–. "Letter – *Immigration and Refugee Protection Regulations.*" 20 November 2002. http://www.web.net/~ccr/statland.htm.

–. "New Bill Is 'Unfair' to Immigrants Says CBA's Immigration Section." News release, 21 February 2001.

–. "New Immigration Bill Reduces Newcomer Rights." News release, 14 March 2001.

–. "New Security Certificate Rules Further Reduce Rights." Press release, 26 January 2004. http://www.web.net/~ccr/relcert.htm.

–. "Reduction in Refugee Levels Must Trigger Reversal of Anti-Refugee Measures." 13 January 2003. http://www.web.net/~ccr/numbersrelease.htm.

–. "Report on Systemic Racism and Discrimination in Canadian Refugee and Immigration Policies." In preparation for the UN World Conference against Racism, Racial Discrimination, Xenophobia, and Related Intolerance. 1 November 2000. http://www.web.net/~ccr/antiracrep.htm.

–. "Resolutions." December 2000. http://www.web.net/%7Eccr/resd00.htm.

–. "Resolutions." May 2001. http://www.web.net/%7Eccr/resm01.html.

–. "Responding to Questions about the 'None Is Too Many' Agreement." 10 June 2002.

–. "Submission on Bill C-44." November 1994.

–. "Submission on *Immigration and Refugee Protection Regulations* Parts 1-17." January 2002. http://www.cba.org/pdf/2002-01-31_immigration.pdf.

Canadian Press/Leger Marketing. "Canadians and Immigration." 18 March 2002. http://www.legermarketing.com/documents/spclm/020318eng.pdf.

Castel, Robert. "From Dangerousness to Risk." In Burchell, Gordon, and Miller, eds., *The Foucault Effect,* 281-98.

Ceyhan, Ayse, and Anastassia Tsoukala. "The Securitization of Migration in Western Societies: Ambivalent Discourses and Policies." *Alternatives* 27 (2002): 21-39.

Clear, Todd, and Natasha Frost. "Private Prisons." *Criminology and Public Policy* 1, 3 (2002): 425-27.

Clifford, James. "Diasporas." *Cultural Anthropology* 9, 3 (1994): 302-38.

Cohen, Russell. "Fundamental (in)Justice: The Deportation of Long-Term Residents from Canada." *Osgoode Hall Law Journal* 32, 3 (1994): 457-80.

Commission on Systemic Racism in the Ontario Criminal Justice System. *Report of the Commission on Systemic Racism in the Ontario Criminal Justice System.* Ottawa: Queen's Printer: 1995.

Constable, Marianne. "Sovereignty and Governmentality in Modern American Immigration Law." *Studies in Law, Politics, and Society* 13 (1993): 249-71.

Corrado, Michael Louis. "Punishment and the Wild Beast of Prey: The Problem of Preventive Detention." *Journal of Criminal Law and Criminology* 86 (1996): 778-81.

Cowan, Jeff G. "Recent Developments in Judicial Review." In Garry J. Smith, ed., *Charter of Rights and Administrative Law 1983-1984,* 7-47. Toronto: Carswell Legal Publications, 1983.

Crépeau, François. "International Cooperation on the Interdiction of Asylum Seekers: A Global Perspective." In Canadian Council for Refugees, *Interdicting Refugees,* 7-22. Montreal: Canadian Council for Refugees, May 1998.

Daniels, Ronald J., Patrick Macklem, and Kent Roach, eds. *The Security of Freedom: Essays on Canada's Anti-Terrorism Bill.* Toronto: University of Toronto Press, 2001.

Dauvergne, Catherine. "Amorality and Humanitarianism in Immigration Law." *Osgoode Hall Law Journal* 37, 3 (1999): 597-623.

Davis, Kenneth Culp. *Discretionary Justice: A Preliminary Inquiry.* Bâton Rouge: Louisiana State University Press, 1969.

Dean, Mitchell. "Always Look on the Dark Side: Politics and the Meaning of Life." In *Proceedings of the 2000 Conference of the Australasian Political Studies Association.* October 2000. http://apsa2000.anu.edu.au/confpapers/Downloadingpapers.htm.

–. *Governmentality: Power and Rule in Modern Society.* London: Sage Publications, 1999.

–. "Liberal Government and Authoritarianism." *Economy and Society* 31 (2002): 37-61.

Defert, Daniel. "Popular Life and Insurance Technology." In Burchell, Gordon, and Miller, eds., *The Foucault Effect,* 211-33.

Dicey, Albert Venn. *Introduction to the Study of the Law of the Constitution.* London: Macmillan, 1985 [1915].

Dictionary of the English Language. 2nd unabridged ed. New York: Random House, 1987.

Dillon, Michael. "Sovereignty and Governmentality: From the Problematics of the 'New World Order' to the Ethical Problematic of the World Order." *Alternatives* 20 (1995): 323-68.

Dirks, Gerald E. *Canada's Refugee Policy: Indifference or Opportunism?* Montreal: McGill-Queen's University Press, 1977.

–. *Controversy and Complexity: Canadian Immigration Policy during the 1980s.* Montreal: McGill-Queen's University Press, 1995.

Dobson-Mack, Ann. "Independent Immigrant Selection Criteria and Equality Rights: Discretion, Discrimination, and Due Process." *Les Cahiers de droit* 34, 2 (1993): 549-72.

Donzelot, Jacques. "The Mobilization of Society." In Burchell, Gordon, and Miller, eds., *The Foucault Effect,* 169-79.

Douglas, Mary. *Risk and Blame: Essays in Cultural Theory.* London: Routledge, 1992.

Dowbiggin, Ian. "Keeping This Young Country Sane: C.K. Clarke, Immigration Restriction, and Canadian Psychiatry, 1890-1925." *Canadian Historical Review* 76, 4 (1995): 598-627.

Dworkin, Ronald. "Judicial Discretion." *Journal of Philosophy* 60, 21 (1963): 624-38.

–. *Taking Rights Seriously.* Cambridge, MA: Harvard University Press, 1977.

Edkins, Jenny. "Sovereign Power, Zones of Indistinction, and the Camp." *Alternatives* 25 (2000): 3-25.

Eliadis, Pearl. "The Swing from Singh." *Immigration Law Reporter* 26 (1995): 130-47.

Emerson, Robert M., and Blair Paley. "Organizational Horizons and Complaint Filing." In Hawkins, ed., *The Uses of Discretion,* 231-48.

Ericson, Richard, and Aaron Doyle, eds. *Risk and Morality.* Toronto: University of Toronto Press, 2003.

Ericson, Richard, and Kevin Haggerty. *Policing the Risk Society.* Toronto: University of Toronto Press, 1997.

Ewald, François. "Risk and Insurance." In Burchell, Gordon, and Miller, eds., *The Foucault Effect,* 197-210.

Falconer, Julian, and Carmen Ellis. "Colour Profiling: The Ultimate Just Desserts." Paper presented at the American Bar Association meeting, August 1998.

Feeley, Malcolm, and Jonathan Simon. "Actuarial Justice: The Emerging New Criminal Law." In David Nelken, ed., *The Futures of Criminology,* 173-201. New Delhi: Sage Publications, 1994.

–. "The New Penology: Notes on the Emerging Strategy for Corrections and Its Implications." *Criminology* 30 (1992): 449-74.

Finkel, Alvin. "Canadian Immigration Policy and the Cold War, 1945-80." *Journal of Canadian Studies* 21 (1986): 53-70.

Fitzgerald, Patrick. "Repelling Borders." *New Statesman and Society* 8 (1995): 16-17.

Fitzpatrick, Peter. *The Mythology of Modern Law.* London: Routledge, 1992.

–. "Racism and the Innocence of Law." *Journal of Law and Society* 14, 1 (1987): 119-32.

–. "The Rise and Rise of Informalism." In Roger Matthews, ed., *Informal Justice?* 178-98. London: Sage, 1988.

–. "Terminal Legality." *Social and Legal Studies* 7, 3 (1998): 431-36.

–, ed. *Nationalism, Racism, and the Rule of Law.* Brookfield: Dartmouth Publishing Company, 1995.

Fitzpatrick, Peter, and Alan Hunt, eds. *Critical Legal Studies.* Oxford: Blackwell, 1987.

Flynn, Stephen E. "Beyond Border Control." *Foreign Affairs* 79, 6 (2000): 57-68.

Forrest, Duncan. "A Study of 95 Sikh Refugees Seeking Asylum in UK." *Lives under Threat.* Medical Foundation for Care of Victims of Torture, 1999. http://www.sikhreview.org/june2000/human2.htm.

Foster, Lorne. *Turnstile Immigration: Multiculturalism, Social Order, and Social Justice in Canada.* Toronto: Thompson Educational Publishing, 1998.

Foster, Steve. "Immigration Detention." *Journal of Law and Social Policy* 8 (1992): 107-41.

Foucault, Michel. *Discipline and Punish: The Birth of the Prison.* Trans. Alan Sheridan. New York: Vintage Books, 1979.

–. "Governmentality." In Burchell, Gordon, and Miller, eds., *The Foucault Effect,* 87-104.

–. *The History of Sexuality: An Introduction.* Vol. 1. Trans. Robert Hurley. New York: Vintage Books, 1990 [1976].

–. *Madness and Civilization: A History of Insanity in the Age of Reason.* New York: Random House, 1965.

–. "Truth and Power." Interview with Michel Foucault, in Rabinow, ed., *The Foucault Reader,* 51-75. New York: Pantheon Books, 1984.

Fraser, Nancy, and Linda Gordon. "A Genealogy of *Dependency*: Tracing a Keyword of the U.S. Welfare State." *Signs* 19, 2 (1994): 309-36.

Gabriel, John. *Racism, Culture, and Markets.* London: Routledge, 1994.

Galligan, Dennis James. *Discretionary Powers: A Legal Study of Official Discretion.* Oxford: Clarendon Press, 1986.

Garland, David. *The Culture of Control: Crime and Social Order in Contemporary Society.* Chicago: University of Chicago Press, 2001.

–. "Governmentality and the Problem of Crime: Foucault, Criminology, Sociology." *Theoretical Criminology* 1, 2 (1997): 173-214.

–. "The Limits of the Sovereign State: Strategies of Crime Control in Contemporary Society." *British Journal of Criminology* 36, 4 (1996): 455-71.

German Embassy, London. "Foreigners in Germany and Europe Compared: Foreigners in the Federal Republic of Germany." June 2002. http://www.german-embassy.org.uk/foreign.html.

Getting Landed Project. "'Protecting the Unprotected': Submission to the House of Commons Standing Committee on Citizenship and Immigration with Respect to the Proposed Regulations under the *Immigration and Refugee Protection Act.*" 14 February 2002. http://www.cpj.ca/getting_landed/docs/brief0202.pdf.

Gilboy, Janet A. "Deciding Who Gets In: Decision-Making by Immigration Inspectors." *Law and Society Review* 25, 3 (1991): 571-99.

–. "Implications of 'Third Party' Involvement in Enforcement: The INS, Illegal Travelers, and International Airlines." *Law and Society Review* 31, 3 (1997): 505-29.

–. "Penetrability of Administrative Systems: Political 'Casework' and Immigration Inspections." *Law and Society Review* 26, 2 (1992): 273-313.

Gilroy, Paul. *There Ain't No Black in the Union Jack: The Cultural Politics of Race and Nation.* Chicago: University of Chicago Press, 1987.

Girard, Philip. "From Subversion to Liberation: Homosexuals and the Immigration Act, 1952-1977." *Canadian Journal of Law and Society* 2 (1987): 1-27.

Global Expertise in Outsourcing (GEO) Group. "Advantages of Working with Us." 2004. http://www.wcc-corrections.com/advantages.asp/.

–. "Chairman's Welcome." 2004. http://www.wcc-corrections.com/.

–. "Fast Facts about GEO." 2004. http://www.wcc-corrections.com/facts.asp/.

–. "History." 2004. *Career Builder.* http://www.careerbuilder.com/JobSeeker/Companies/CompanyDetails.aspx?HHName=geogroup&cbRecursionCnt=1&cbsid=b06527a774174b80a23389328d0ac2b8-143484426-xm-2.

Goodin, Robert. "Welfare, Rights, and Discretion." *Oxford Journal of Legal Studies* 6, 1 (1986): 232-61.

Goodwin-Gill, Guy S., and Judith Kumin. "Refugees in Limbo and Canada's International Obligations." Caledon Institute of Social Policy, Ottawa, September 2000.

Gordon, Colin. "Governmental Rationality: An Introduction." In Burchell, Gordon, and Miller, eds., *The Foucault Effect*, 1-51.

Gorlick, Brian. "The Exclusion of 'Security Risks' as a Form of Immigration Control: Law and Process in Canada-1." *Immigration and Nationality Law and Practice* 5, 3 (1991): 76-82.

–. "The Exclusion of 'Security Risks' as a Form of Immigration Control: Law and Process in Canada-2." *Immigration and Nationality Law and Practice* 5, 4 (1991): 109-15.

Greene, Michael (Chair, National Citizenship and Immigration Law Section, Canadian Bar Association). "Letter to Parliamentary Committee on Citizenship and Immigration and MPs, re: Bill C-11." 2 March 2001.

–. "Submission on *Immigration and Refugee Protection Regulations* Parts 1-17." January 2002. http://www.cba.org/pdf/2002-01-31_immigration.pdf.

Grey, Julius. *Immigration Law in Canada.* Toronto: Butterworths, 1984.

–. "Refugee Status in Canada." In Nash and Humphrey, *Human Rights and Refugees under International Law*, 299-319.

Grover, Kelly. "The Social Organization of a High-Rise Neighbourhood: The Influence of Race, Culture, Economic Class, and Tenure on the Community Sentiments of Kingsview Park." Master's thesis, Queen's University, June 1995.

Hacking, Ian. *The Taming of Chance.* Cambridge: Cambridge University Press, 1990.

Haigh, Richard, and Jim Smith. "Return of the Chancellor's Foot? Discretion in Permanent Resident Deportation Appeals under the *Immigration Act*." *Osgoode Hall Law Journal* 36, 1 (1998): 245-92.

Hanks, Peter, and John D. McCamus, eds. *National Security: Surveillance and Accountability in a Democratic Society.* Cowansville: Les Éditions Yvon Blais, 1989.

Hannah-Moffat, Kelly. "Criminogenic Need and the Transformative Risk Subject: Hybridizations of Risk/Need in Penality," *Punishment and Society* 7, 1 (2002): 29-51.

Hathaway, James, and Alexander Neve. "Fundamental Justice and the Deflection of Refugees from Canada." *Osgoode Hall Law Journal* 34 (1996): 213-70.

Hawkes, Jim. "Panel of Canadian Parliamentarians." In Nash and Humphrey, *Human Rights and Refugees under International Law*, 253-56.

Hawkins, Freda. *Canada and Immigration: Public Policy and Public Concern.* Montreal: McGill-Queen's University Press, 1972.

Hawkins, Keith. *Law as Last Resort: Prosecution Decision-Making in a Regulatory Agency.* Oxford: Oxford University Press, 2002.

–, ed. *The Uses of Discretion.* Oxford: Clarendon Press, 1992.

Heap, Dan. "Panel of Canadian Parliamentarians." In Nash and Humphrey, *Human Rights and Refugees under International Law*, 253-66.

Heyman, Josiah. "Why Interdiction? Immigration Control at the United States-Mexico Border." *Regional Studies* 33, 7 (1999): 619-30.

Heyman, Michael. "Judicial Review of Discretionary Immigration Decision-Making." *San Diego Law Review* 31, 4 (1994): 861-910.

Holsten, James, and Arjun Appadurai. "Cities and Citizenship." *Public Culture* 8, 2 (1996): 187-204.

Holton, Robert, and Michael Lanphier. "Public Opinion, Immigration, and Refugees." In Adelman et al., eds., *Immigration and Refugee Policy*, 125-48.

Hudson, Barbara. "Punishment and Governance." *Social and Legal Studies* 7, 4 (1998): 553-59.

Hunt, Alan. *Explorations in Law and Society: Toward a Constitutive Theory of Law.* New York: Routledge, 1993.

–. "Foucault's Expulsion of Law: Toward a Retrieval." *Law and Social Inquiry* 17, 2 (1992): 1-38.
–. *Governing Morals: A Social History of Moral Regulation.* Cambridge: Cambridge University Press, 1999.
Hunt, Alan, and Gary Wickham. *Foucault and Law: Towards a Sociology of Law as Governance.* London: Pluto Press, 1994.
Hurwitz, Paula. "The New Detention Provisions of the *Immigration Act:* Can They Withstand a Charter Challenge?" *University of Toronto Faculty of Law Review* 47, 2 (1989): 587-606.
Huysmans, Jef. "Migrants as a Security Problem: Dangers of 'Securitizing' Societal Issues." In Miles and Thränhardt, eds., *Migration and European Integration,* 53-72.
Hyndman, Jennifer, and Margaret Walters Roberts. "Transnational Migration and Nation: Burmese Refugees in Vancouver." Unpublished paper, December 1998, 4.
Inda, Jonathan Xavier, and Renato Rosaldo. "A World in Motion." In Jonathan Xavier Inda and Renato Rosaldo, eds., *The Anthropology of Globalization: A Reader,* 1-12. Malden, MA: Blackwell, 2002.
Inter-American Commission on Human Rights. "Report on the Situation of Human Rights of Asylum Seekers within the Canadian Refugee Determination System." February 2000.
Ipsos-Reid Group. "Canadians and Immigration." 6 May 2000. http://www.ipsos-reid.com/search/pdf/media/mr000506.pdf.
–. "Canadians Split on Illegal Immigration Issue." 31 August 1999. http://www.ipsos-reid.com/search/pdf/media/pr990831%5F1.pdf.
–. "Globus: International Affairs Poll." Associated Press poll conducted by Ipsos-Public Affairs. Interview dates 7-17 May 2004. http://www.ipsos-na.com/news/pdf/media/mr040527-2tbzz.pdf.
–. "Poll on Canadian Attitudes towards Immigrants and Immigration." 22 November 1999. http://www.ipsos-reid.com/search/pdf/media/pr991122%5F1.pdf.
Isin, Engin, ed. *Democracy, Citizenship, and the Global City.* London: Routledge, 2000.
Jackman, Barbara. "Canada's Refugee Crisis: Planned Mismanagement." In Nash and Humphrey, *Human Rights and Refugees under International Law,* 321-26.
Jakubowski, Lisa Marie. *Immigration and the Legalization of Racism.* Halifax: Fernwood Publishing, 1997.
–. "'Managing' Immigration: Immigration, Racism, Ethnic Selectivity, and the Law." In Elizabeth Comack, ed., *Locating Law: Race/Class/Gender Connections,* 98-124. Halifax: Fernwood Publishing, 1999.
Johnson, Andrew, Stephen McBride, and Patrick Smith, eds. *Continuities and Discontinuities: The Political Economy of Social Welfare and Labour Market Policy in Canada.* Toronto: University of Toronto Press, 1994.
Kafka, Franz. "Before the Law." Trans. Ian Johnston, Malaspina University-College, Nanaimo, British Columbia, 2003. http://www.mala.bc.ca/~johnstoi/kafka/beforethelaw/htm.
–. "In the Penal Colony." In Neugroschel, trans., *The Metamorphosis, In the Penal Colony, and Other Stories,* 191-230.
–. *The Trial.* London: Penguin Books, 1994 [1925].
Kellerman, Robert (Law Union of Ontario). Submission to Standing Committee on Legal and Constitutional Affairs. 13 December 1995.
Kelley, Ninette, and Michael Trebilcock. *The Making of the Mosaic: A History of Canadian Immigration Policy.* Toronto: University of Toronto Press, 1998.
Kendall, Perry (President and CEO, Addiction Research Foundation). "Submission to the Standing Committee on Legal and Constitutional Affairs Hearings on Bill C-8." 13 December 1995.
Kinsman, Gary. "'Character Weakness' and 'Fruit Machines': Towards an Analysis of the Anti-Homosexual Security Campaign in the Canadian Civil Service." *Labour/Le Travail* 35 (1995): 133-62.
Kinsman, Gary, Dieter K. Buse, and Mercedes Steedman. "Constructing Gay Men and Lesbians as National Security Risks, 1950-1970." In *Whose National Security? Canadian State Surveillance and the Creation of Enemies,* 143-53. Toronto: Between the Lines, 2000.
Koziebrocki, Irwin, and Peter Copeland. "Bill C-55: 'High-Risk Offender' Amendments to the *Criminal Code* Submissions to the Standing Committee on Justice and Legal Affairs,

on Behalf of the Criminal Lawyers' Association." *Criminal Lawyers' Association Newsletter* 18, 3 (1997).

Lacey, Nicola. "The Jurisprudence of Discretion: Escaping the Legal Paradigm." In Hawkins, ed., *The Uses of Discretion,* 361-88.

Lahav, Gallya. "Migration and Security: The Role of Non-State Actors and Civil Liberties in Liberal Democracies." Paper prepared for the Second Coordination Meeting on International Migration, Population Division, Department of Economic and Social Affairs, United Nations Secretariat, New York, 15-16 October 2003.

Larner, Wendy, and William Walters, eds. *Global Governmentality: Governing International Spaces.* London: Routledge, 2004.

Latour, Bruno. *Science in Action.* Cambridge, MA: Harvard University Press, 1987.

Law Society of Upper Canada. *Charter of Rights and Administrative Law.* Toronto: Law Society of Upper Canada, 1986.

Leddy, Mary Jo. "Comments on Detentions and Removals: Brief to the Standing Committee on Citizenship and Removals." Toronto: Romero House, 1998.

Li, Peter. "The Racial Subtext in Canada's Immigration Subtext." *Journal of International Migration and Integration* 2, 1 (2001): 77-97.

Lippert, Randy. "Governing Refugees: The Relevance of Governmentality to Understanding the International Refugee Regime." *Alternatives* 24 (1999): 295-328.

–. "Policing Property and Moral Risk through Promotions, Anonymization, and Rewards: Crime Stoppers Revisited." *Social and Legal Studies* 11 (2000): 475-502.

– "Sanctuary Practices, Rationalities, and Sovereignties." *Alternatives: Global, Local, Political* 29, 5 (2004): 535-55.

Lipschutz, Ronnie D., ed. *On Security.* New York: Columbia University Press, 1995.

Luke, Timothy. "Governmentality and Contragovernmentality: Rethinking Sovereignty and Territoriality after the Cold War." *Political Geography* 15, 6-7 (1996): 491-507.

Macklin, Audrey. "Borderline Security." In Daniels, Macklem, and Roach, eds., *The Security of Freedom,* 383-404.

–. "Mr. Suresh and the Evil Twin." *Refuge* 20, 4 (2002): 15-22.

Mahtani, Minelle, and Alison Mountz. "Immigration to British Columbia: Media Representation and Public Opinion." Research on Immigration and Integration in the Metropolis, Working Paper Series 02-15, August 2002.

Malarek, Victor. *Haven's Gate: Canada's Immigration Fiasco.* Toronto: Macmillan, 1987.

Mandel, Michael. *The Charter of Rights and the Legalization of Politics in Canada.* Toronto: Wall and Thompson, 1989.

Manning, Peter. "'Big Bang' Decisions: Notes on a Naturalistic Approach." In Hawkins, ed., *The Uses of Discretion,* 249-85.

Marrocco, Frank N., and Henry M. Goslett. *The 1996 Annotated Immigration Act of Canada.* Toronto: Carswell, 1995.

Matas, David. "The Credibility of Refugee Claimants." *Immigration Law Reporter* 21 (1994): 134-54.

–. "Immigration Removals: A Submission to the House of Commons Standing Committee on Citizenship and Immigration." March 1998.

–. "The Struggle for Justice: Nazi War Criminals in Canada." *From Immigration to Integration: The Canadian Jewish Experience: A Millennium Edition.* Institute for International Affairs, B'nai Brith Canada, 2000. http://www.bnaibrith.ca/institute/millennium/millennium00.html.

Maytree Foundation. "Brief to the Standing Committee on Citizenship and Immigration Regarding Proposed Immigration and Refugee Protection Regulations." 31 January 2002. http://www.maytree.com/HTMLFiles/RegulationsBrief.htm.

McLachlin, Beverly. "Rules and Discretion in the Governance of Canada." *Saskatchewan Law Review* 56 (1992): 167-79.

Meissner, Doris (Commissioner, Immigration and Naturalization Service, Department of Justice). "Concerning INS Reform: Detention Issues." Testimony before the Subcommittee on Immigration Committee on the Judiciary, US Senate. 16 September 1998. http://www.fas.org/irp/congress/1998_hr/98091631_llt.html.

Menzies, Robert, Dorothy Chunn, and Christopher Webster, eds. "Risky Business: The Classification of Dangerous People in the Canadian Carceral Enterprise." In Kevin R.E. McCormick and Livy A. Visano, eds., *Canadian Penology: Advanced Perspectives and Research,* 61-94. Toronto: Canadian Scholars' Press, 1992.

Metro Toronto Chinese and Southeast Asian Legal Clinic. "Submission to the Standing Committee on Citizenship and Immigration." 1998.

Miles, Robert, and Dietrich Thränhardt, eds. *Migration and European Integration: The Dynamics of Inclusion and Exclusion.* London: Pinter Publishers, 1995.

Morris, Lydia. "Governing at a Distance: The Elaboration of Controls in British Immigration." *International Migration Review* 32, 4 (1998): 949-73.

Mosher, Janet C. *Discrimination and Denial: Systemic Racism in Ontario's Legal and Criminal Justice Systems, 1892-1961.* Toronto: University of Toronto Press, 1998.

Mullaly, Robert. "Social Welfare and the New Right: A Class Mobilization Perspective." In Johnson, McBride, and Smith, eds., *Continuities and Discontinuities,* 76-94.

Muszynski, Leon. "Defending the Welfare State and Labour Market Policy." In Johnson, McBride, and Smith, eds., *Continuities and Discontinuities,* 306-26.

Nash, Alan, ed., and John P. Humphrey, *rapporteur. Human Rights and the Protection of Refugees under International Law: Proceedings of a Conference held in Montreal November 29-December 2, 1987.* Halifax: Canadian Human Rights Foundation and Institute for Research on Public Policy, 1988.

Nasrulla, Amber. "*Khat:* Harmless Stimulant or Addictive Drug?" *Journal of Addiction and Mental Health* (now *CrossCurrents*) 3, 3 (2000): 5.

Nathanson Centre for the Study of Organized Crime. "Chinese Organized Crime." *Organized Crime in Canada: A Quarterly Summary of Recent Events, July to September 2000.* http://www.yorku.ca/nathanson/CurrentEvents/Jul-Sept2000.htm#Chinese.

Navasky, Victor S. "Deportation as Punishment." *University of Kansas Law Review* 27 (1959): 213-32.

Neugroschel, Joachim, trans. *The Metamorphosis, In the Penal Colony, and Other Stories.* New York: Scribner, 1995.

Newman, Edward, and Joannes van Selm, eds. *Refugees and Forced Displacement: International Security, Human Vulnerability, and the State.* Tokyo: United Nations University Press, 2003.

O'Malley, Pat. *Crime and the Risk Society.* The International Library of Criminology, Criminal Justice, and Penology. Australia: Ashgate Dartmouth, 1998.

–. "Genealogy, Systematisation, and Résistance in 'Advanced Liberalism.'" In Gary Wickham and George Pavlich, eds., *Rethinking Law, Society, and Governance: Foucault's Bequest,* 13-25. Oxford: Hart Publishing, 2001.

–. "Introduction: Configurations of Risk." *Economy and Society* 29, 4 (2000): 457-59.

–. "Risk, Power, and Crime Prevention." *Economy and Society* 21, 3 (1992): 252-75.

–. "Risk and Responsibility." In Andrew Barry, Thomas Osborne, and Nikolas Rose, eds., *Foucault and Political Reason: Liberalism, Neo-Liberalism, and Rationalities of Government,* 189-208. Chicago: University of Chicago Press, 1996.

–. "Uncertain Subjects: Risks, Liberalism, and Contract." *Economy and Society* 29, 4 (2000): 460-84.

–. *Uncertainty and Government.* London: Glasshouse Press, 2004.

–. "Volatile and Contradictory Punishment." *Theoretical Criminology* 3, 2 (1999): 175-96.

Oscapella, Eugene L.M. "The War on Drugs and the Crime Control Industry: 'Profiteers and Prohibition.'" Notes for an address to the International Society for the Reform of Criminal Law conference on Drugs, Criminal Justice, and Social Policy, St. Michael, Barbados, 11 August 1998.

Parkdale Legal Services. "Memorandum on Metro West Detention Centre Hunger Strike by Immigration Detainees." Toronto, 22 July 1997.

Parkin, Andrew. "Attitudes toward Immigration Unchanged." *Opinion Canada* 4, 34 (2002). http://cric.ca/en_html/opinion/opv4n34.html.

–. "Reacting to Terrorism: A Review of Canadian Public Opinion." *Opinion Canada* 3, 36 (2001). http://www.cric.ca/en_html/opinion/opv3n36.html#file.

Pavlich, George C. *Justice Fragmented: Mediating Community Disputes under Postmodern Conditions.* London: Routledge, 1996.

Pearce, Frank, and Steve Tombs. "Foucault, Governmentality, and Marxism." *Social and Legal Studies* 7, 4 (1998): 567-75.

Poulton, Ron, and Barbara Jackman. "Detention of Asylum Seekers: The Canadian Perspective." In Jane Hughes and Fabrice Liebaut eds., *Detention of Asylum Seekers in Europe: Analysis and Perspectives*, 113-23. The Hague: Martinus Nijhoff Publishers, 1998.

Pratt, Anna. "Dunking the Doughnut: Discretionary Power, Law, and the Administration of the Canadian *Immigration Act*." *Social and Legal Studies* 8, 2 (1999): 199-226.

–. "New Immigrant and Refugee Battered Women: The Intersection of Immigration and Criminal Justice Policy." In Mariana Valverde et al., eds., *Wife Assault and the Criminal Justice System*, 84-103. Toronto: Centre of Criminology, University of Toronto, 1995.

–. "Sovereign Power, Carceral Conditions, and Penal Practices: Detention and Deportation in Canada." *Studies in Law, Politics, and Society* 23 (1998): 45-78.

Pratt, Anna, and Mariana Valverde. "From Deserving Victims to 'Masters of Confusion': Redefining Refugees in the 1990s." *Canadian Journal of Sociology* 27, 2 (2002): 135-61.

Pratt, John. "Dangerousness and Modern Society." In Mark Brown and John Pratt, eds., *Dangerous Offenders: Punishment and Social Order*, 35-48. London: Routledge, 2000.

Razack, Sherene. "Domestic Violence as Gender Persecution: Policing the Borders of Nation, Race, and Gender." *Canadian Journal of Women and the Law* 8 (1995): 45-88.

–. "Simple Logic: Race, the Identity Documents Rule, and the Story of a Nation Besieged and Betrayed." *Journal of Law and Social Policy* 15 (2000). 183-211.

Refugee Council On-Line. "UK Asylum Law and Process." http://www.refugeecouncil.org.uk/infocentre/asylumlaw/legis_overview.html.

Reisig, Michael, and Travis Pratt. "The Ethics of Correctional Privatization: A Critical Examination of the Delegation of Coercive Authority." *Prison Journal* 80, 2 (2000): 210-23.

Resnick, Philip. "Neo-Conservatism and Beyond." In Johnson, McBride, and Smith, eds., *Continuities and Discontinuities*, 25-35.

Rexdale Community Health Centre, *Khat* Awareness Project Committee. "*Khat* Awareness in Toronto: A Preliminary Review of the Social, Economic, and Health Effects of *Khat* Use in Toronto." July 1998.

Richmond, Anthony. "Refugees and Racism in Canada." *Refuge* 19, 6 (2001): 8-13.

Riley, Diane. "Drugs and Drug Policy in Canada: A Brief Review and Commentary." Canadian Foundation for Drug Policy and International Harm Reduction Association, November 1998. http://www.cfdp.ca/sen8ex1.htm.

–. "Drugs and Drug Policy in Canada: A Study Prepared for Senator Pierre Claude Nolin as a Background Document for His June 1999 Motion to Have Canada's Senate Conduct a Thorough Review of Canadian Drug Law and Policy." Canadian Foundation for Drug Policy, 1999. http://www.parl.gc.ca/36/2/parlbus/commbus/senate/com-e/ille-e/rep-e/rep-nov98-e.htm.

Roach, Kent, and Sujit Choudry. "Racial and Ethnic Profiling: Statutory Discretion, Constitutional Remedies, and Democratic Accountability." *Osgoode Hall Law Journal* 41, 1 (2003): 1-36.

Roberts, Barbara. *Whence They Came: Deportation from Canada 1900-1935*. Ottawa: University of Ottawa Press, 1988.

Robinson, Daniel, and David Kimmel. "The Queer Career of Homosexual Security Vetting in Cold War Canada." *Canadian Historical Review* 75, 3 (1994): 319-45.

Rose, Nikolas. "Beyond the Public/Private Division: Law, Power, and the Family." In Fitzpatrick and Hunt, eds., *Critical Legal Studies*, 61-76.

–. "Governing 'Advanced' Liberal Democracies." In Andrew Barry, Thomas Osborne, and Nikolas Rose, eds., *Foucault and Political Reason*, 37-64. London: UCL Press, 1996.

–. "Government Authority and Expertise in Advanced Liberalism." *Economy and Society* 22, 3 (1993): 283-99.

–. "Government and Control." In David Garland and Richard Sparks, eds., *Criminology and Social Theory*, 183-208. Oxford: Oxford University Press, 2000.

–. "Inventiveness in Politics." *Economy and Society* 28, 3 (1999): 467-93.

–. *Powers of Freedom: Reframing Political Thought*. Cambridge: Cambridge University Press, 1999.

Rose, Nikolas, and Peter Miller. "Political Power beyond the State: Problematics of Government." *British Journal of Sociology* 43, 2 (1992): 173-205.

Rose, Nikolas, and Mariana Valverde. "Governed by Law?" *Social and Legal Studies* 7, 4 (1998): 541-51.

Royal Commission on the Donald Marshall Jr. Inquiry. *Discrimination against Blacks in Nova Scotia: The Investigation of the Criminal Justice System.* Halifax: Queen's Printer, 1989.

Said, Edward. *Orientalism.* New York: Vintage Books, 1979.

Sarat, Austin. *When the State Kills: Capital Punishment and the American Condition.* Princeton: Princeton University Press, 2001.

Sassen, Saskia. *Global Networks, Linked Cities.* London: Routledge, 2002.

–. *Losing Control: Sovereignty in an Age of Globalization.* New York: Columbia University Press, 1996.

Satzewich, Vic, ed. *Deconstructing a Nation: Immigration, Multiculturalism, and Racism in 90s Canada.* Halifax: Fernwood Publishing, 1992.

Schmitt, Carl. *Political Theology: Four Chapters on the Concept of Sovereignty.* Cambridge, MA: MIT Press, 1988.

Schwartz, Bryan. "Factum: The Preventative Function of Section 15 of the Charter and the Danger Certificate System." *Manitoba Law Journal* 27 (1999): 115-39.

Shearing, Clifford, and Richard Ericson. "Culture as Figurative Action." *British Journal of Sociology* 42, 4 (1991): 481-506.

Sheptycki, James. "The Governance of Organized Crime in Canada." *Canadian Journal of Sociology* 28, 4 (2003): 489-516.

Simalchik, Joan. "Is This Canada? A Report on Refugee Detention in the Celebrity Inn Immigration Holding Centre." Prepared for the Toronto Refugee Affairs Council Detention Committee, January 1998.

Simmons, Alan. "Racism and Immigration Policy." In Victor Satzewich, ed., *Racism and Social Inequality in Canada,* 87-114. Toronto: Thompson Educational Publishing, 1998.

Simon, Jonathan. "The Emergence of a Risk Society: Insurance, Law, and the State." *Socialist Review* 95 (1987): 61-89.

–. "Ghosts of the Disciplinary Machine: Lee Harvey Oswald, Life History, and the Truth of Crime." *Yale Journal of Law* 10, 1 (1998): 75-113.

–. "Governing through Crime." In Lawrence M. Friedman and George Fisher, eds., *The Crime Conundrum: Essays on Criminal Justice,* 171-89. New York: Westview Press, 1997.

–. "The Ideological Effects of Actuarial Practices." *Law and Society Review* 22, 4 (1988): 771-800.

–. "Refugees in a Carceral Age: The Rebirth of Immigration Prisons in the US." *Public Culture* 10, 3 (1998): 577-606.

Simon, Jonathan, and M. Feeley. "True Crime: The New Penology and Public Discourse on Crime." In Thomas Blomberg and Stanley Cohen, eds., *Punishment and Social Control,* 147-80. New York: Aldine de Gruyter, 1995.

Singer, Colin R. (Canadian Bar Association, National Citizenship and Immigration Law Section). "Key Concerns Respecting Bill C-31, *Immigration and Refugee Protection Act.*" Speaking notes, National Congress of Italian-Canadians, Montreal, 10 June 2000.

Somali Immigrant Aid Association. Background information, October 1999. http://webhome.idirect.com/~siao/background.html.

Sossin, Lorne. "The Rule of Policy: *Baker* and the Impact of Judicial Review on Administrative Discretion." In D. Dyzenhaus et al., eds., *The Unity of Public Law,* 87-112. London: Hart, 2004.

Stenson, Kevin. "Beyond Histories of the Present." *Economy and Society* 27, 4 (1998): 333-52.

–. "Community Policing as Governmental Technology." *Economy and Society* 22, 3 (1993): 373-89.

Stoffman, Daniel. "Dispatch from Dixon." *Toronto Life,* August 1995: 40-47.

–. "Towards a More Realistic Immigration Policy for Canada." *Backgrounder.* C.D. Howe Institute, June 1993.

–. *Who Gets In: What's Wrong with Canada's Immigration Policy – and How to Fix It.* Toronto: Macfarlane, Walter, and Ross, 2002.

Strange, Carolyn, ed. *Qualities of Mercy: Justice, Punishment, and Discretion.* Vancouver: UBC Press, 1996.

Struthers, James. *No Fault of Their Own: Unemployment and the Canadian Welfare State, 1914-1941.* Toronto: University of Toronto Press, 1983.

Sullum, Jacob. "Drugs: *Khat* Calls." *Reason Magazine* 24, 10 (1993): 42-44.

–. "Voodoo Social Policy: Exorcising the Twin Demons, Guns and Drugs." *Reason Magazine* 26, 5 (1994): 26-31. http://reason.com/9410/fe.sullum.shtml.

Thobani, Sunera. "Closing Ranks: Racism and Sexism in Canada's Immigration Policy." *Race and Class* 41, 1 (2000): 35-55.

Thomas, Derrick. "The Foreign Born in the Federal Prison Population." Ottawa: Employment and Immigration Canada, Strategic Planning and Research, June 1993.

Thompson, Paul. "Private Prison Partnerships in Criminal Justice." *New Economy* 7, 3 (2000): 150-55.

Toronto Refugee Affairs Council. "Brief to the Government of Canada about Recommendations by the Legislative Review Committee." March 1998.

Torpey, John. "Coming and Going: On the State Monopolization of the Legitimate Means of Movement." *Sociological Theory* 16, 3 (1998): 239-59.

–. *The Invention of the Passport.* Cambridge: Cambridge University Press, 2000.

United States Committee for Refugees. "Country Report: Australia." *World Wide Refugee Information.* 2002. http://www.refugees.org/world/countryrpt/easia_pacific/australia.htm.

–. "Country Report: France." *World Wide Refugee Information.* 2002. http://www.refugees.org/world/countryrpt/europe/2002/france.cfm.

–. "Country Report: Germany." *World Wide Refugee Information.* 2002. http://www.refugees.org/world/countryrpt/europe/2002/germany.cfm.

–. "Country Report: United States." *World Wide Refugee Information.* 2002. http://www.refugees.org/world/countryrpt/amer_carib/us.html.

Valverde, Mariana. *The Age of Light, Soap, and Water: Moral Reform in English Canada, 1885-1925.* Toronto: McClelland and Stewart, 1993.

–. "'Despotism' and Ethical Governance." *Economy and Society* 25, 3 (1996): 357-72.

–. "Governing Security, Governing through Security." In Daniels, Macklem, and Roach, eds., *The Security of Freedom,* 84-91.

–. *Law's Dream of a Common Knowledge.* Princeton: Princeton University Press, 2003.

Valverde, Mariana, Ron Levi, and Dawn Moore. "Legal Knowledges of Risks." Report to the Law Commission of Canada. Presented at the Joint Session of the Canadian Association of Law Teachers and Canadian Law and Society Association, Halifax, 2 June 2003.

Valverde, Mariana, Ron Levi, Clifford Shearing, Mary Condon, and Pat O'Malley. "Democracy in Governance: Toward a Socio-Legal Framework." Report for the Law Commission of Canada, 1999.

Valverde, Mariana, Linda Macleod, and Kirsten Johnson, eds. *Wife Assault and the Criminal Justice System.* Toronto: Centre of Criminology, University of Toronto, 1995.

Wackenhut Corrections Corporation. "Deliver Global Services." 2002.

Waever, Ole. "Securitization and Desecuritization." In Lipschutz, ed., *On Security,* 46-86.

Waever, Ole, Barry Buzan, Morten Kelstrup, and Pierre Lemaitre. *Identity, Migration, and the New Security Agenda in Europe.* London: Pinter Publishers, 1993.

Walker, David M. *The Oxford Companion to Law.* Oxford: Clarendon Press, 1980.

Walters, Paul. "Baylis/Leone Lawsuit against Federal Immigration Now in Full Swing." *Metropolitan Police Association Bulletin,* Fall 1997.

Walters, William. "Deportation, Expulsion, and the International Police of Aliens." *Citizenship Studies* 6, 3 (2002): 265-92.

–. "Mapping Schengenland: Denaturalizing the Border." *Environment and Planning D: Society and Space* 20 (2002): 561-80.

Weiner, Gerry. "Canada's Refugee Policy." In Nash and Humphrey, *Human Rights and the Protection of Refugees,* 237-38.

Weinreb, Arthur, and Rocco Galati. *The Criminal Lawyer's Guide to Immigration and Citizenship Law.* Aurora: Canada Law Book, 1996.

Welch, Michael. *Detained: Immigration Laws and the Expanding I.N.S. Jail Complex.* Philadelphia: Temple University Press, 2003.

–. "Questioning the Utility and Fairness of Immigration and Naturalization Service Detention: Criticisms of Poor Institutional Conditions and Protracted Periods of Confinement for Undocumented Immigrants." *Journal of Contemporary Criminal Justice* 13, 1 (1997): 41-54.

Whitaker, Reg. "Designing a Balance between Freedom and Security." In Joseph F. Fletcher, ed., *Ideas in Action: Essays on Politics and Law in Honour of Peter Russell,* 126-49. Toronto: University of Toronto Press, 1999.

–. *Double Standard: The Secret History of Canadian Immigration.* Toronto: Lester and Orpen Dennys, 1987.

–. "Refugee Policy after September 11th: Not Much New." *Refuge* 20, 4 (2002): 29-33.

–. "Refugees: The Security Dimension." *Citizenship Studies* 2, 3 (1998): 413-34.

–. "Security and Intelligence in the Post-Cold War World." In Ralph Miliband and Leo Panitch, eds., *Socialist Register 1992: New World Order?* 111-30. London/New York: The Merlin Press/Monthly Review Press, 1992.

Wortley, Scot. "Justice for All? Race and Perceptions of Bias in the Ontario Criminal Justice System: A Toronto Survey." *Canadian Journal of Criminology* 38, 4 (1996): 439-67.

Yeager, Matthew. "Immigrants and Criminality: A Meta-Survey." Prepared for Strategic Policy, Planning and Research, and Metropolis Project, Citizenship and Immigration Canada, January 1996.

Young, Alison. *Imagining Crime.* London: Sage Publications, 1996.

Young, Robert. *Hybridity in Theory, Culture, and Race.* London: Routledge, 1995.

Index

immigration officers, 30, 199, 202; coercive powers, 68, 106, 248n3; detention powers, 31, 32, 62; discretionary powers, 62-4, 67, 107; enforcement mentality, 179-80; forgeries by, 179-80; risk assessment, 144-5; screening activities, 164, 165, 175, 198, 202; senior immigration officers (SIOs), 32, 63, 107; temporary resident permits, 180-3
immigration penality, 1-2, 9-12. *See also* crime-security nexus; deportation; detention; neoliberalism
Immigration Reform and Control Act, 1986 (United States), 50
Immigration and Refugee Board (IRB), 30, 32, 65, 66-7, 96; Bill C-55 and, 66, 99-100
Immigration and Refugee Protection Act (IRPA), 2001 (Canada), 3, 4-5, 65, 164; crime-security nexus and, 3, 60, 61, 163, 165; detention and, 31, 49, 51, 133; discretionary powers, 4, 61-2, 71; security provisions, 153, 154, 155; serious criminality and, 141-2, 145, 176; temporary resident permit, 180, 182
immigration statistics, 95, 245n35
Integrated Border Enforcement Teams (IBETs), 197, 199
intelligence services, 164-72. *See also* Canadian Security Intelligence Service (CSIS); organized crime
interdiction, 4, 5, 8, 68, 149, 196, 199, 200-5, 222; risk management and, 203-4
International Criminal Court (ICC), 173

jail: for criminality based immigration detentions, 27; statistics, 43, 45; transfer to, 40-1, 49;
Jamaican migrants, 116, 117, 140, 141, 145, 148
Johnson, Glenford, 189
Joint Statement on Cooperation and Regional Migration Issues, 4
Jones, Mark, 140
judicial review: and administrative discretion, 60-1; danger to the public, 140-4; discretionary powers and, 149-52, 157-8; Immigration Appeal Board, 82, 86, 89; refugee decisions 100; security certificates, 153; security provisions 78, 79; *Suresh v. Canada,* 155-9; *Williams v. Canada,* 149-52
Just Desserts Bill. *See* Bill C-44
Justice Prisoner and Alien Transportation System, 35

Kendall, Perry, 137
khat, 134-7
Kidane, Derar v. Canada, 31
King, Mackenzie, 75

Lacey, Nicola: quoted, 55
law: administration and, 57-8, 60-2, 71-2; civil suits, 161-2; vs discretion, 53-8, 63-4, 65, 68-9, 70-1, 81, 87, 140, 146, 147, 158, 214-15, international human rights, 110, 117, 153-5, 158, 159, 172, 173; liberalism and, 16-17, 57-8, 87, 140, 160, 214-15; and order, 18, 19, 92-3, 97, 103, 109, 110, 117, 131-2, 138, 221; sovereign power, 12; the state and, 9-10. *See also* judicial review; legislation
legislation: Australia, 7; European Union, 5-7; France, 6; Germany, 6; against organized crime, 165-6; United Kingdom, 6-7; United States, 7-8. *See also* law, *names of specific Canadian acts and bills*
Leimonis, Georgina, 116, 140, 161
Lewis, Doug, 108
liberal legality, 16-17, 235n20; and coercive practices, 141, 160; discretion and, 54-8, 151, 214-15
liberalism: discretionary powers and, 16, 57-8, 79, 87; governmentality and, 15-17; law and, 16-17, 57-8, 87, 140, 160, 214-15. *See also* neoliberalism
Lippert, Randy: quoted, 210-11
LRAG. *See* Immigration Legislative Review Advisory Group (LRAG)

Marchi, Sergio, 64, 122, 140
McAdam, Brian, 171
McLeod, Lyn, 120-1
medical exclusions, 77, 256n7
Metropolis Project, 176-9
Metropolitan Police Association, 161-2
Miller, Peter: quoted, 10, 15
Mississauga, Ont. *See* Celebrity Inn Immigration Holding Centre
multiple authorities, 14, 26, 32, 185; detention and, 39, 52; RCMP/CSIS cooperation, 168. *See also* governing at a distance; governmentality; partnerships
municipalities, 117-18. *See also* Toronto, Ont.
Muslim travellers, 208-9

national security, 85, 187-96; Canada-United States issues, 196-200; deportation and, 105, 152-9; liberal legality and, 154-5, 160; security certificate process, 89, 152-3; Sedgwick Report, 81-2; shifts